NAT TURNER

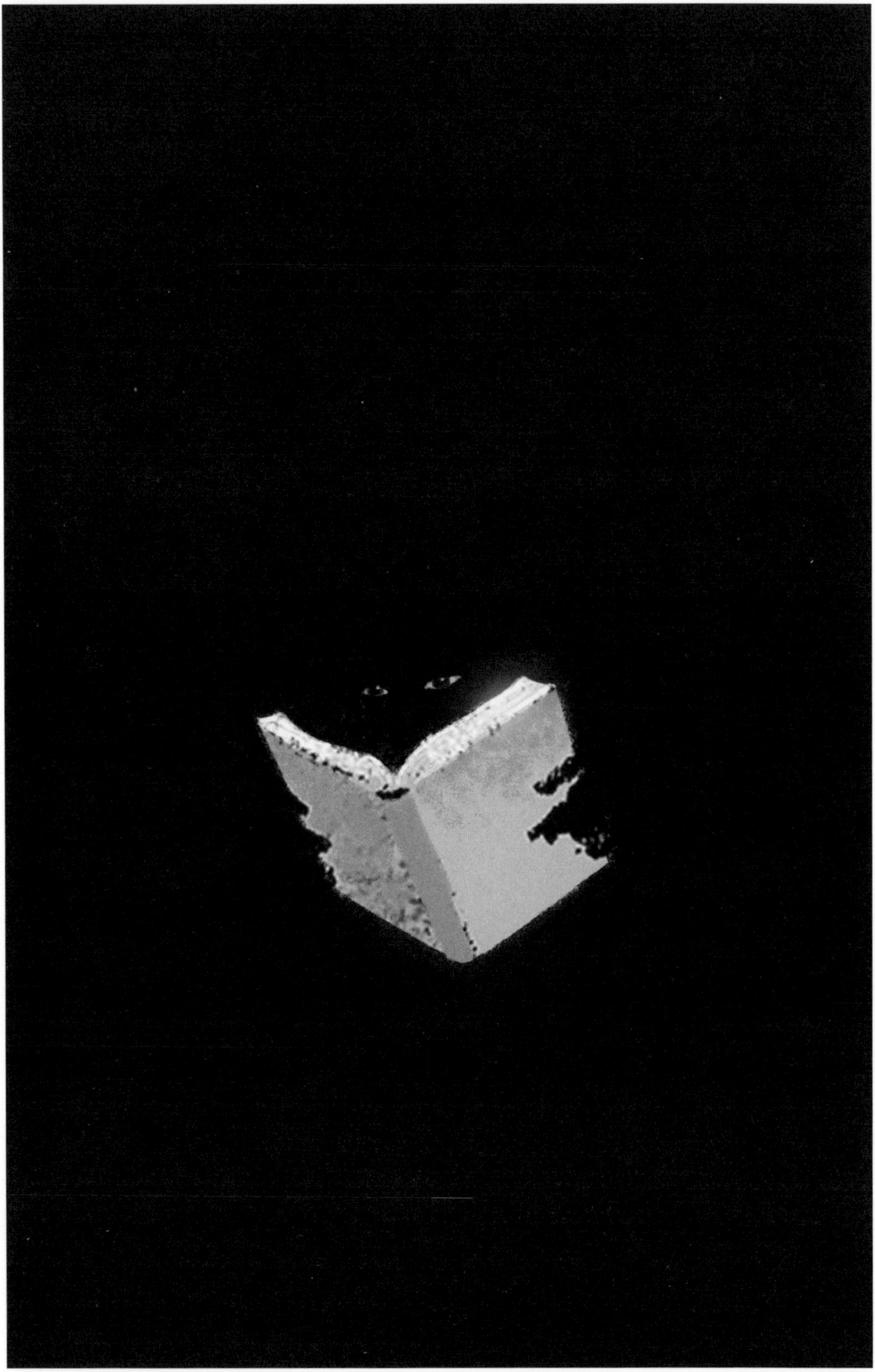

KYLE BAKER

NAT TURNER™

ABRAMS, NEW YORK

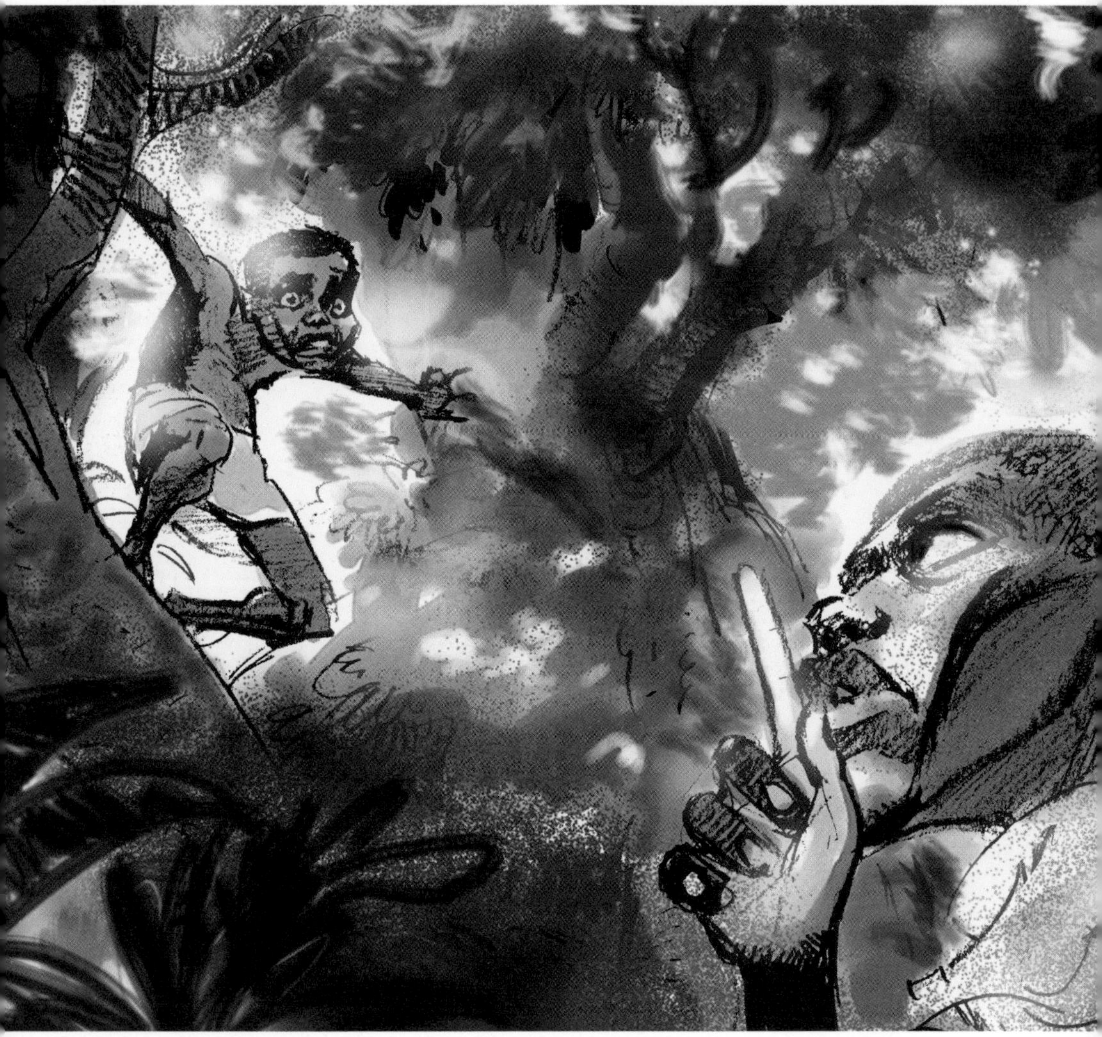

PREFACE

I first learned the name Nat Turner as a child in school. In my American history textbook was one paragraph, which basically said that Nat Turner led a slave rebellion in 1831, and that it was a significant event.

Over the years I would encounter the name Nat Turner in various books. None of the entries was longer than a few sentences mentioning the name, the date, and that it was important.

I became curious: Who was this man who was important enough to be mentioned in *all* the history books, yet is never spoken about at length?

Most of history's great people and events are examined in novels, plays, film, even art. I can go to a bookstore and find dozens of books about Harriet Tubman, Abraham Lincoln, or George Washington Carver. I may find one about Nat Turner. I can rent dozens of films about the Civil War, Martin Luther King, Rosa Parks, and Jackie Robinson. But there are no Hollywood Nat Turner films.

While many battle sites of the Civil War have plaques, statues, and even gift shops, the sites of Turner's rebellion are unmarked.

Many of history's greatest people, including Frederick Douglass, Harriet Tubman, and Malcolm X all cite Nat Turner as an inspiration. Talk about important! In fact, it was in Malcom X's autobiography where I first read a longer narrative of the Turner Rebellion. Reading Malcolm X's description of Turner's story made me realize it was the perfect subject for a comic book.

Comic books/graphic novels are a visual medium, so it's most important for an artist to choose a subject with opportunities for compelling graphics. The Nat Turner story has lots of action and suspense, also a hero with superhuman abilities.

I often choose to write books on subjects I wish to know more about. I wanted to know how a person nobody wanted to talk about could be arguably one of the most important men in American history.

One thing that's always mystified me about slavery is this: If slaves were selected and bred for size and strength, slavemasters must very quickly have found themselves outnumbered by their bigger, stronger slave population. How does a weaker minority dominate a physically superior majority?

In my research I learned that this is accomplished by destroying the slave's mind. More effective than whips and guns was the simple act of outlawing the teaching of slaves to read or to write.

Think I'm exaggerating? Nat Turner broke the law, learned to read and write, and the rest is history.

Turner was a lousy fighter, an inept swordsman, and most of the people he tried to kill didn't die by his hand. His sole strength was his superior brain. He became a leader of men because he had developed his mind by reading, which happened to be illegal. Coincidence?

We are fortunate today to live in a free country where access to books is unlimited. If a man in Nat Turner's circumstances was able to change history, imagine what you can do with the freedom you have today.

I originally chose to publish Nat Turner myself, rather than through the comic book publishers I usually work for (the two largest). I liked that one of my first books as an independent publisher would be about a self-freed slave. I knew nothing about publishing, having only worked as an artist before. In the tradition of my hero Nat Turner, I went out and found books about being a publisher. I learned how to start a business, get printing, and distribution. I found books about sales and marketing.

My self-published book ended up selling through two printings thanks to reviews in *Entertainment Weekly* and *The Washington Post*. It was so successful that one of my all-time favorite publishers, Harry N. Abrams, picked it up and published the lovely edition you are now holding.

That's just one example of what free access to reading has given me. You can do it, too. Did you know there are books about how to find a diamond mine? Think about it.

—Kyle Baker

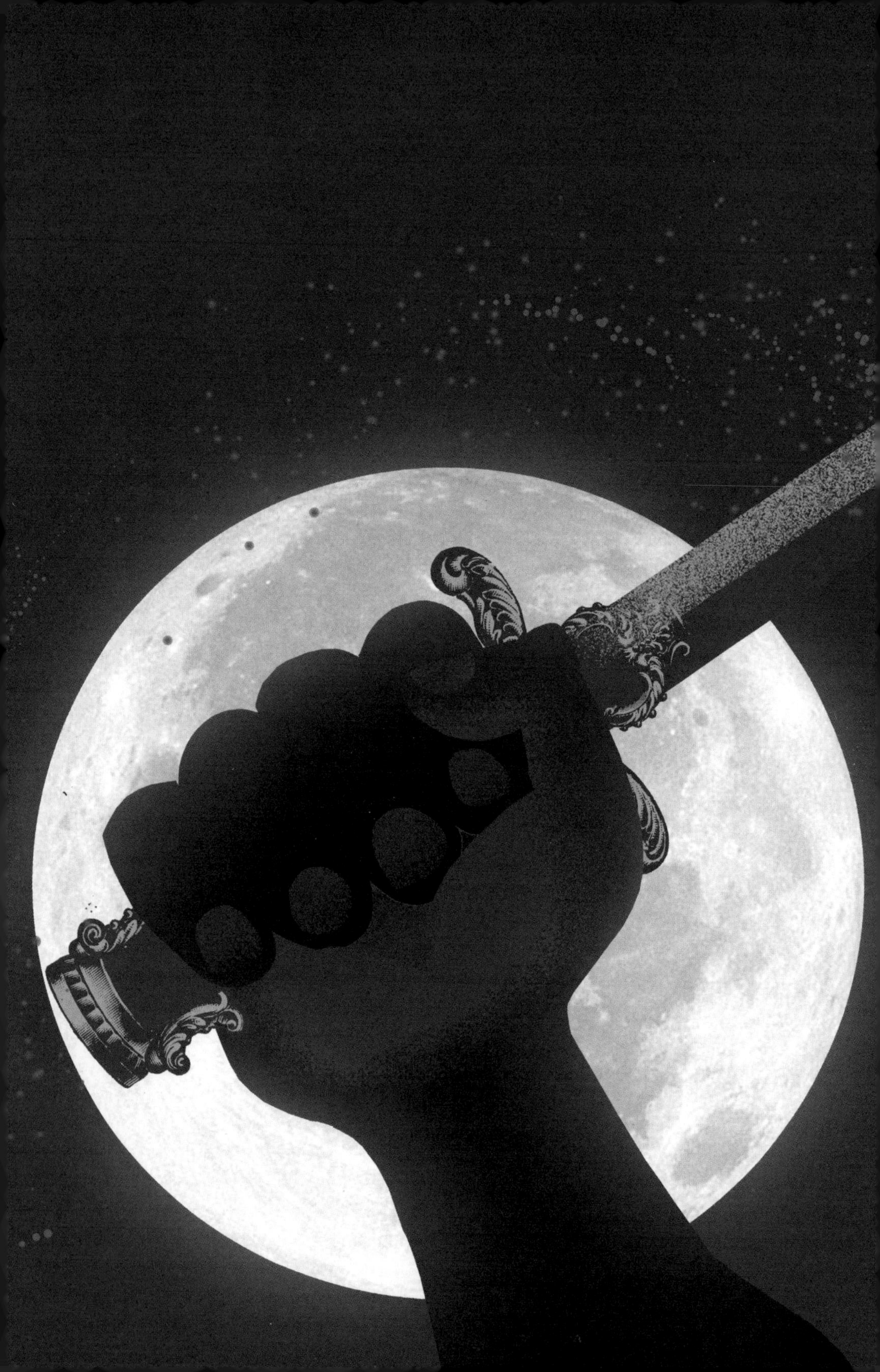

I

HOME

THE

CONFESSIONS

OF

NAT TURNER,

THE LEADER

OF

THE LATE INSURRECTION

IN SOUTHAMPTON, VA.

AS FULLY AND VOLUNTARILY MADE TO

THOMAS R. GRAY,

In the prison where he was confined, and acknowledged by him to be such
when read before the Court of Southampton: with the
certificate, under seal of the Court convened at
Jerusalem, Nov. 5, 1831, for his trial.

ALSO,

AN AUTHENTIC ACCOUNT

OF THE

WHOLE INSURRECTION,

WITH

Lists of the Whites who were Murdered,

AND OF THE

*Negroes brought before the Court of Southampton,
and there sentenced, &c.*

———

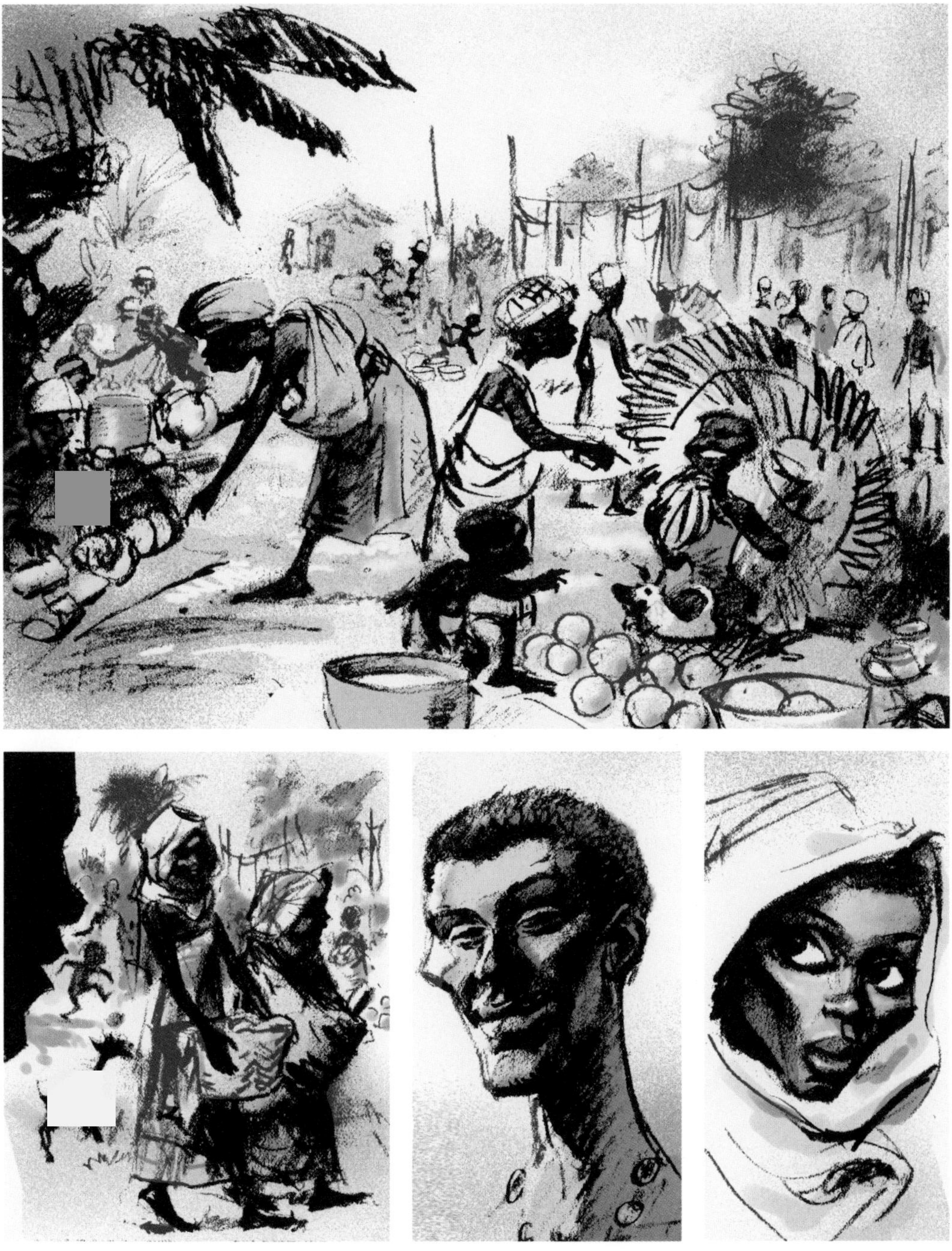

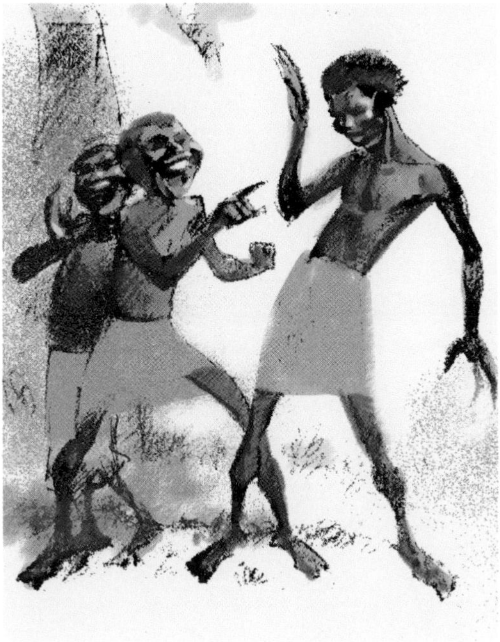

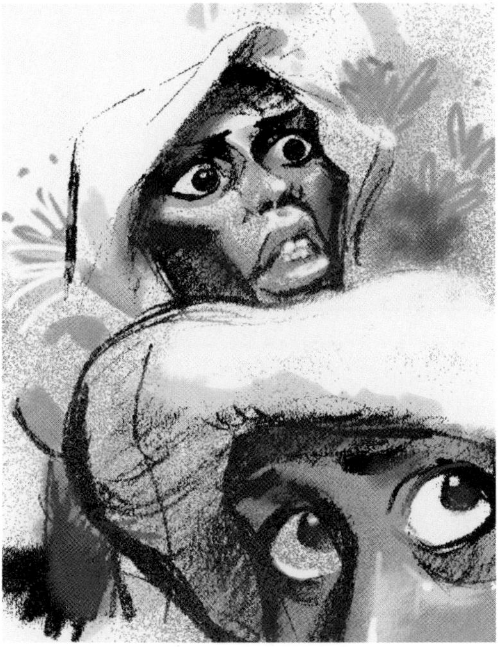

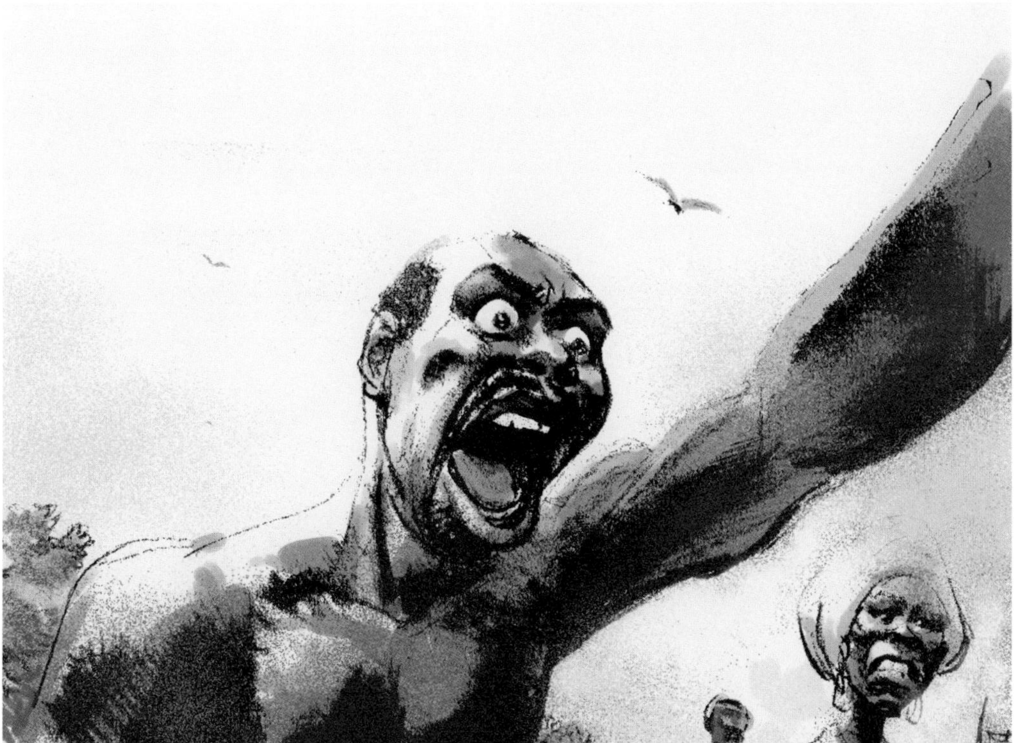

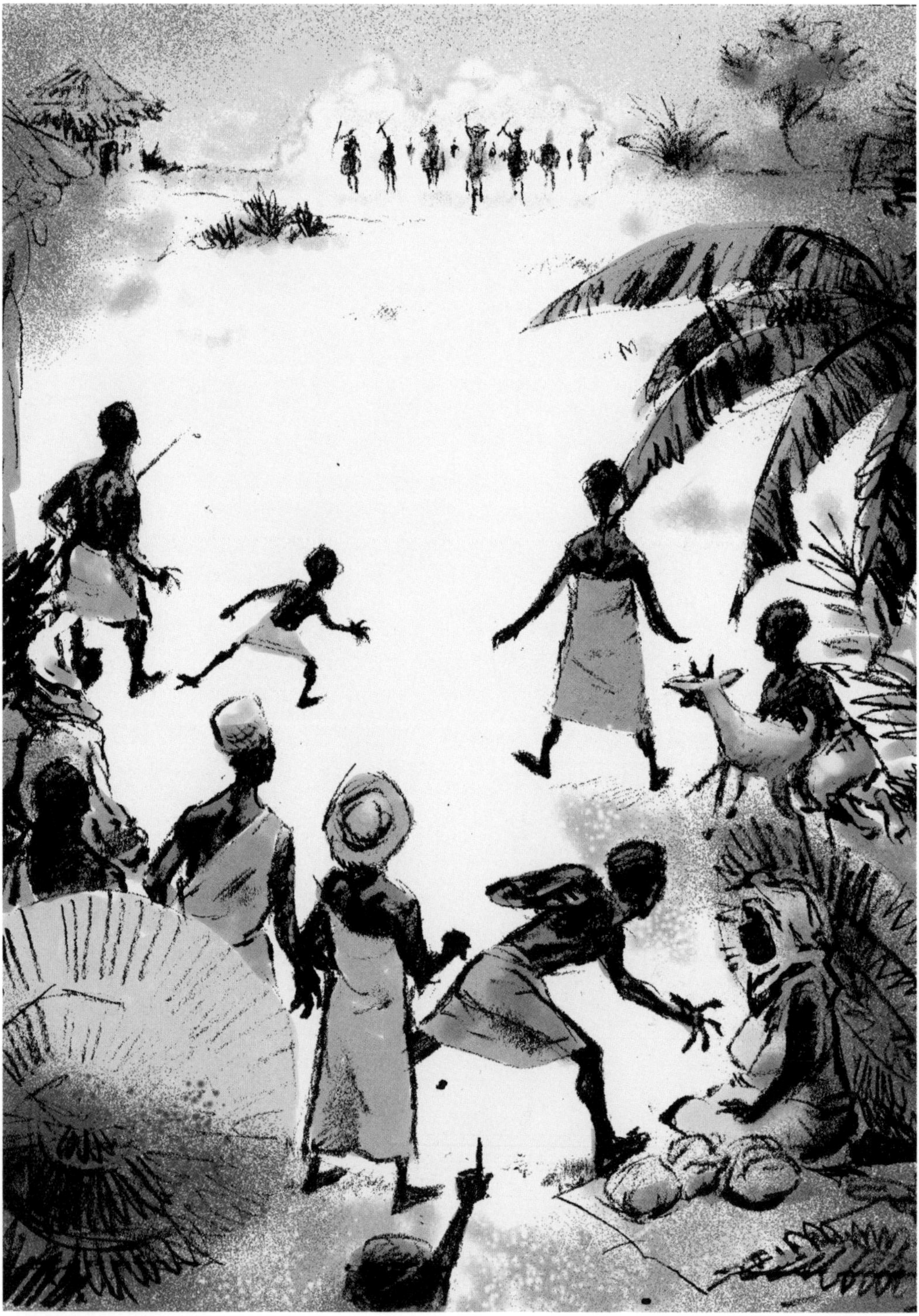

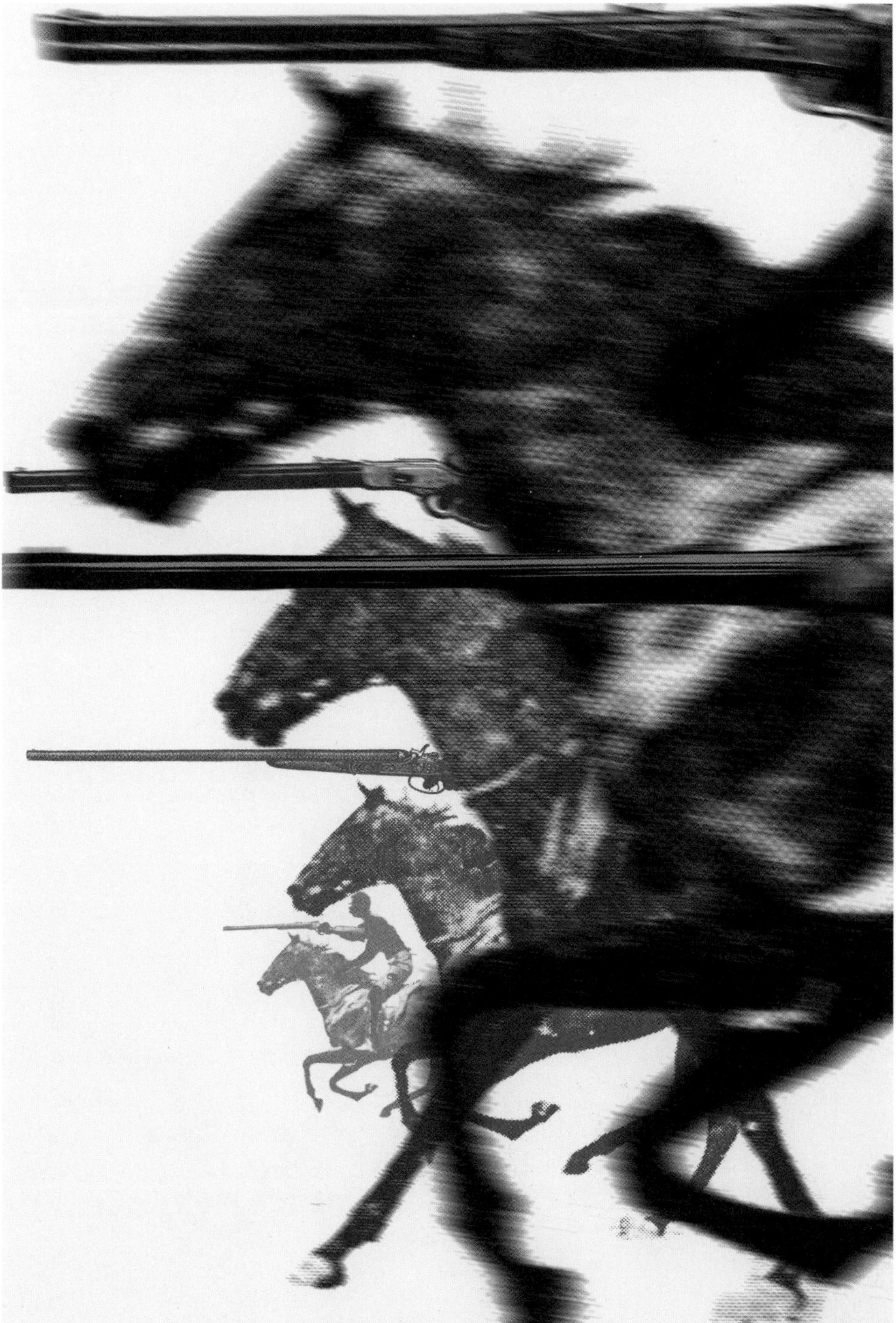

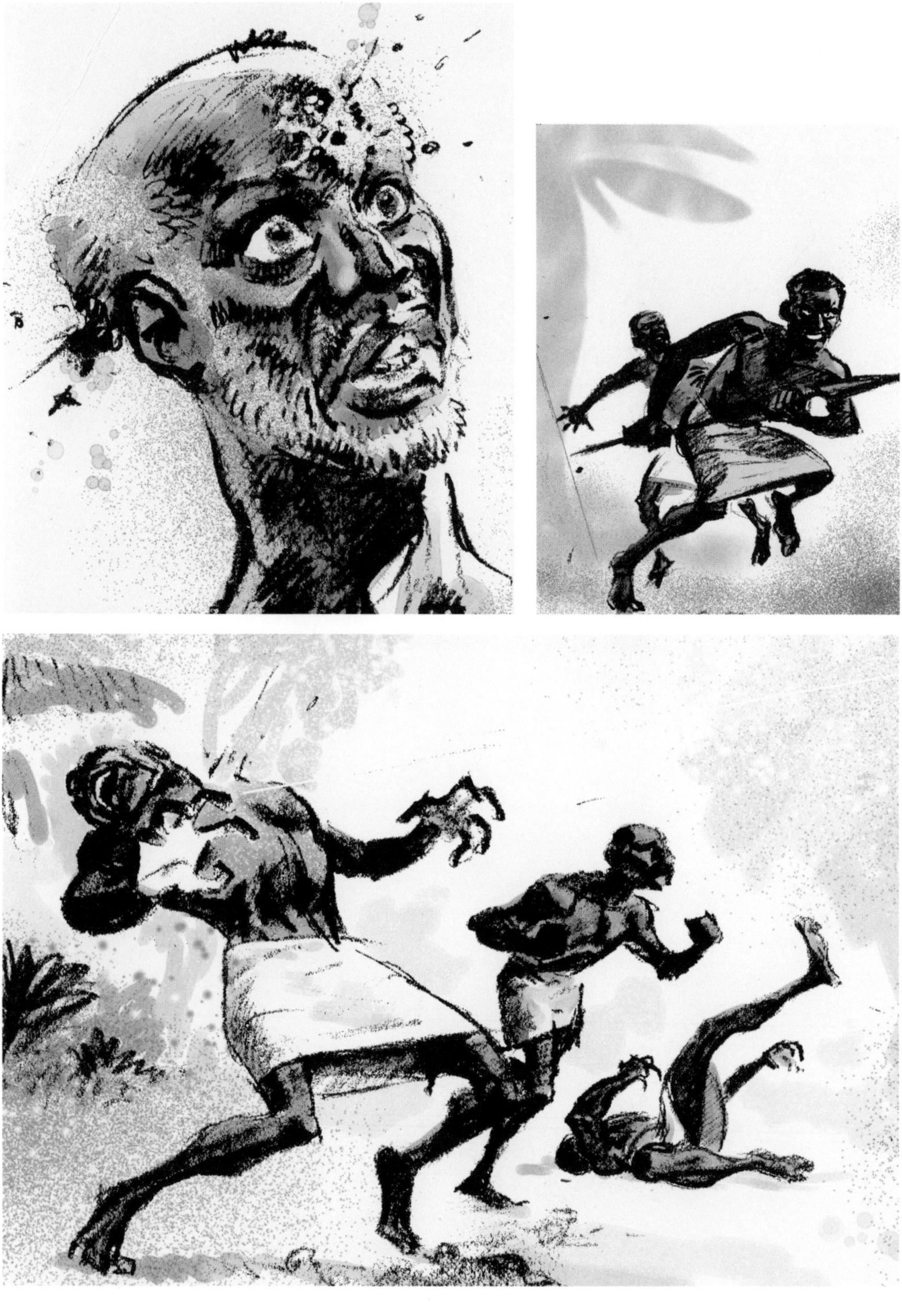

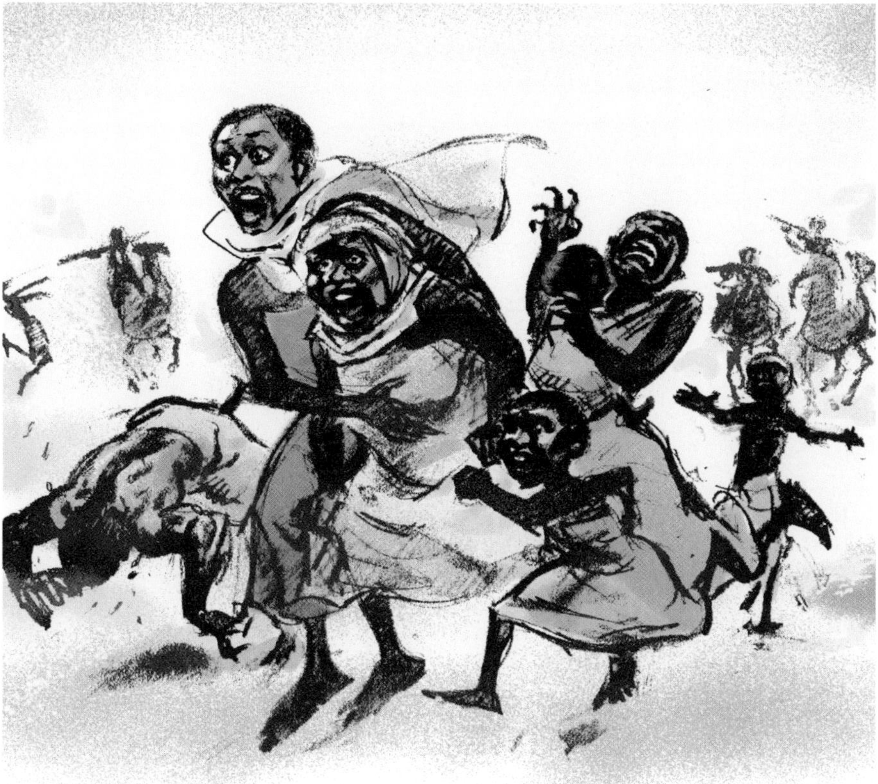

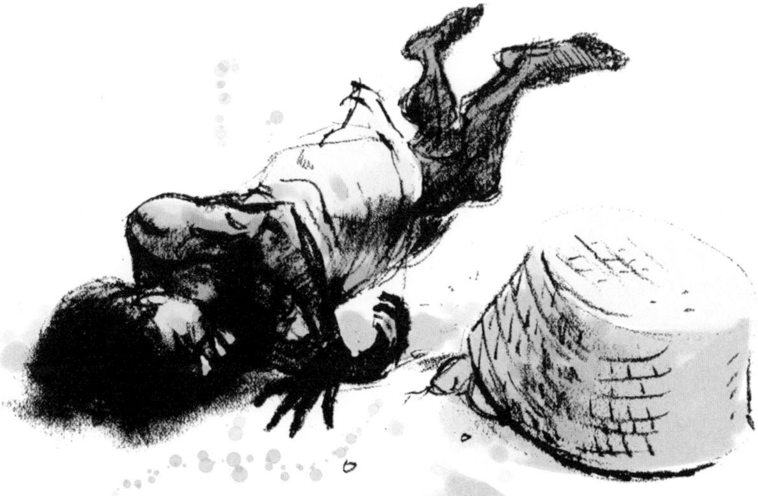

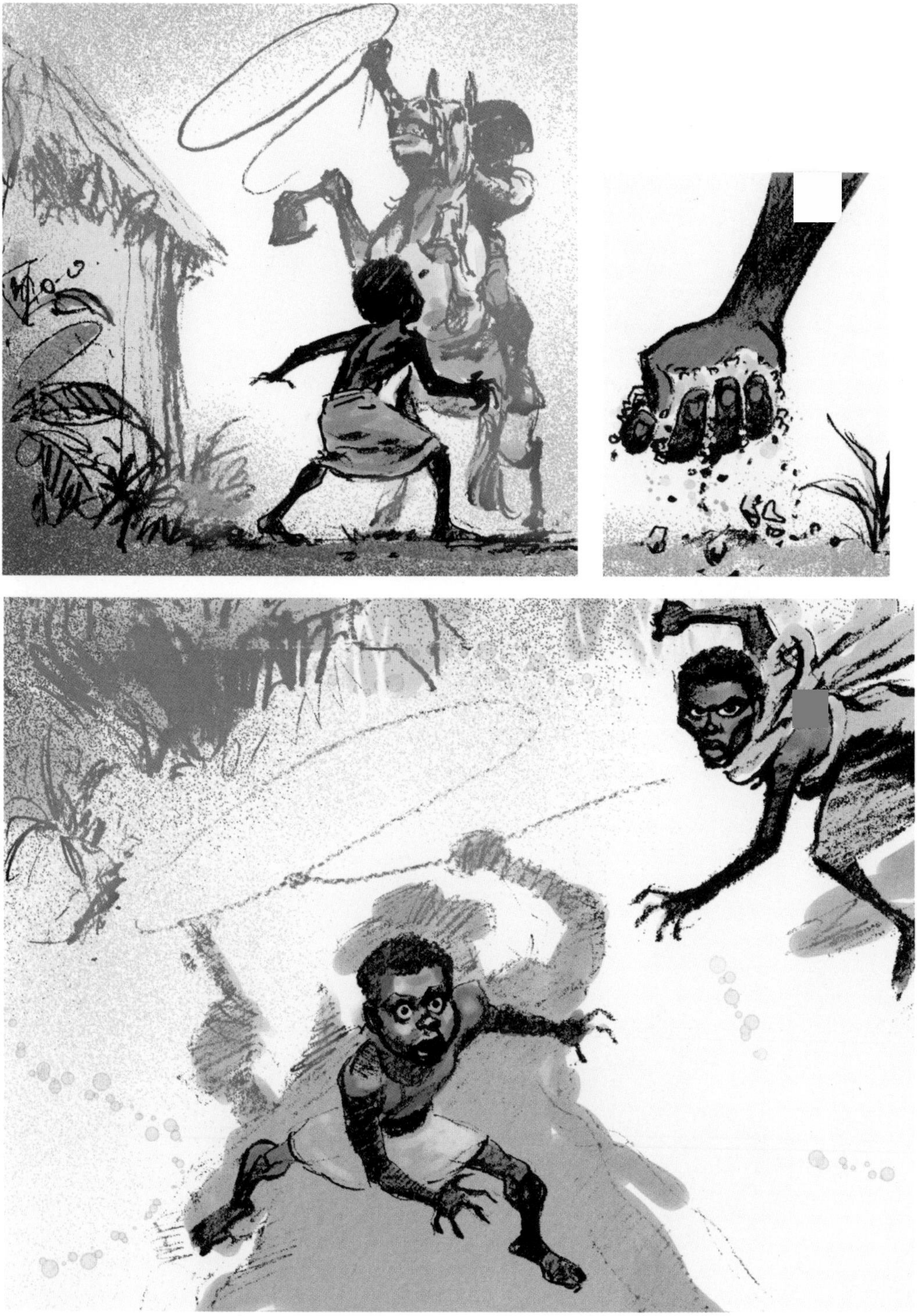

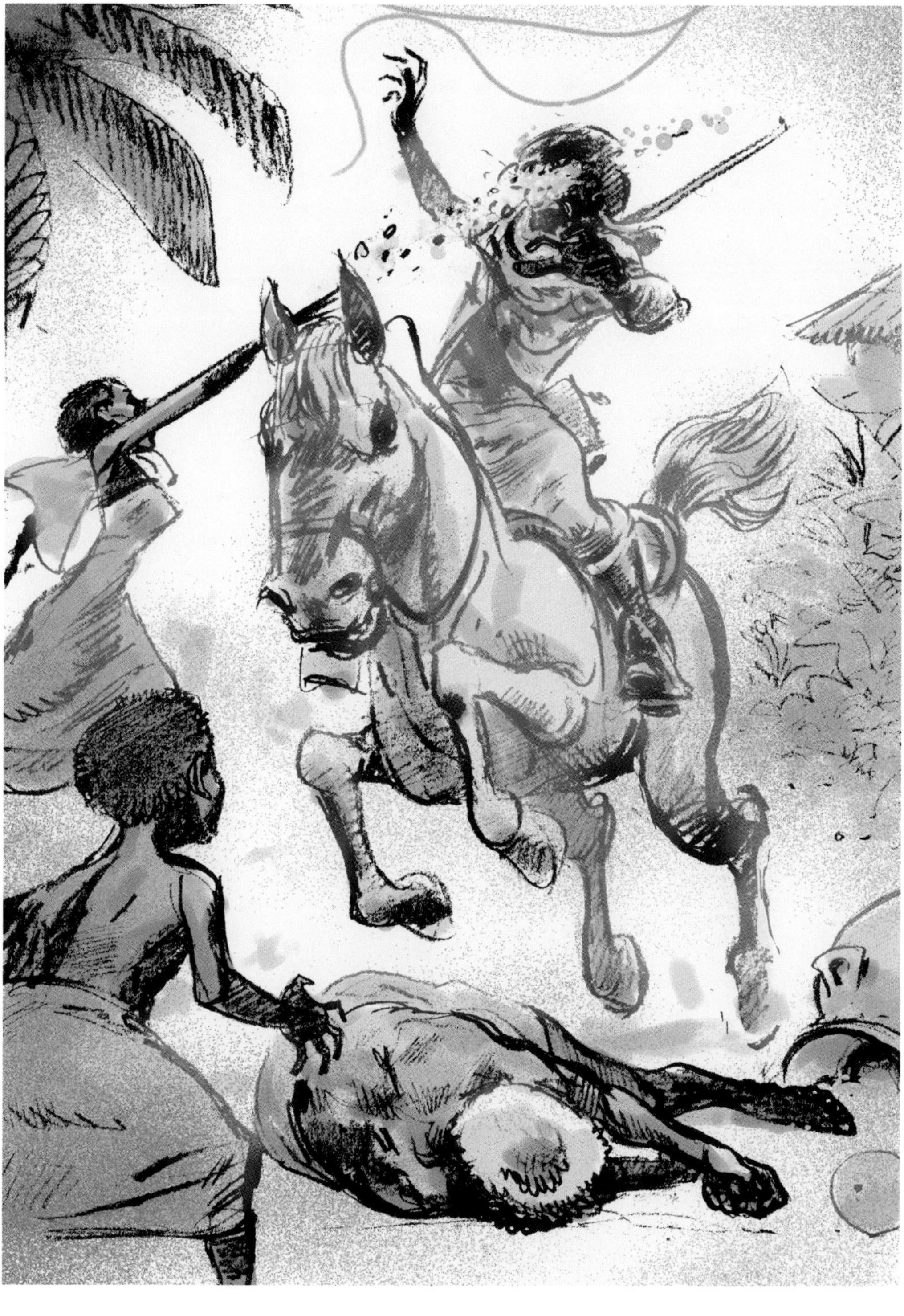

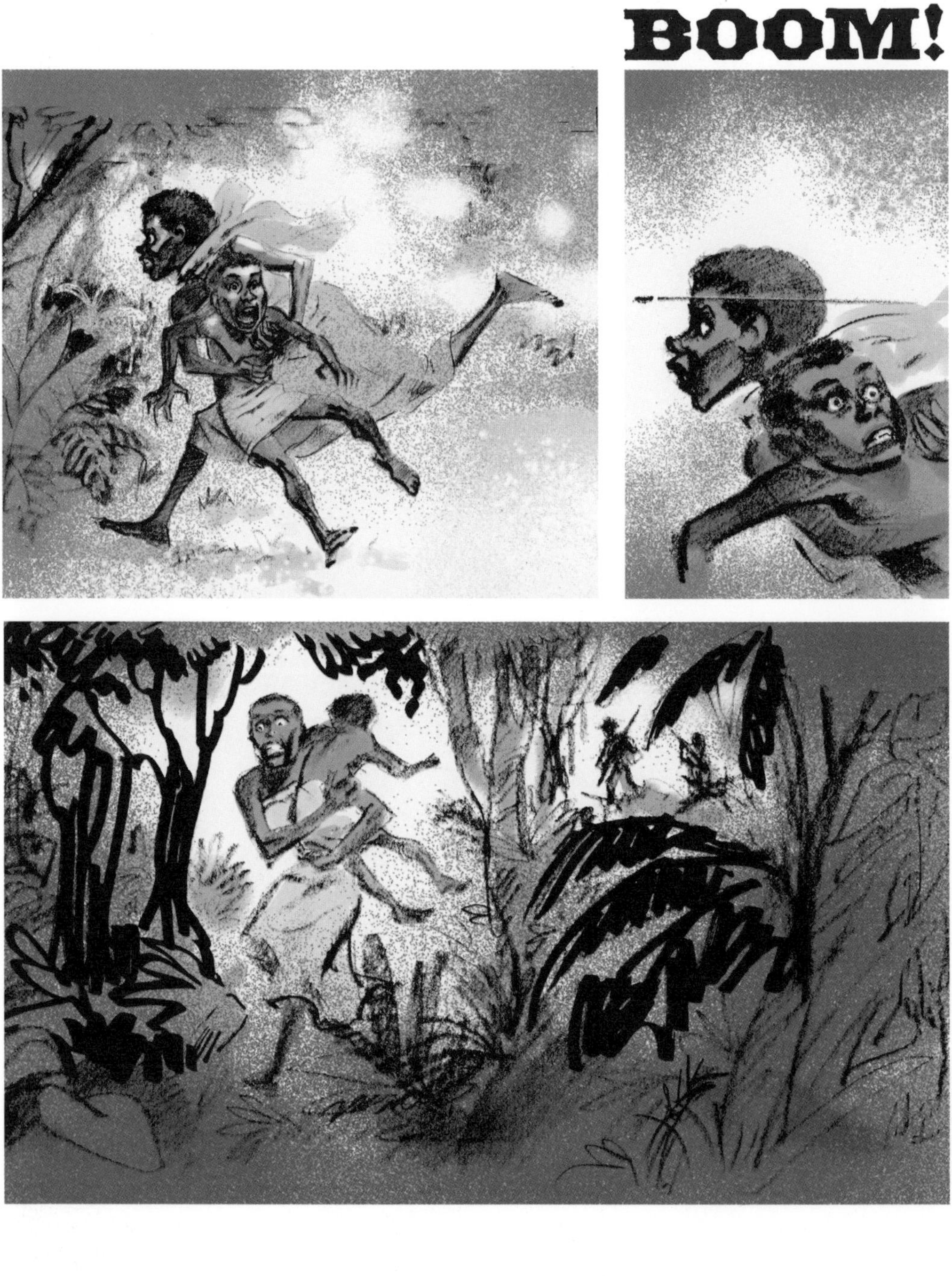
BOOM!

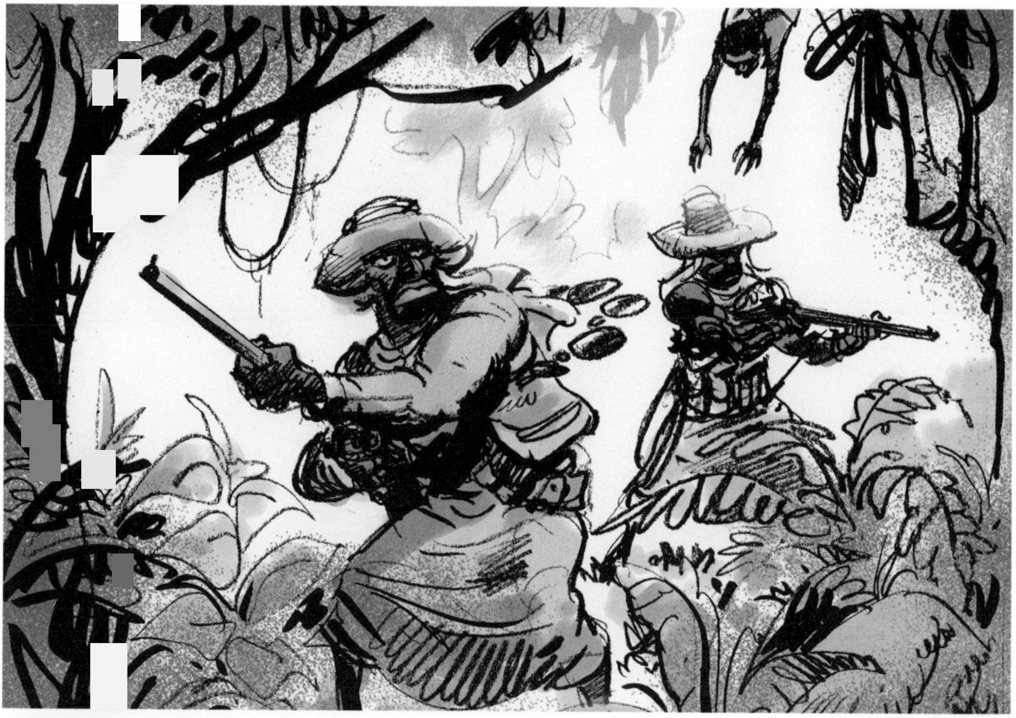

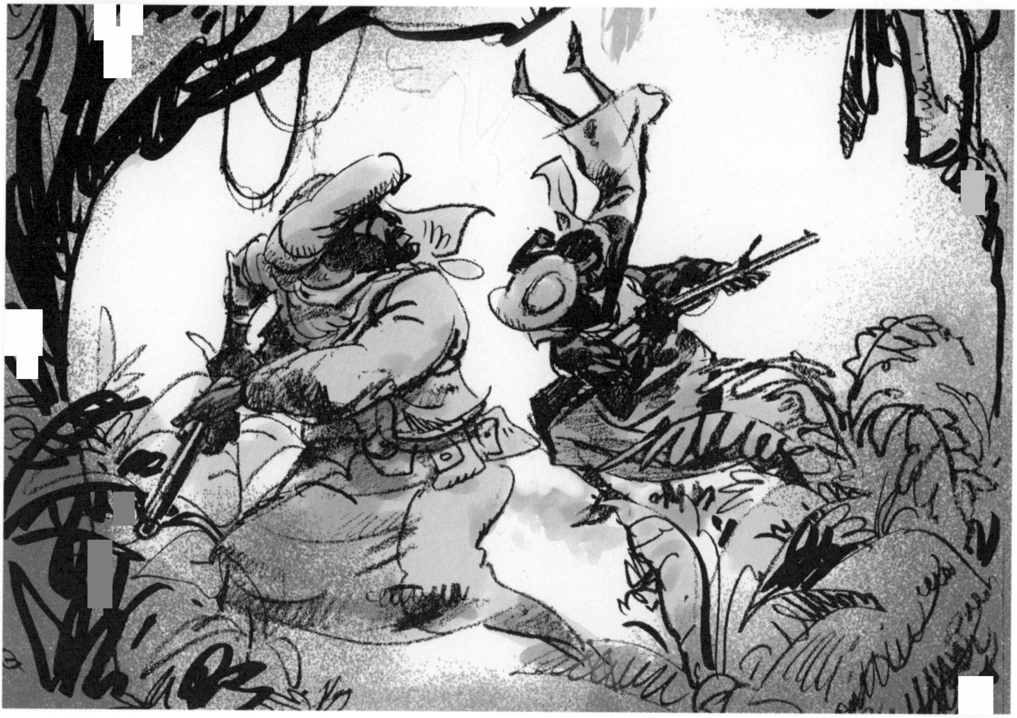

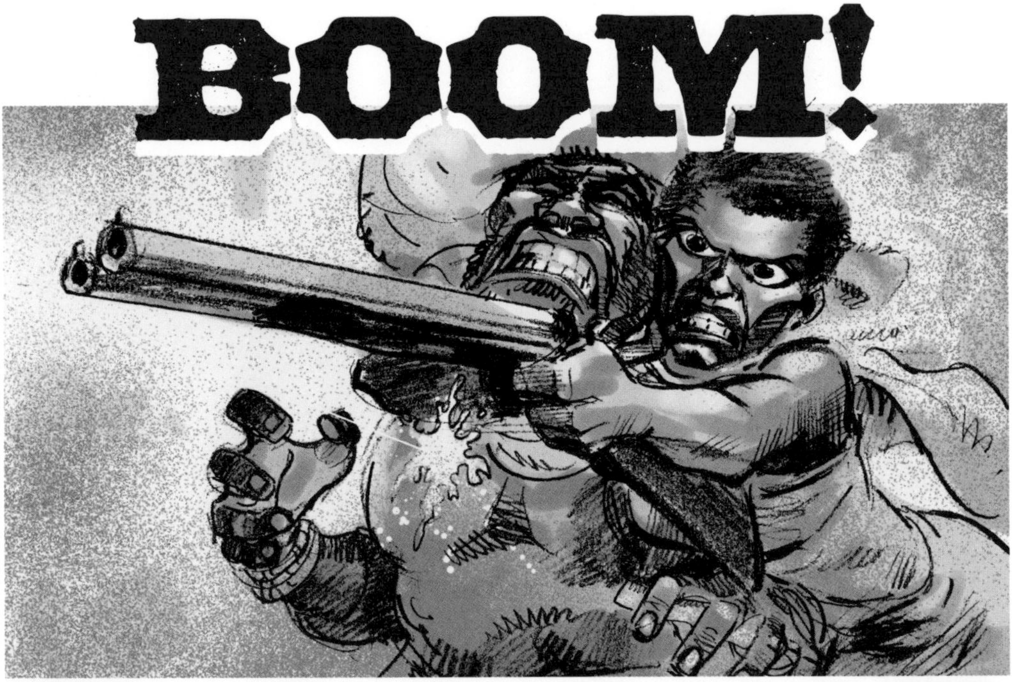
BOOM!

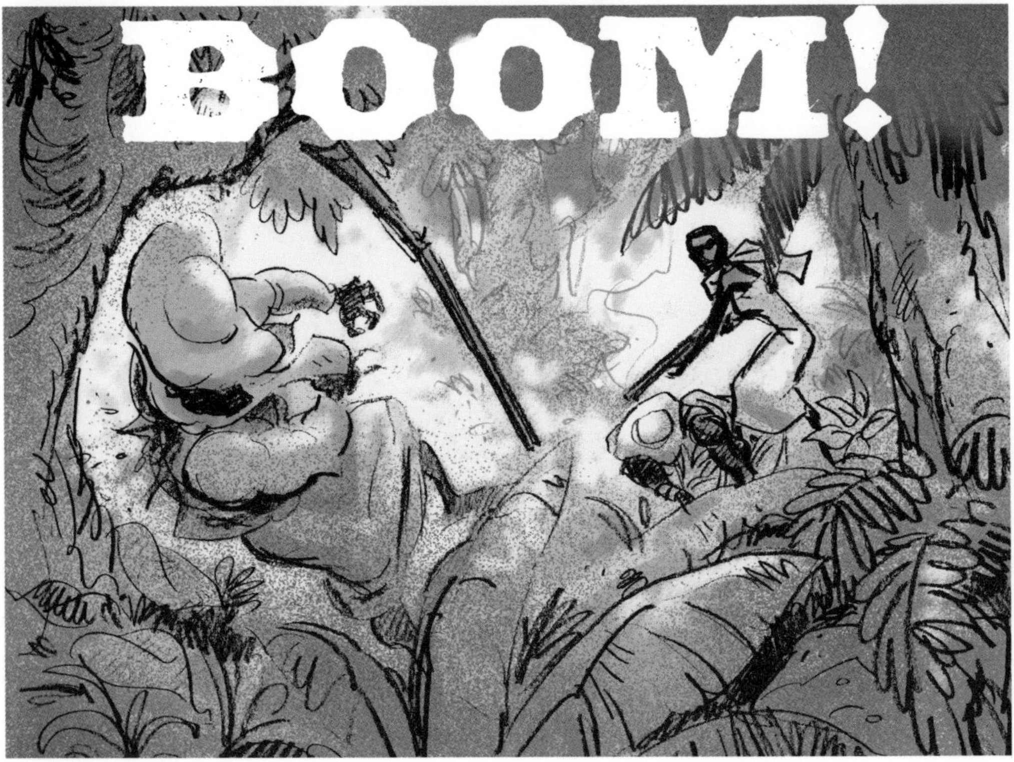
BOOM!

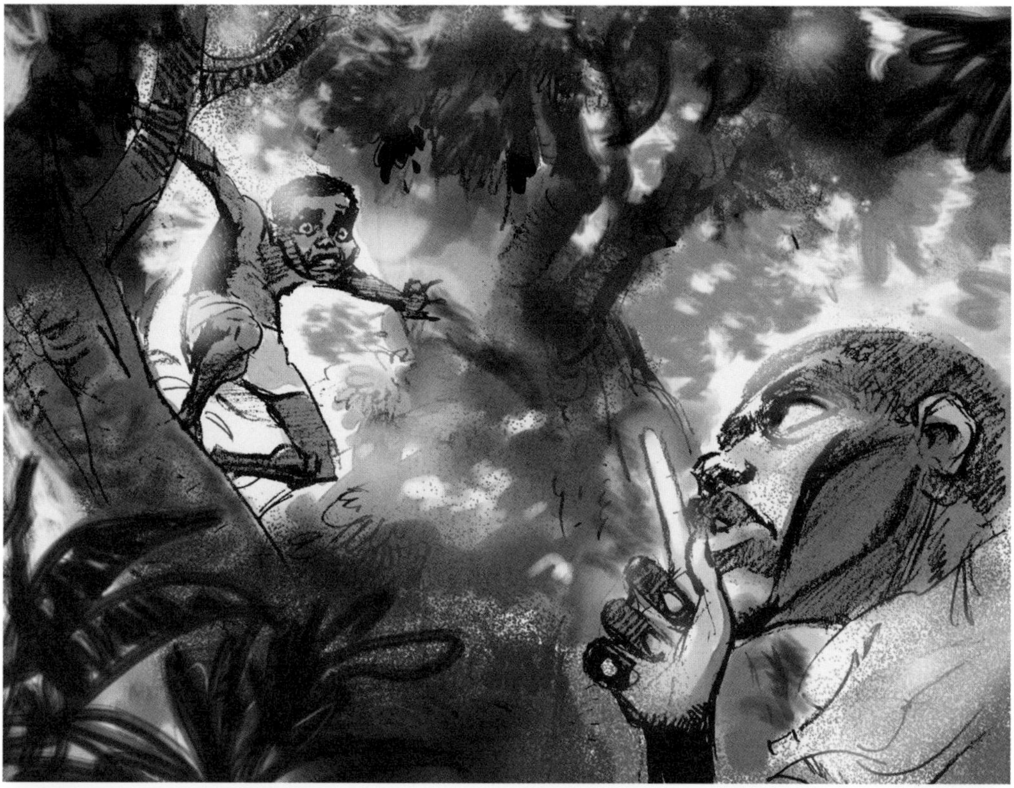

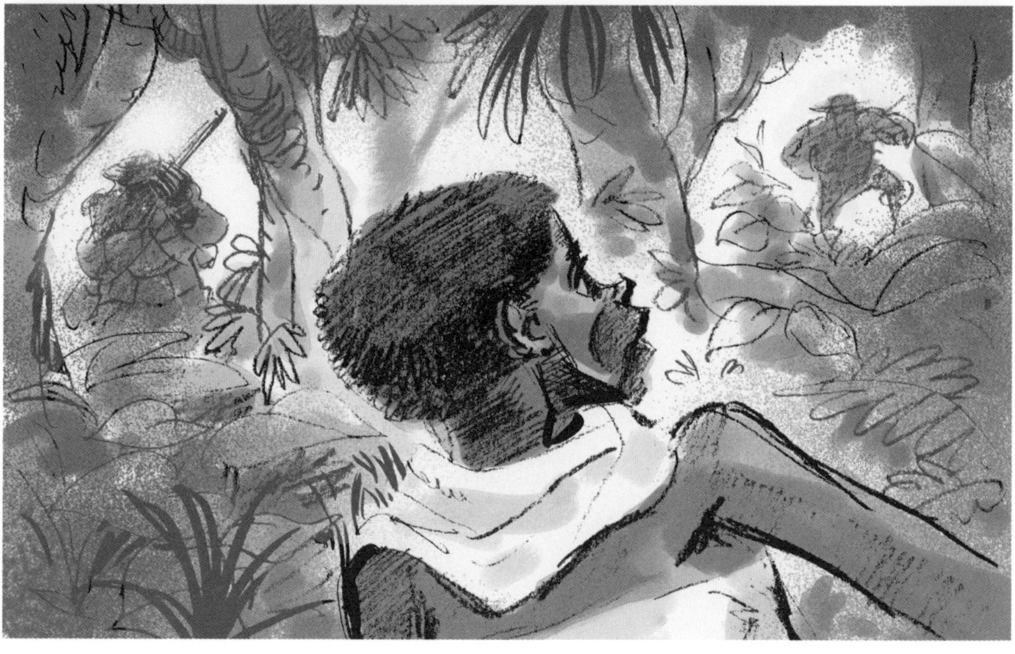

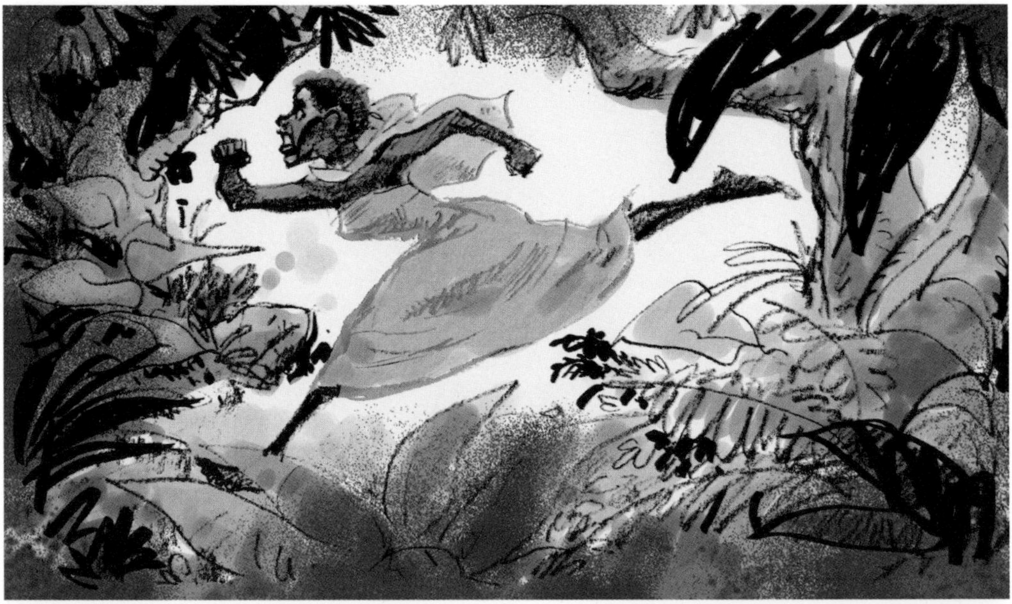

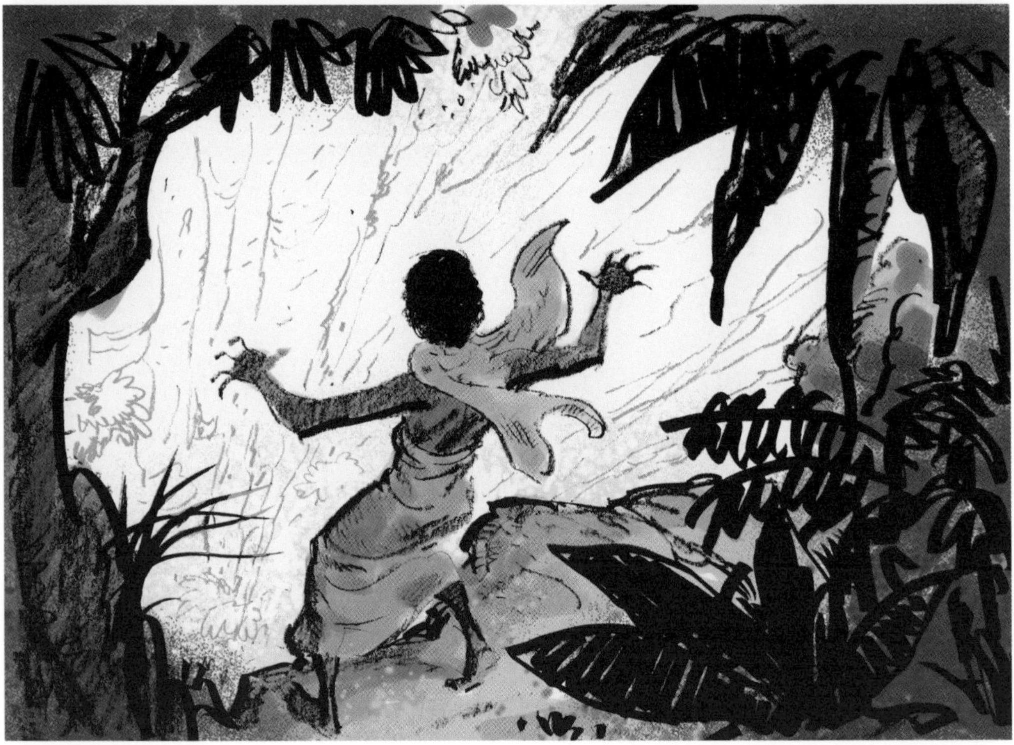

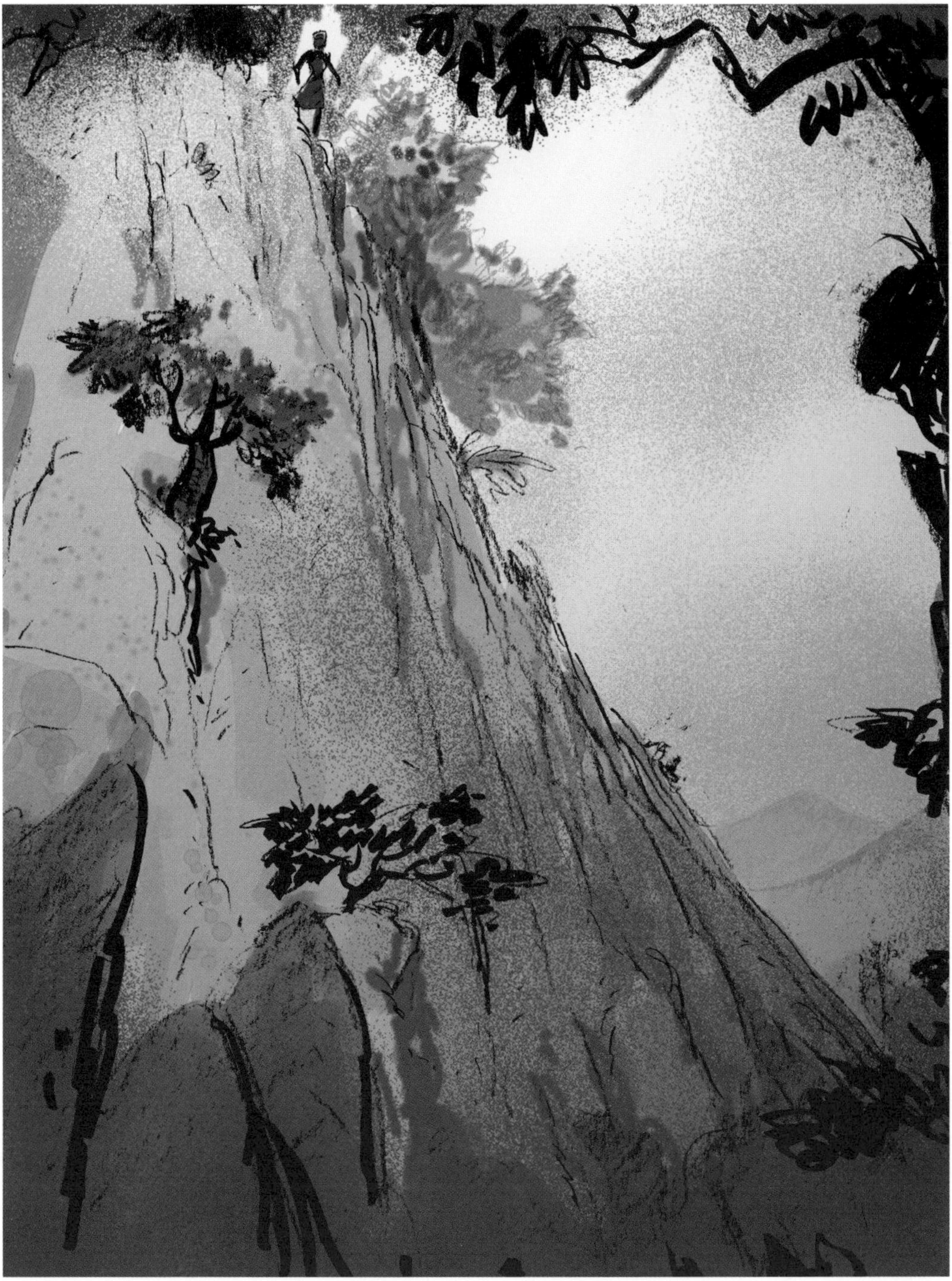

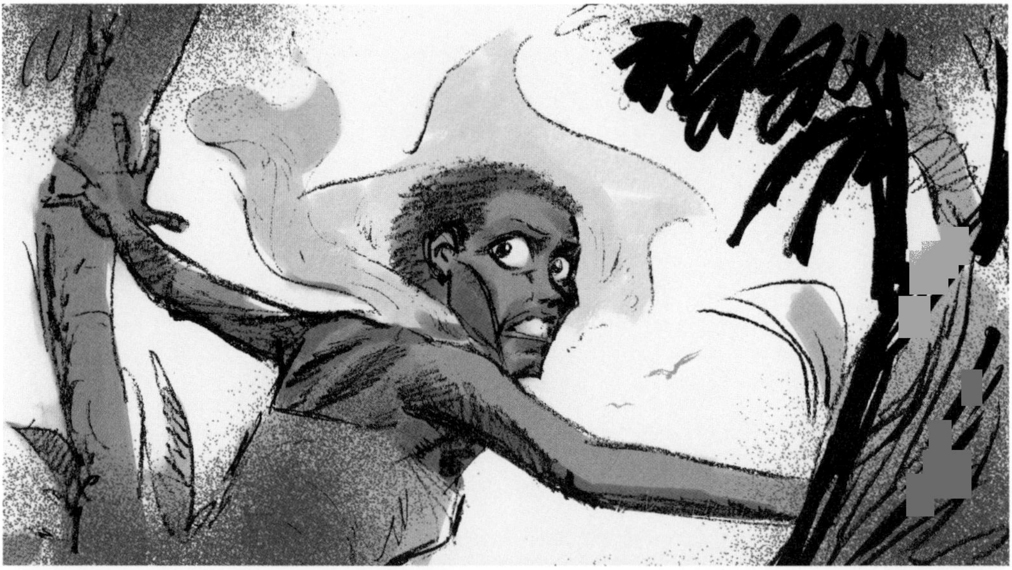

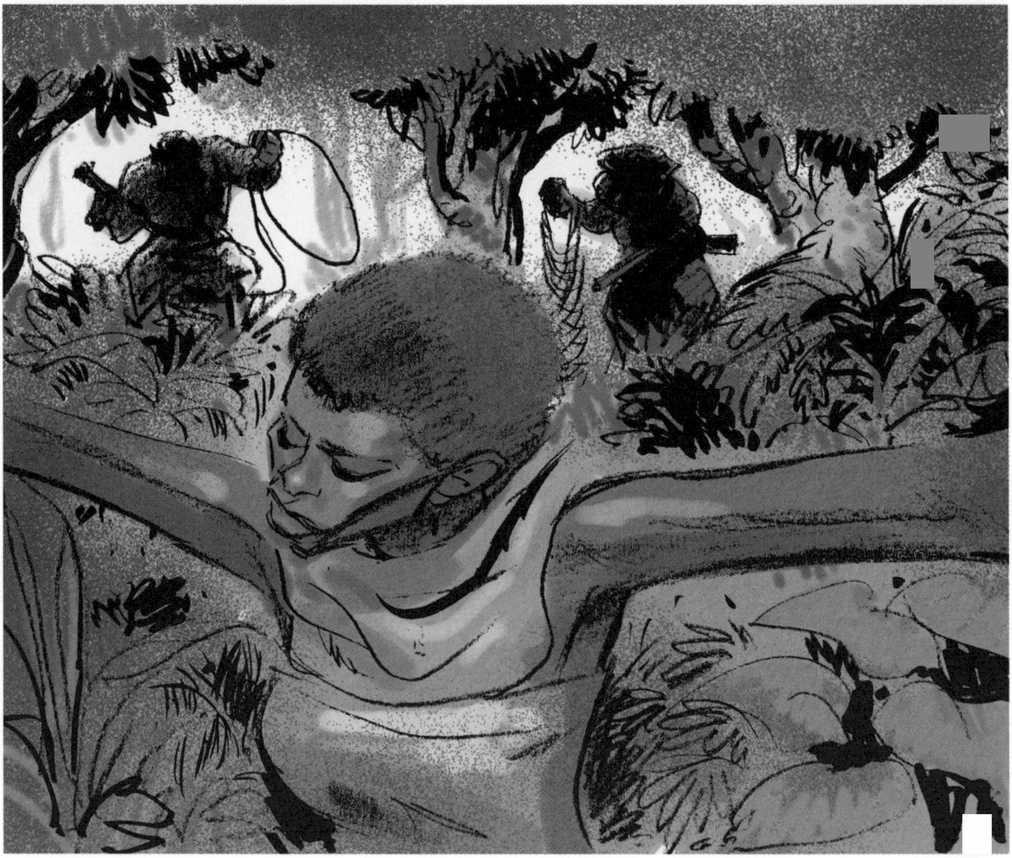

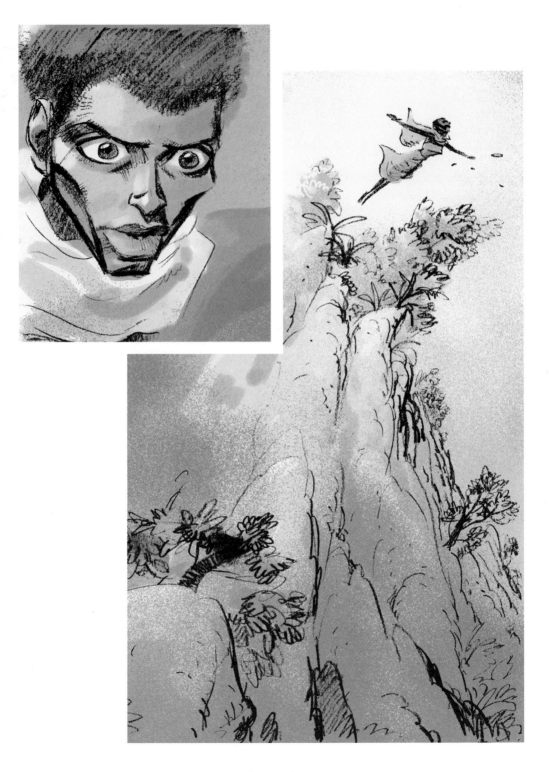

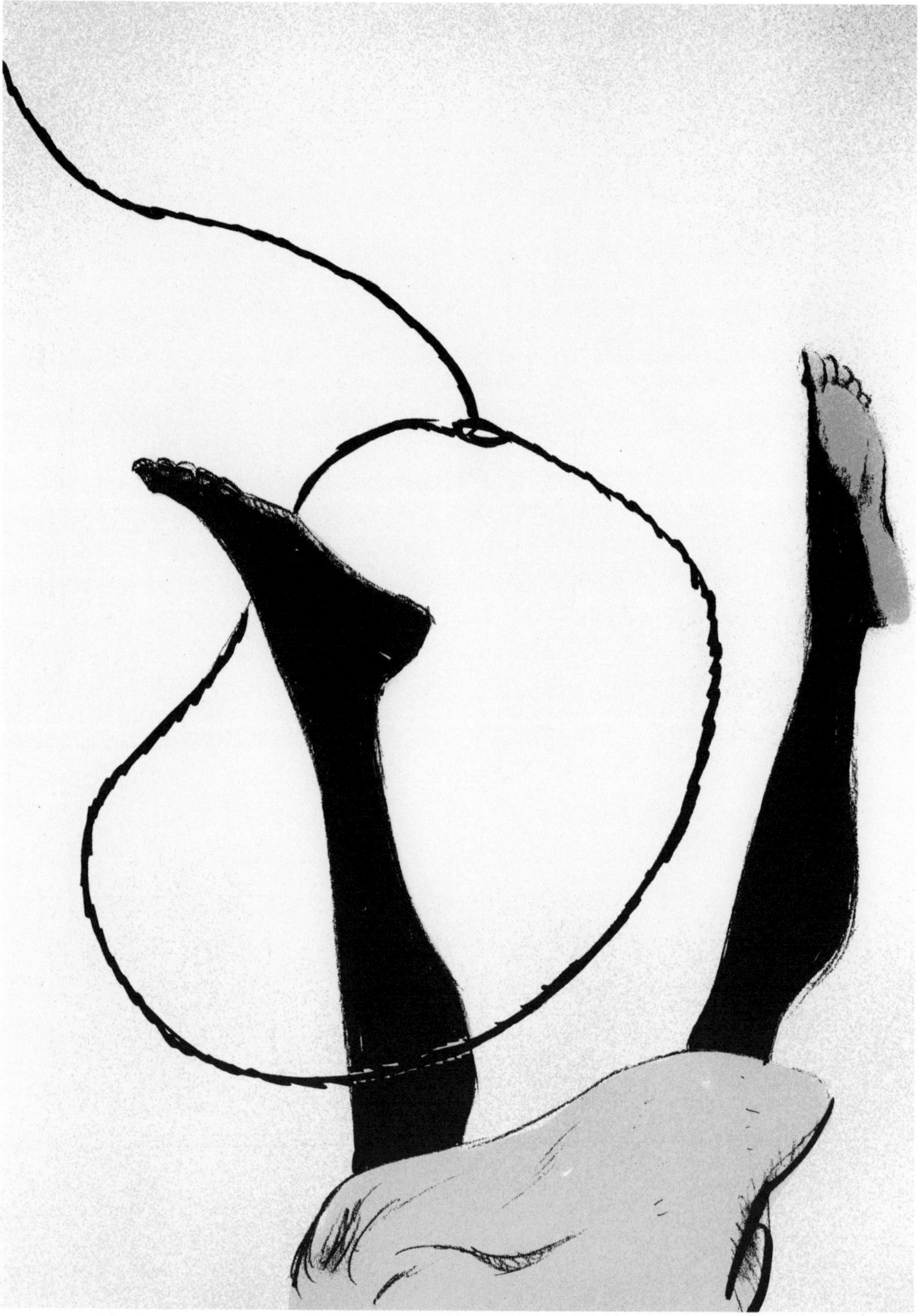

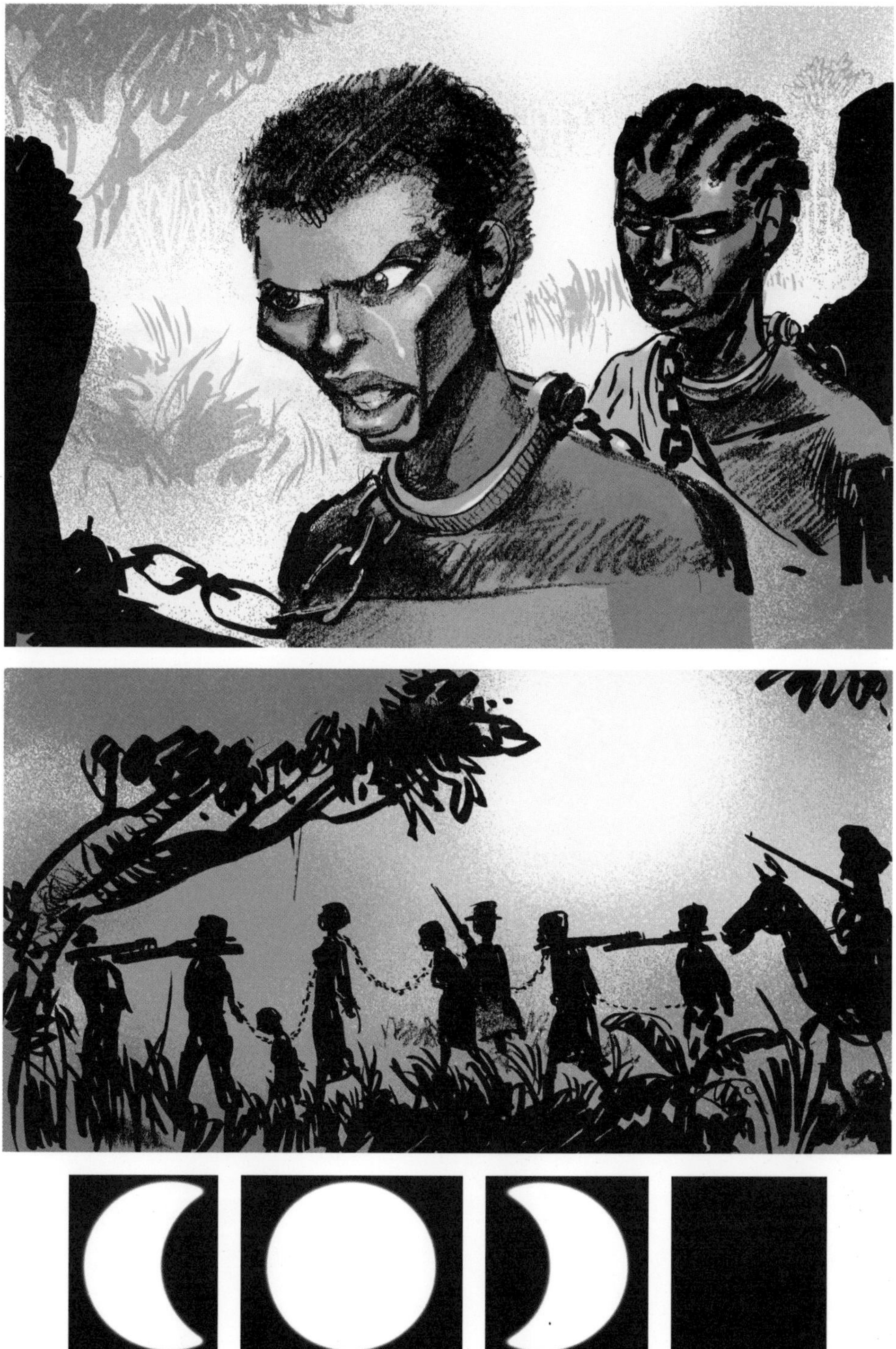

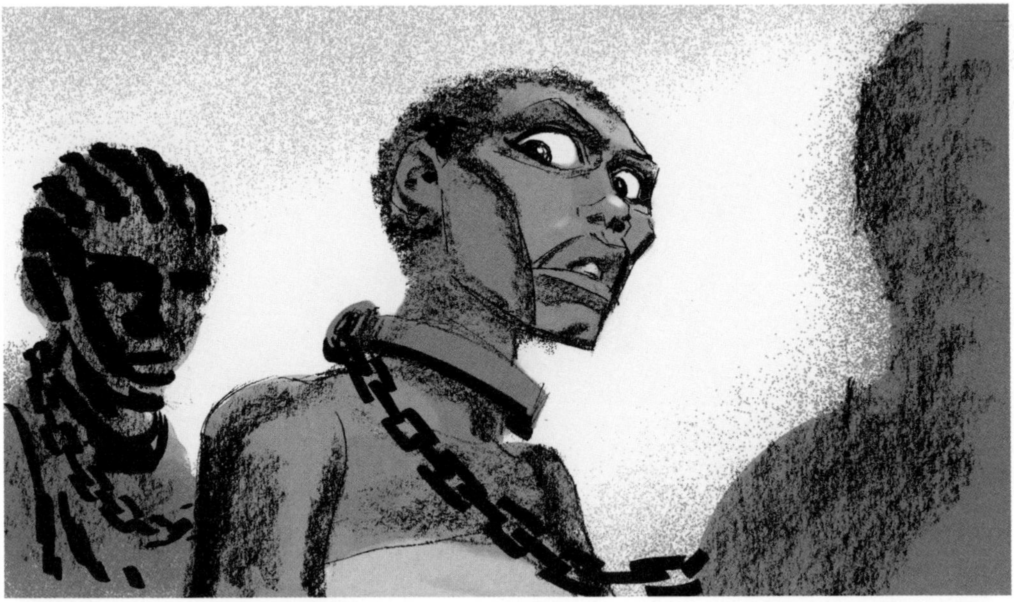

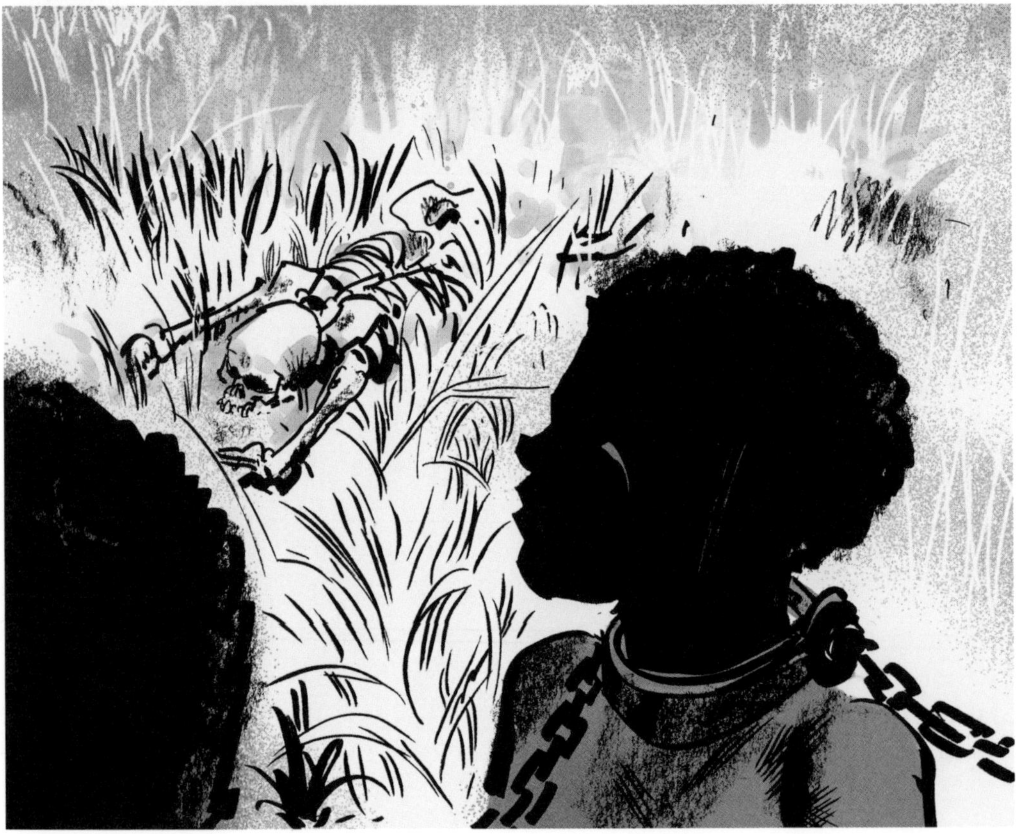

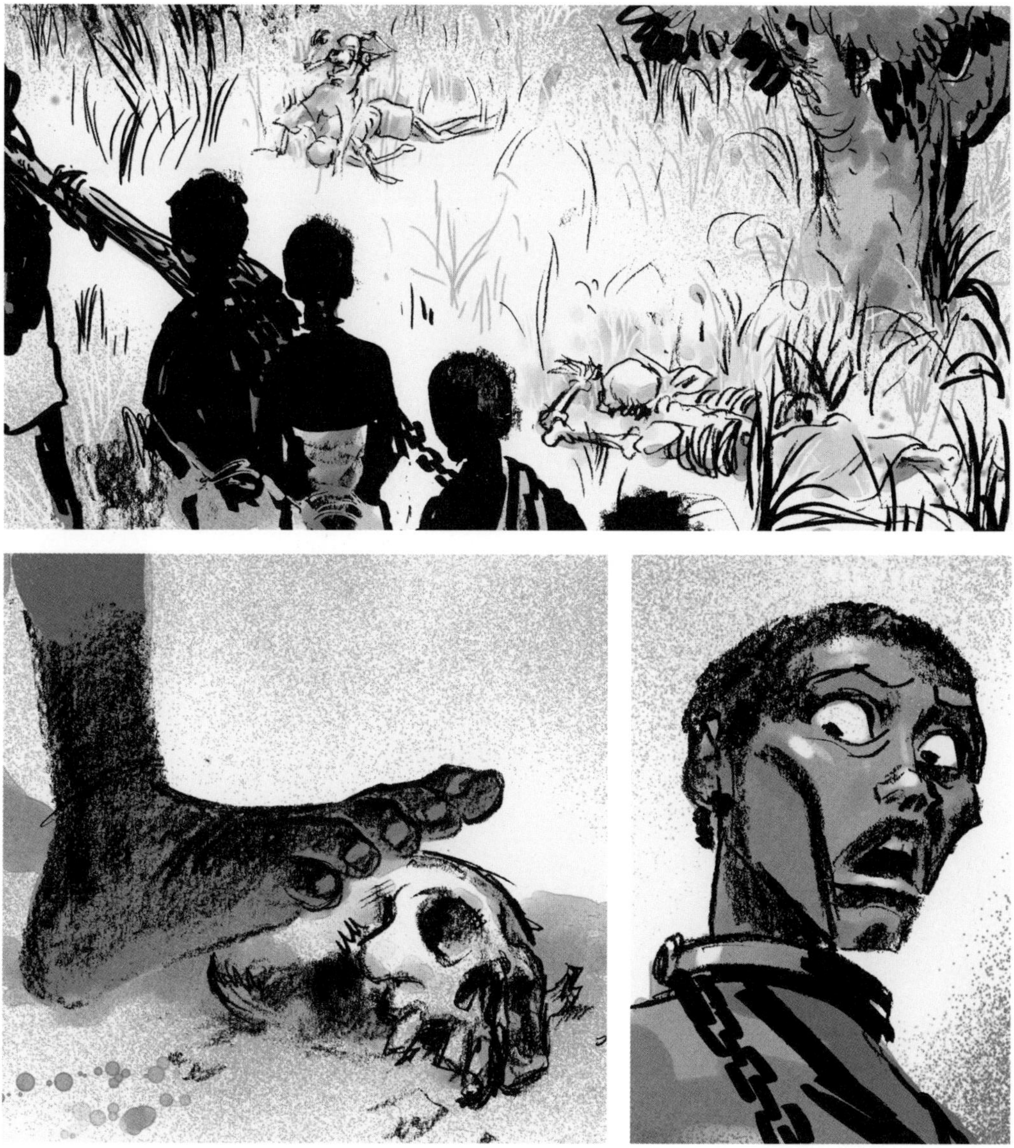

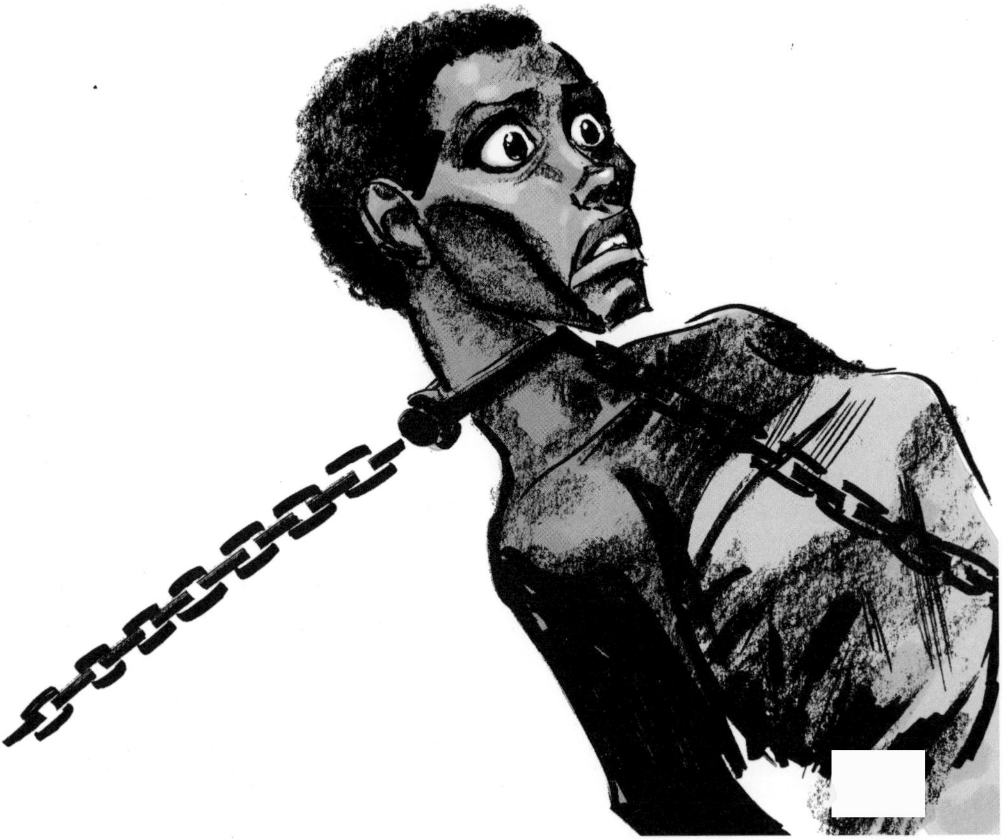

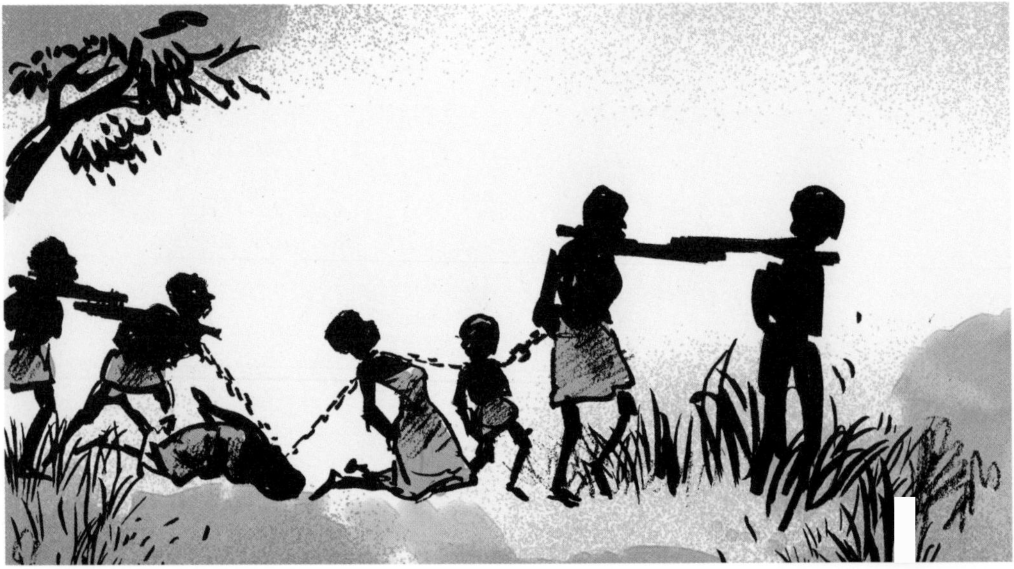

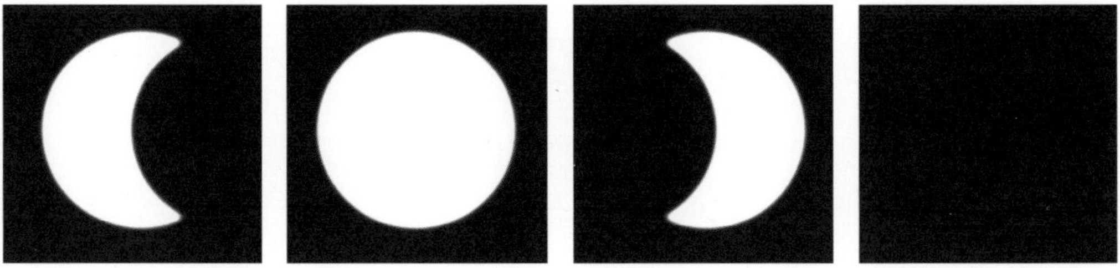

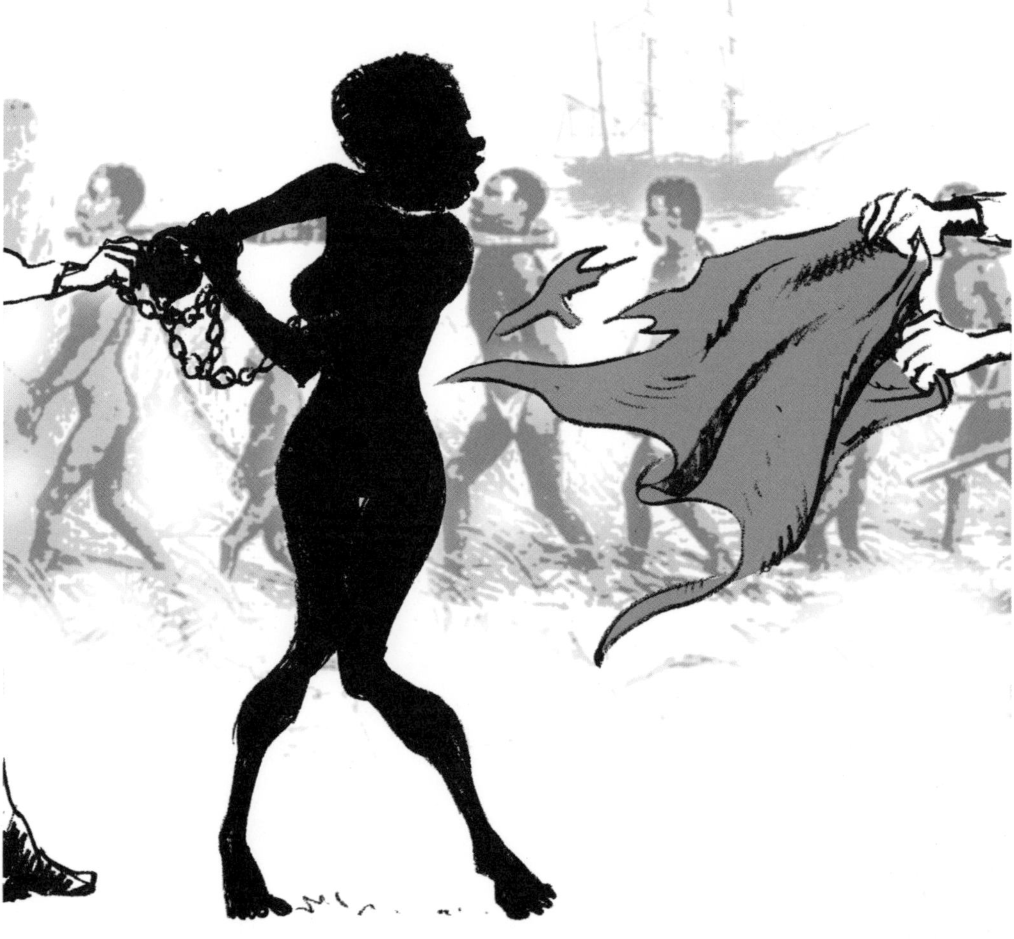

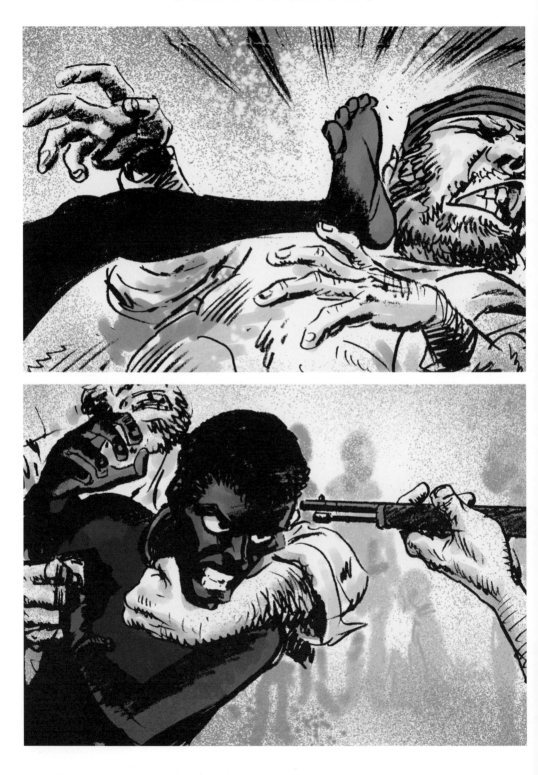

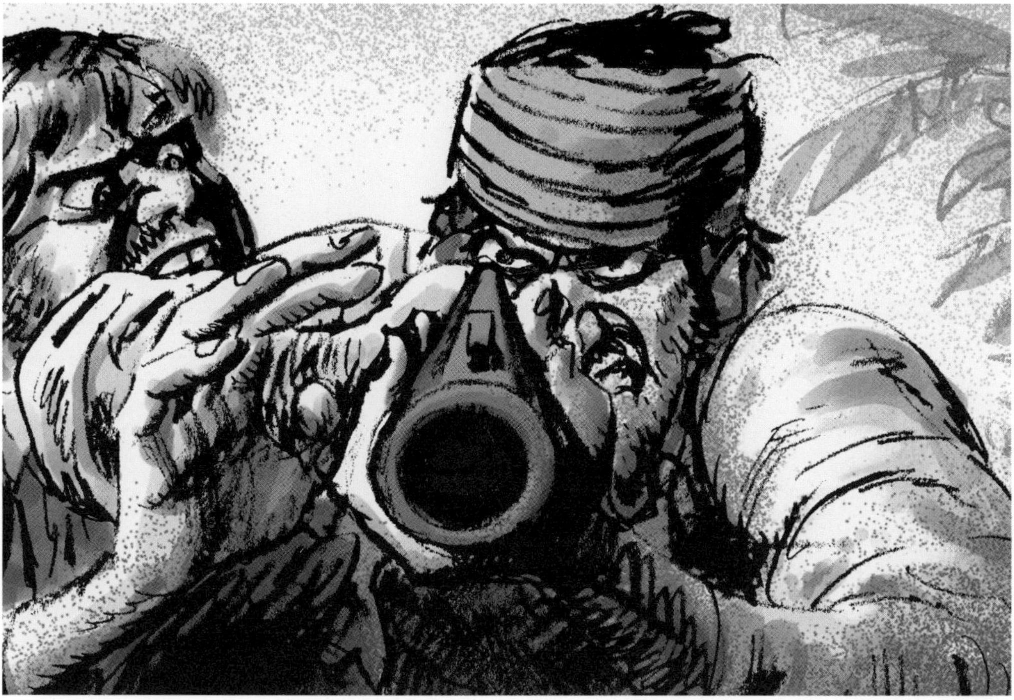

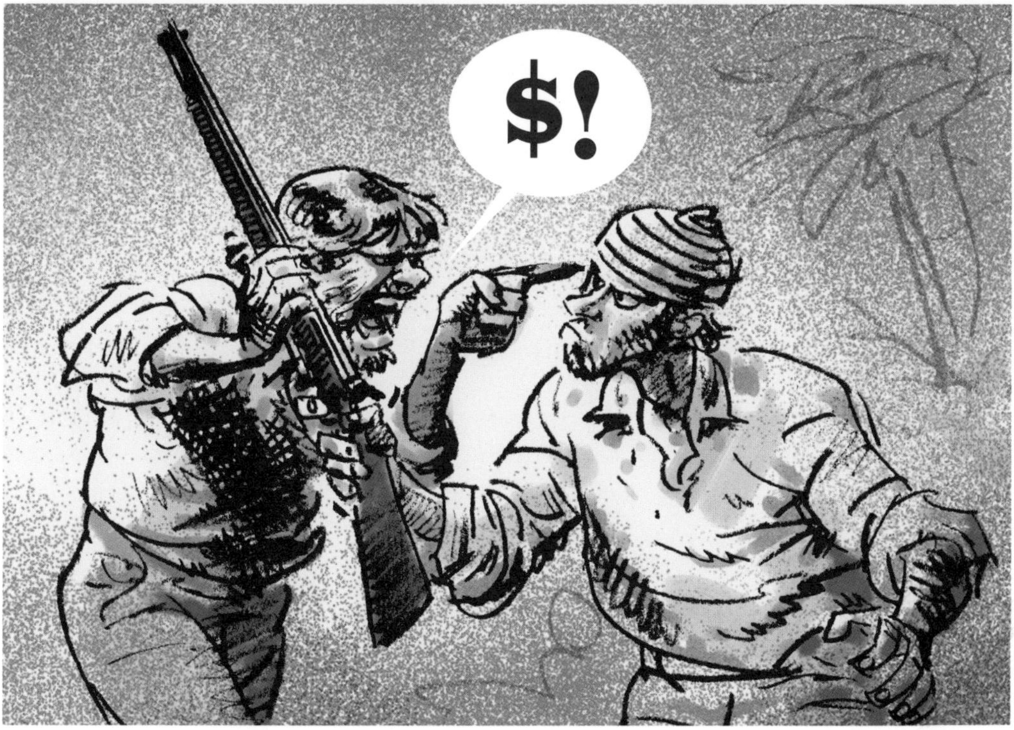
$!

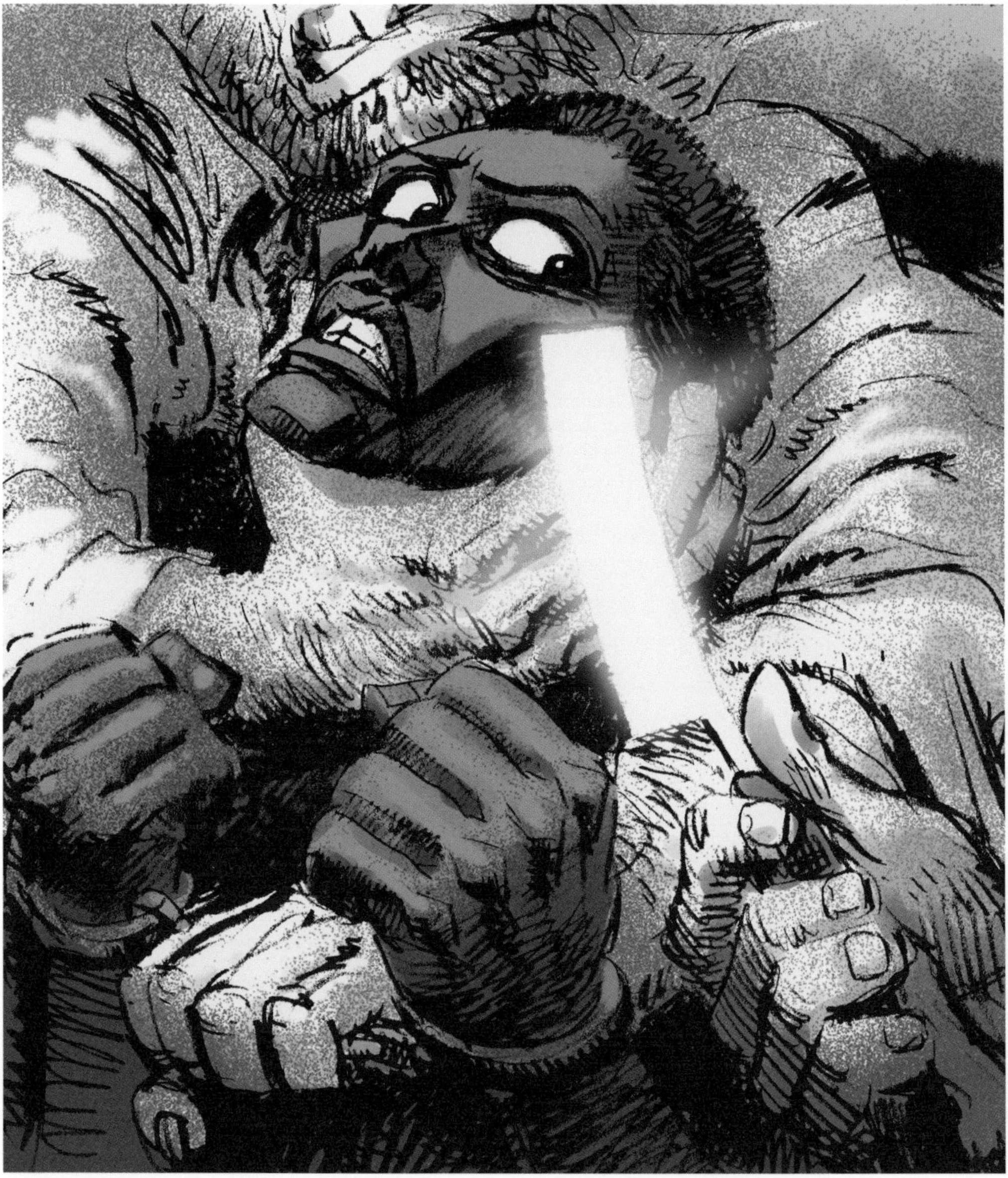

FROM THE MEMOIR OF CAPTAIN THEODORE CANOT: TWENTY YEARS OF AN AFRICAN SLAVER

"The head of every male and female is neatly shaved; and, if the cargo belongs to several owners, each man's brand is impressed on the body of his respective negro.... They are entirely stripped, so that women as well as men go out of Africa as they came into it—naked."

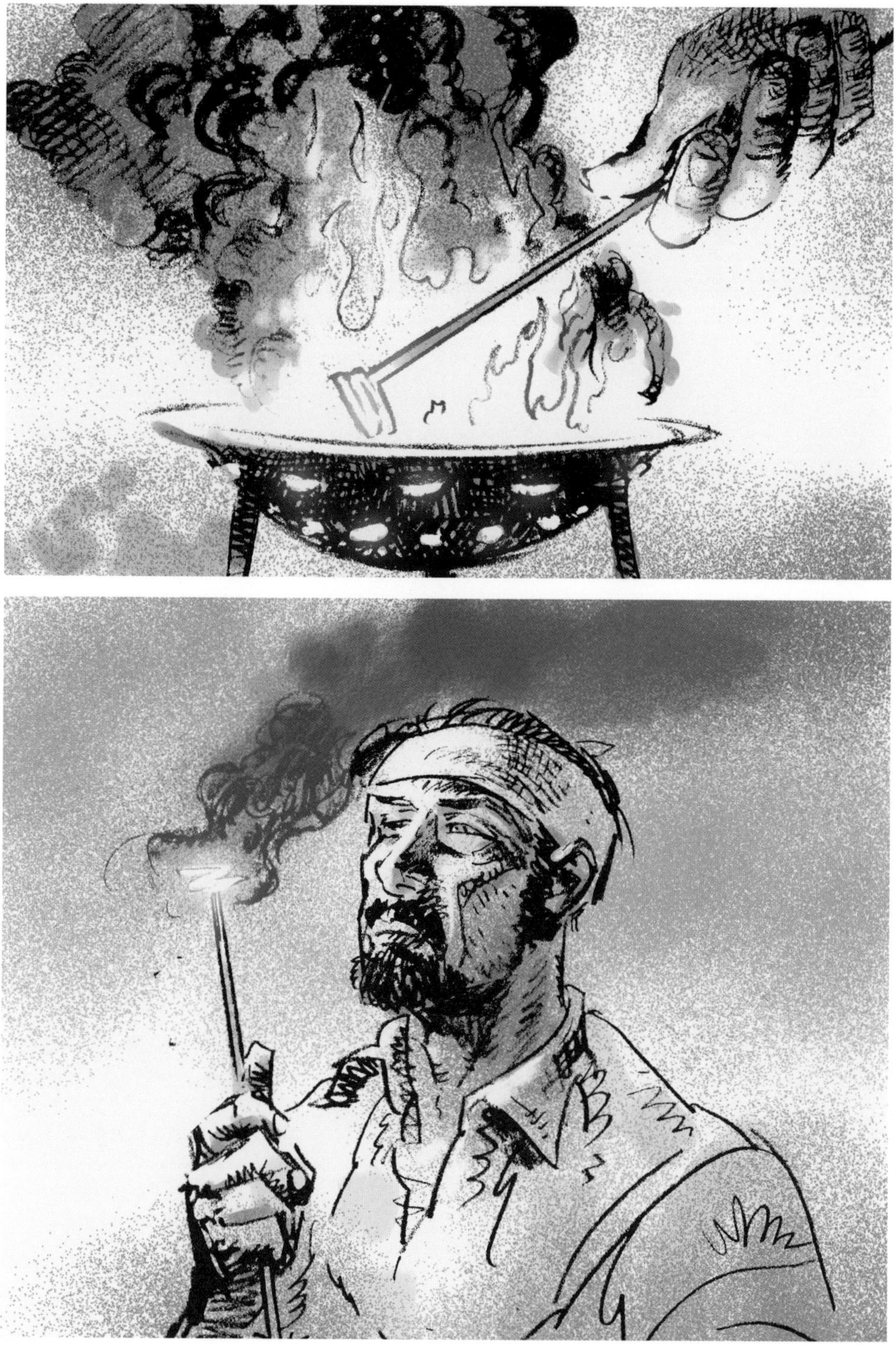

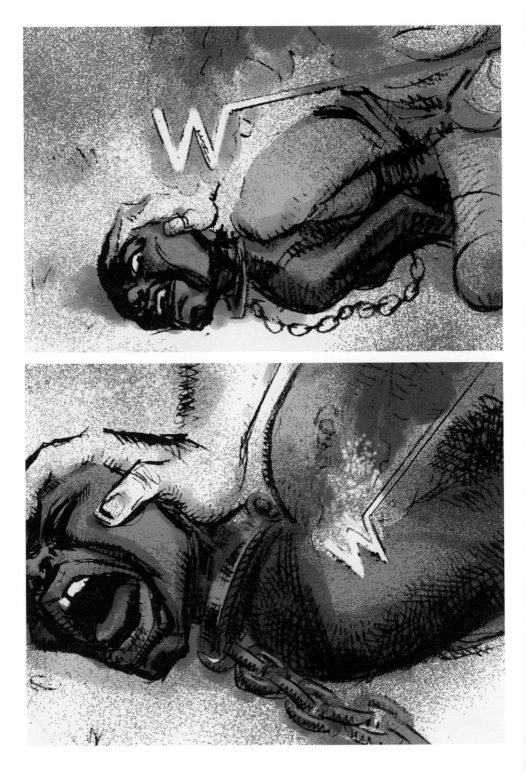

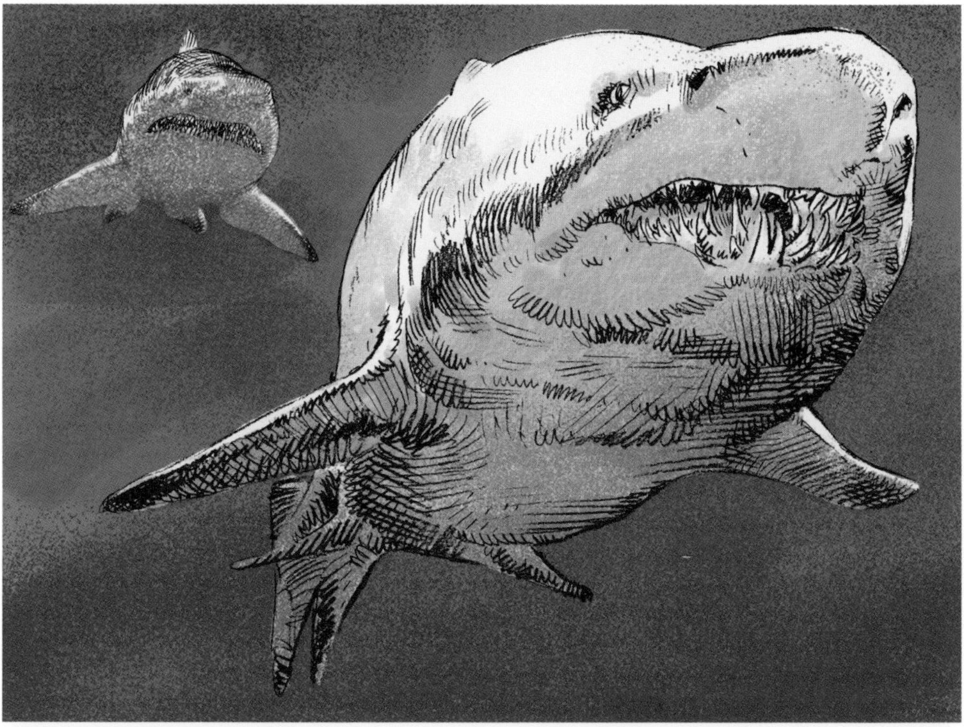

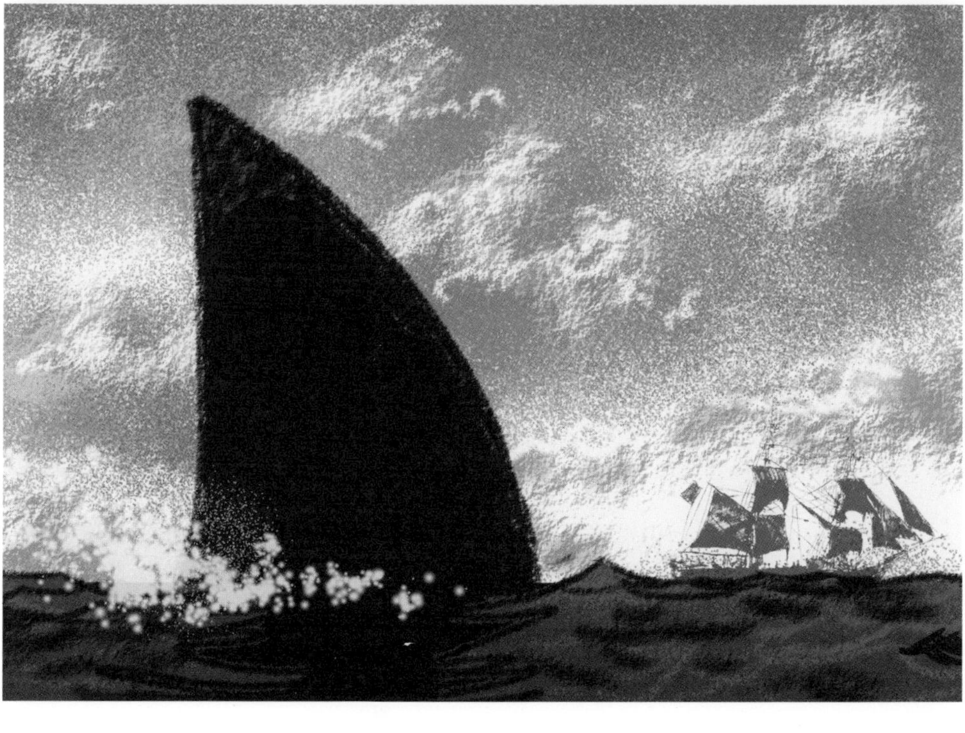

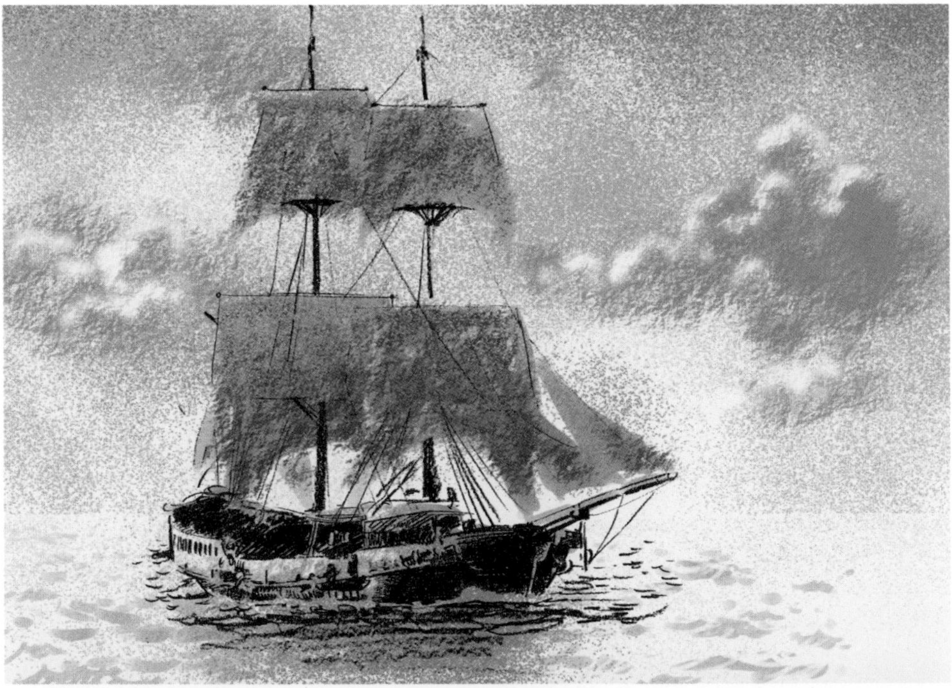

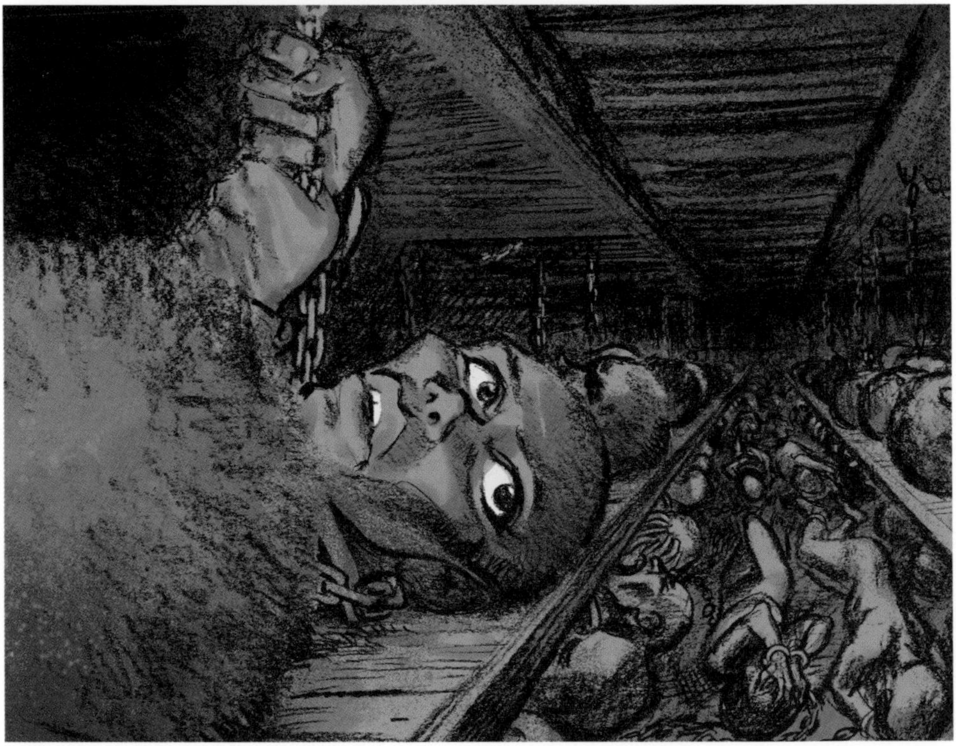

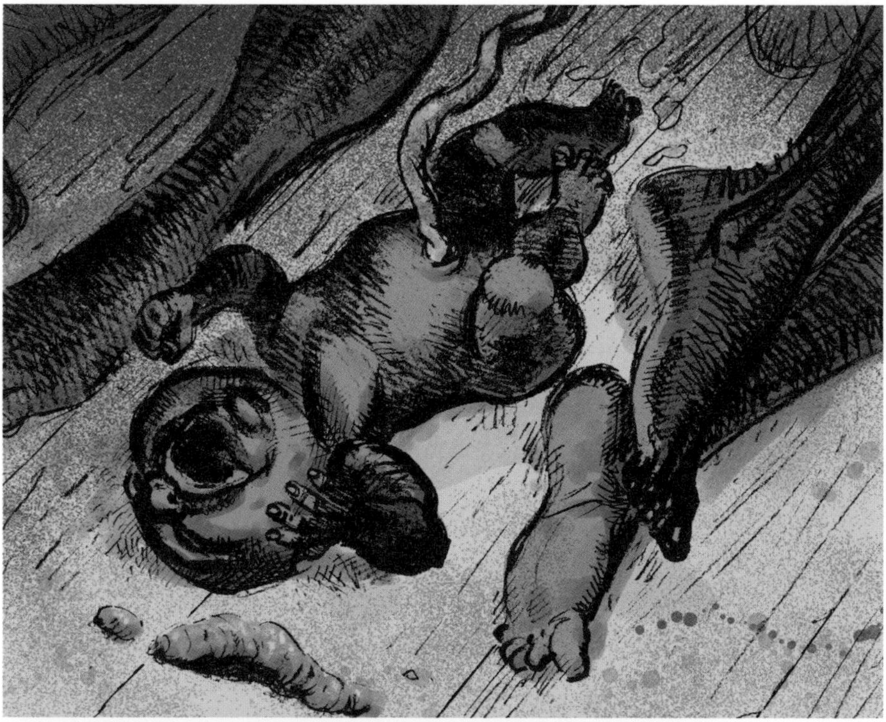

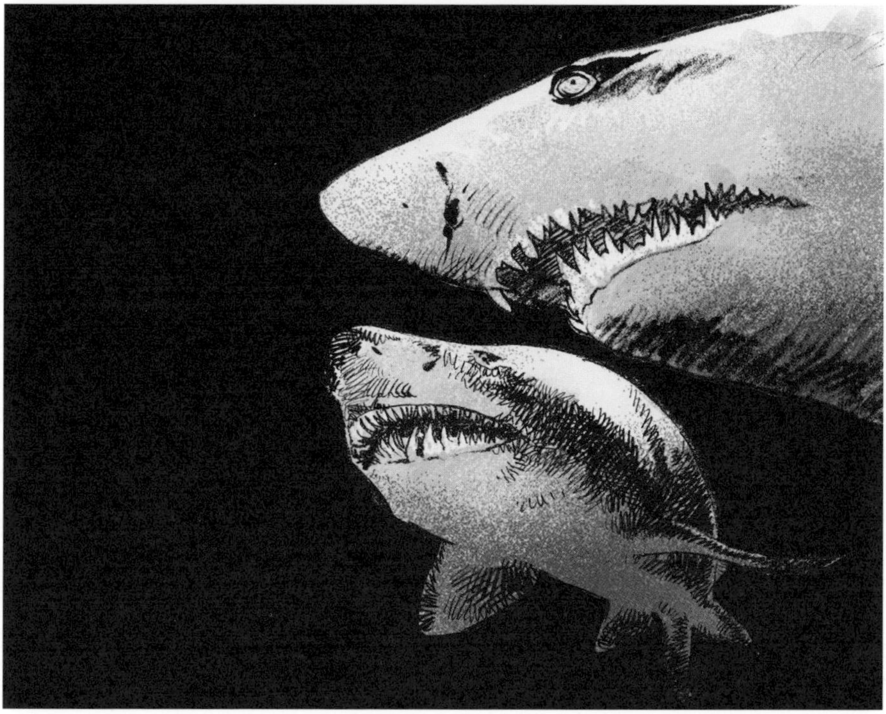

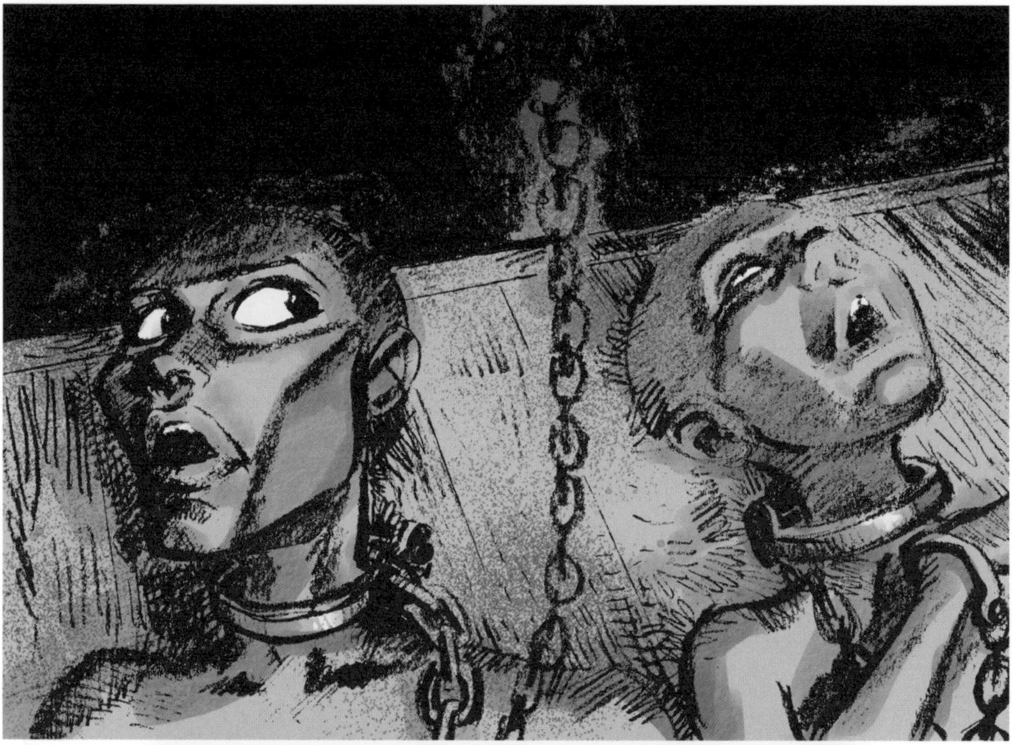

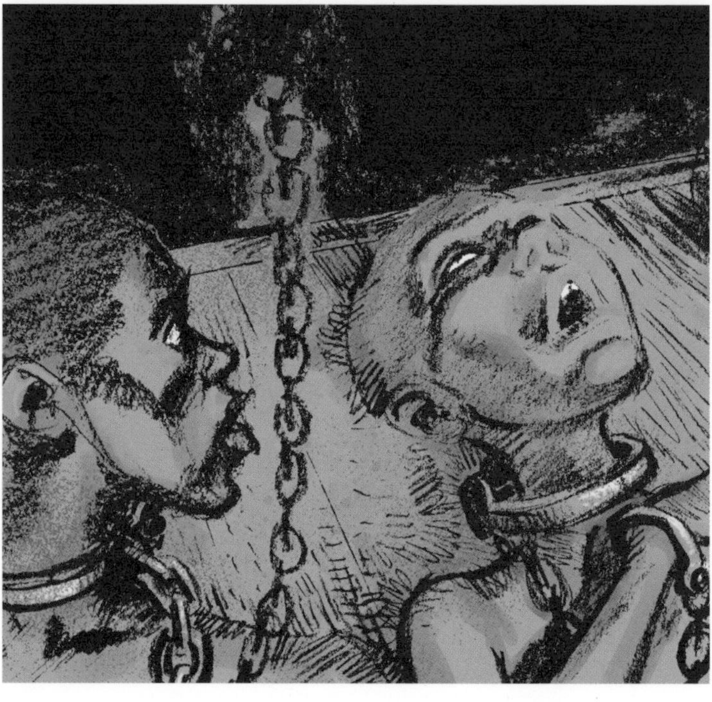

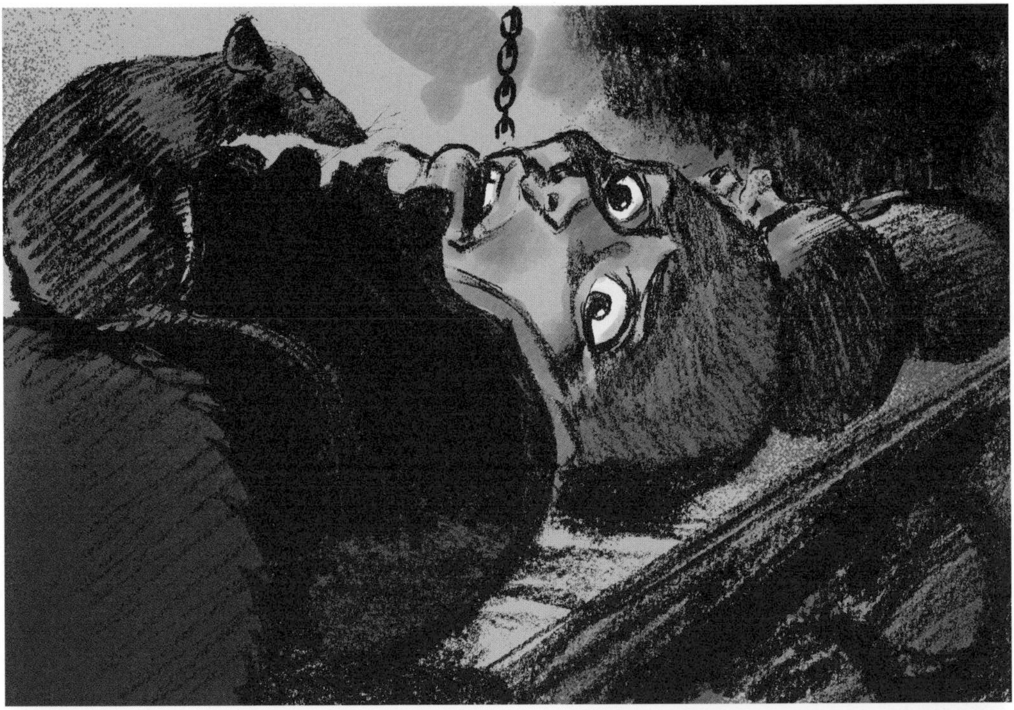

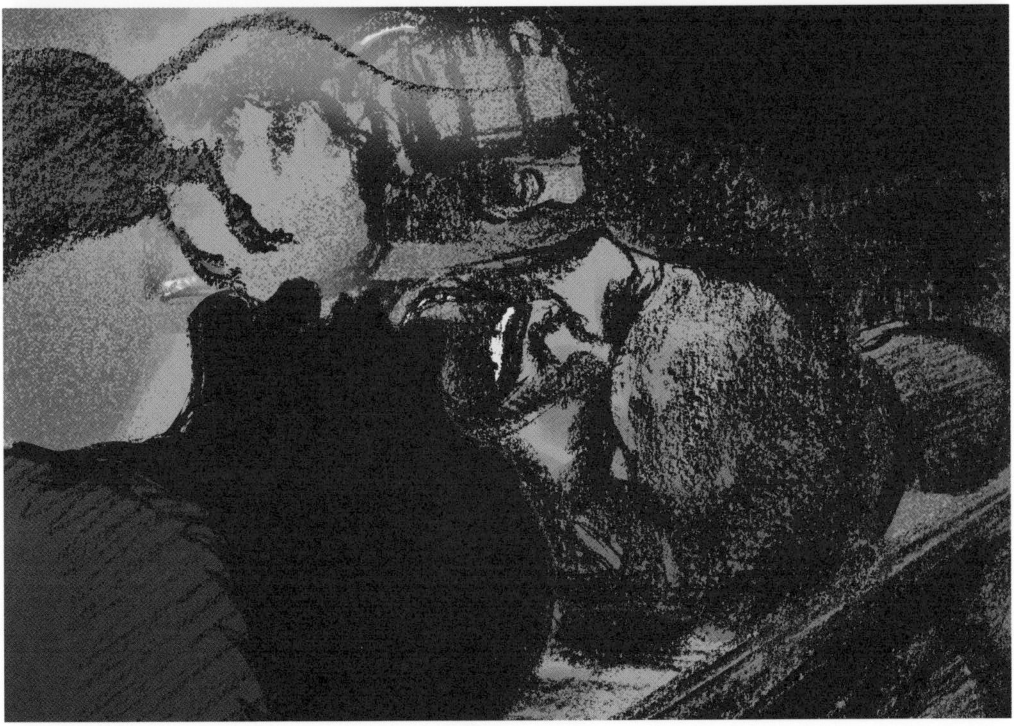

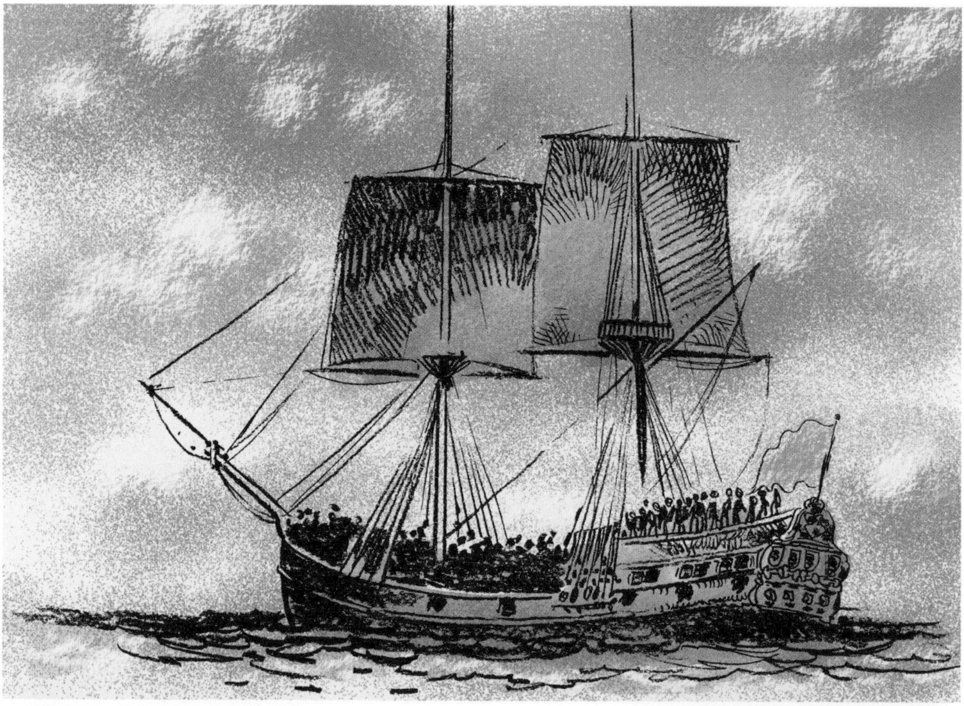

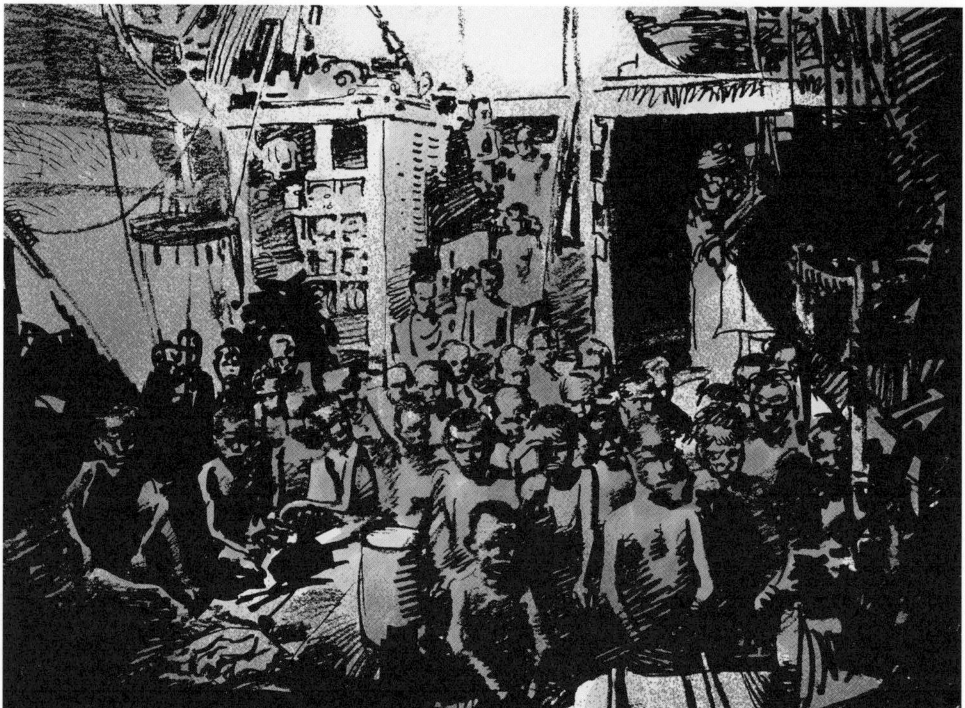

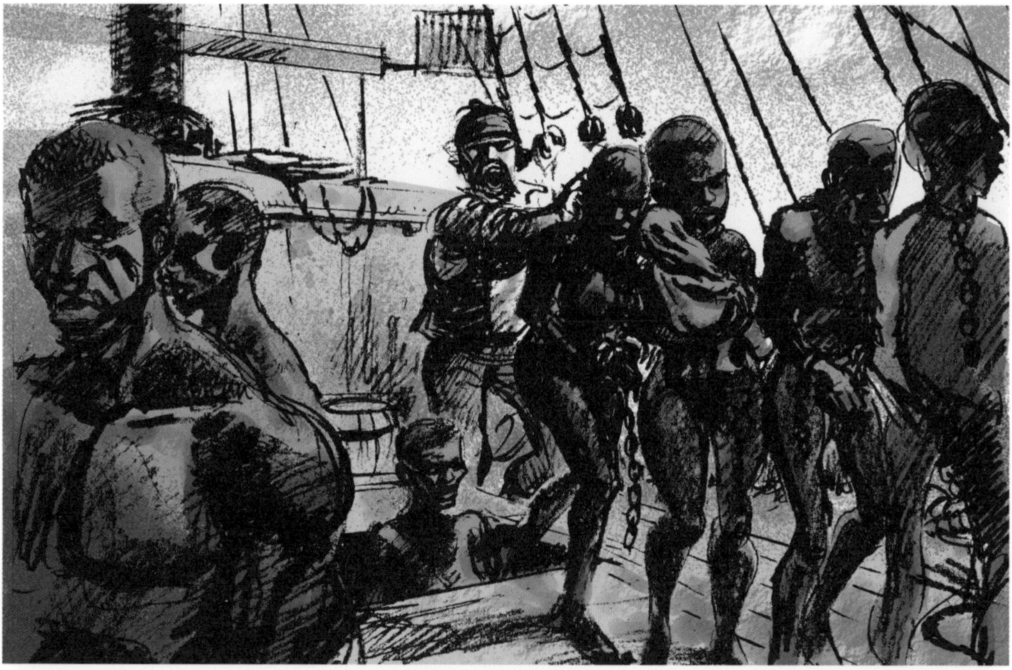

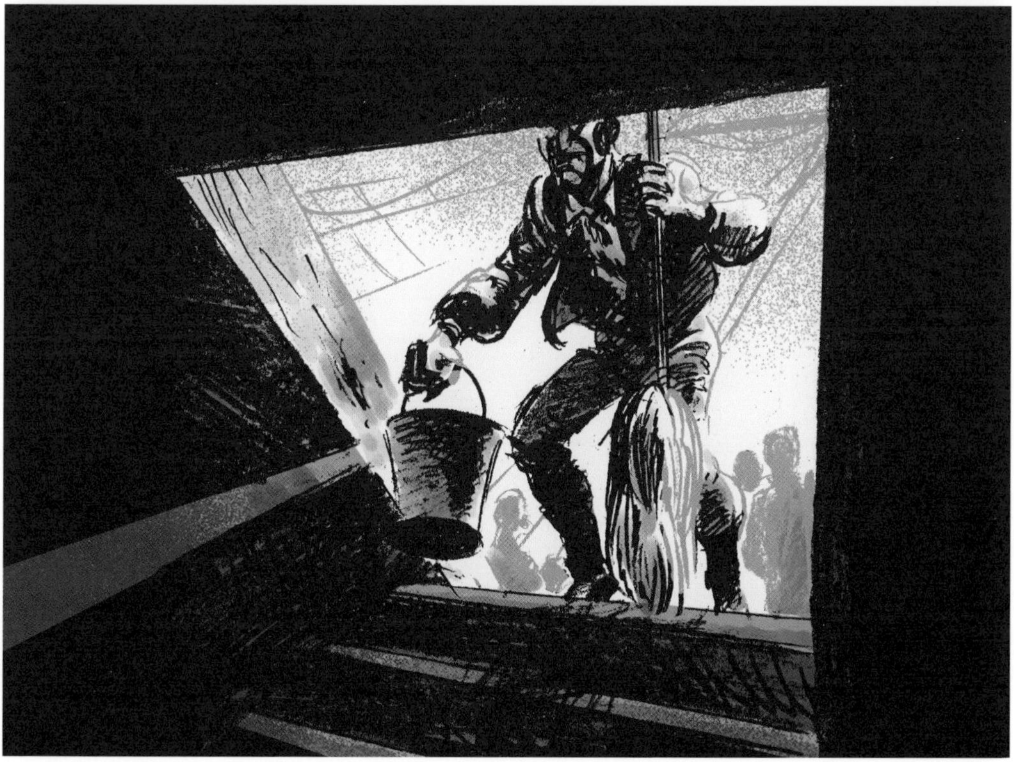

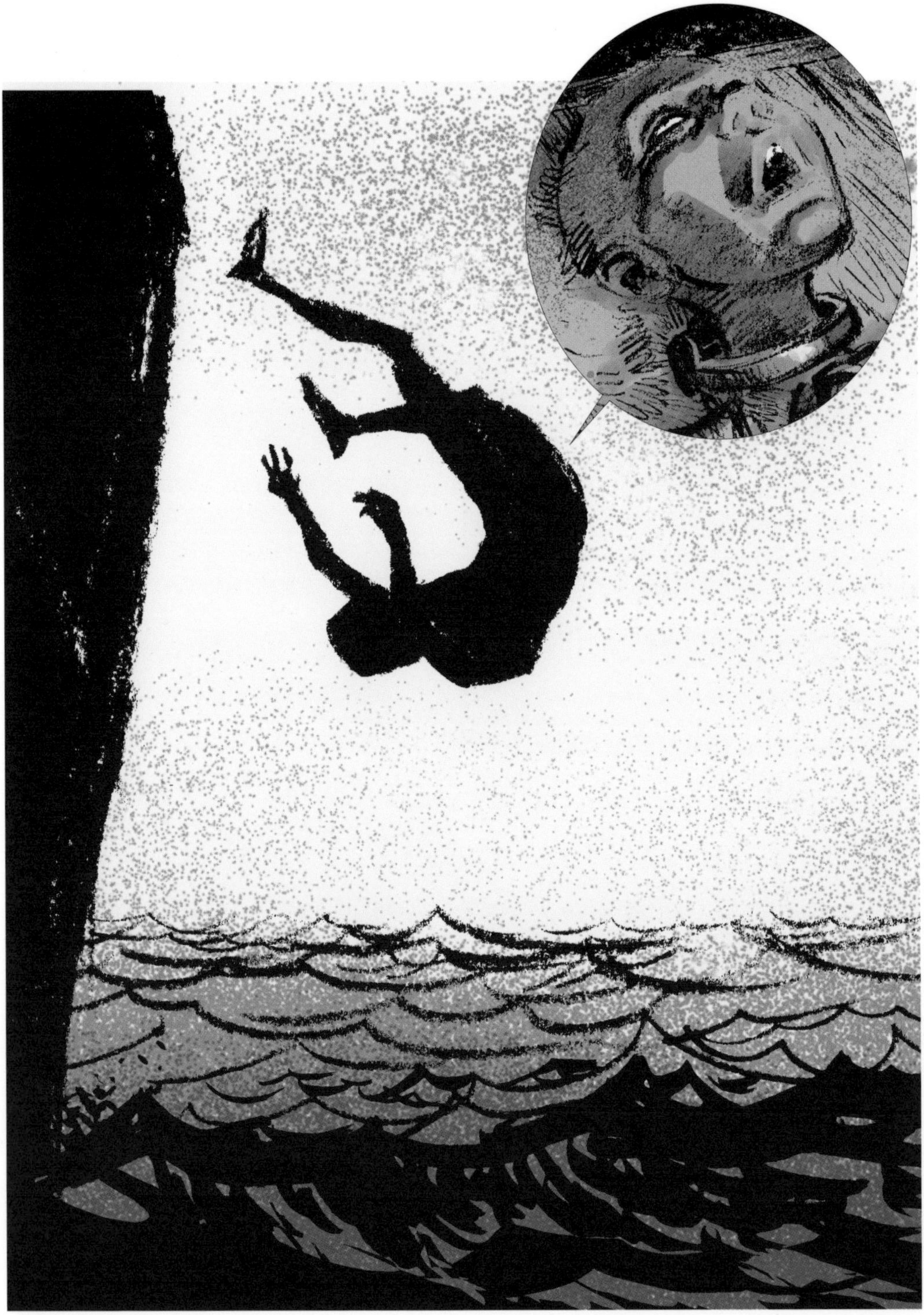

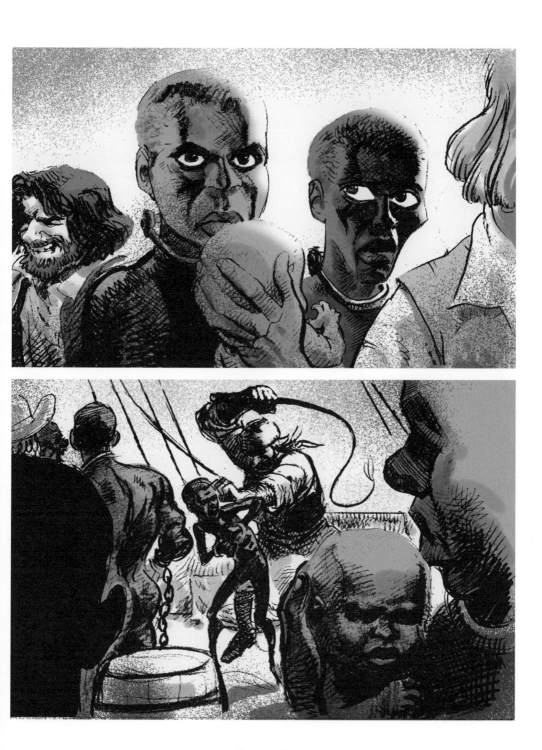

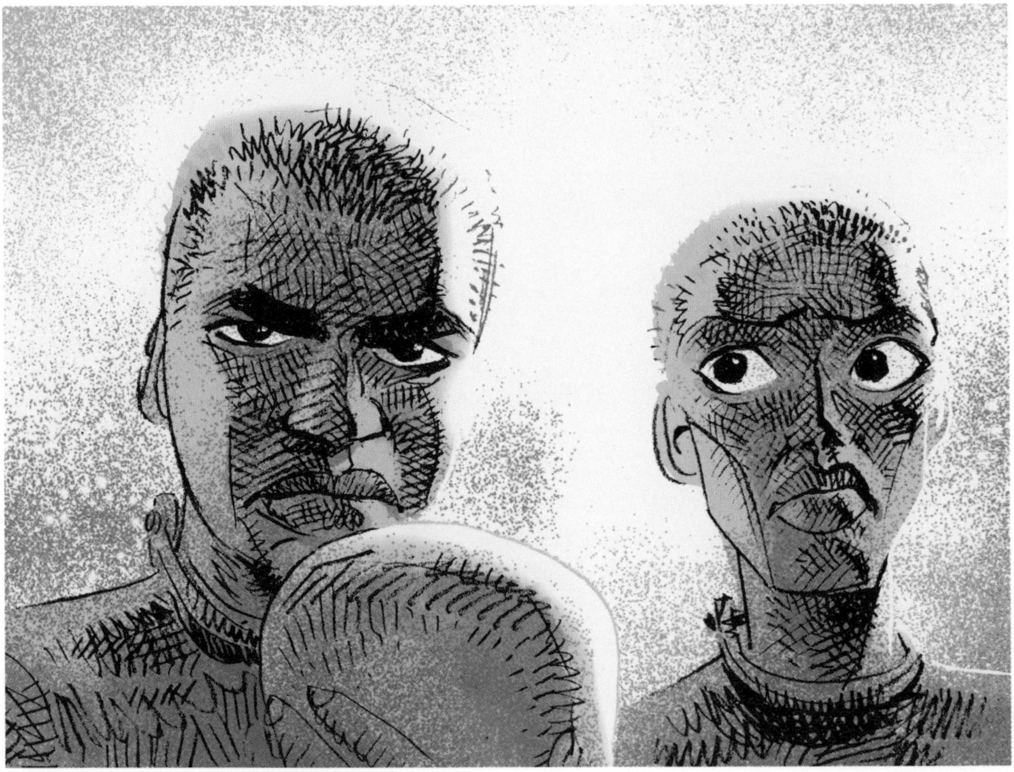

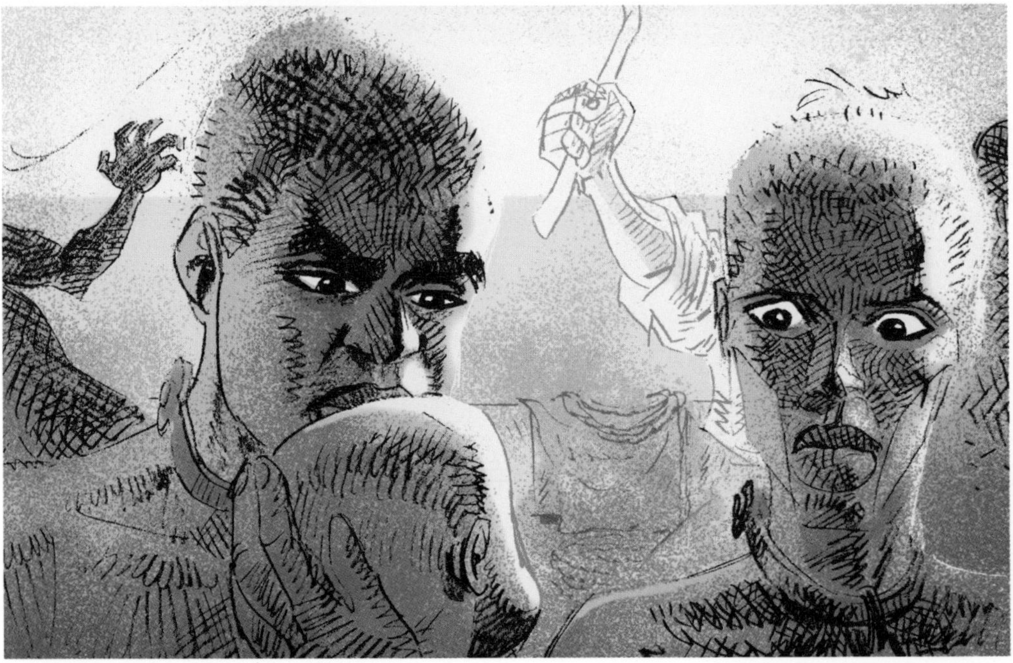

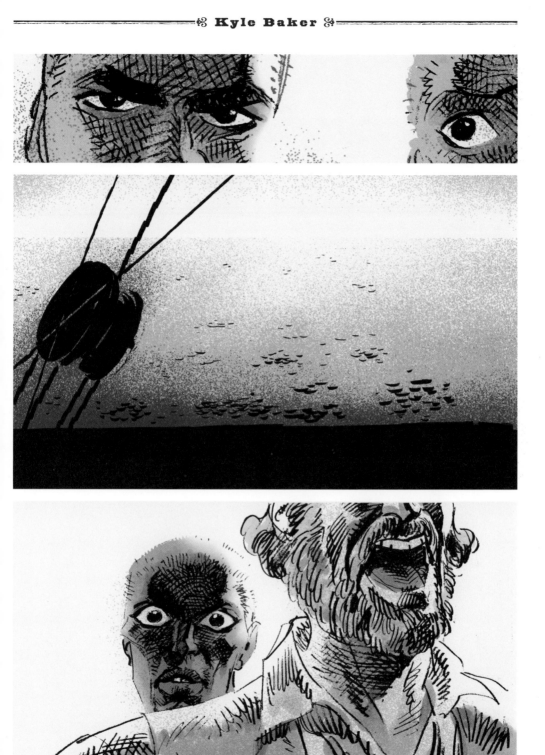

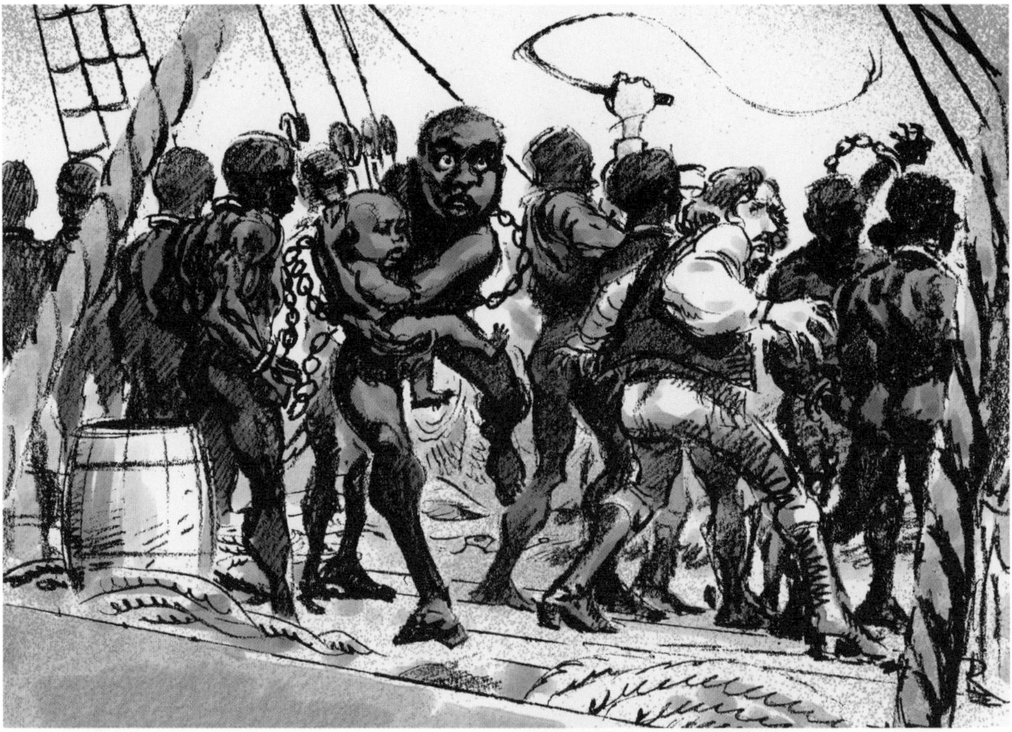

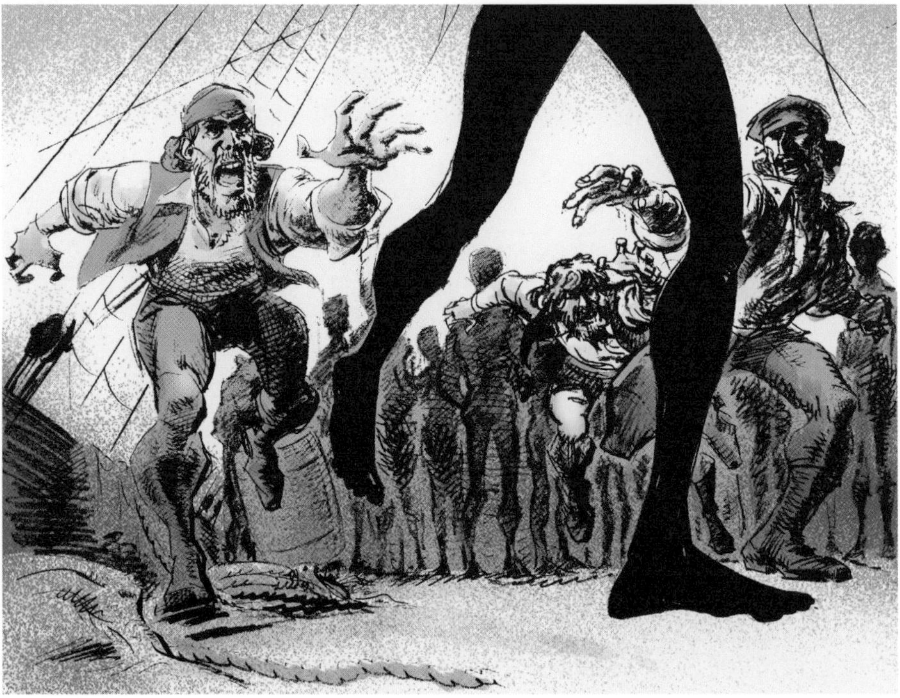

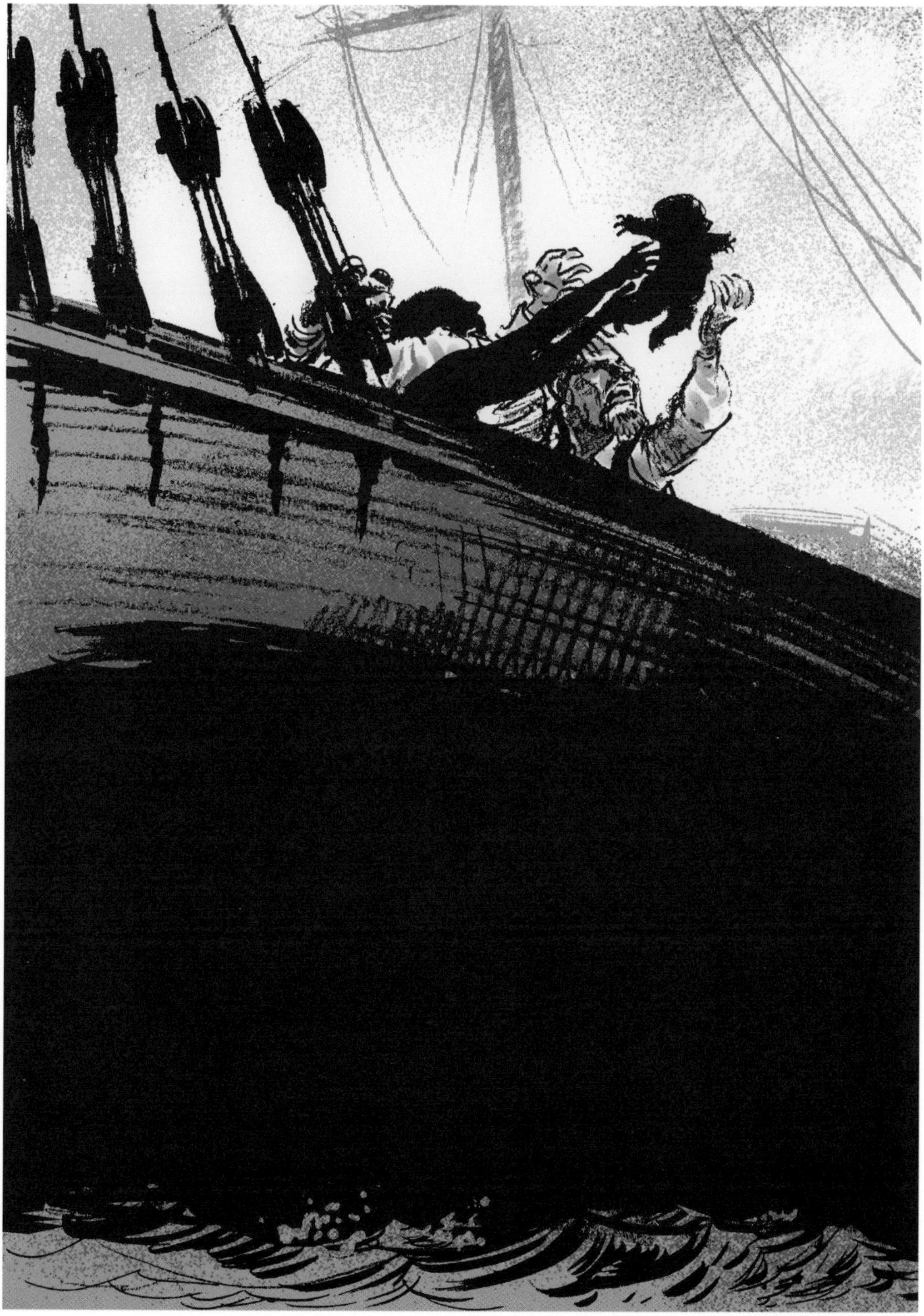

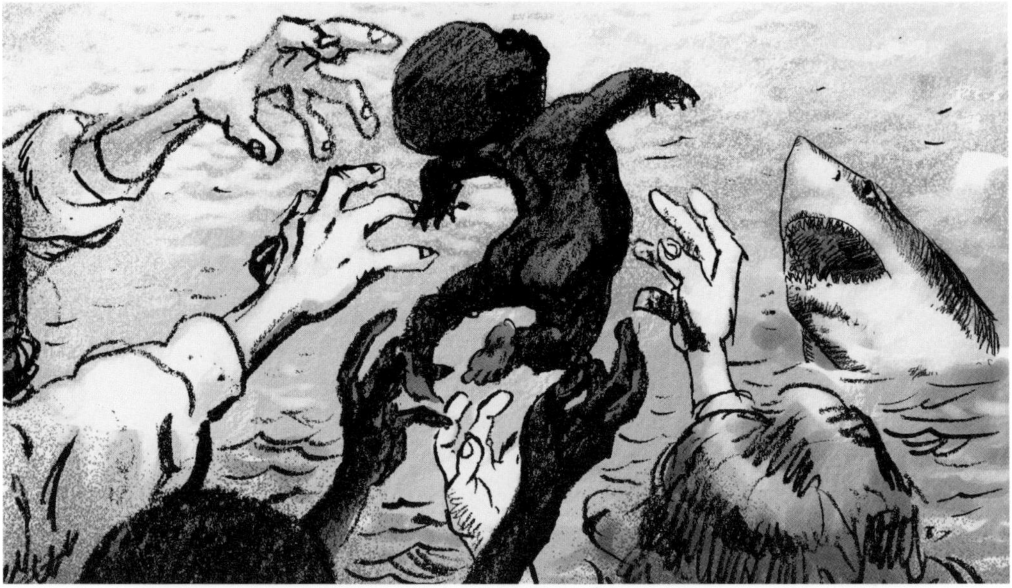

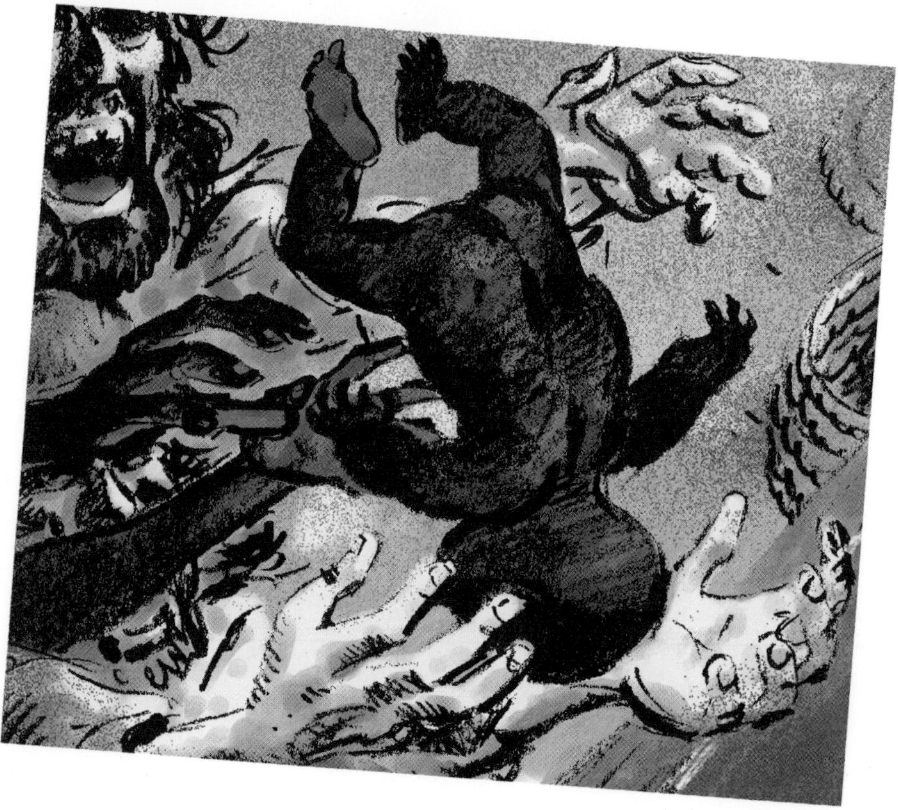

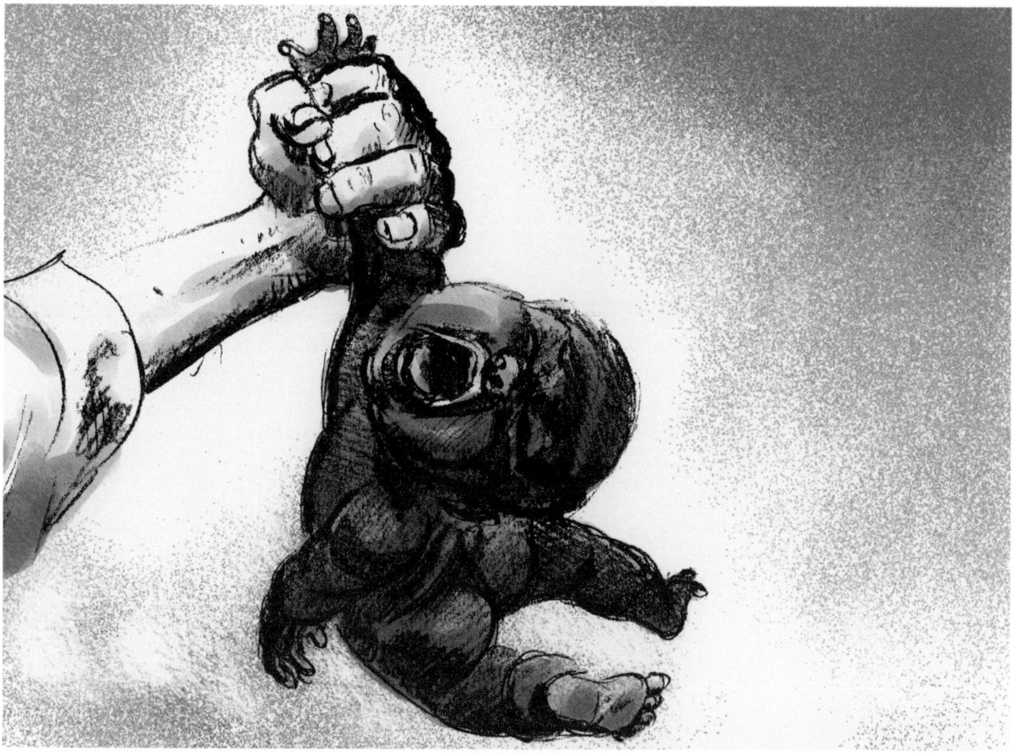

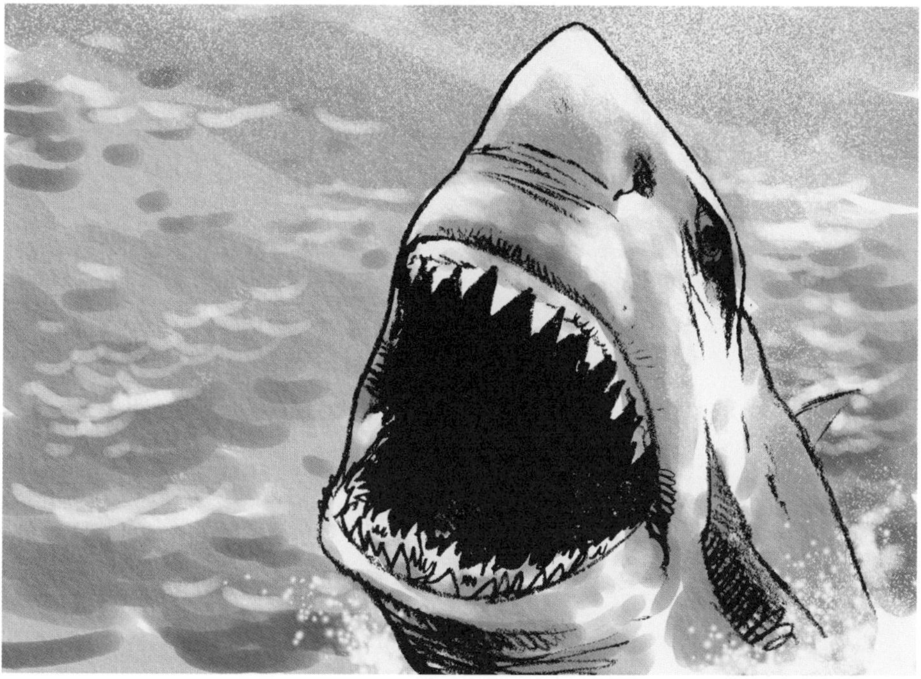

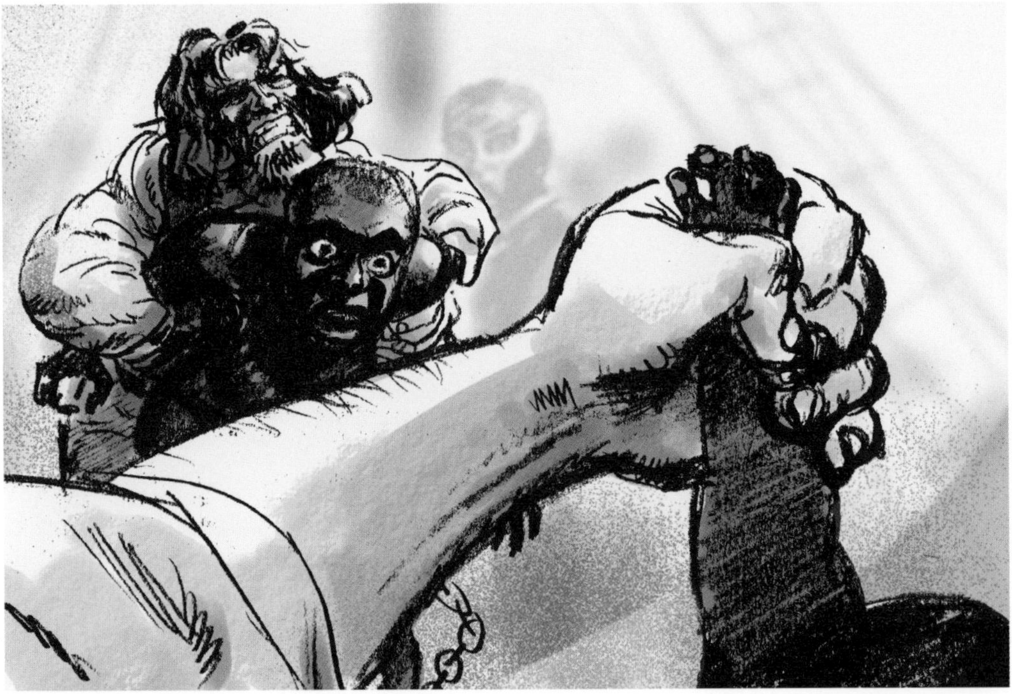

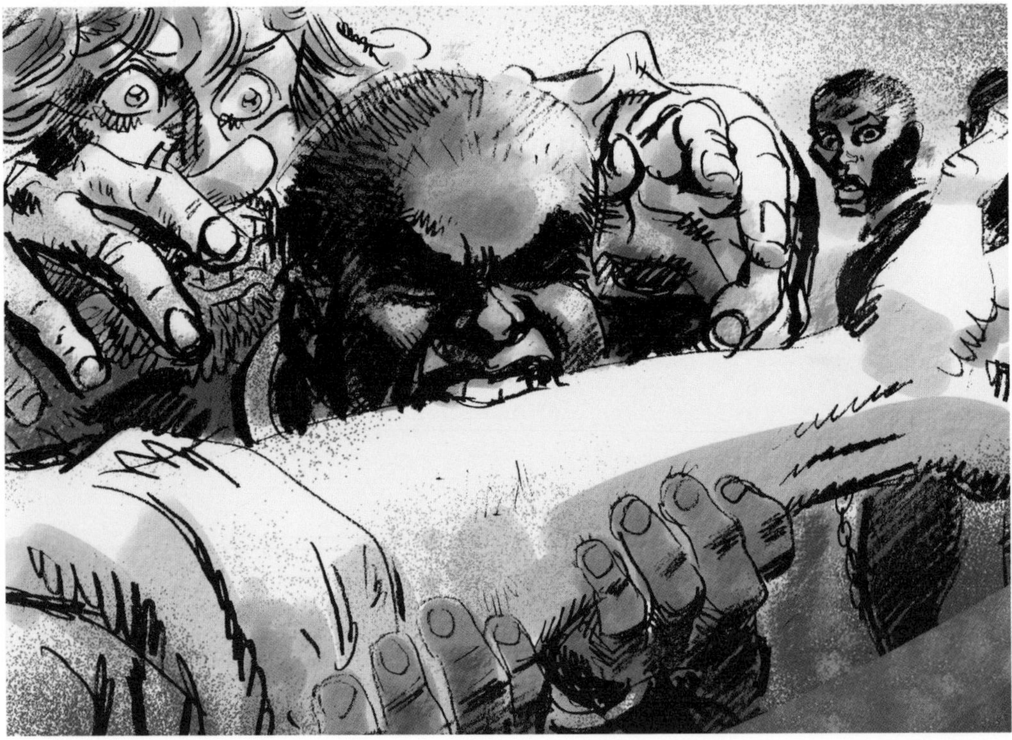

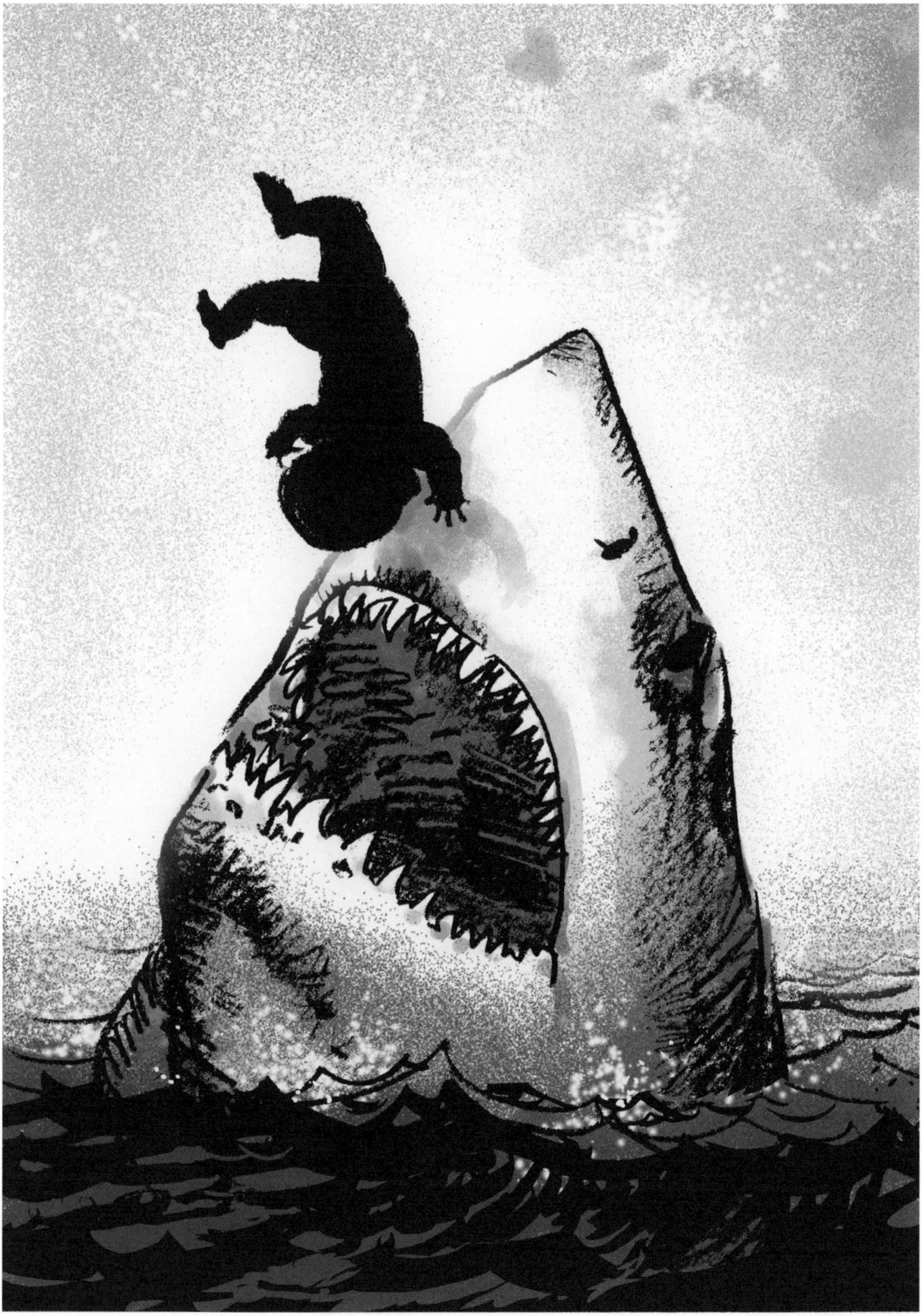

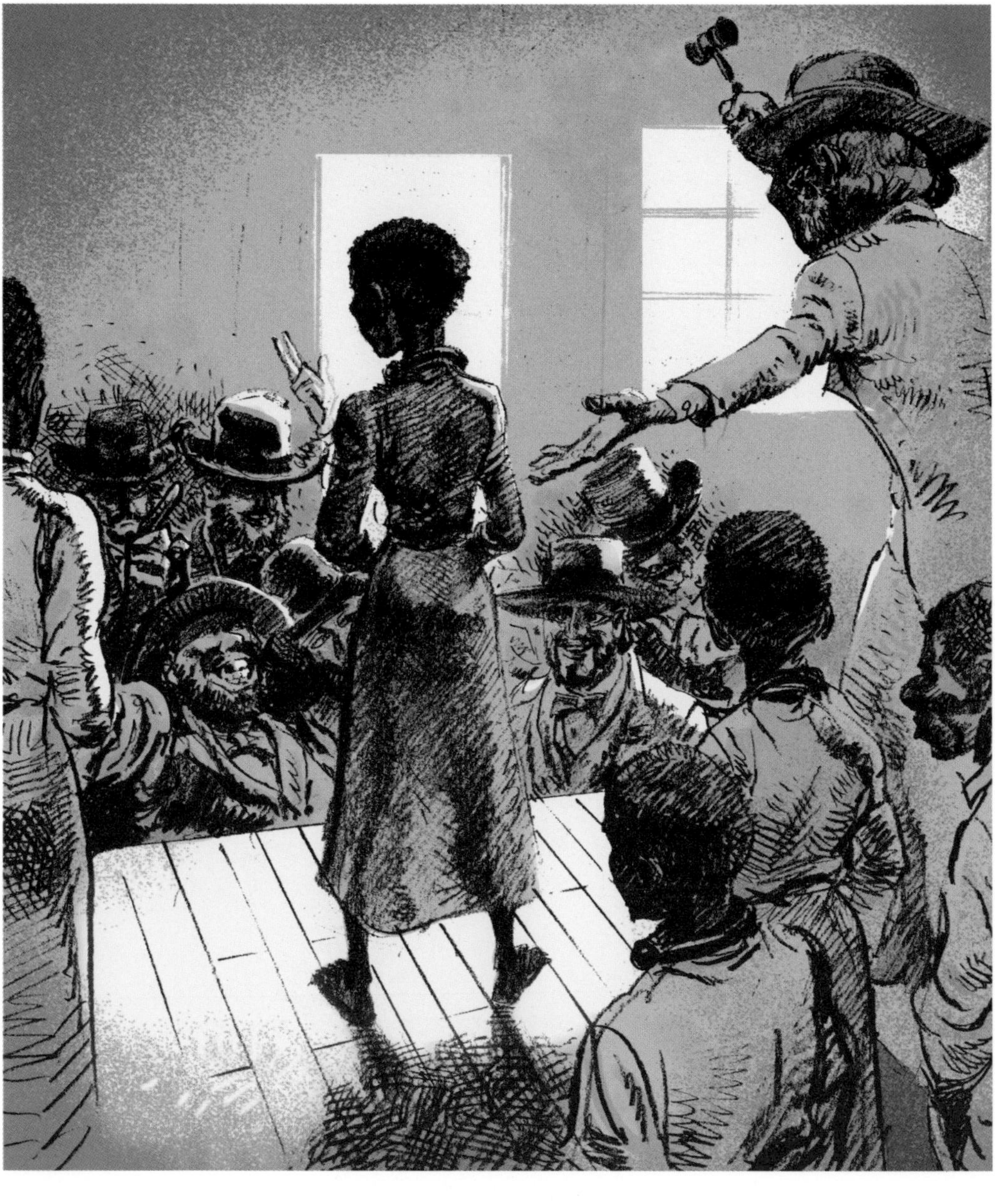

FROM THE CONFESSIONS OF NAT TURNER

"It is here necessary to relate this circumstance—trifling as it may seem, it was the commencement of that belief which has grown with time, and even now, sir, in this dungeon, helpless and forsaken as I am, I cannot divest myself of it. Being at play with other children, when three or four years old, I was telling them something which my mother, overhearing, said it had happened before I was born— I stuck to my story, however, and related some things which went, in her opinion, to confirm it—others being called on were greatly astonished, knowing that these things had happened, and caused them to say in my hearing, I surely would be a prophet, as the Lord had shown me things that had happened before my birth."

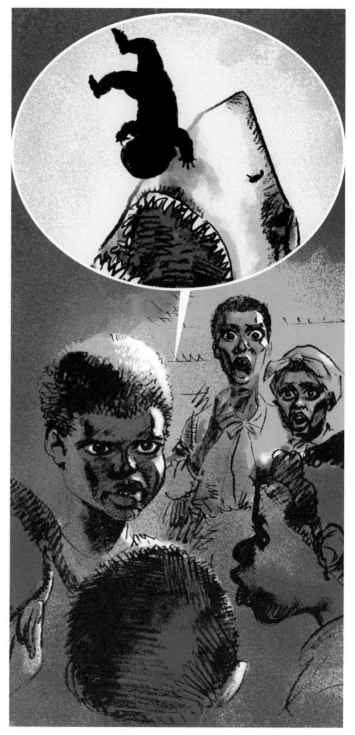

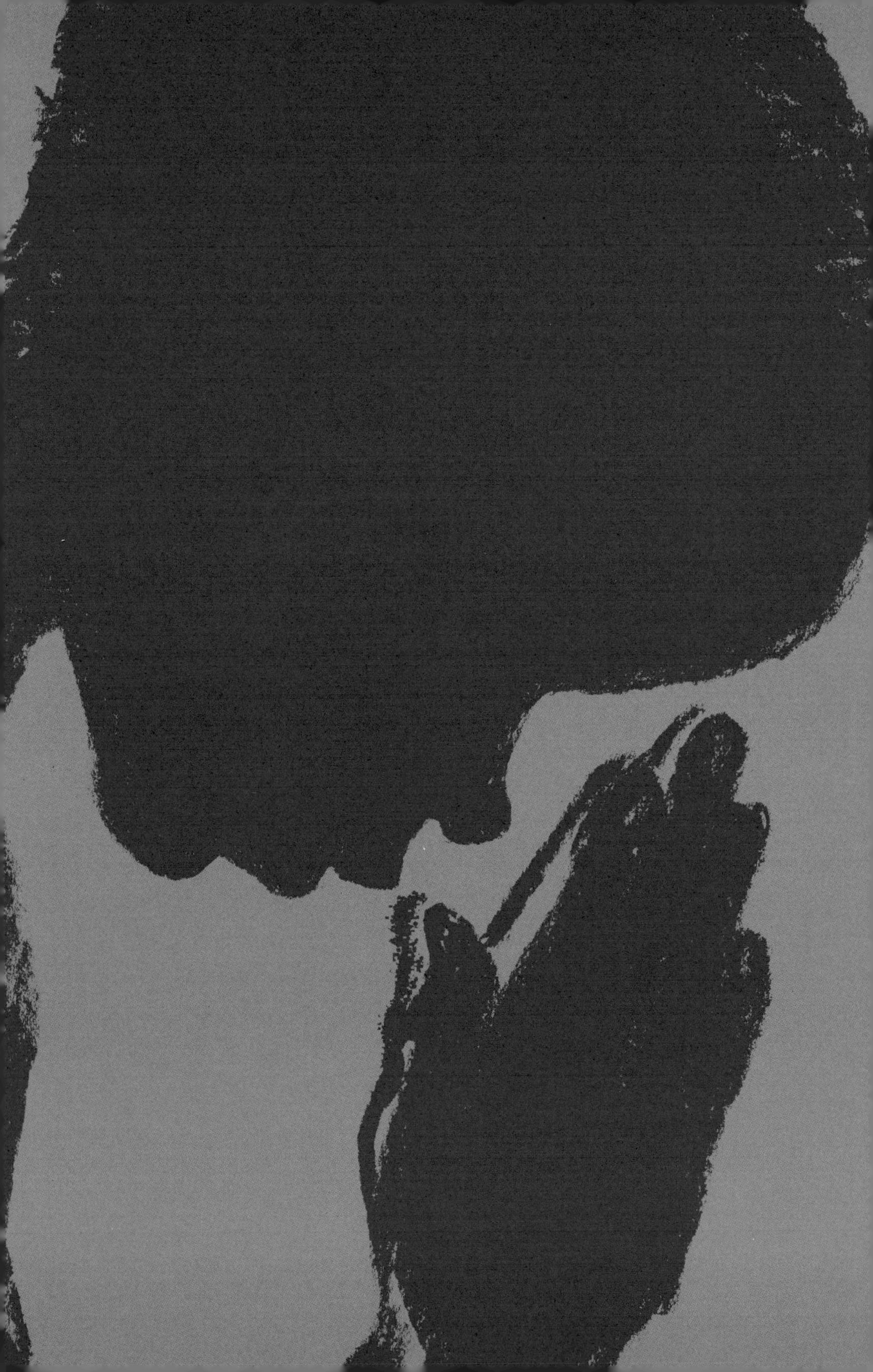

II

EDUCATION

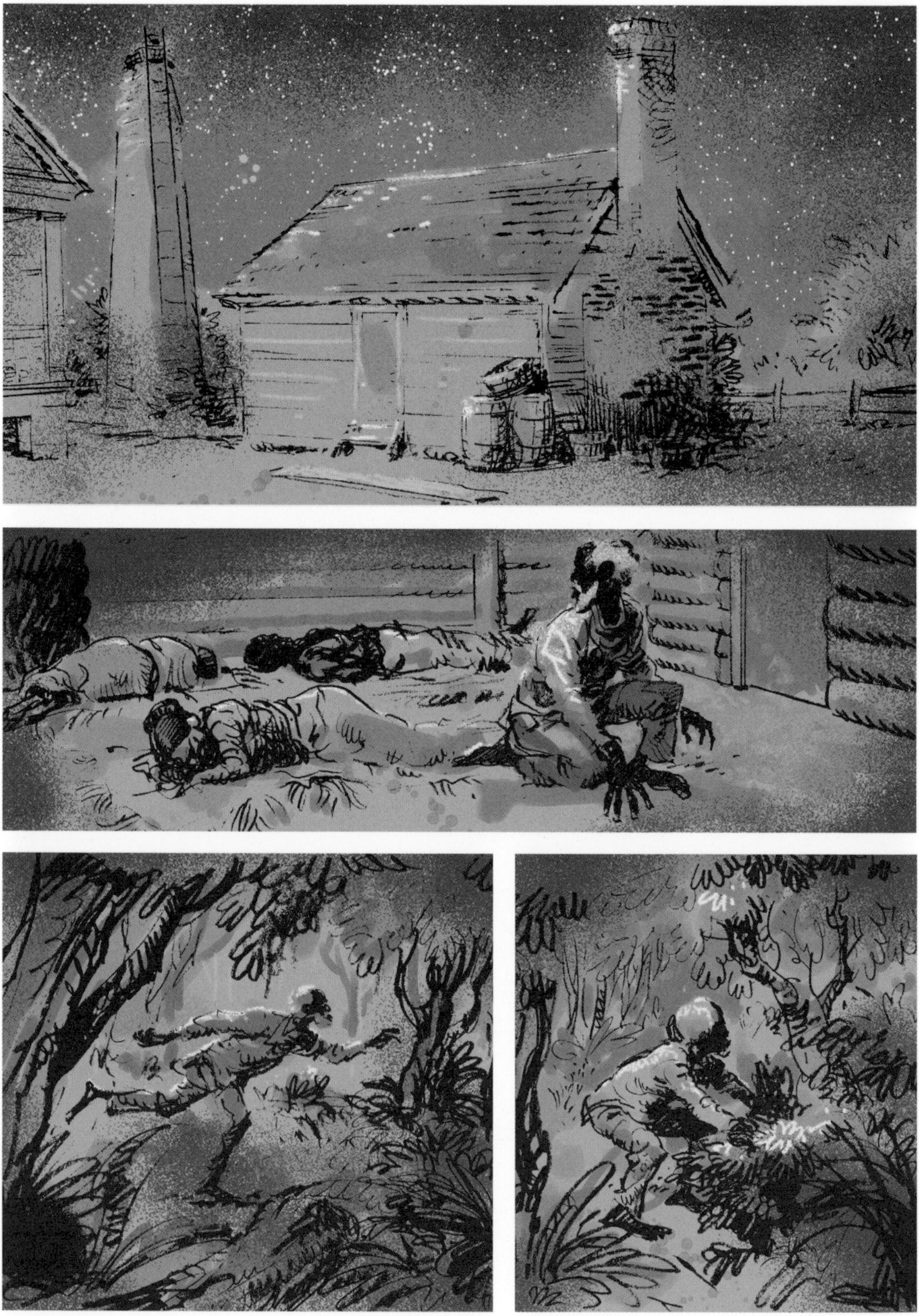

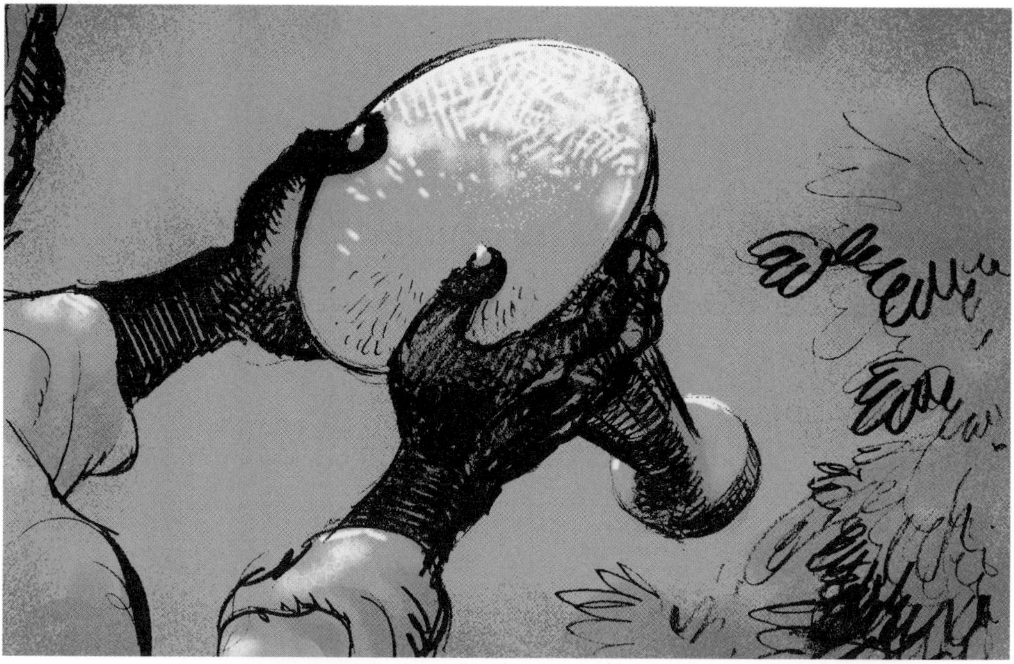

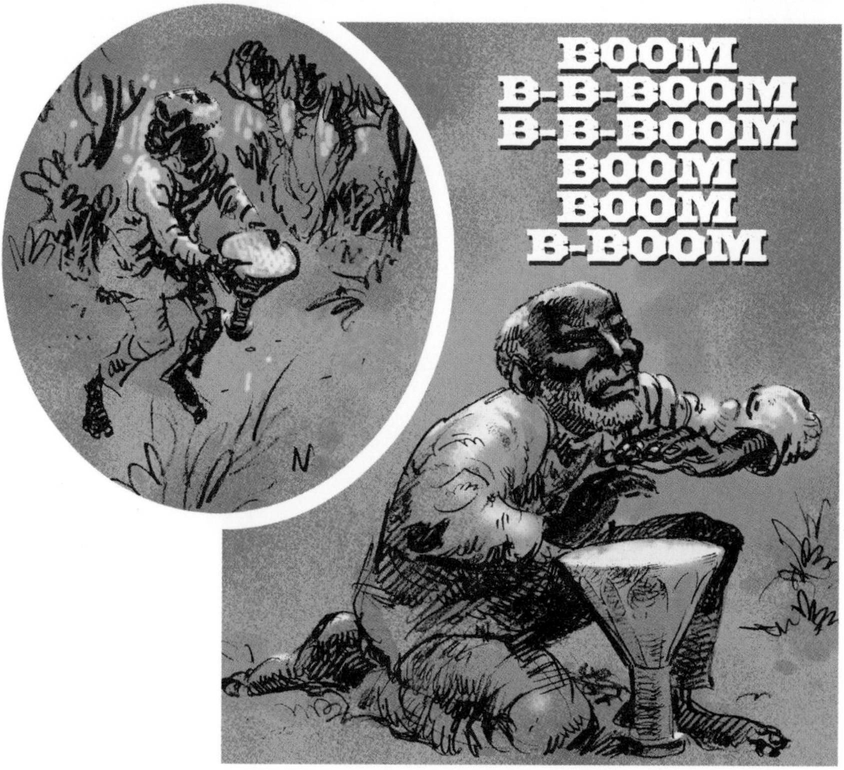
BOOM
B-B-BOOM
B-B-BOOM
BOOM
BOOM
B-BOOM

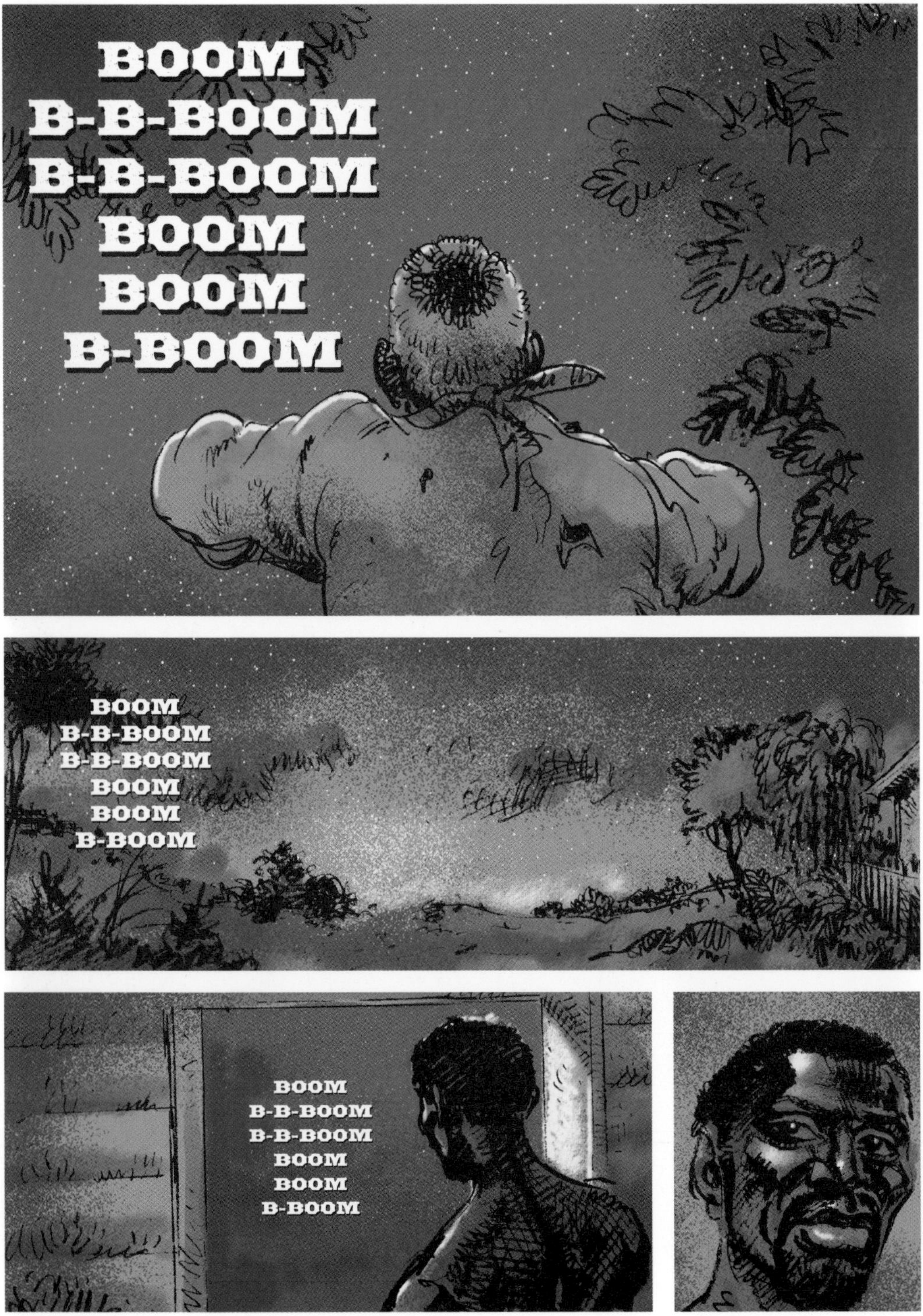
BOOM
B-B-BOOM
B-B-BOOM
BOOM
BOOM
B-BOOM
BOOM
B-B-BOOM
B-B-BOOM
BOOM
BOOM
B-BOOM
BOOM
B-B-BOOM
B-B-BOOM
BOOM
BOOM
B-BOOM

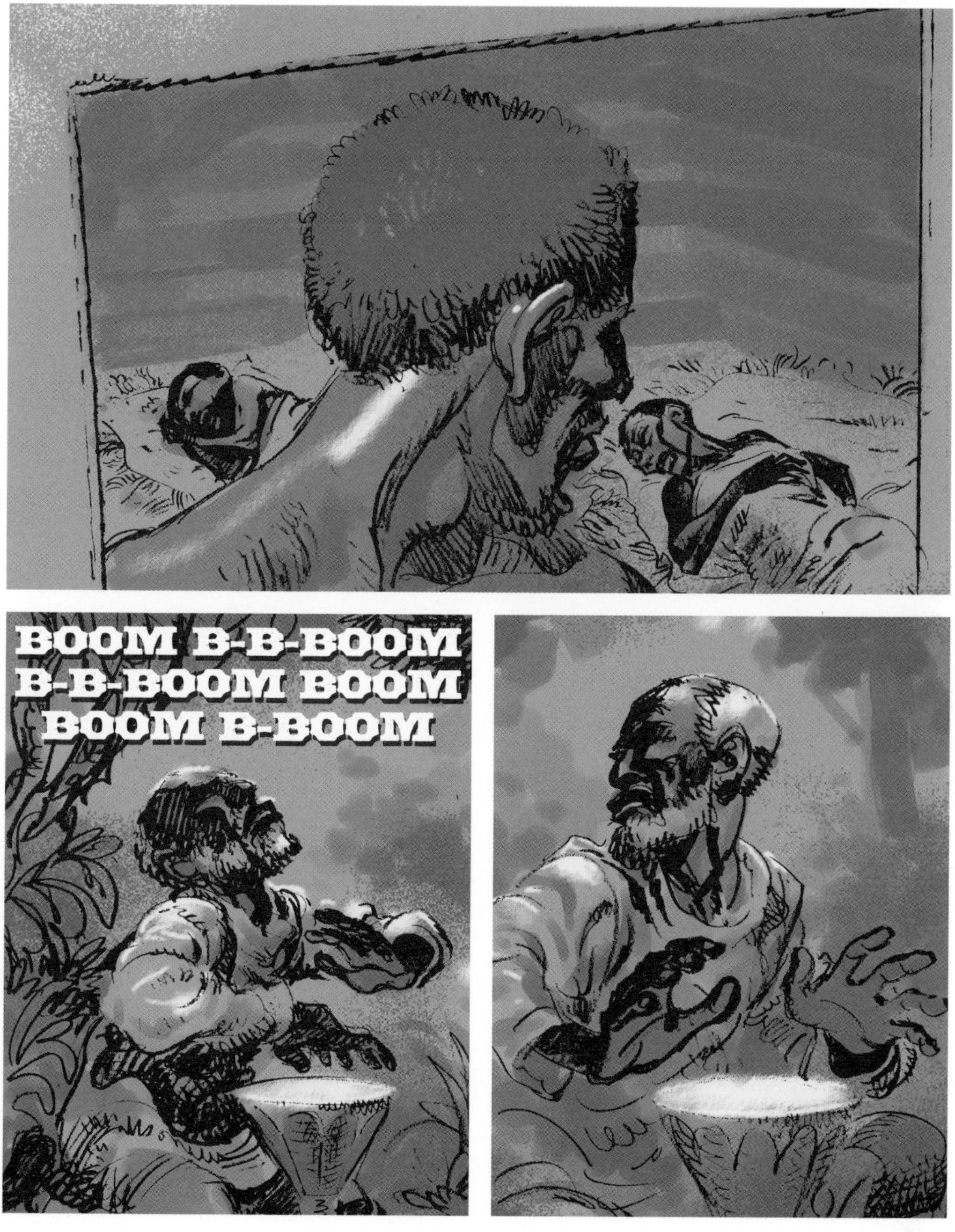
BOOM B-B-BOOM
B-B-BOOM BOOM
BOOM B-BOOM

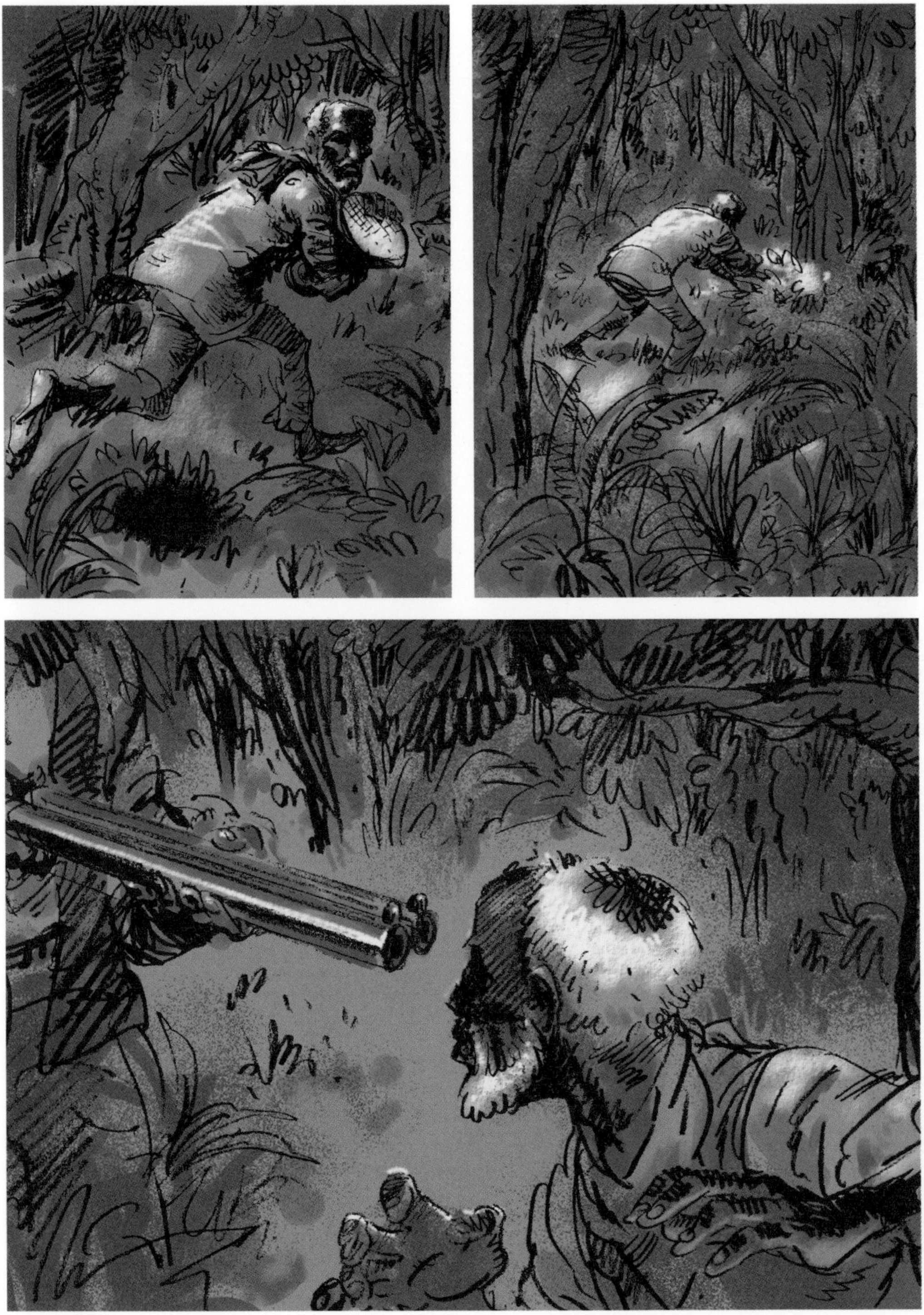

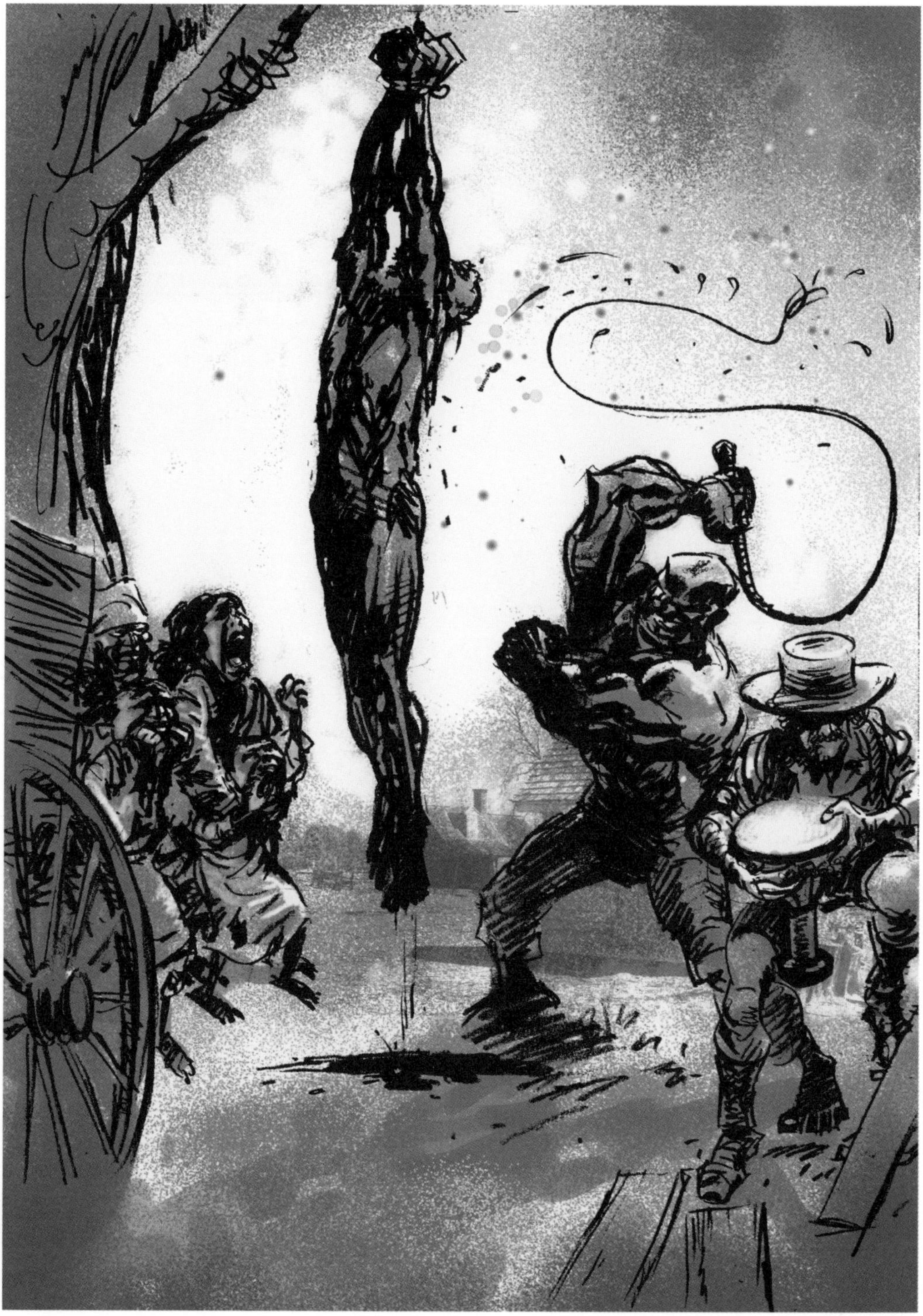

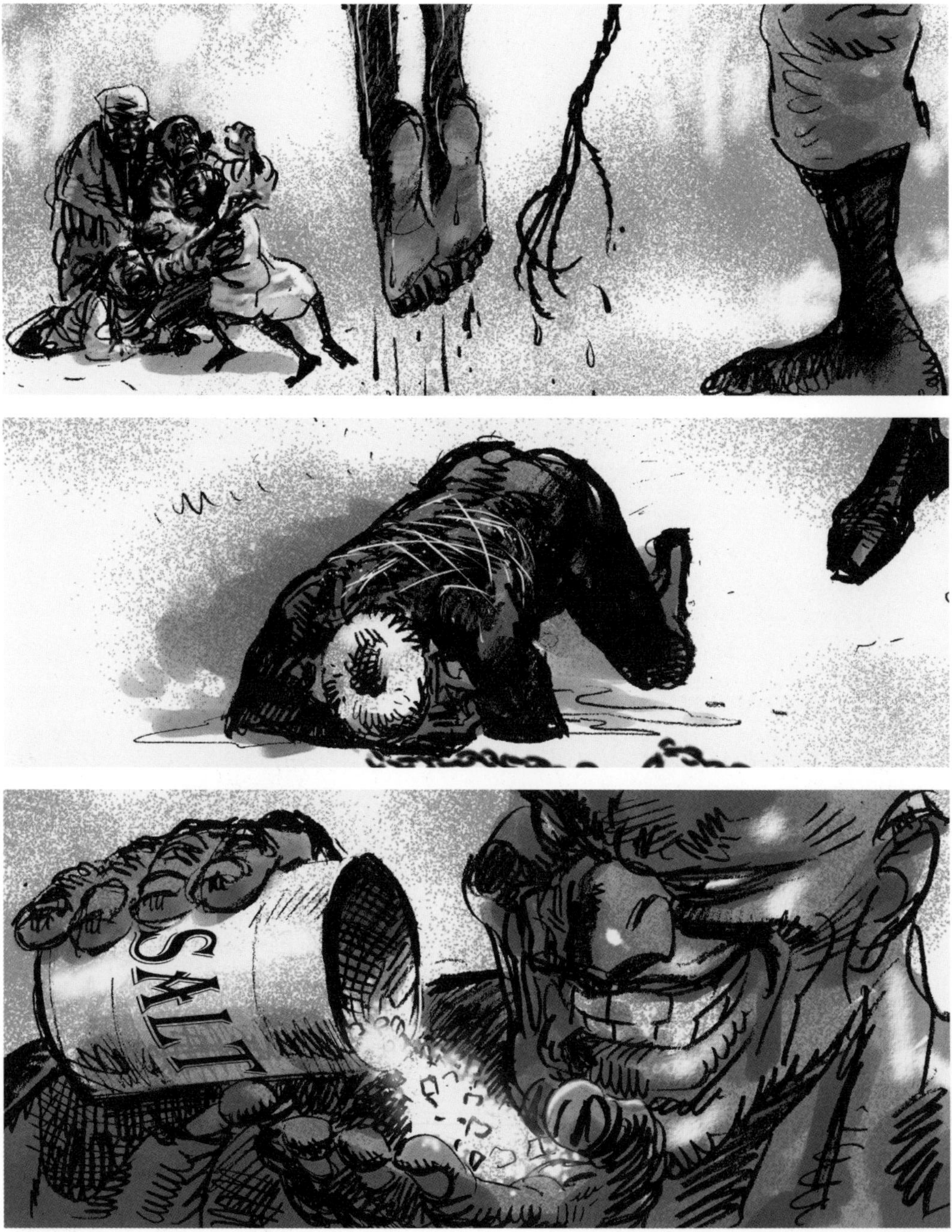
SALT

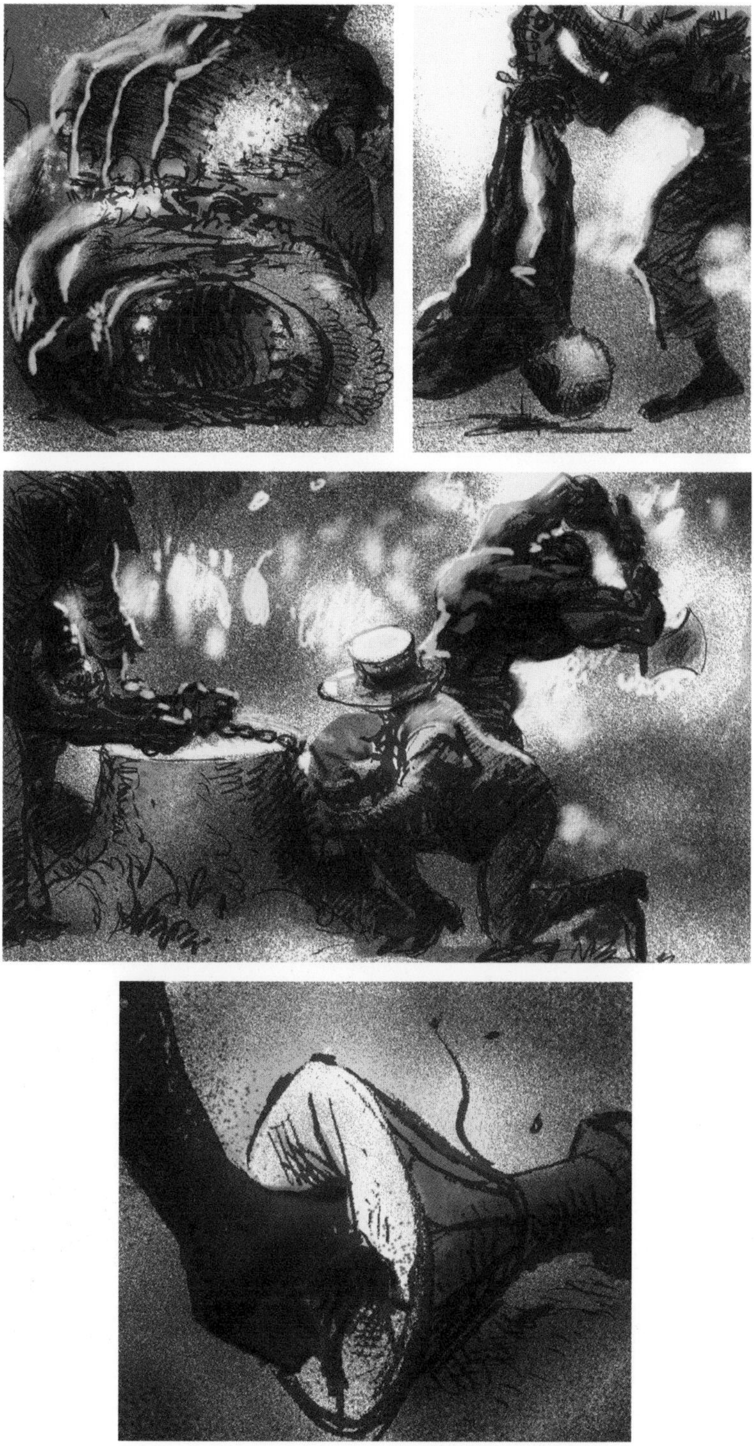

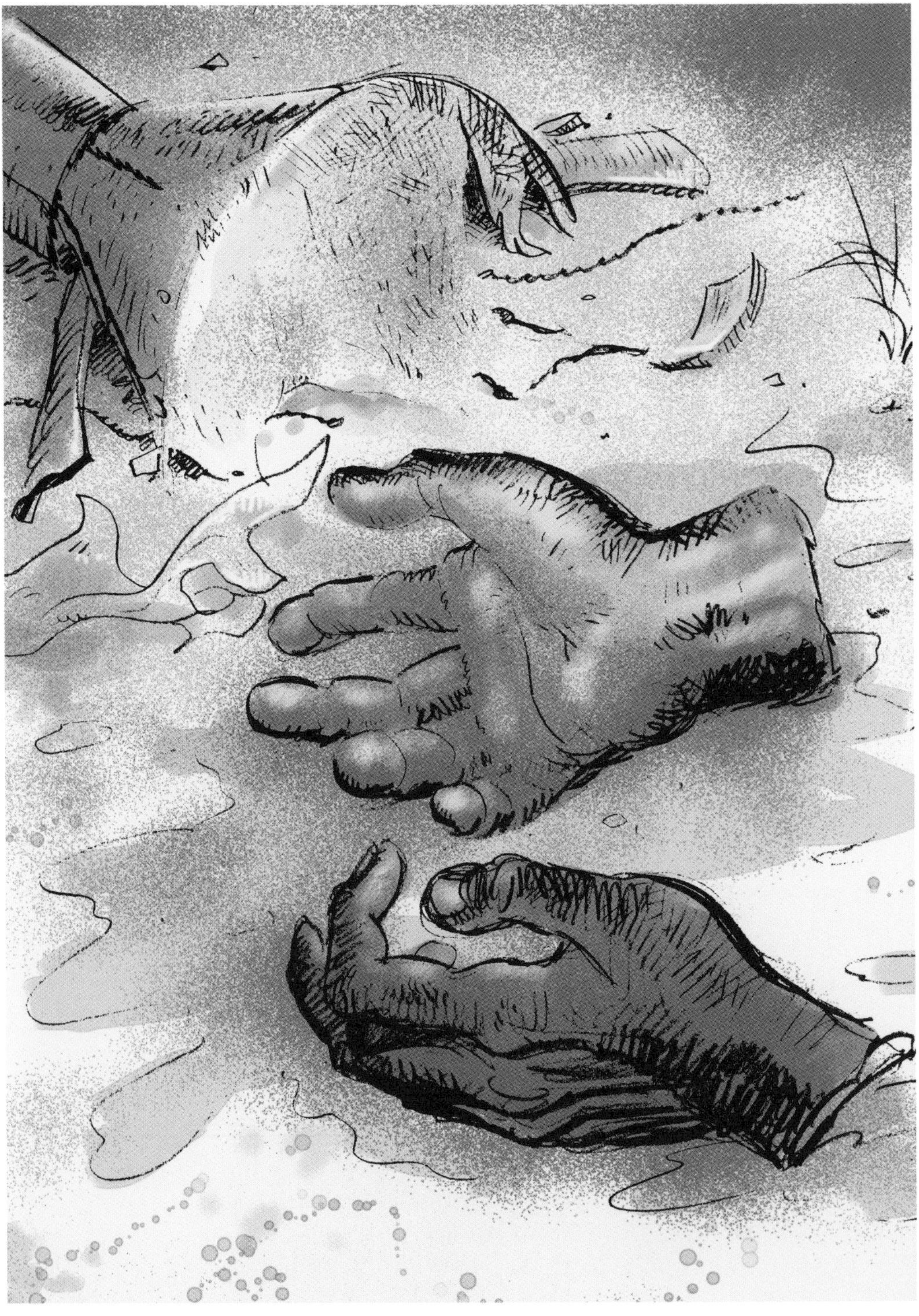

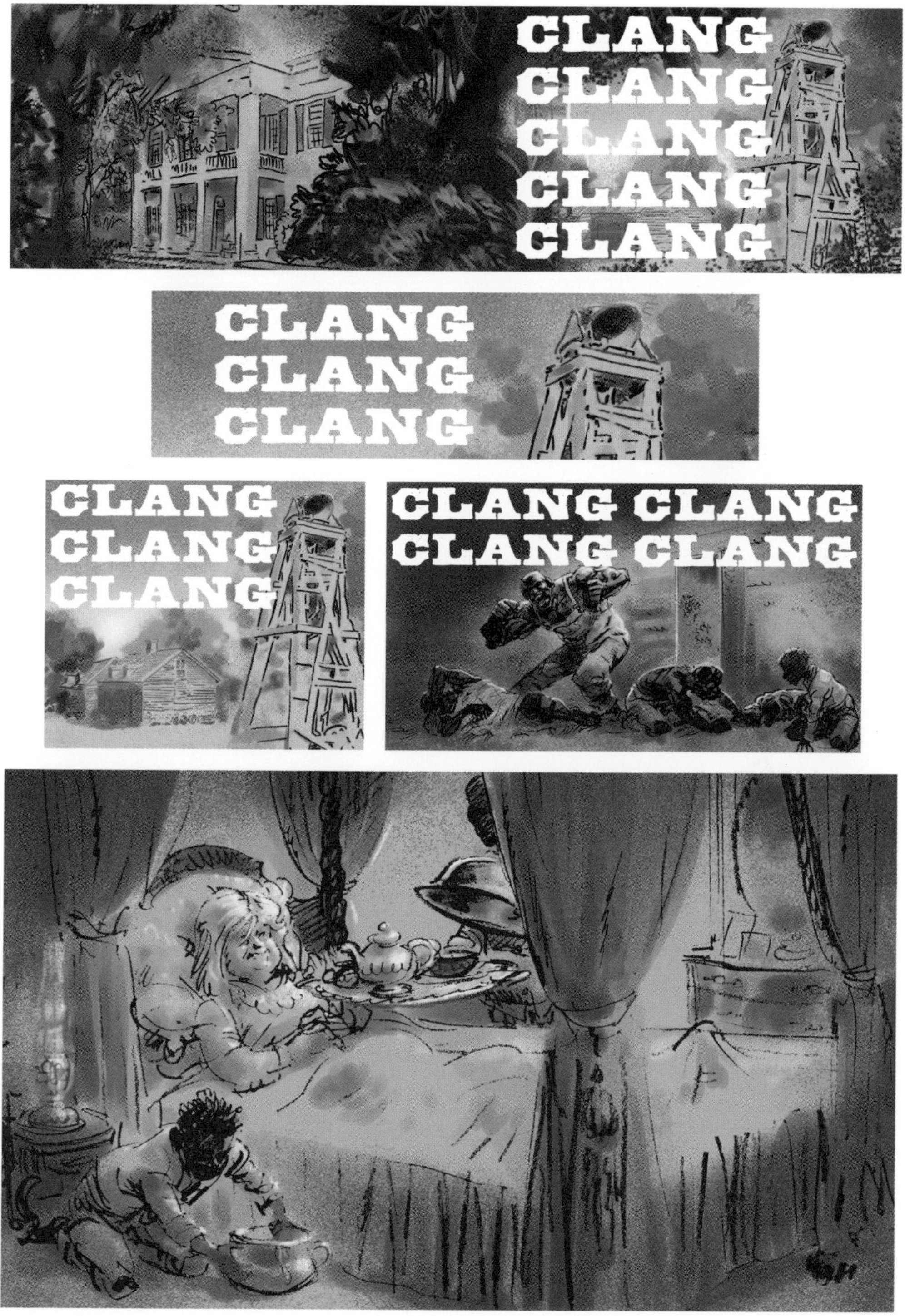
CLANG
CLANG
CLANG
CLANG
CLANG
CLANG
CLANG
CLANG
CLANG
CLANG
CLANG
CLANG CLANG
CLANG CLANG

FROM THE CONFESSIONS OF NAT TURNER

"My father and mother strengthened me in this, my first impression, saying in my presence I was intended for some great purpose, which they had always thought from certain marks on my head and breast.... My grandmother, who was very religious, and to whom I was much attached—my master, who belonged to the church, and other religious persons who visited the house, and whom I often saw at prayers, noticing the singularity of my manners, I suppose, and my uncommon intelligence for a child, remarked I had too much sense to be raised, and if I was, I would never be of any service to any one as a slave..."

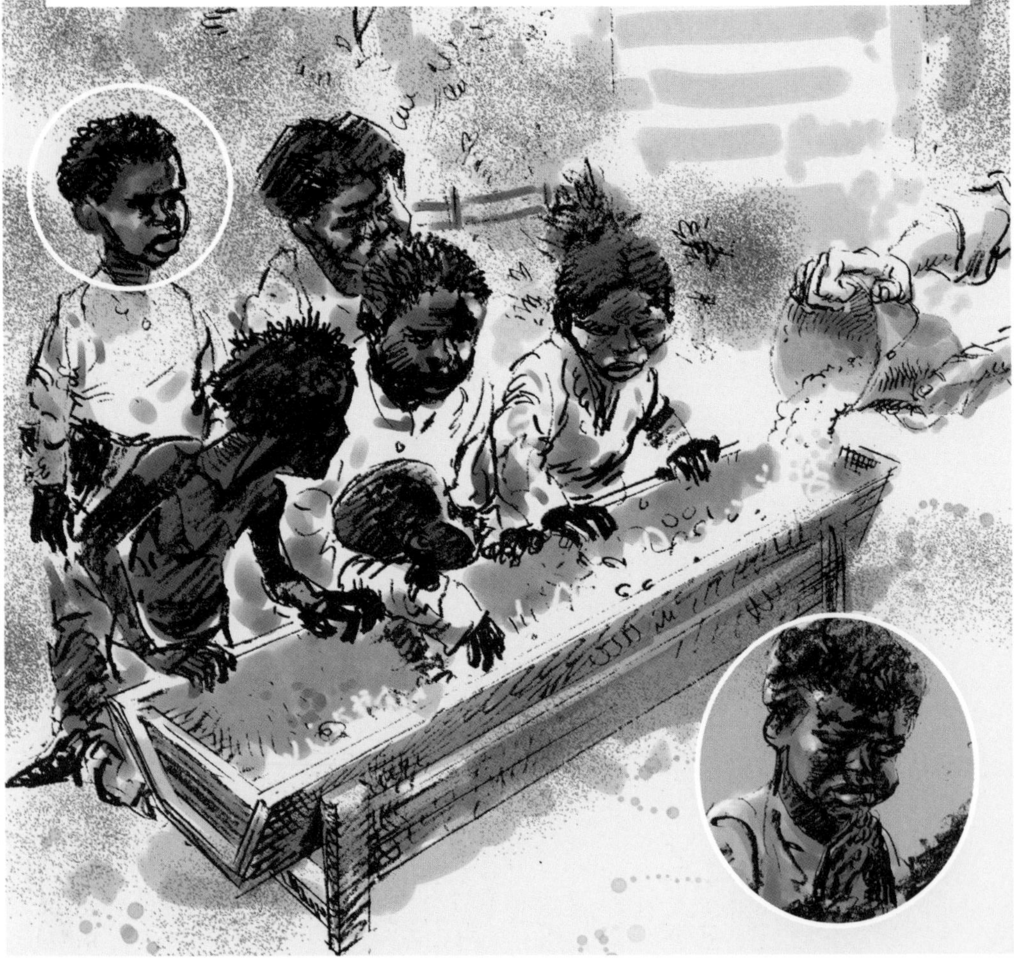

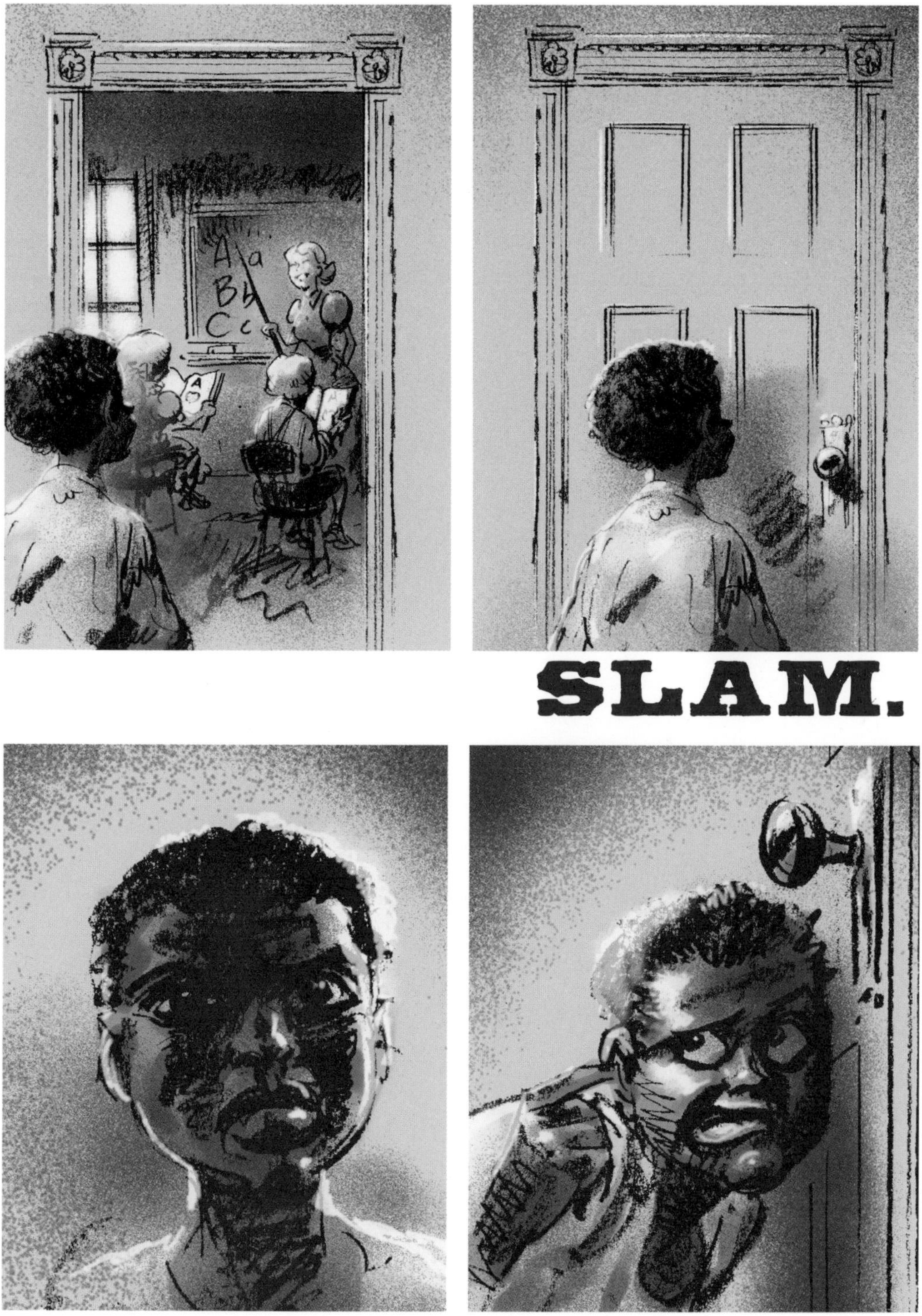
Aa
Bb
Cc
SLAM.

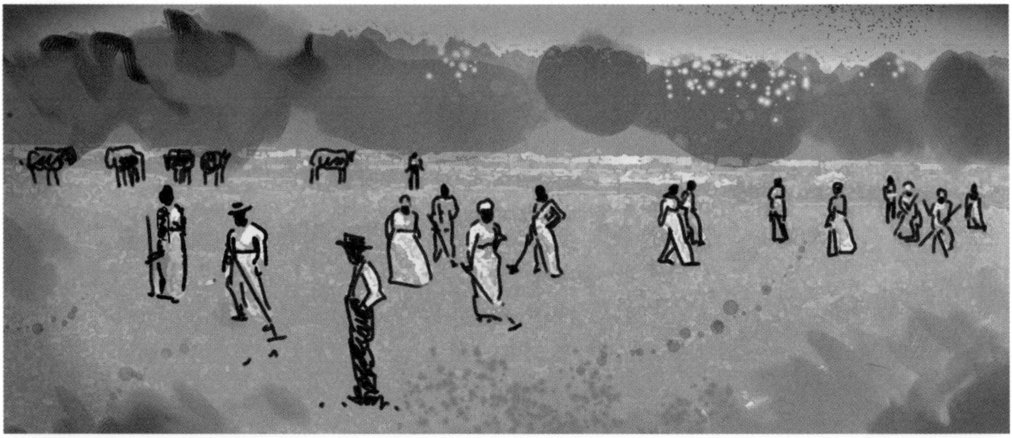

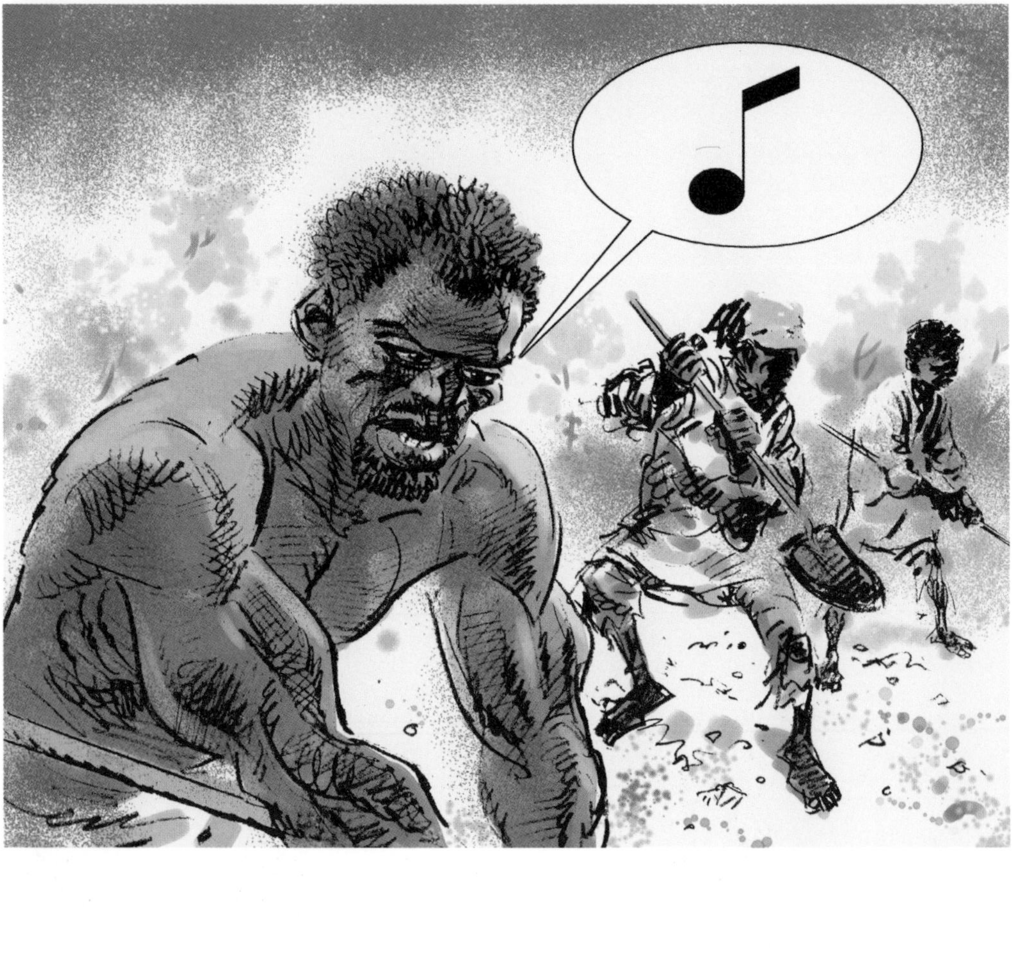

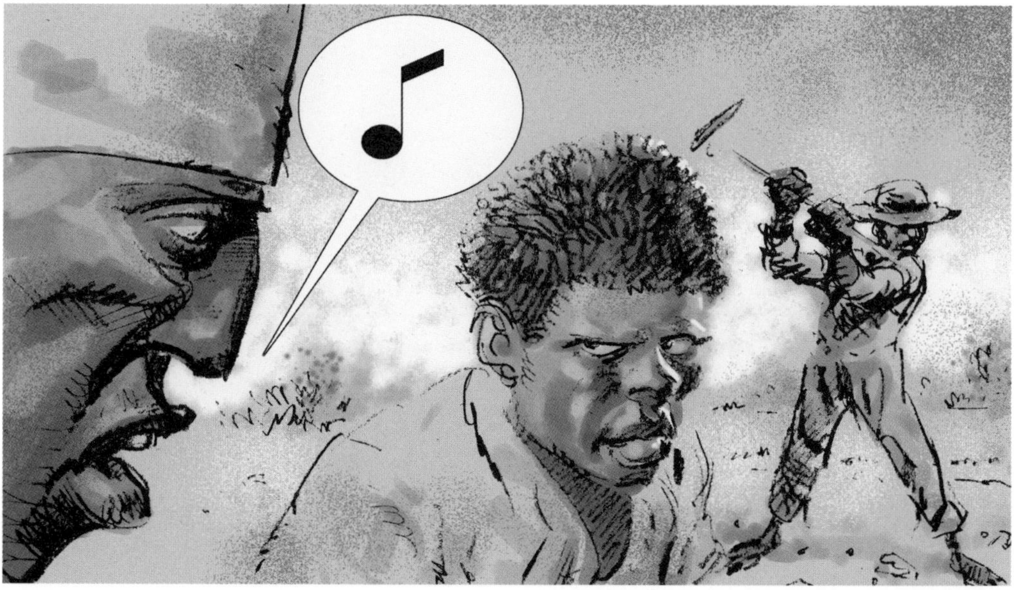

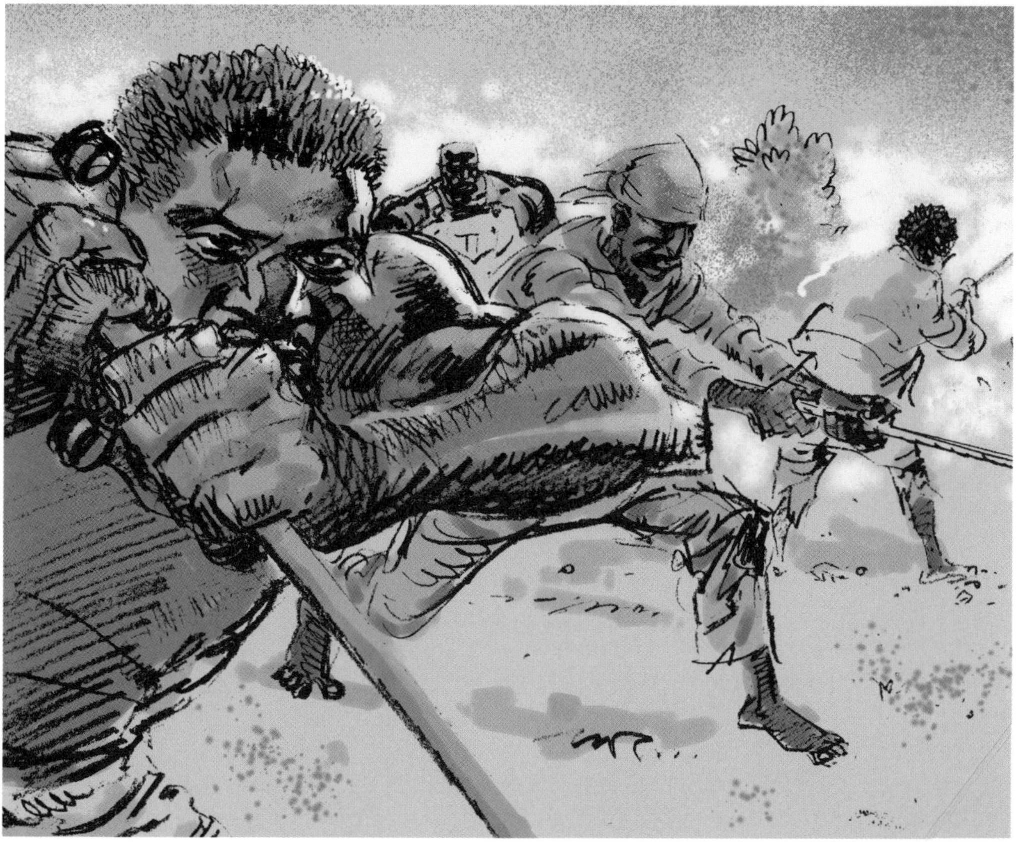

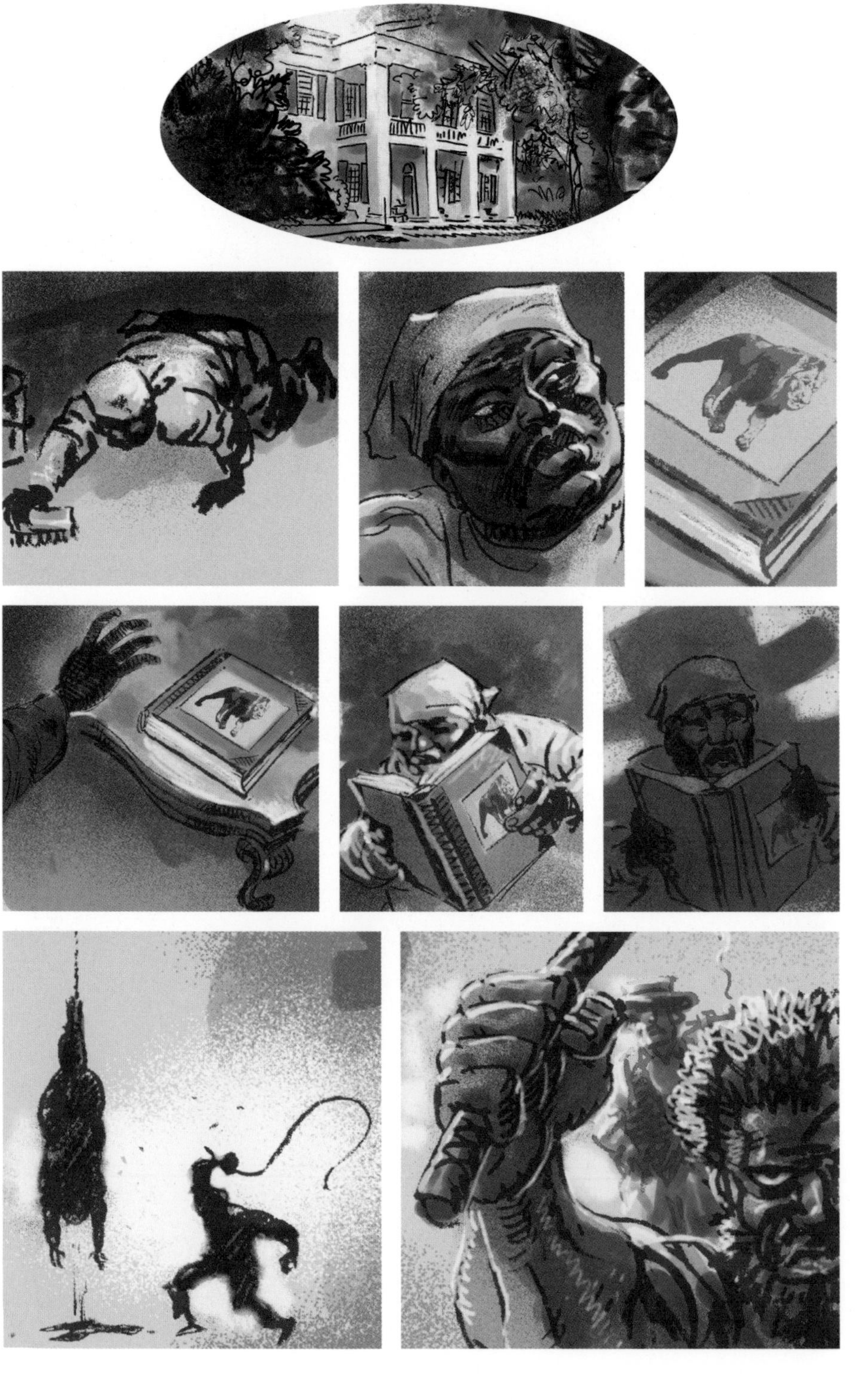

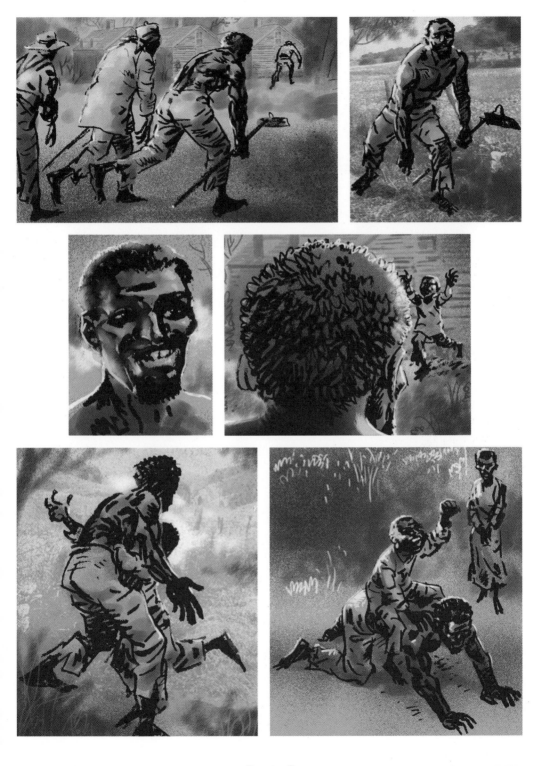

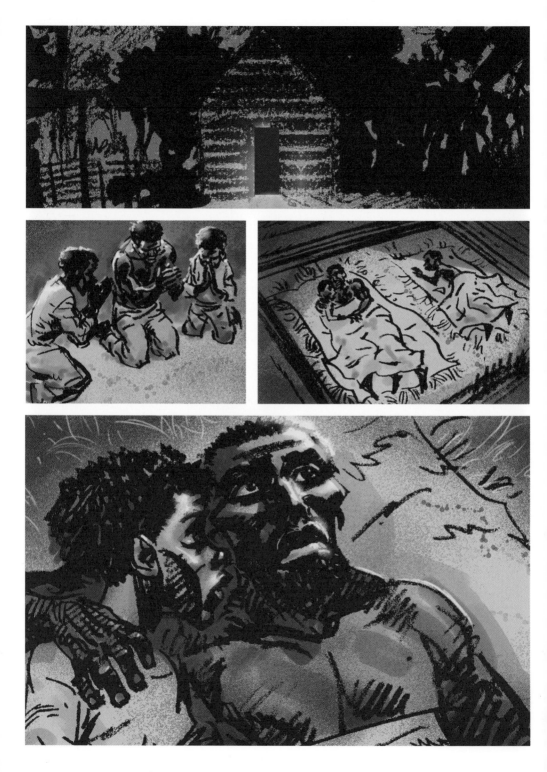

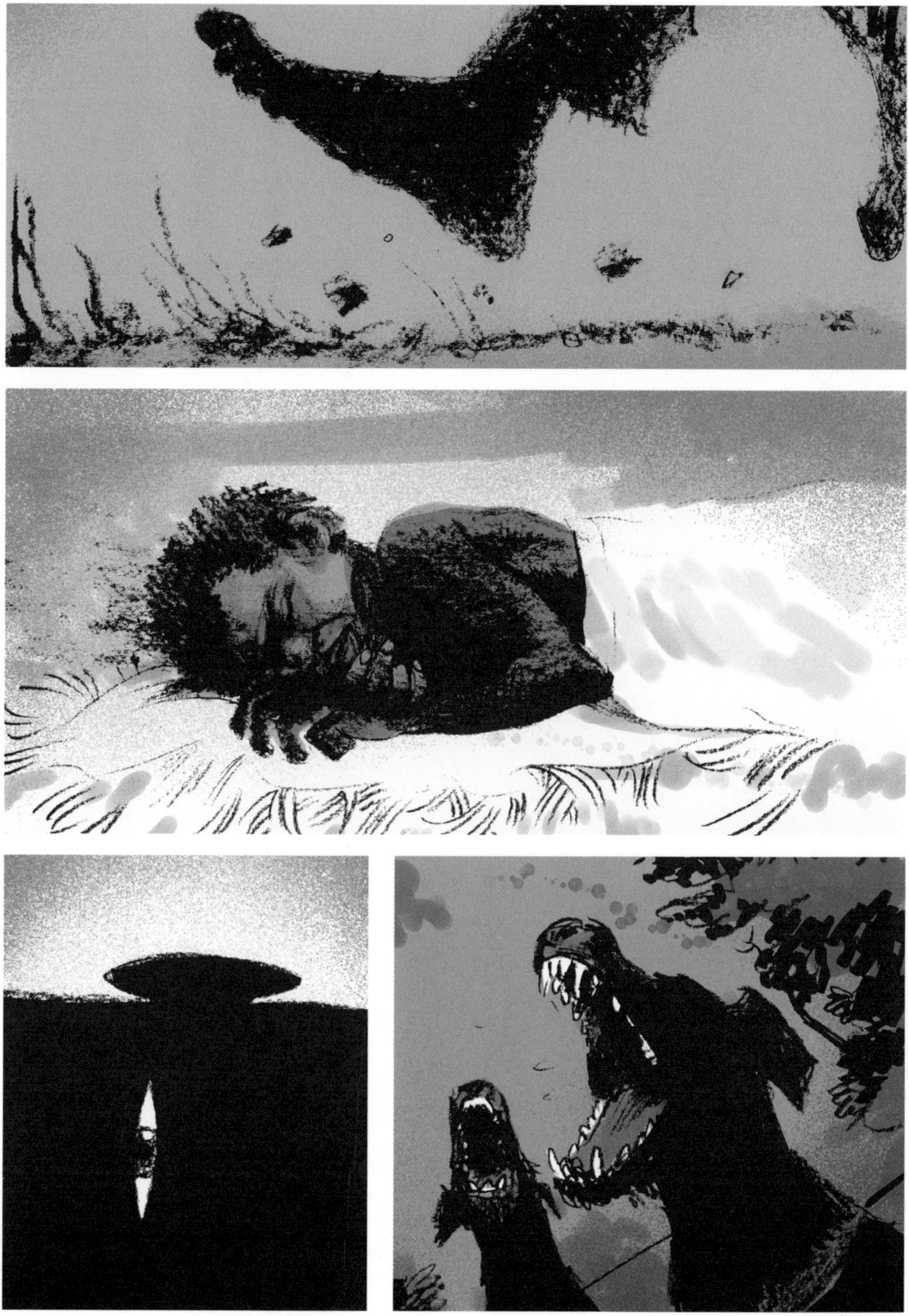

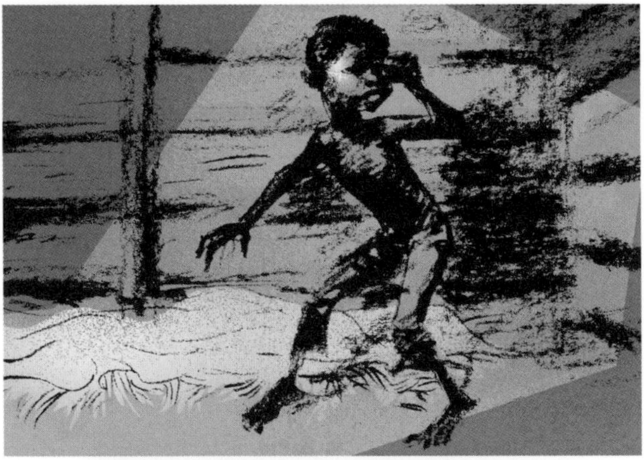

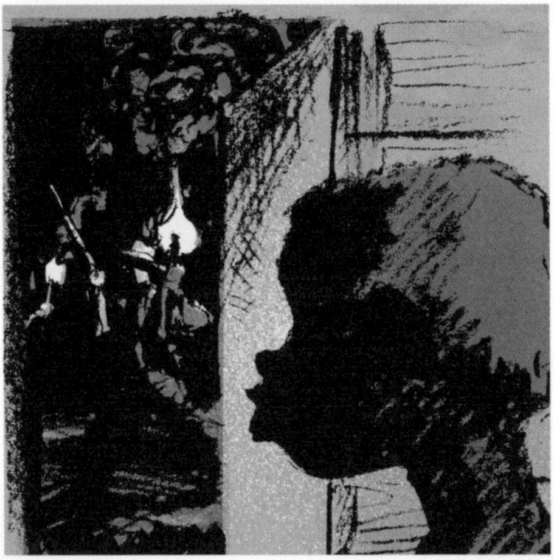

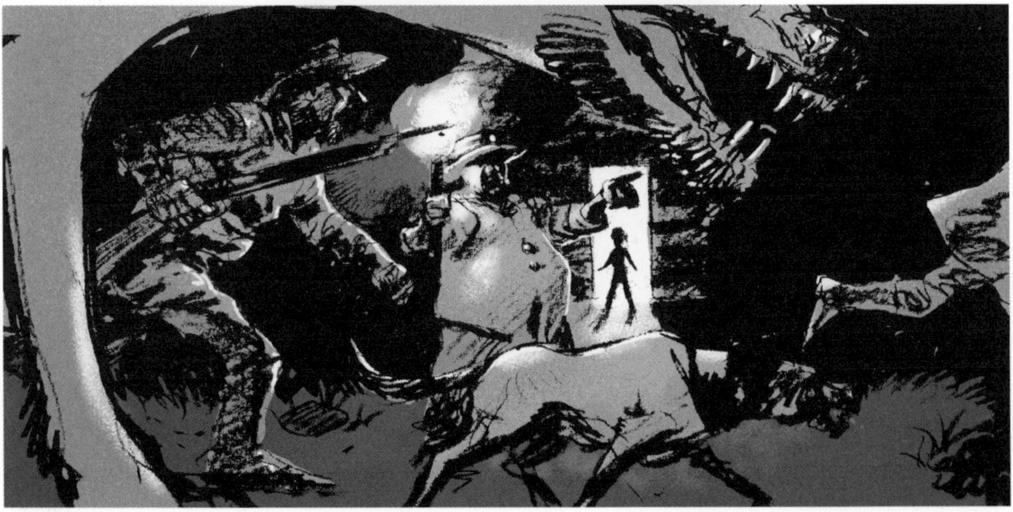

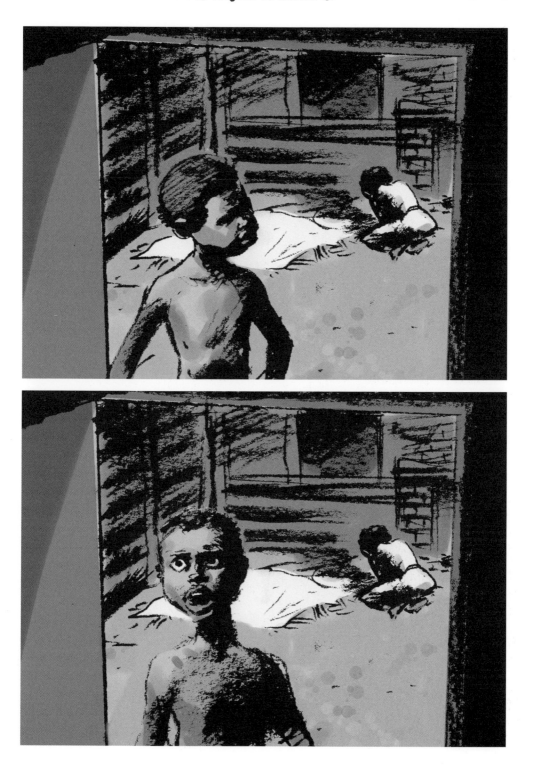

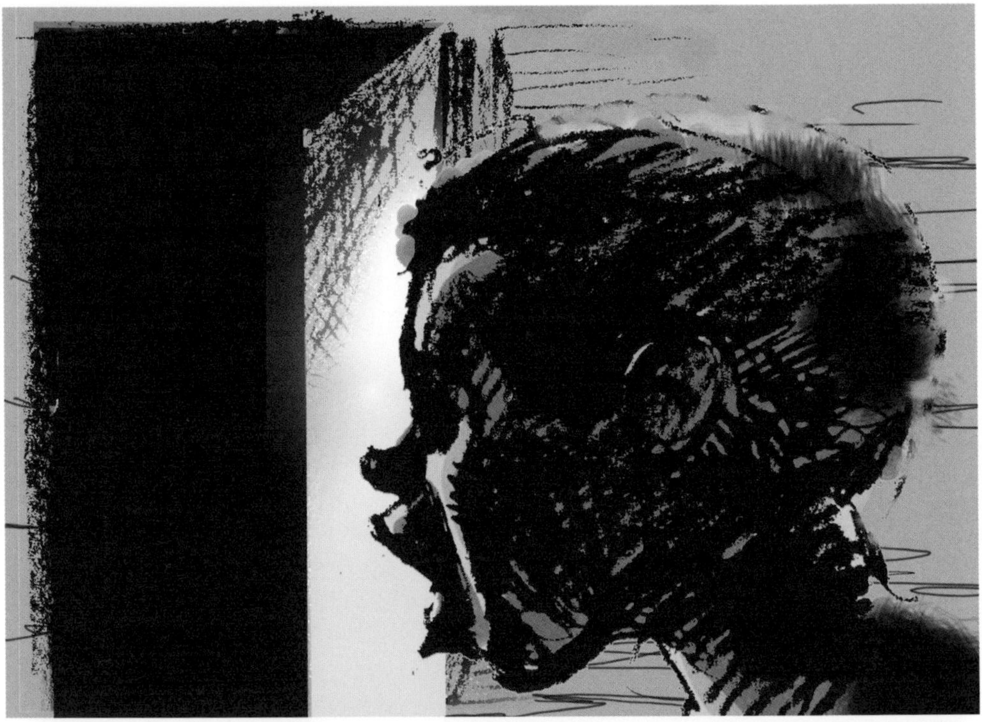

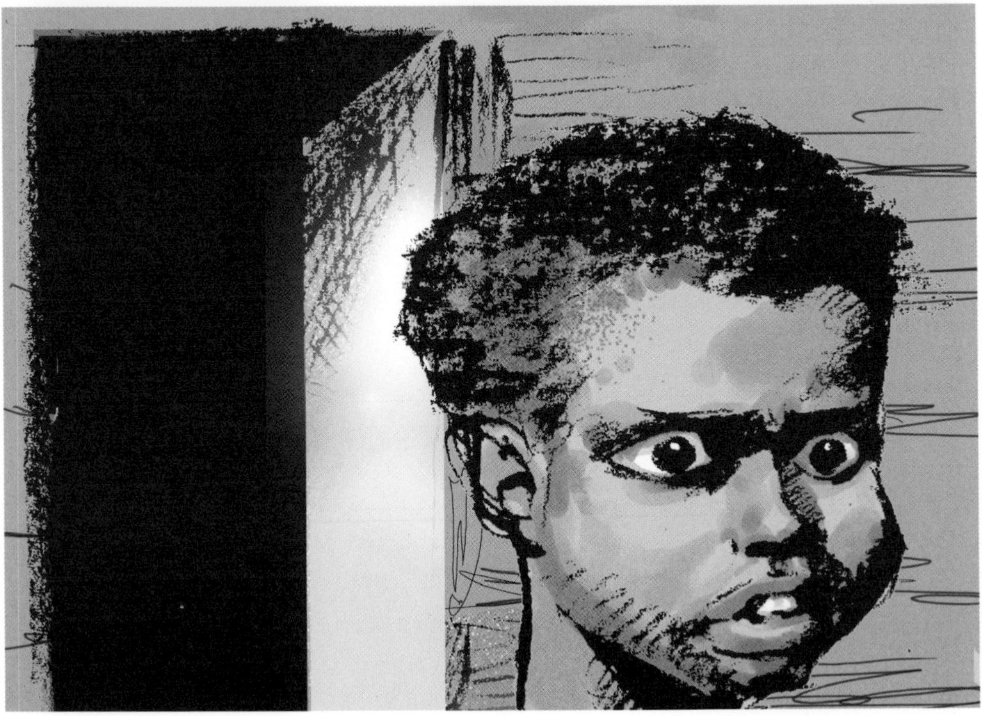

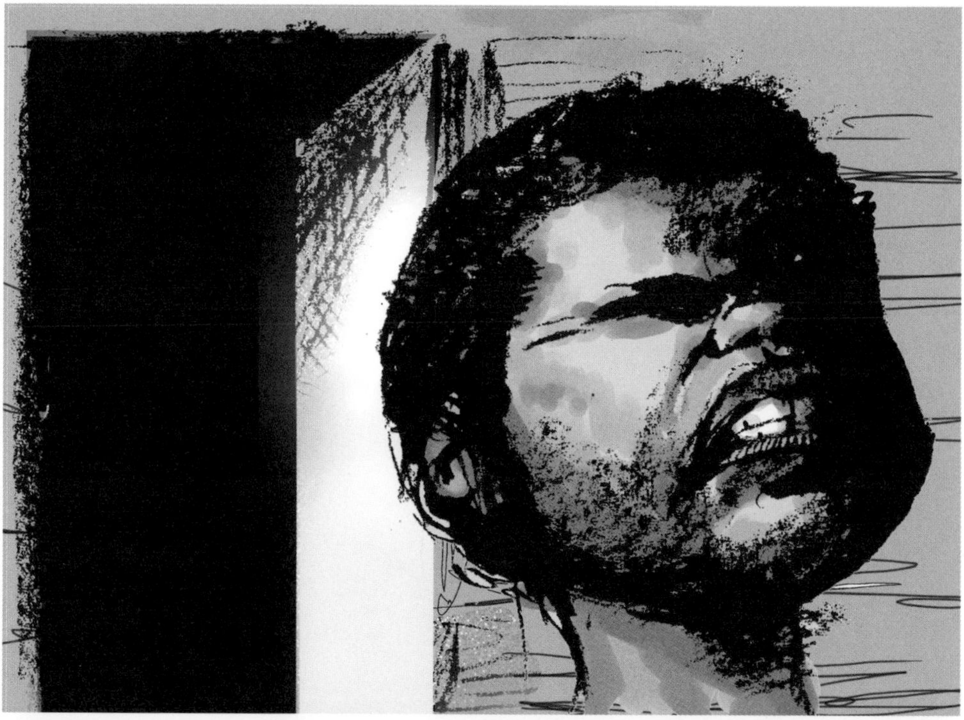

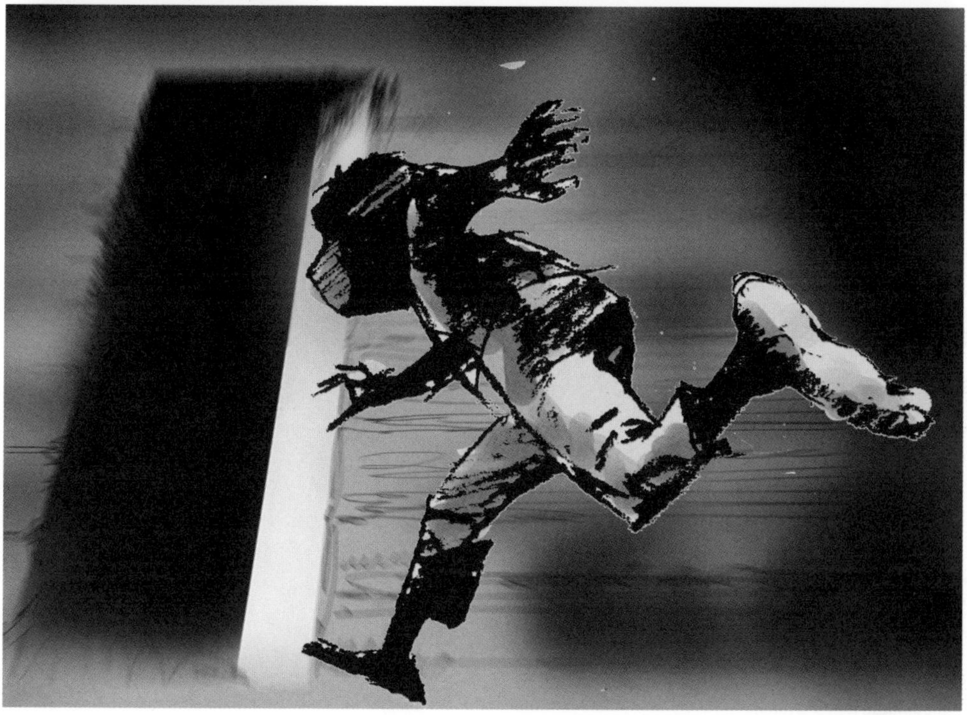

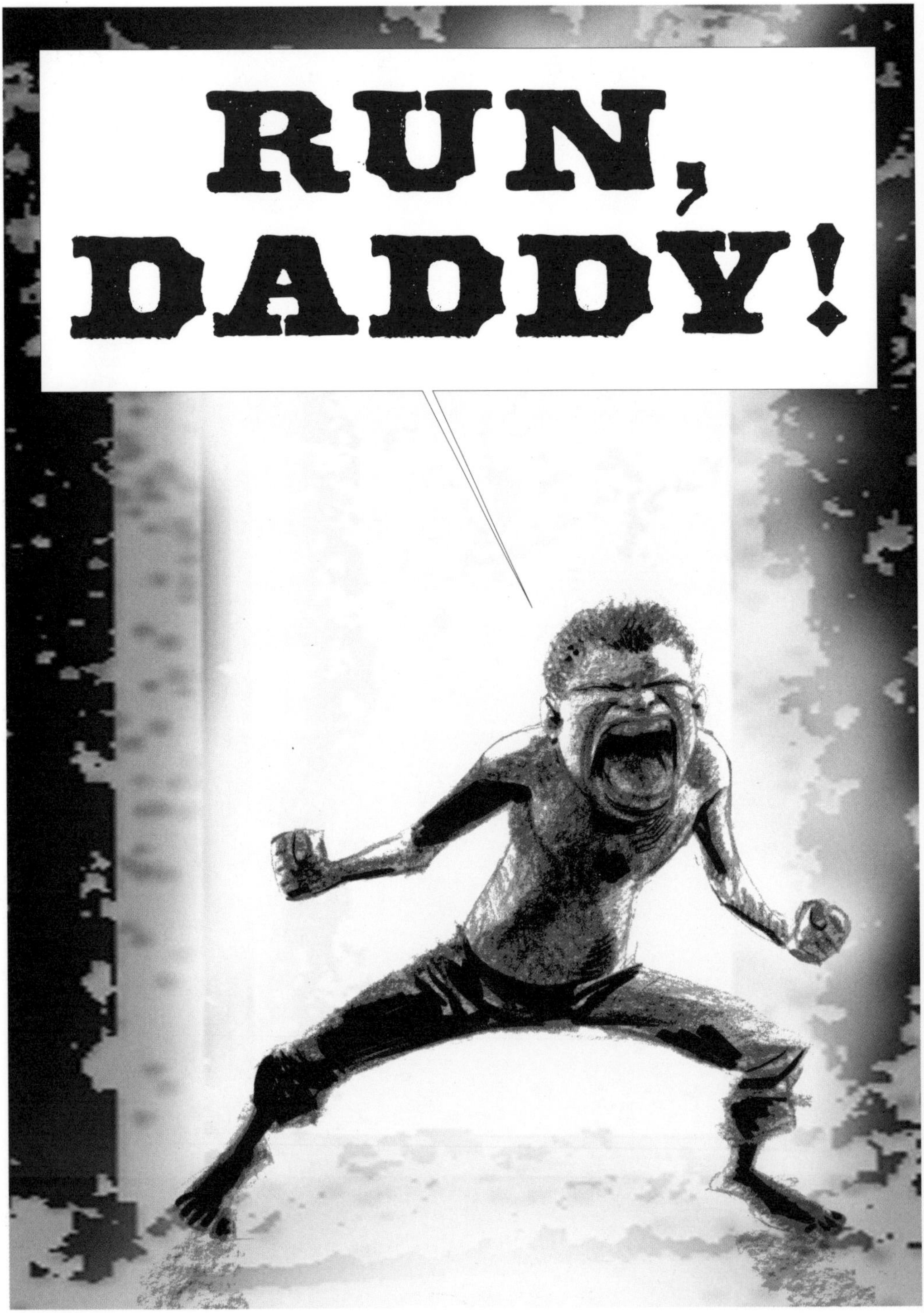
RUN, DADDY!

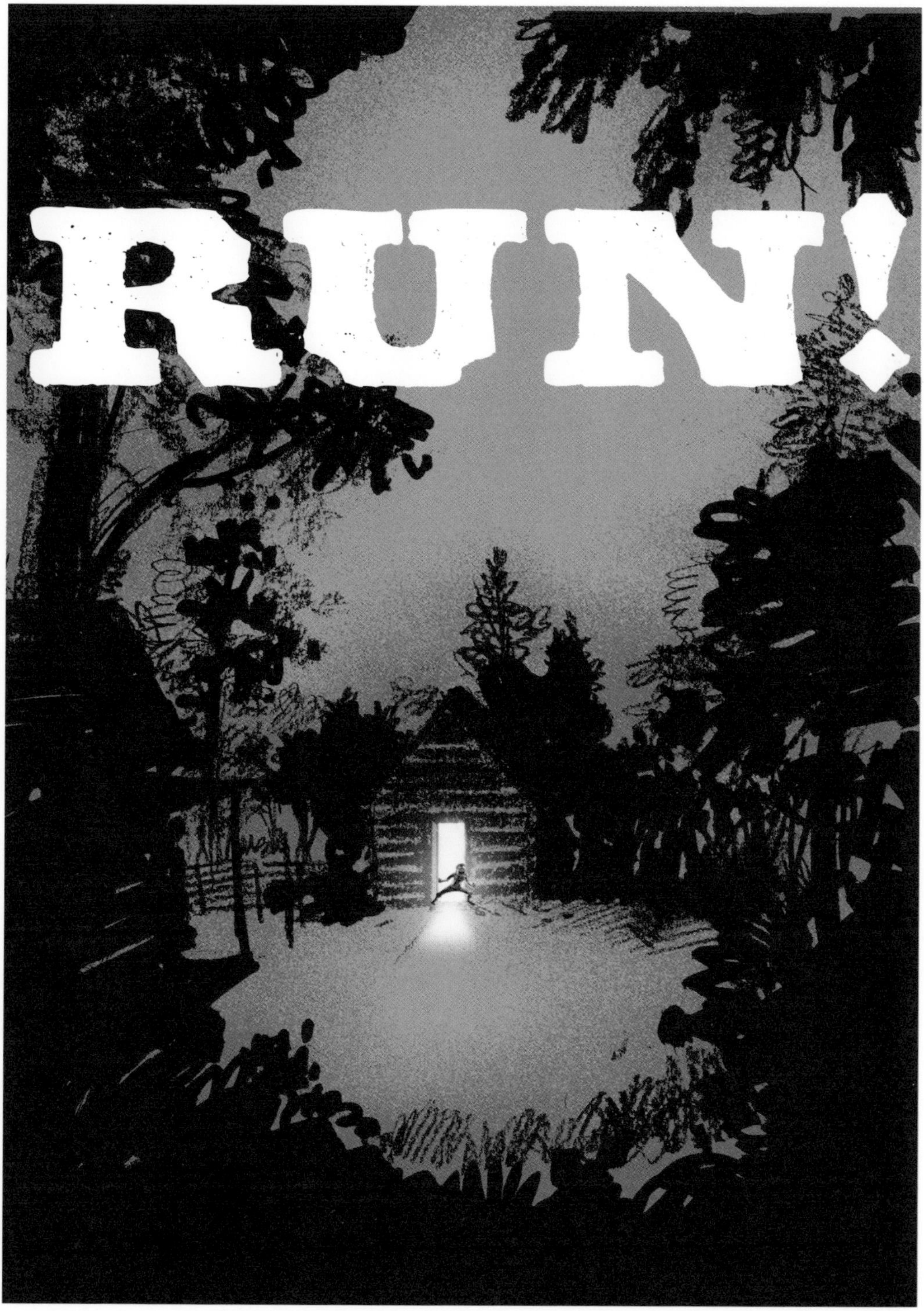
RUN!

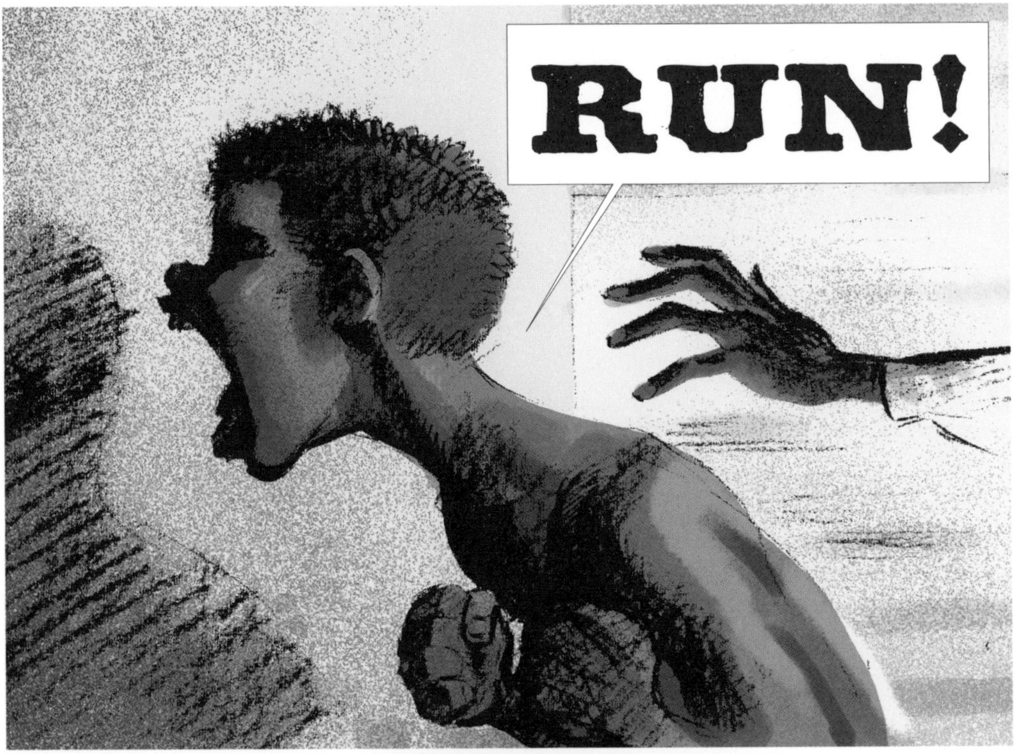
RUN!

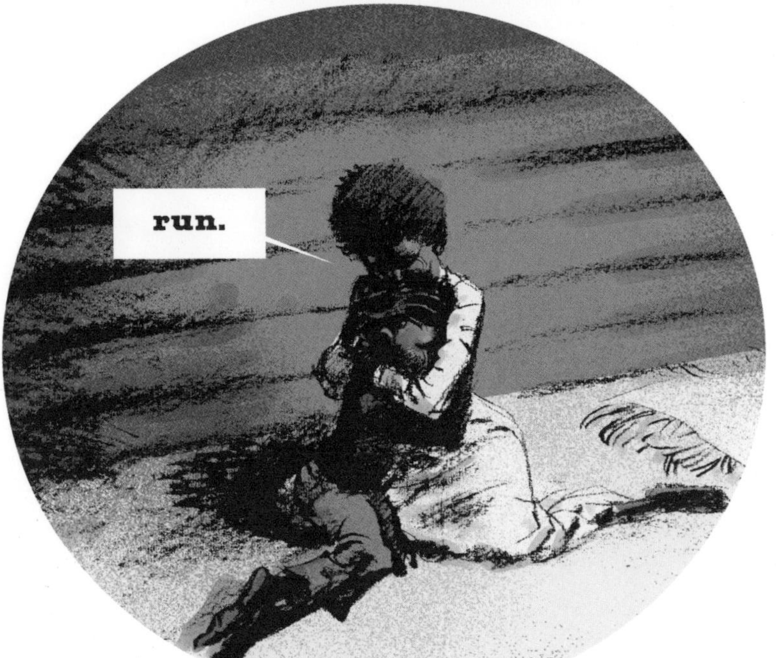
run.

"TO A MIND LIKE mine, restless, inquisitive and observant of every thing that was passing, it is easy to suppose that religion was the subject to which it would be directed, and although this subject principally occupied my thoughts—there was nothing that I saw or heard of to which my attention was not directed.

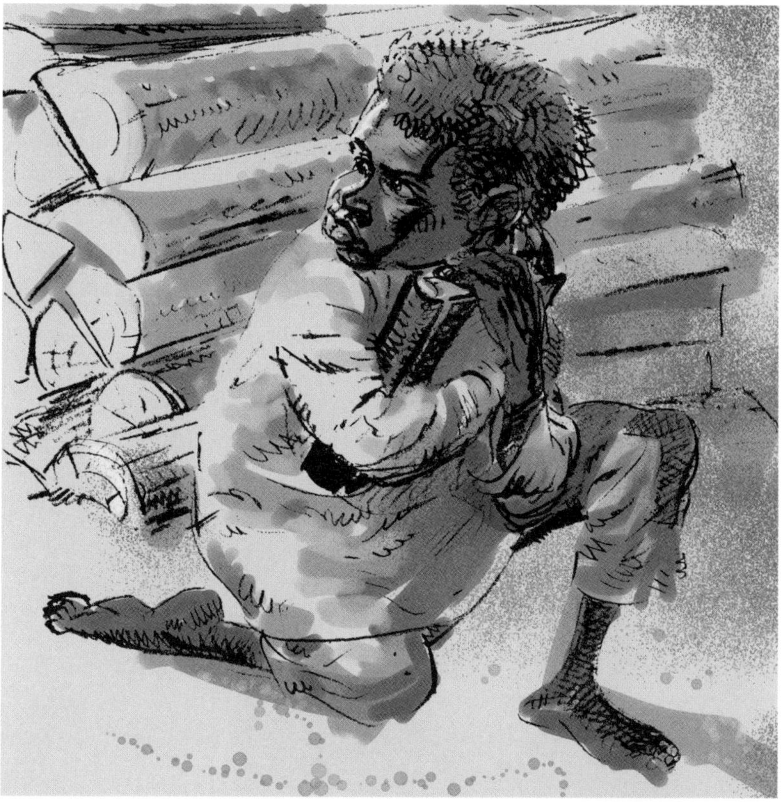

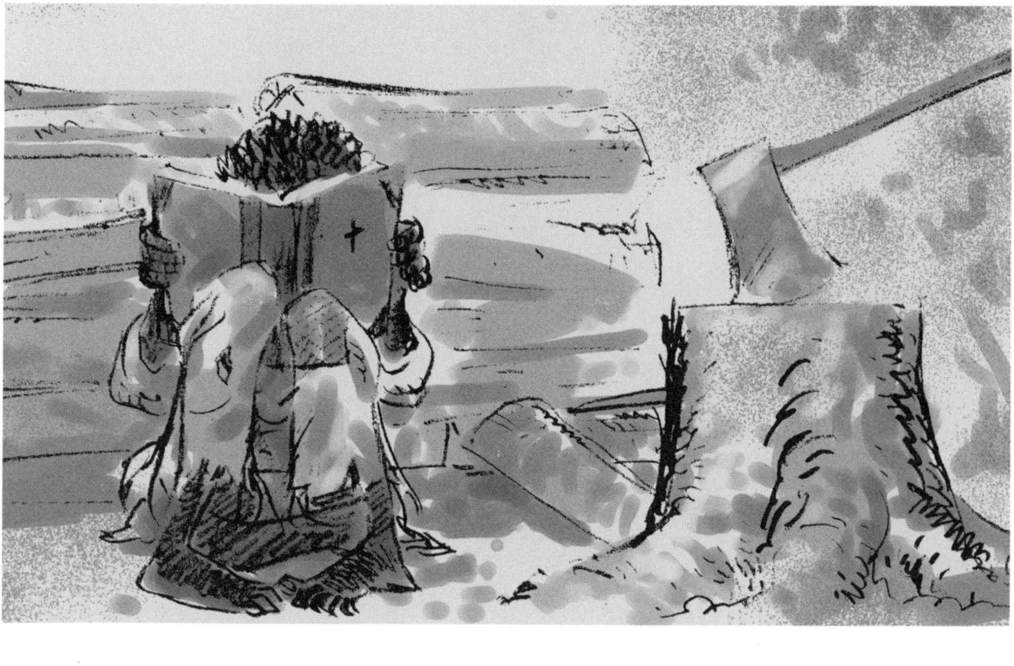

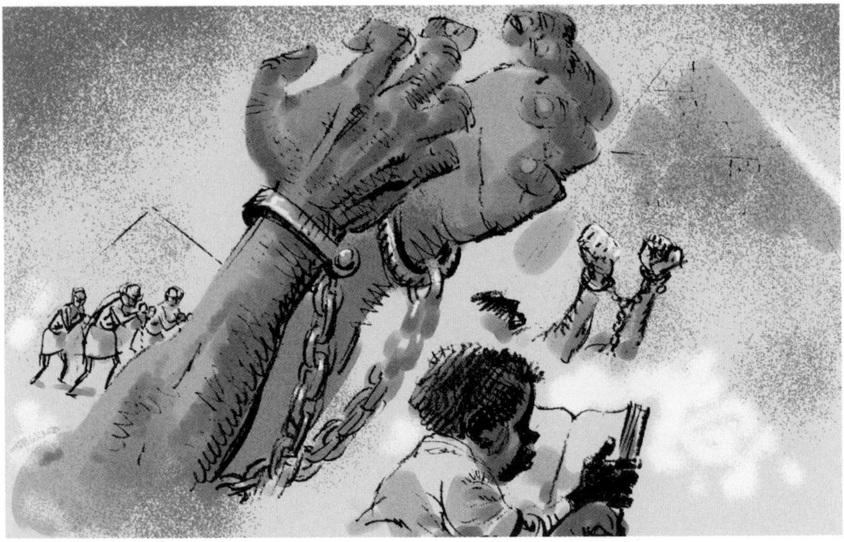

"THE MANNER IN WHICH I LEARNED TO READ AND WRITE, NOT ONLY HAD great influence on my own mind, as I acquired it with the most perfect ease, so much so, that I have no recollection whatever of learning the alphabet.

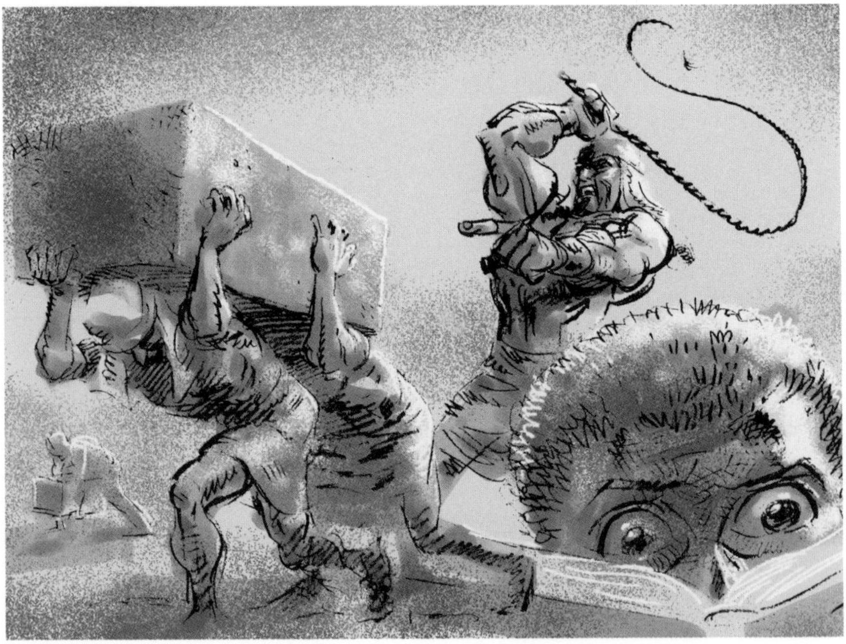

"BUT TO THE ASTONISHMENT OF THE FAMILY, ONE DAY WHEN A BOOK WAS shown to me to keep me from crying, I began spelling the names of different objects.

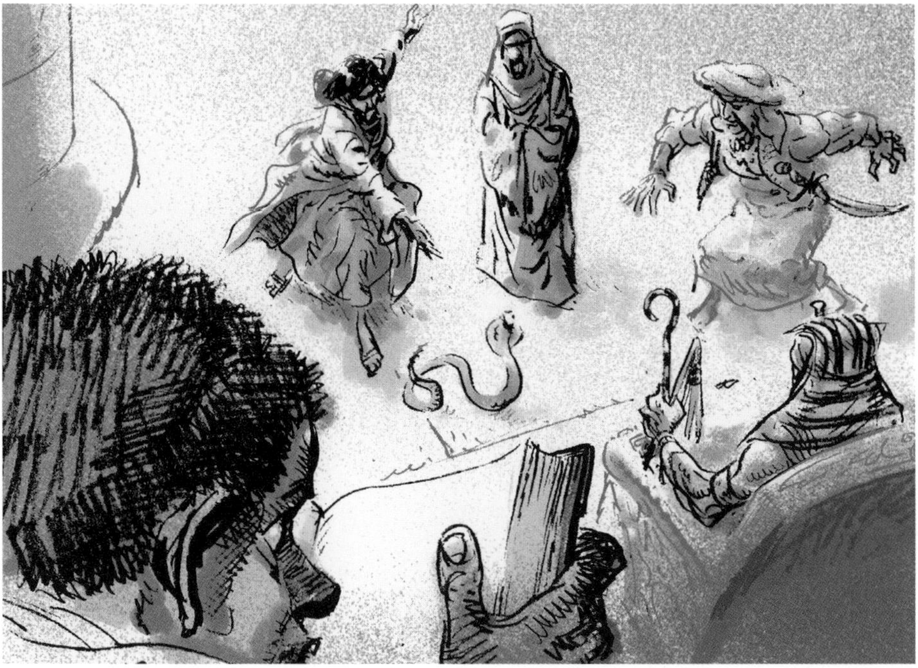

"THIS WAS A SOURCE OF WONDER TO ALL IN THE NEIGHBORHOOD, PARTICULARLY the blacks—and this learning was constantly improved at all opportunities.

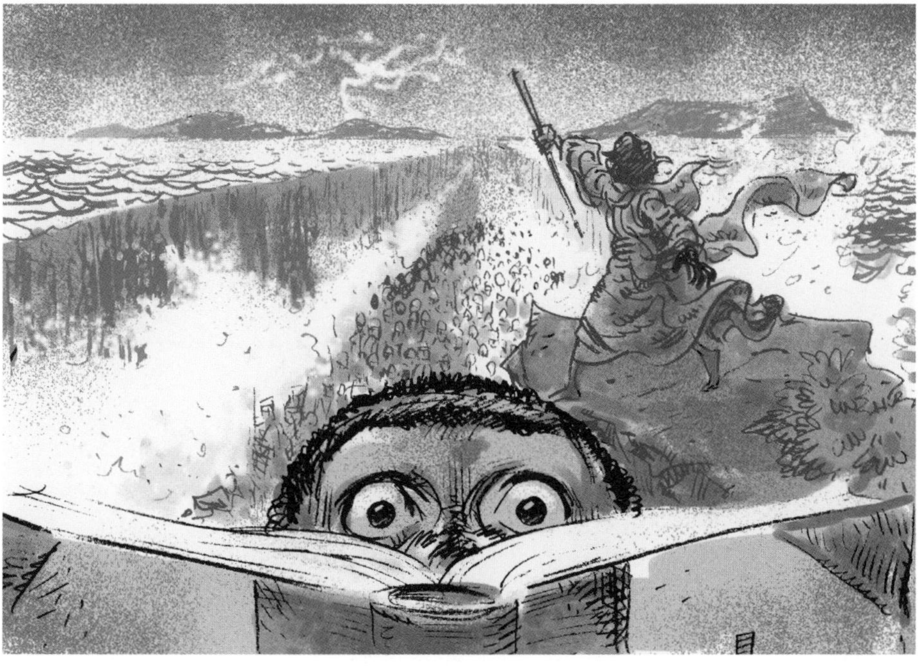

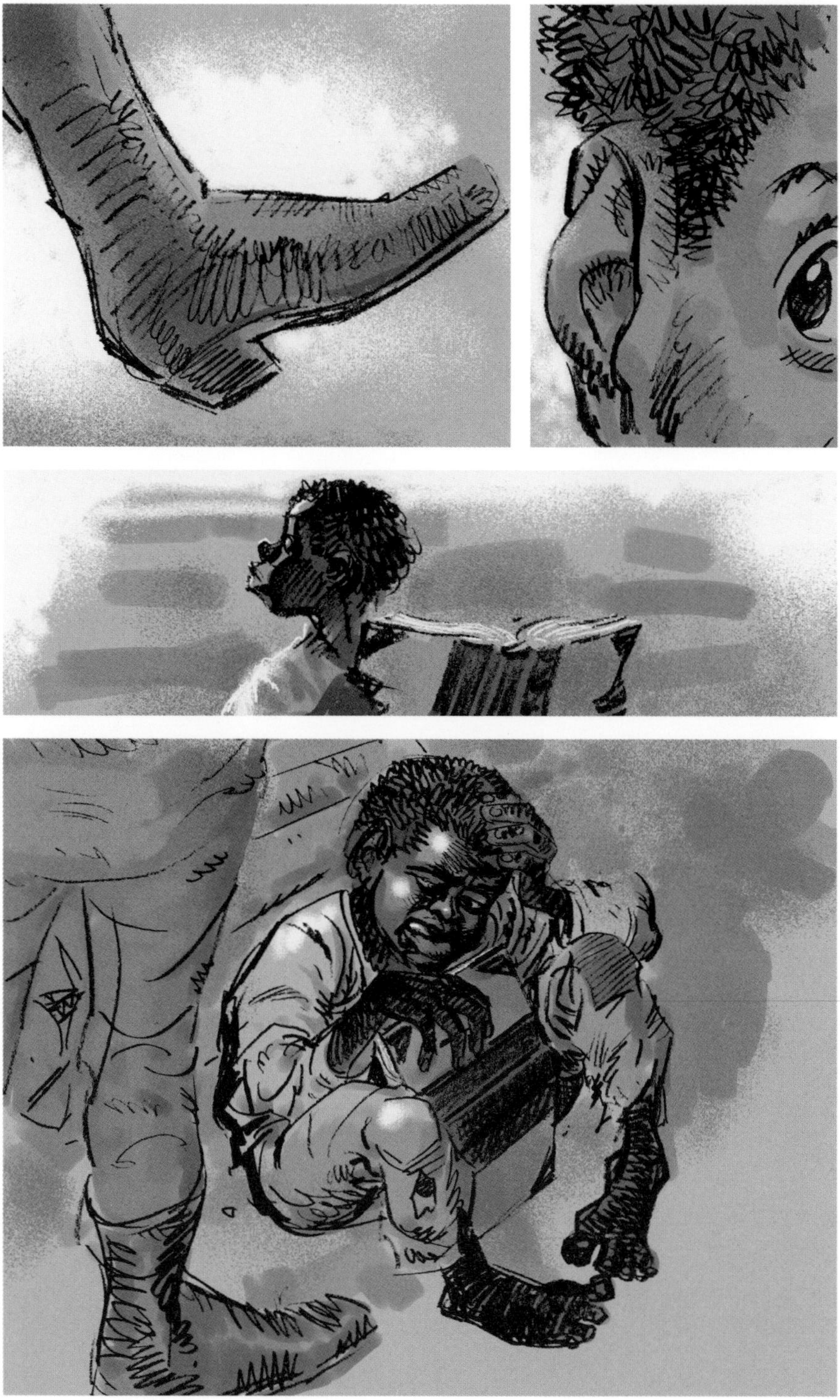

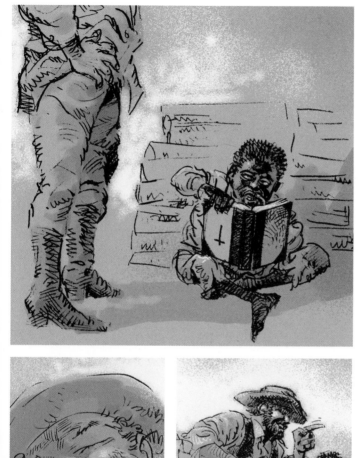

"WHEN I GOT LARGE ENOUGH to go to work, while employed, I was reflecting on many things that would present themselves to my imagination, and whenever an opportunity occurred of looking at a book, when the school children were getting their lessons, I would find many things that the fertility of my own imagination had depicted to me before; all my time, not devoted to my master's service, was spent either in prayer, or in making experiments in casting different things in molds made of earth, in attempting to make paper, gunpowder, and many other experiments, that although I could not perfect, yet convinced me of its practicability if I had the means.

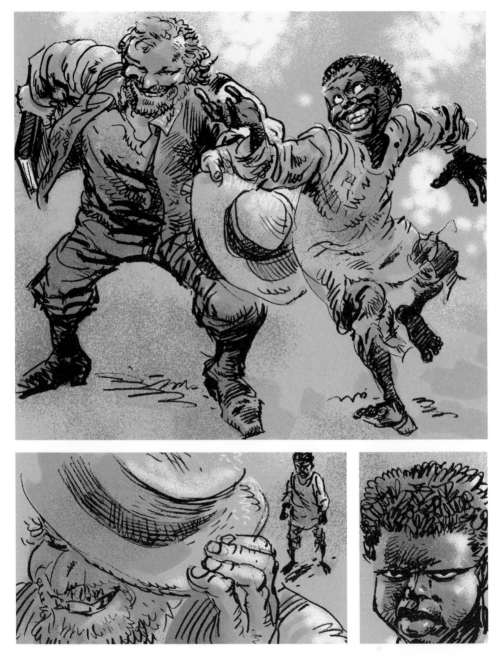

"I WAS NOT ADDICTED TO STEALING IN MY YOUTH, NOR HAVE EVER BEEN—YET SUCH was the confidence of the Negroes in the neighborhood, even at this early period of my life, in my superior judgment, that they would often carry me with them when they were going on any roguery, to plan for them.

"GROWING UP AMONG THEM WITH THIS CONFIDENCE IN MY SUPERIOR judgment, and when this, in their opinions, was perfected by Divine inspiration, from the circumstances already alluded to in my infancy, and which belief was ever afterwards zealously inculcated by the austerity of my life and manners, which became the subject of remark by white and black.

"HAVING SOON DISCOVERED TO BE GREAT, I MUST APPEAR SO, AND therefore studiously avoided mixing in society, and wrapped myself in mystery, devoting my time to fasting and prayer.

"BY THIS TIME, HAVING ARRIVED TO MAN'S estate, and hearing the scriptures commented on at meetings, I was struck with that particular passage which says: 'Seek ye the kingdom of Heaven and all things shall be added unto you.' I reflected much on this passage, and prayed daily for light on this subject. As I was praying one day at my plough, the spirit spoke to me, saying 'Seek ye the kingdom of Heaven and all things shall be added unto you.'" *Question: What do you mean by the Spirit?* "The Spirit that spoke to the prophets in former days. I was greatly astonished, and for two years prayed continually, whenever my duty would permit— and then again I had the same revelation, which fully confirmed me in the impression

that I was ordained for some great purpose in the hands of the Almighty. Several years rolled round, in which many events occurred to strengthen me in this my belief. At this time I reverted in my mind to the remarks made of me in my childhood, and the things that had been shown me—and as it had been said of me in my childhood by those by whom I had been taught to pray, both white and black, and in whom I had the greatest confidence, that I had too much sense to be raised, and if I was, I would never be of any use to any one as a slave. Now finding I had arrived to man's estate, and was a slave, and these revelations being made known to me, I began to direct my attention to this great object, to fulfill the purpose for which, by this time, I felt assured I was intended.

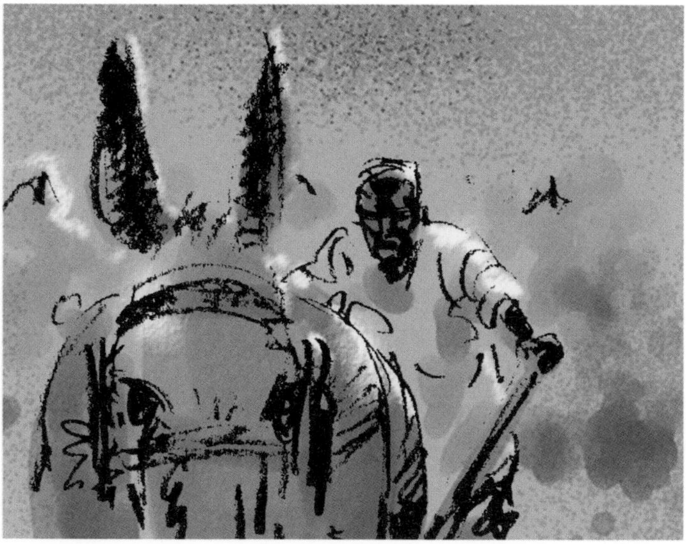

"KNOWING THE INFLUENCE I HAD OBTAINED OVER THE MINDS OF MY FELLOW SERVANTS, (not by the means of conjuring and such like tricks—for to them I always spoke of such things with contempt) but by the communion of the Spirit whose revelations I often communicated to them, and they believed and said my wisdom came from God. I now began to prepare them for my purpose, by telling them something was about to happen that would terminate in fulfilling the great promise that had been made to me.

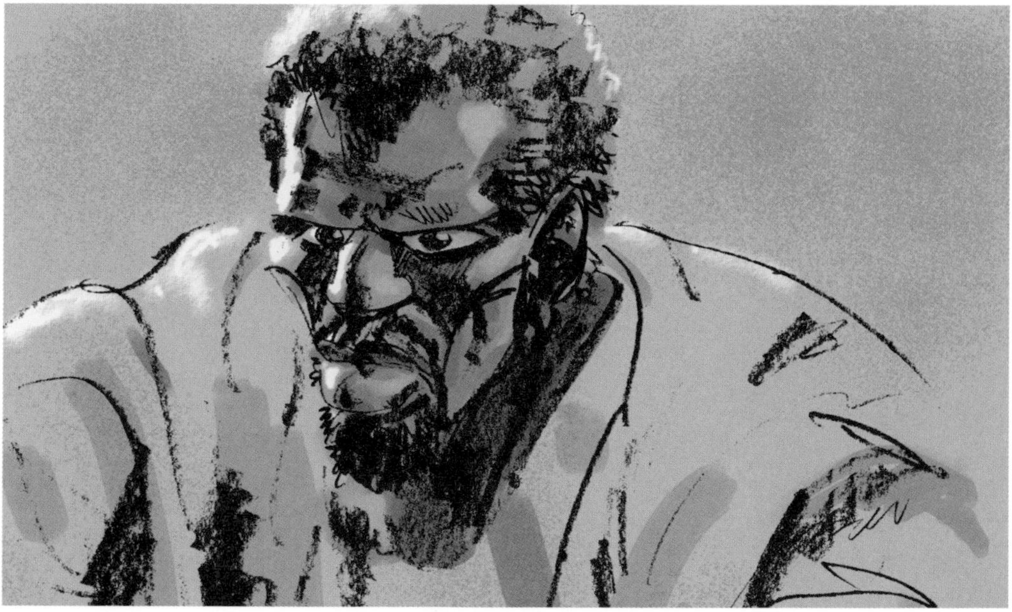

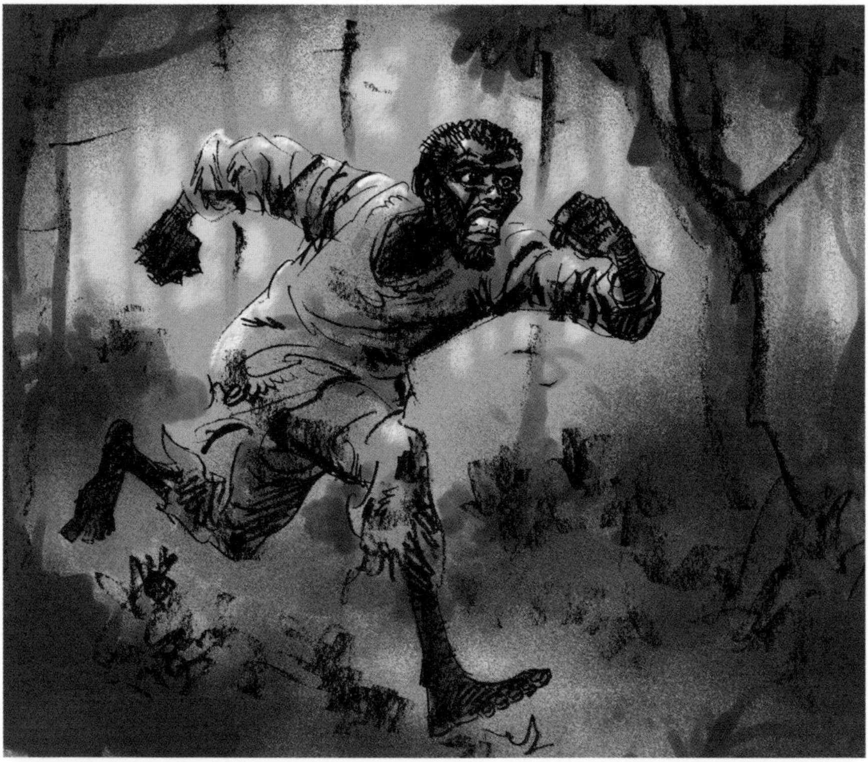

"ABOUT THIS TIME I WAS PLACED UNDER AN OVERSEER, FROM WHOM I RAN AWAY.

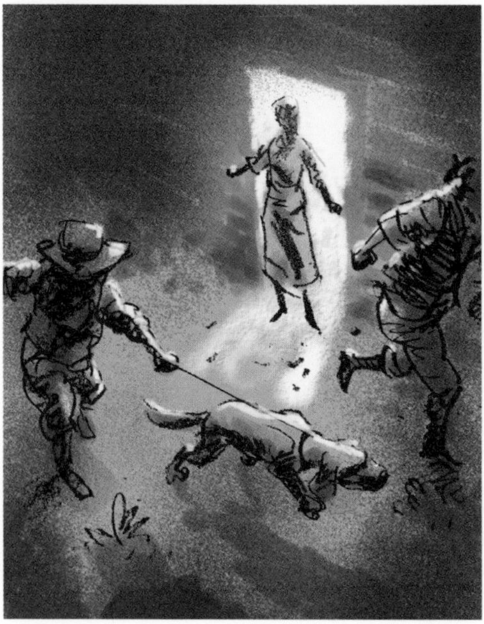

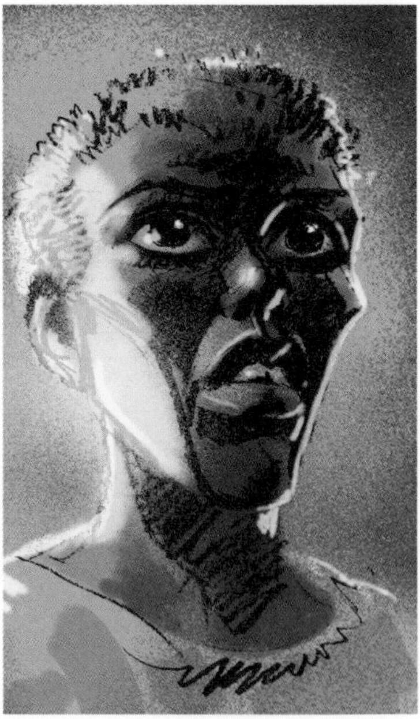

"**AFTER REMAINING** in the woods thirty days, I returned, to the astonishment of the Negroes on the plantation, who thought I had made my escape to some other part of the country, as my father had done before. But the reason of my return was that the Spirit appeared to me and said I had my wishes directed to the things of this world, and not to the kingdom of Heaven, and that I should return to the service of my earthly master—'For he who knoweth his Master's will, and doeth it not, shall be beaten with many stripes, and thus have I chastened you.' And the Negroes found fault, and murmured against me, saying that if they had my sense they would not serve any master in the world.

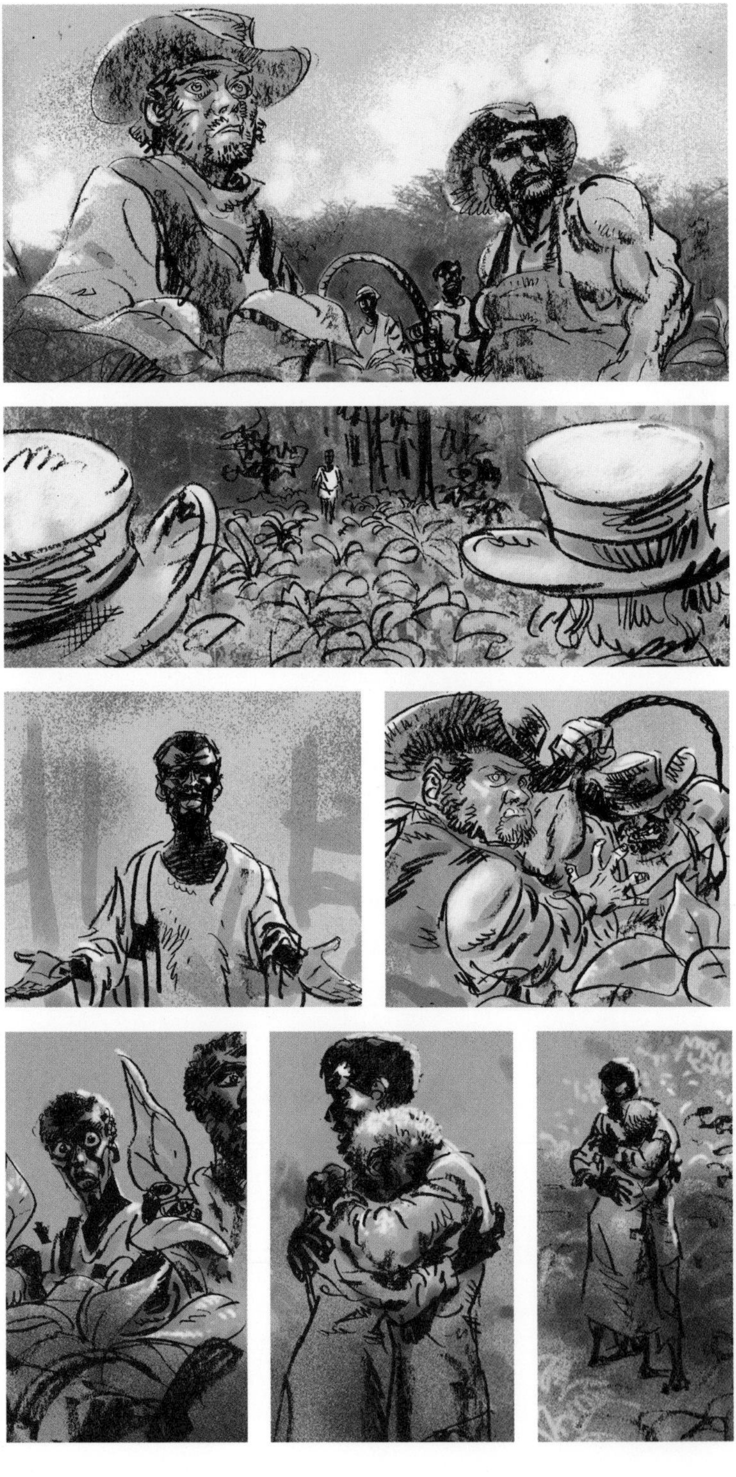

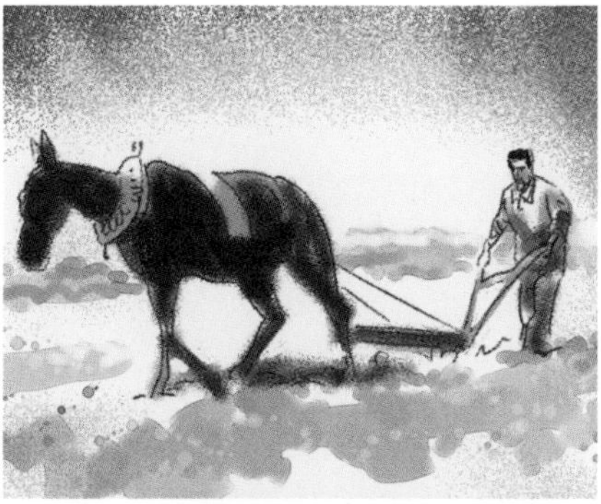

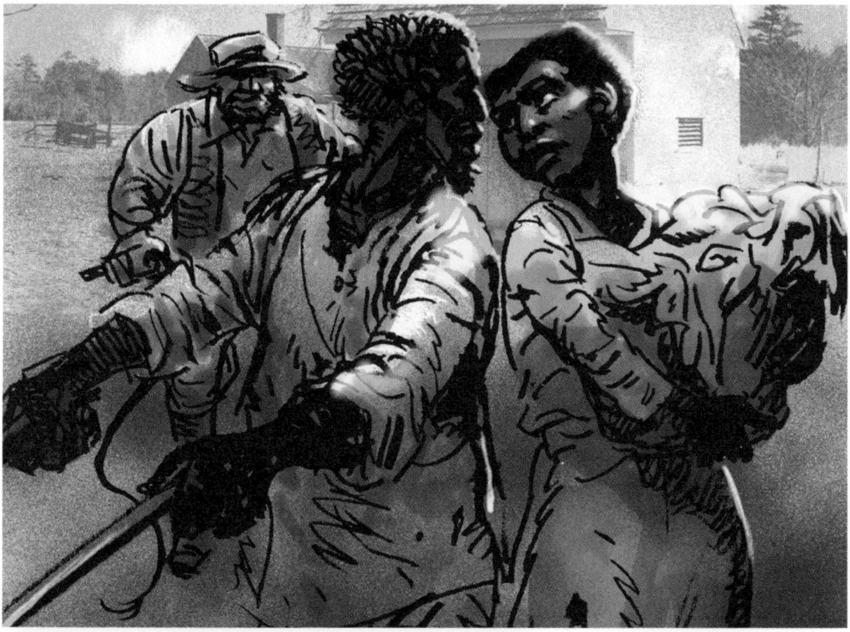

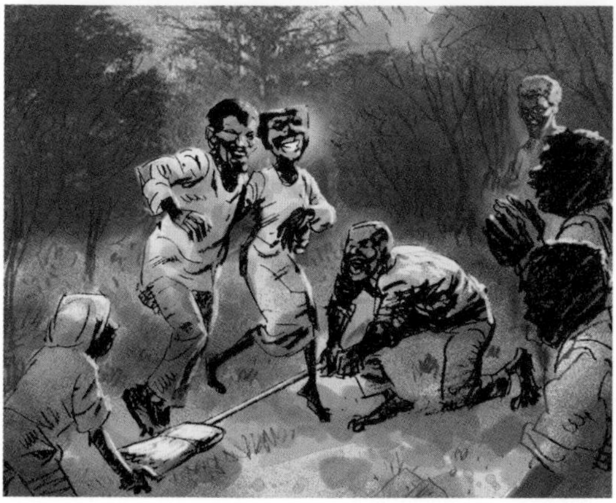

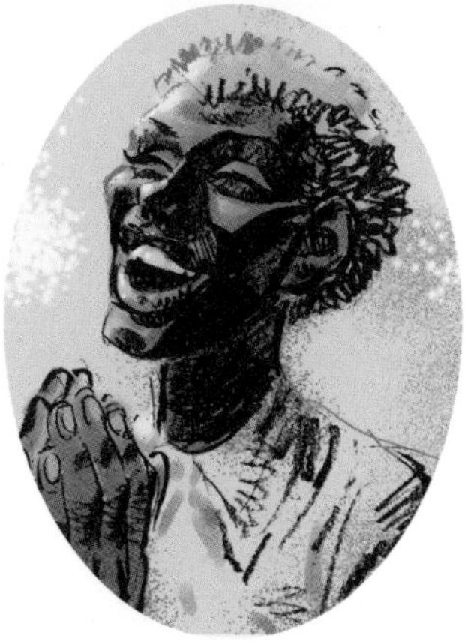

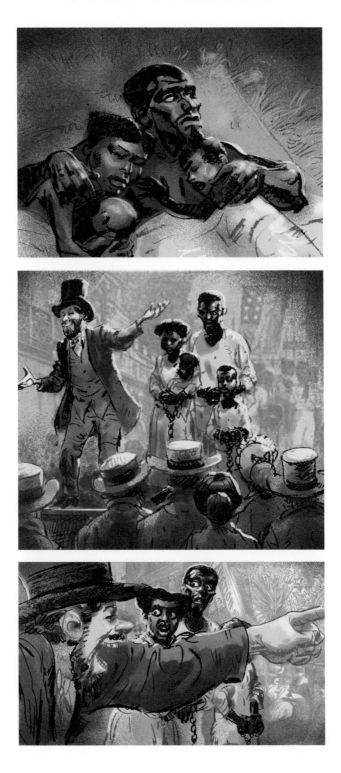

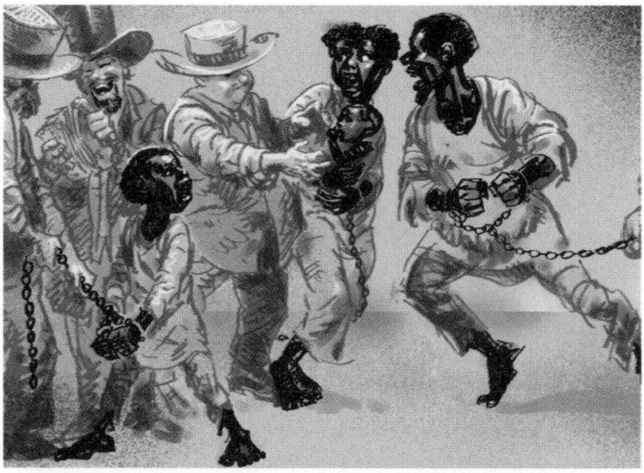

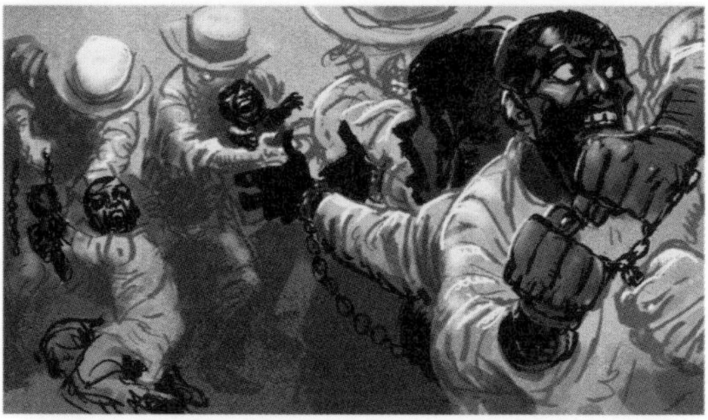

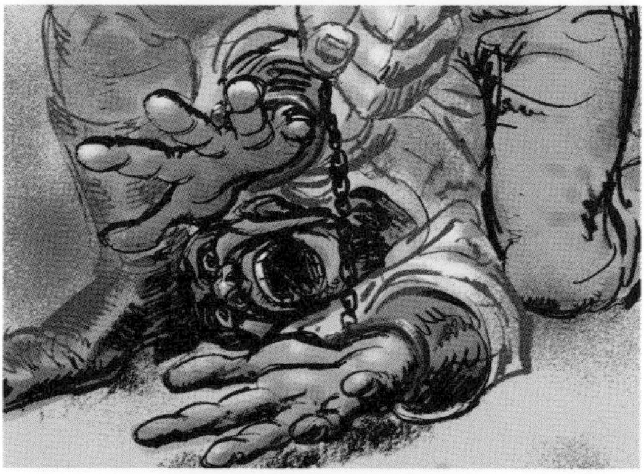

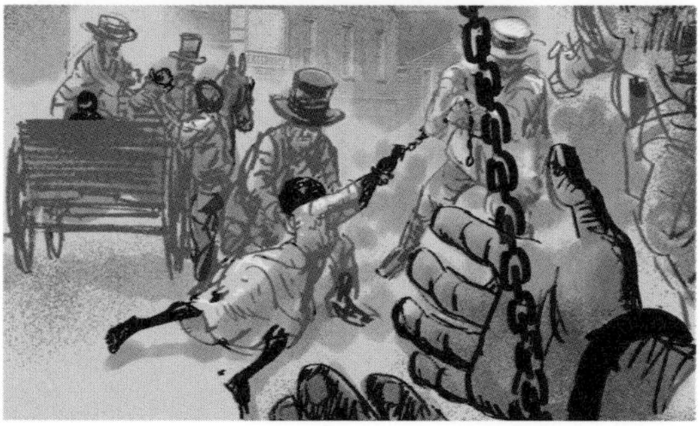

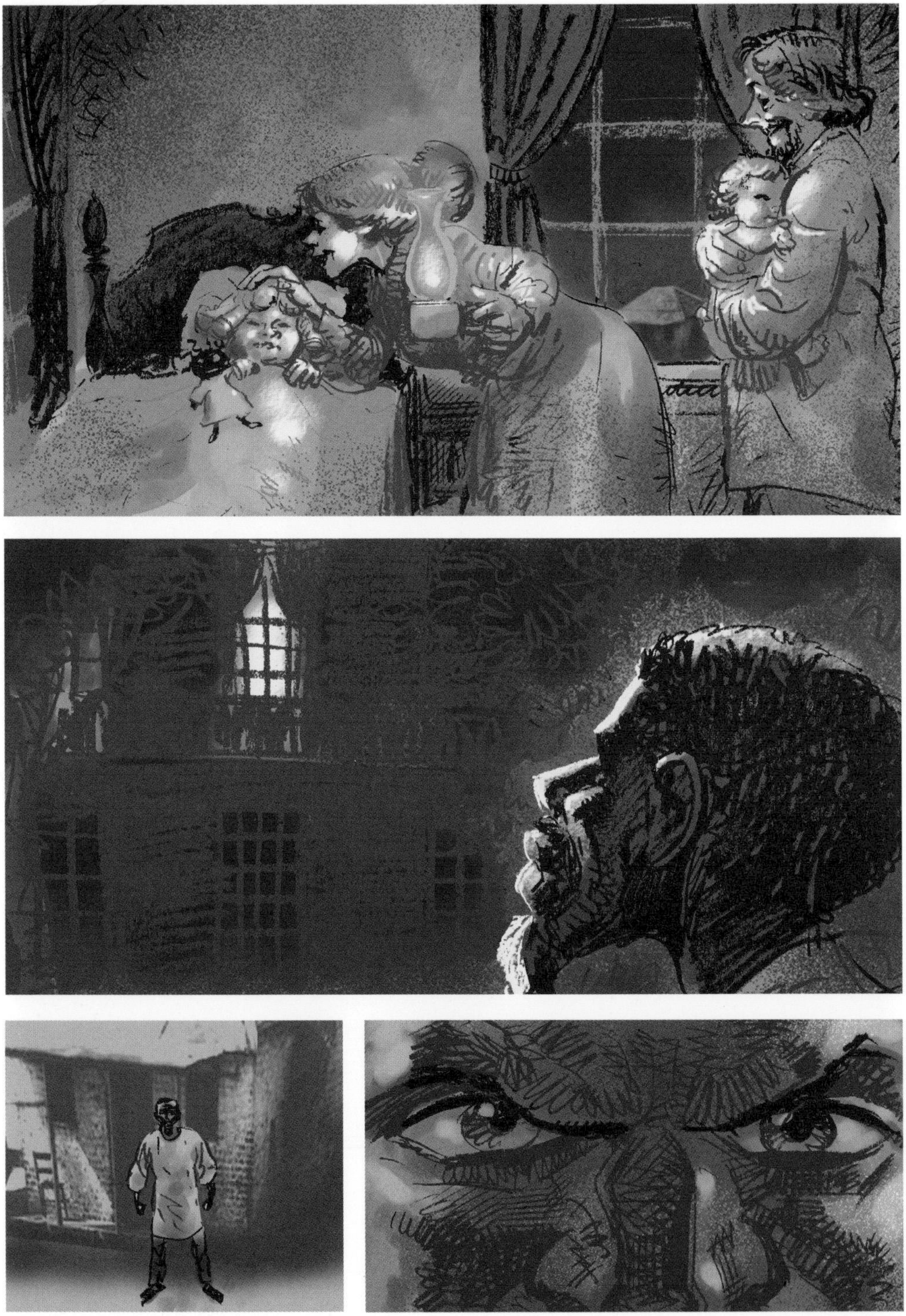

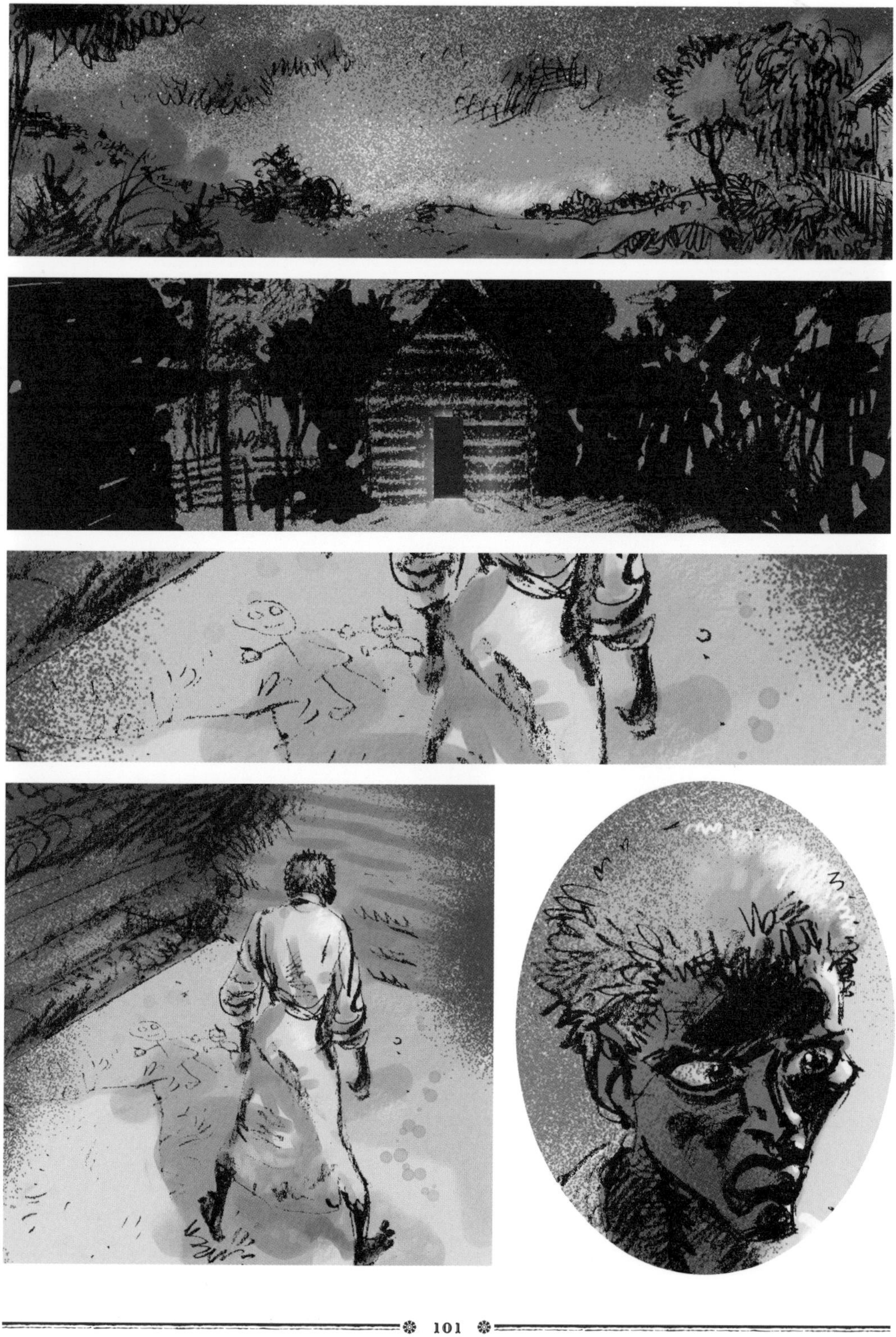

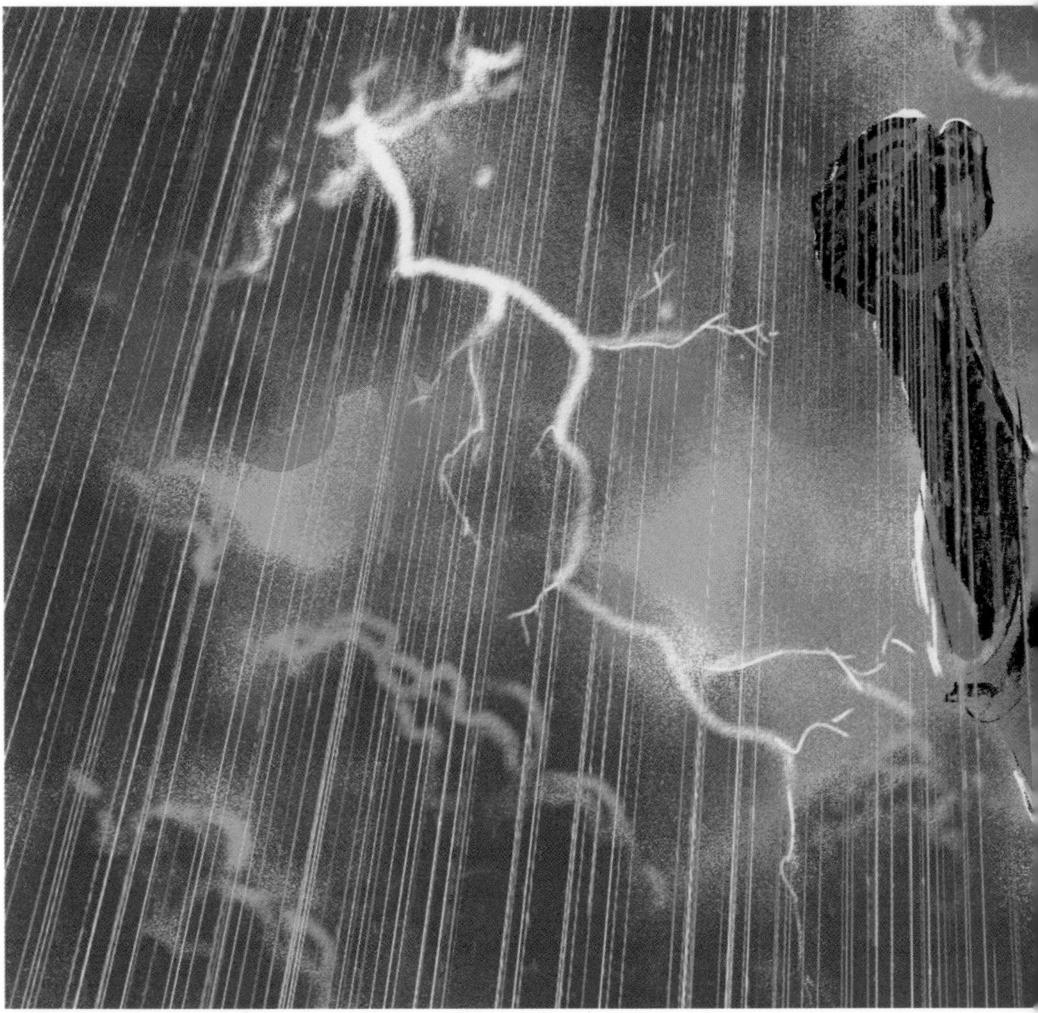

"AND ABOUT THIS TIME I HAD A VISION—AND I SAW WHITE SPIRITS AND BLACK SPIRITS engaged in battle, and the sun was darkened—the thunder rolled in the Heavens, and blood flowed in streams, and I heard a voice saying, 'Such is your luck, such you are called to see, and let it come rough or smooth, you must surely bear it.' I now withdrew myself as much as my situation would permit, from the intercourse of my fellow servants, for the avowed purpose of serving the Spirit more fully—and it appeared to me, and reminded me of the things it had already shown me, and that it would then reveal to me the knowledge of the elements, the revolution of the planets, the operation of tides, and changes of the seasons. After this revelation in the year of 1825, and the knowledge of the elements being made known to me, I sought more than ever to obtain true holiness before the great day of judgment should appear,

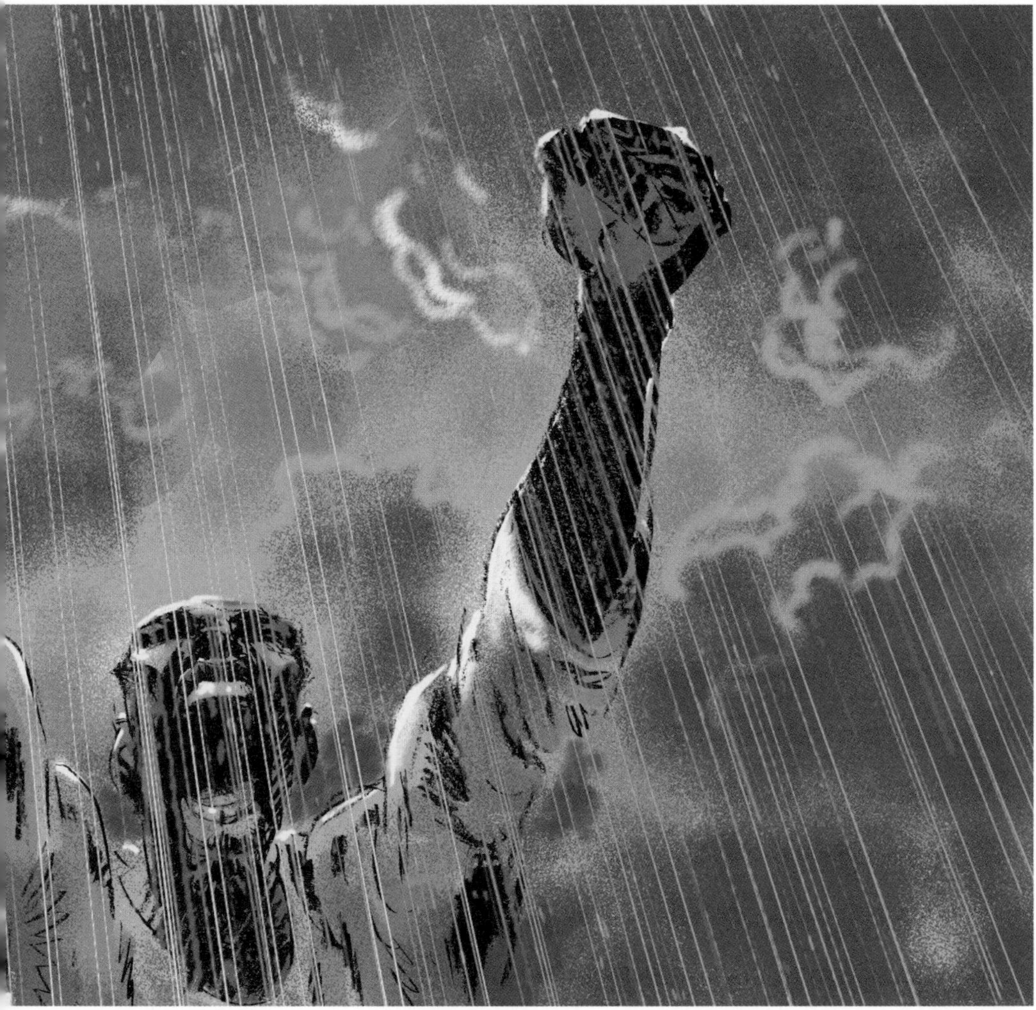

and then I began to receive the true knowledge of faith. And from the first steps of righteousness until the last, was I made perfect; and the Holy Ghost was with me, and said, 'Behold me as I stand in the Heavens'—and I looked and saw the forms of men in different attitudes—and there were lights in the sky to which the children of darkness gave other names than what they really were—for they were the lights of the Savior's hands, stretched forth from east to west, even as they were extended on the cross on Calvary for the redemption of sinners. And I wondered greatly at these miracles, and prayed to be informed of a certainty of the meaning thereof—and shortly afterward, while laboring in the field, I discovered drops of blood on the corn as though it were dew from heaven—and I communicated it to many, both white and black, in the neighborhood.

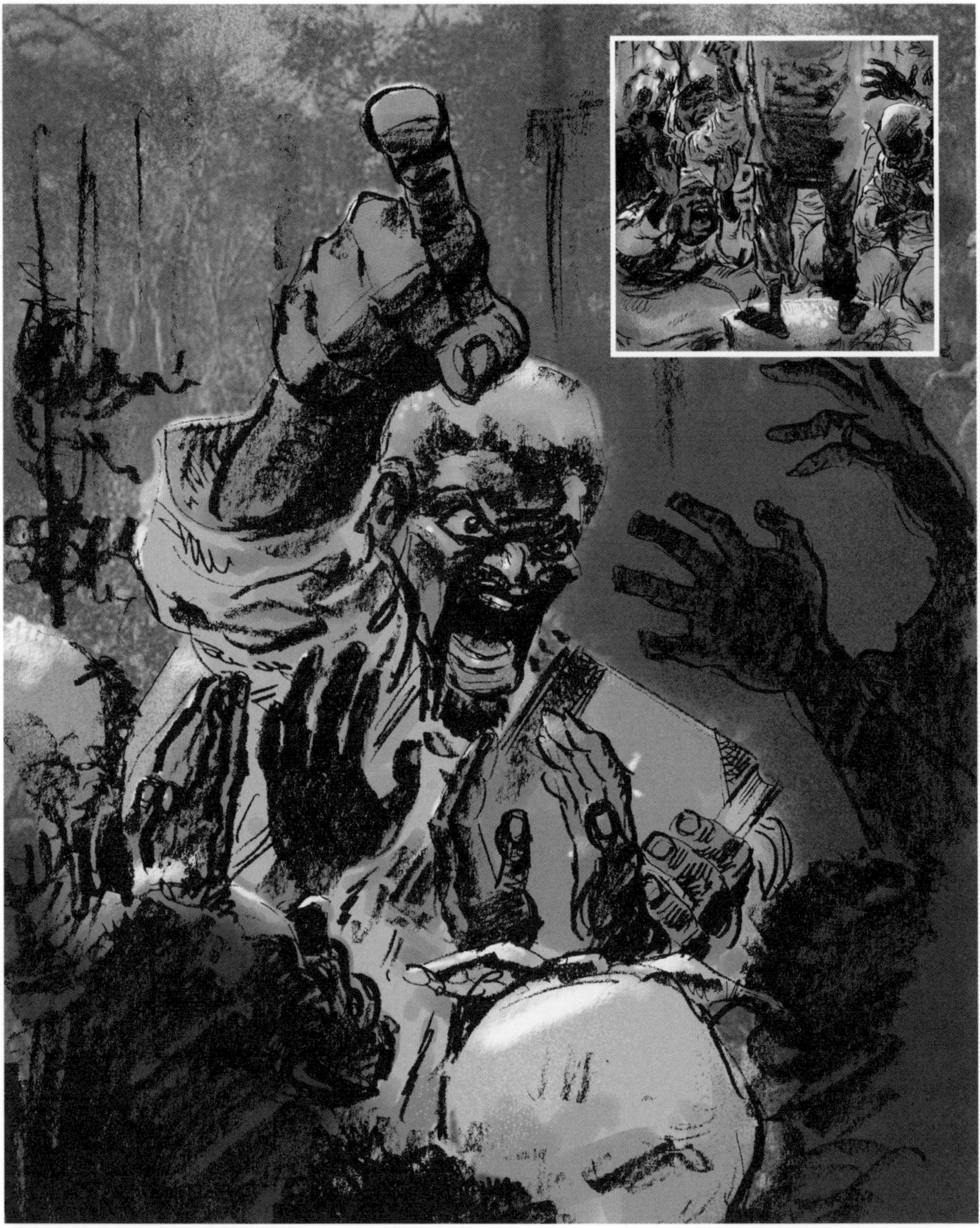

"AND ON THE 12TH OF MAY, 1828, I HEARD A LOUD NOISE IN THE HEAVENS, AND THE SPIRIT instantly appeared to me and said the Serpent was loosened, and Christ had laid down the yoke He had borne for the sins of men, and that I should take it on and fight against the Serpent, for the time was fast approaching when the first should be last and the last should be first."

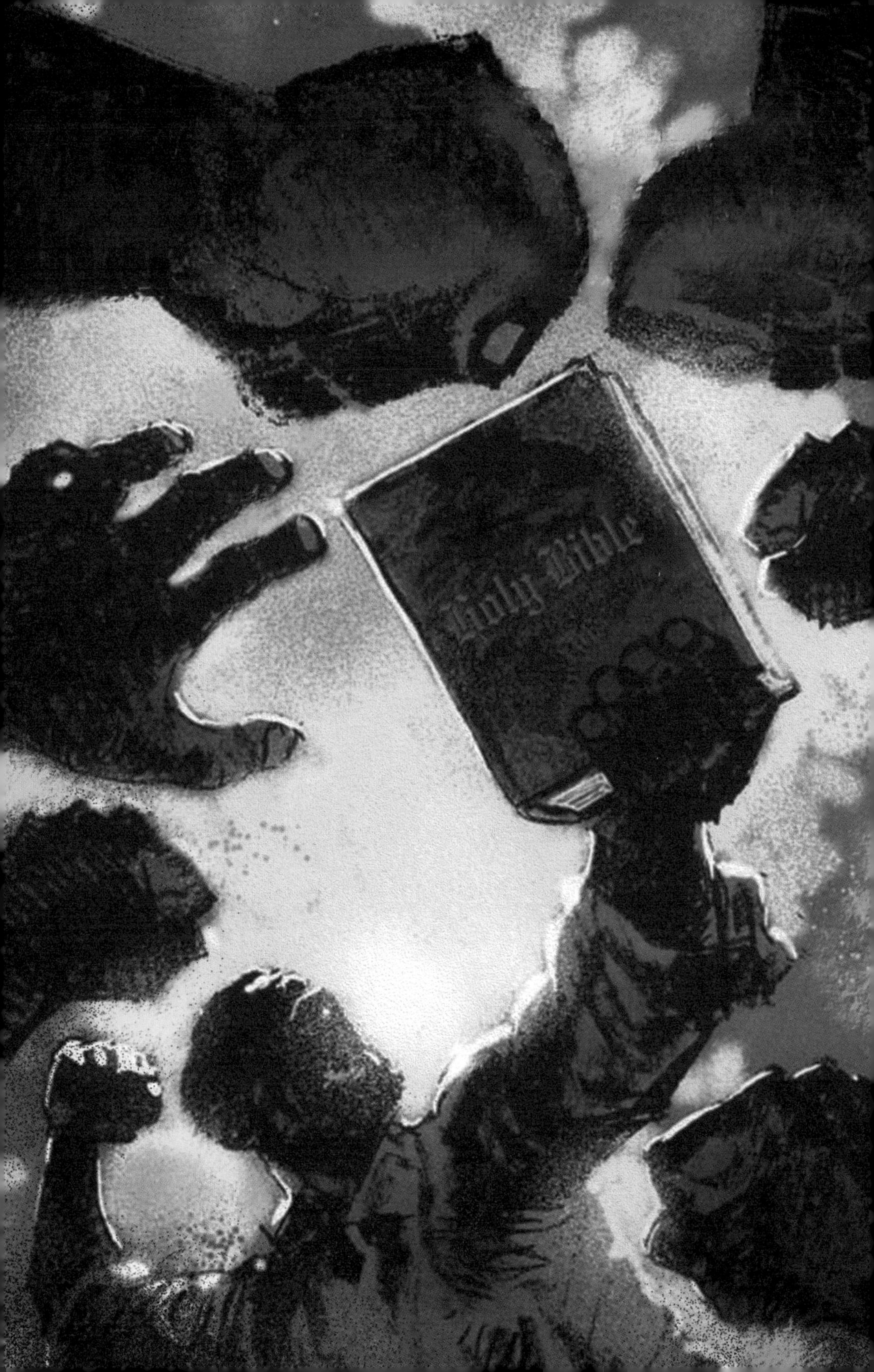
Holy Bible

III

FREEDOM

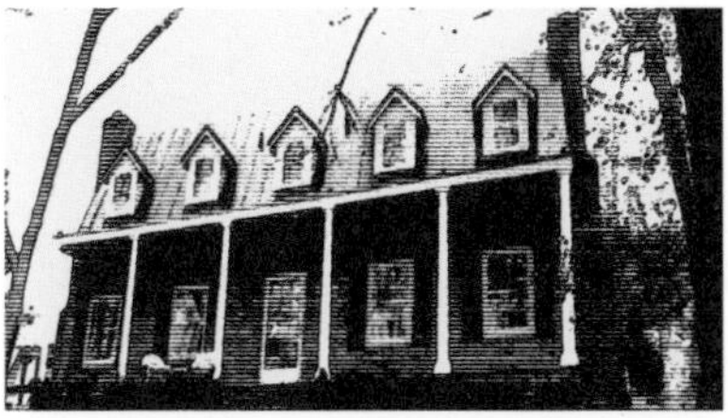

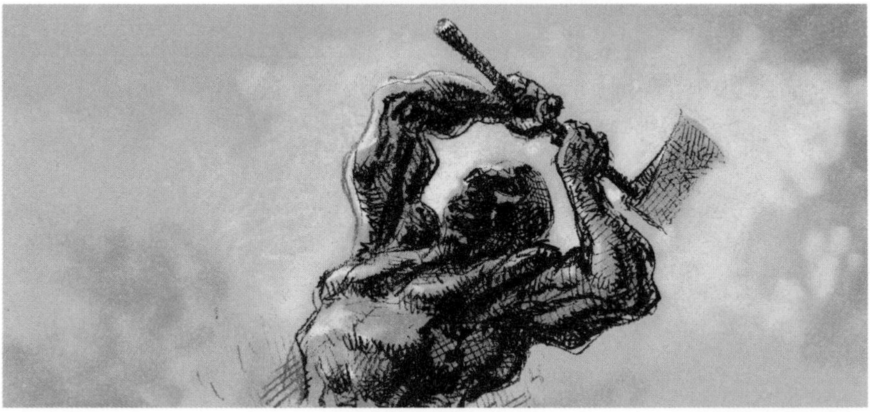

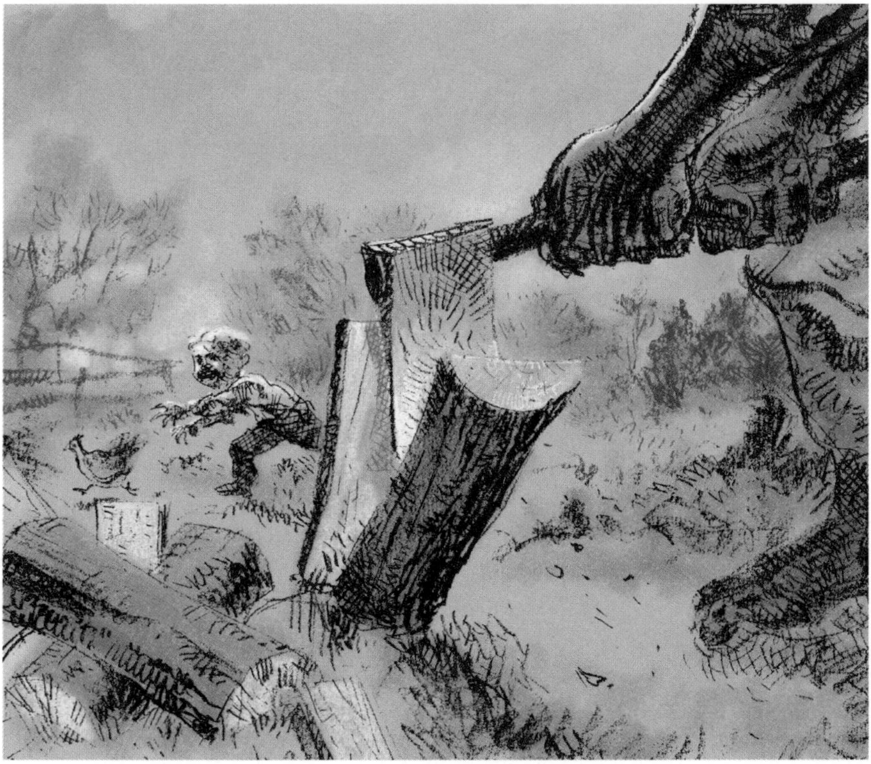

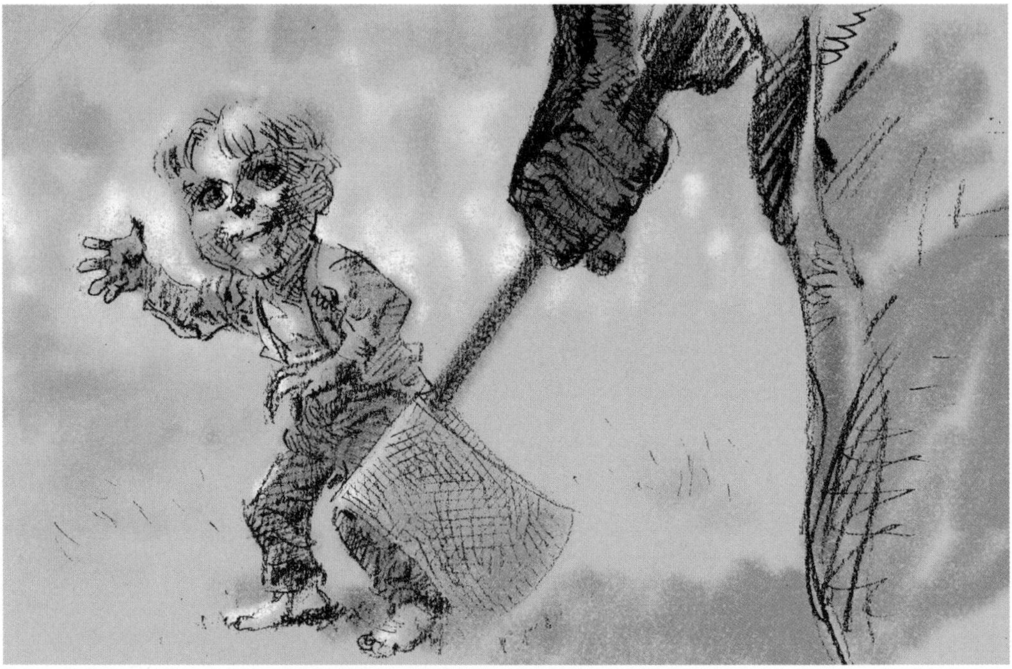

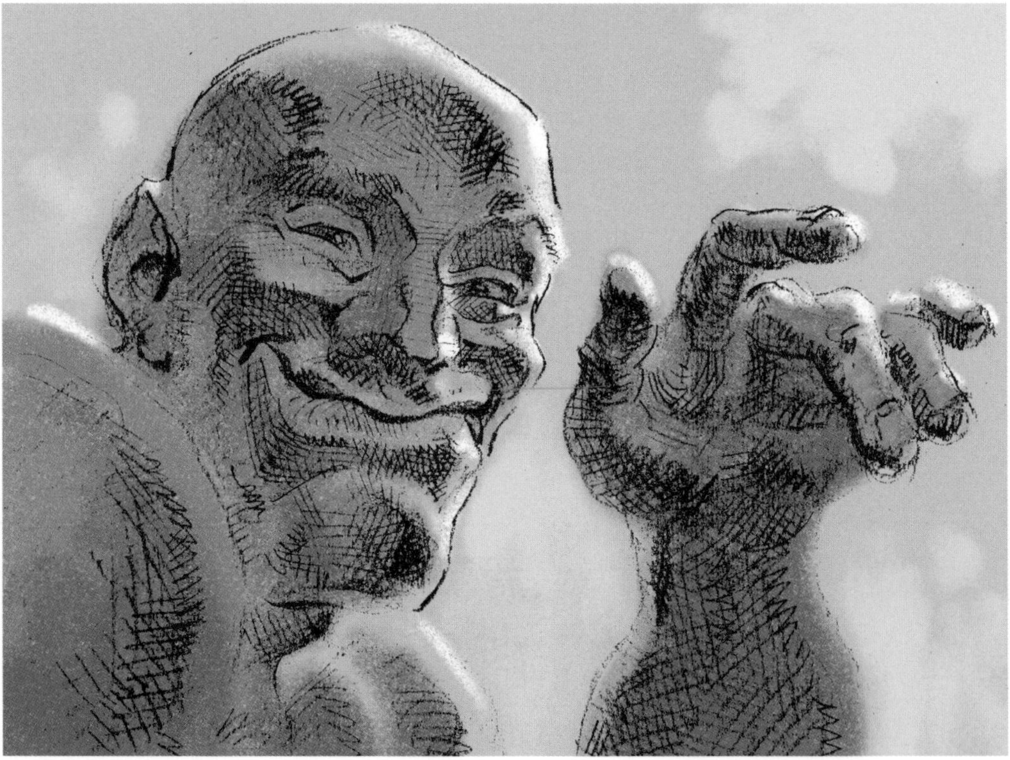

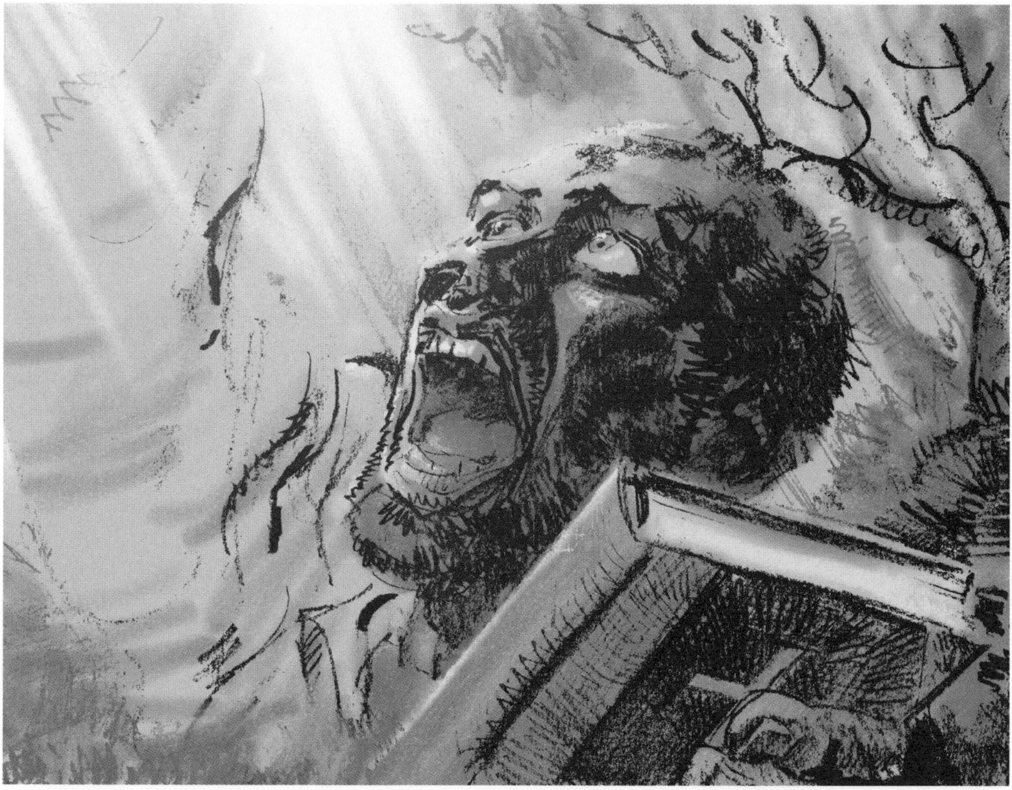

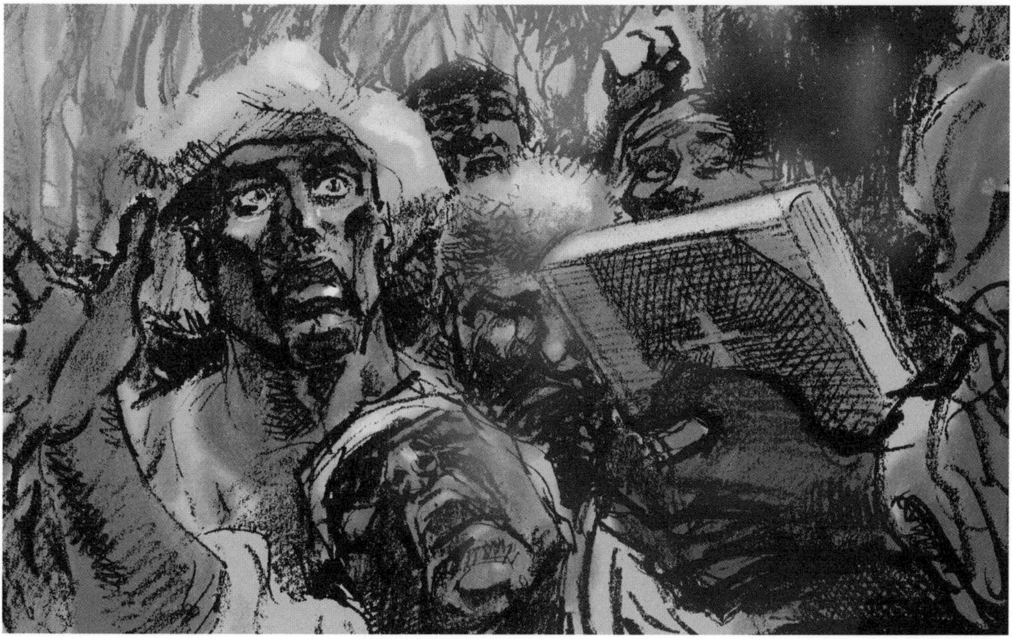

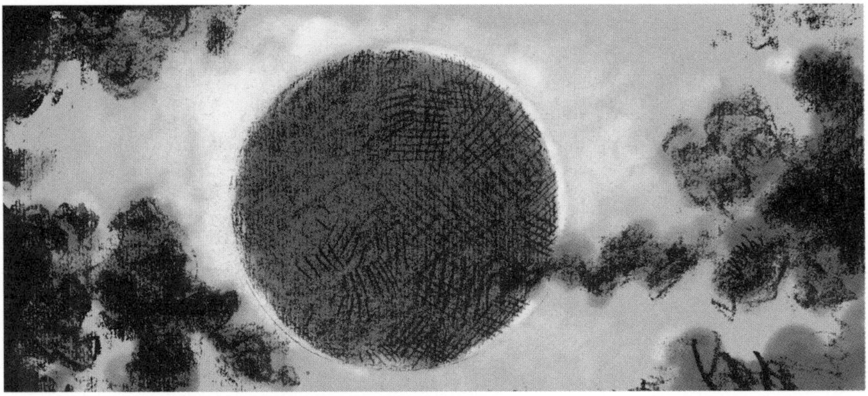

FROM THE CONFESSIONS OF NAT TURNER

"And by signs in the heavens that it would make known to me when I should commence the great work—and until the first sign appeared, I should conceal it from the knowledge of men—and on the appearance of the sign, (the eclipse of the sun last February) I should arise and prepare myself, and slay my enemies with their own weapons.

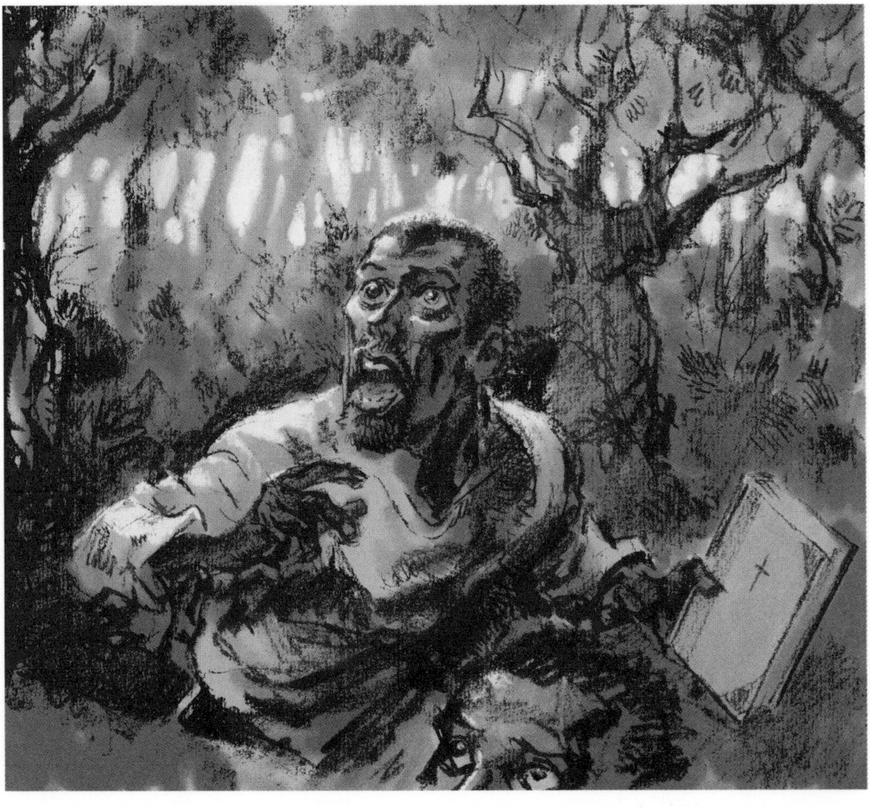

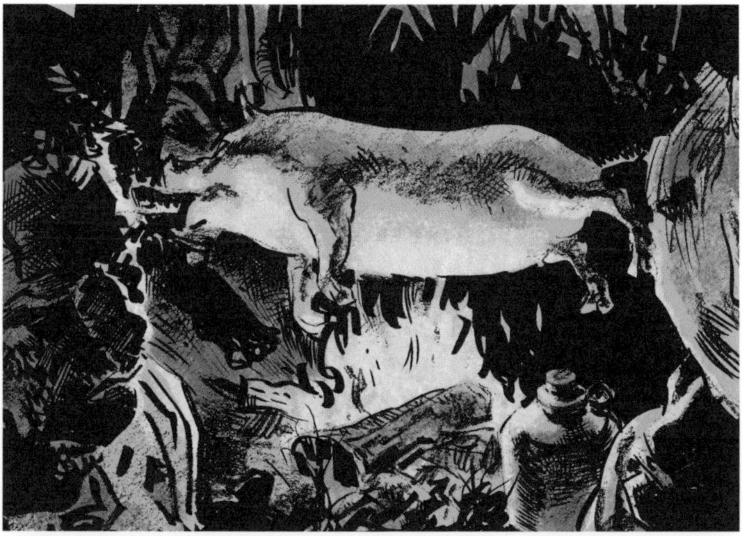

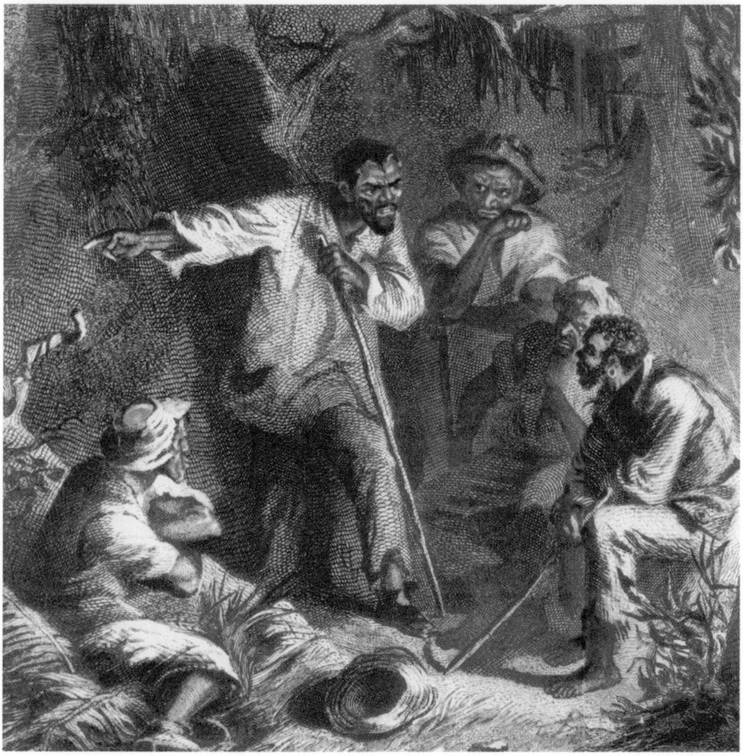

"AND IMMEDIATELY on the sign appearing in the heavens, the seal was removed from my lips, and I communicated the great work laid out for me to do, to four in whom I had the greatest confidence—it was intended by us to have begun the work of death on the 4th of July last. Many were the plans formed and rejected by us, and it affected my mind to such a degree that I fell sick, and the time passed without our coming to any determination how to commence. Still forming new schemes and rejecting them, when the sign appeared again, which determined me not to wait longer.

"IT WAS QUICKLY AGREED WE SHOULD COMMENCE AT HOME (MR. J. TRAVIS'S) ON THAT NIGHT and until we had armed and equipped ourselves, and gathered sufficient force, neither age nor sex was to be spared, (which was invariably adhered to). We remained at the feast until about two hours in the night, when we went to the house and found Austin; they all went to the cider press and drank, except myself. On returning to the house, Hark went to the door with an axe, for the purpose of breaking it open, as we knew we were strong enough to murder the family, if they were awakened by the noise; but reflecting that it might create an alarm in the neighborhood, we determined to enter the house secretly, and murder them whilst sleeping.

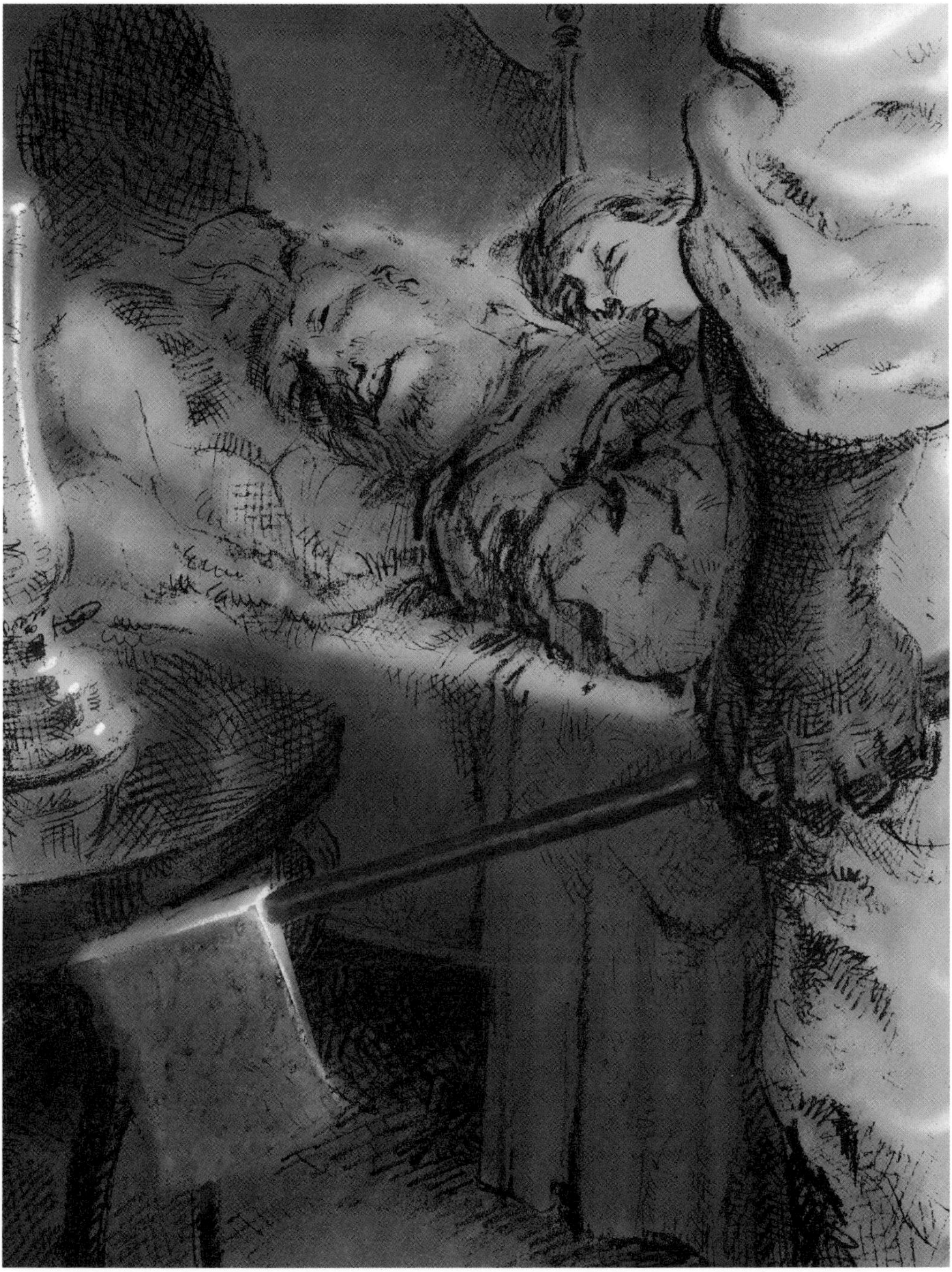

"IT WAS THEN OBSERVED THAT I MUST SPILL THE FIRST BLOOD. ON WHICH, ARMED WITH a hatchet, and accompanied by Will, I entered my master's chamber.

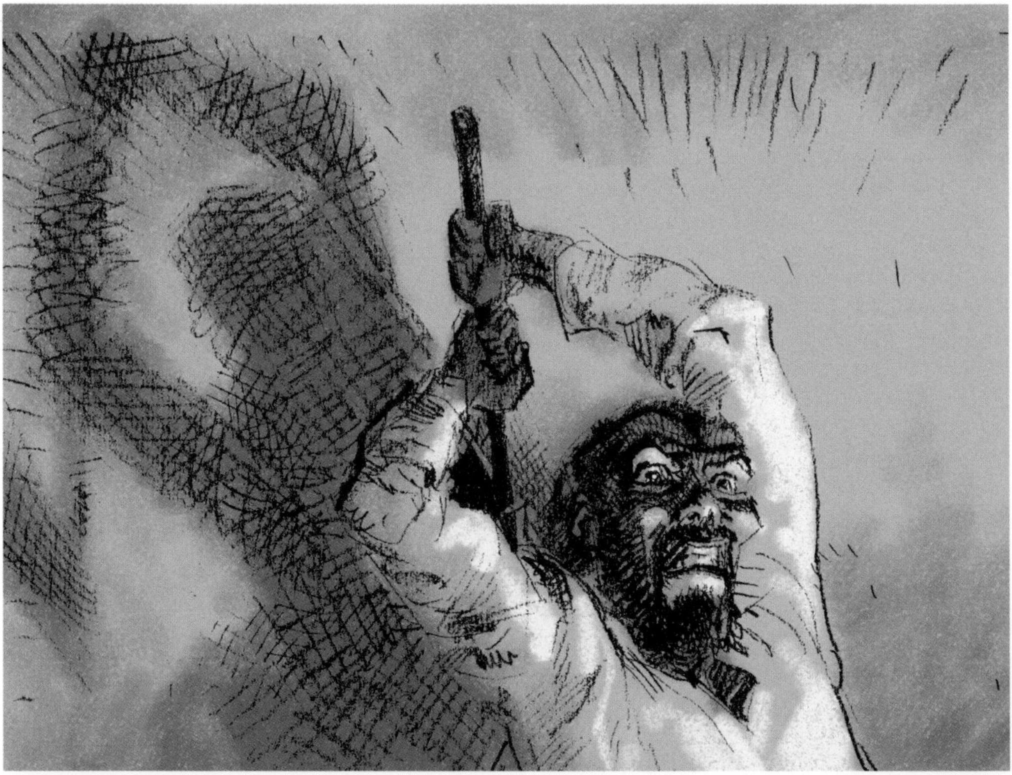

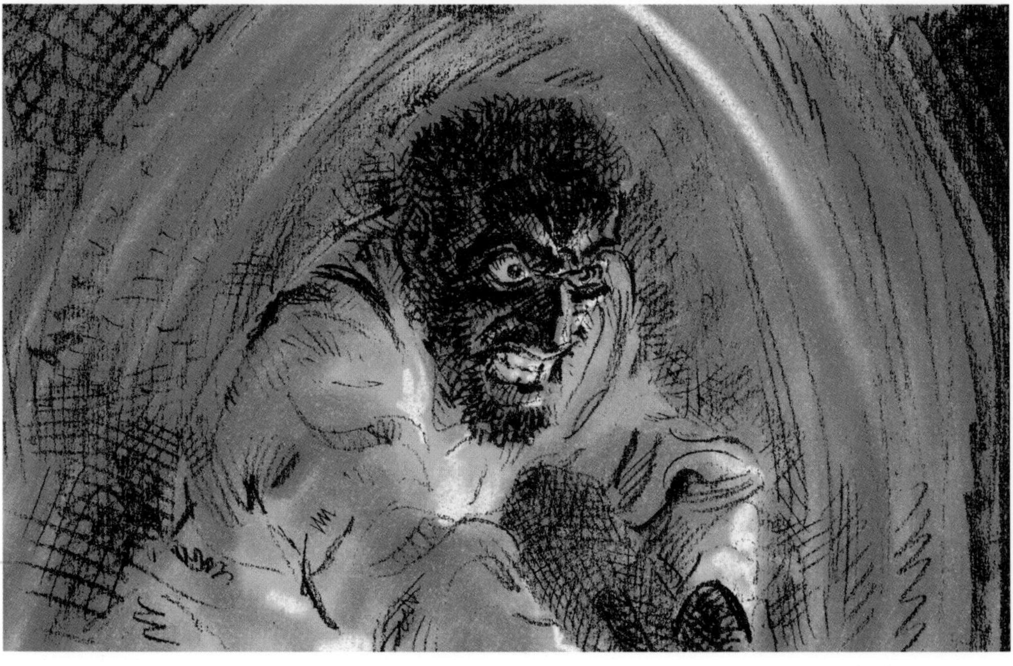

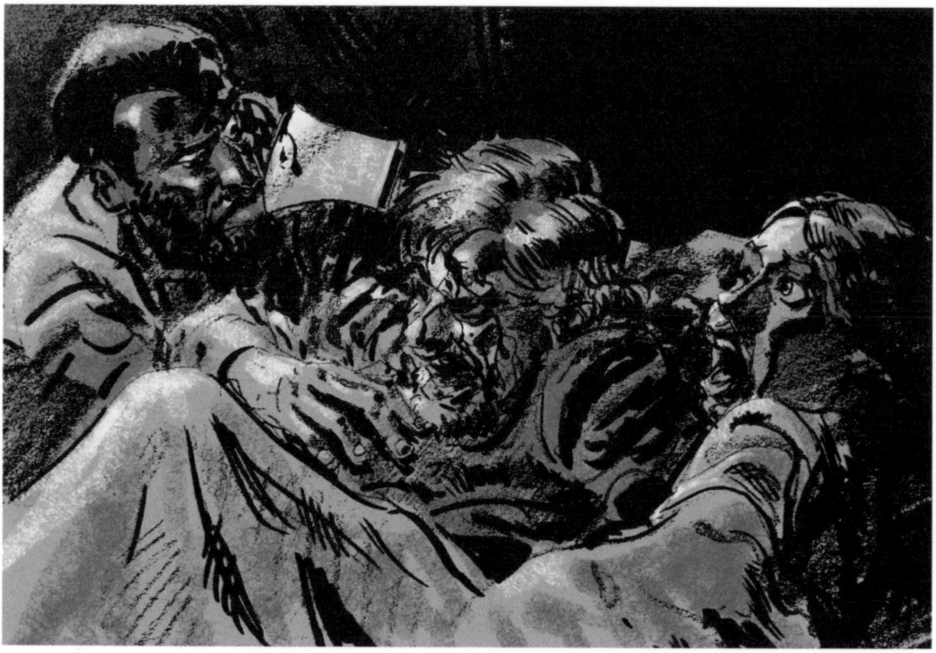

"IT BEING DARK, I COULD NOT GIVE A DEATH BLOW. THE HATCHET GLANCED FROM his head, he sprang from the bed and called his wife—it was his last word. Will laid him dead with a blow of his axe, and Mrs. Travis shared the same fate.

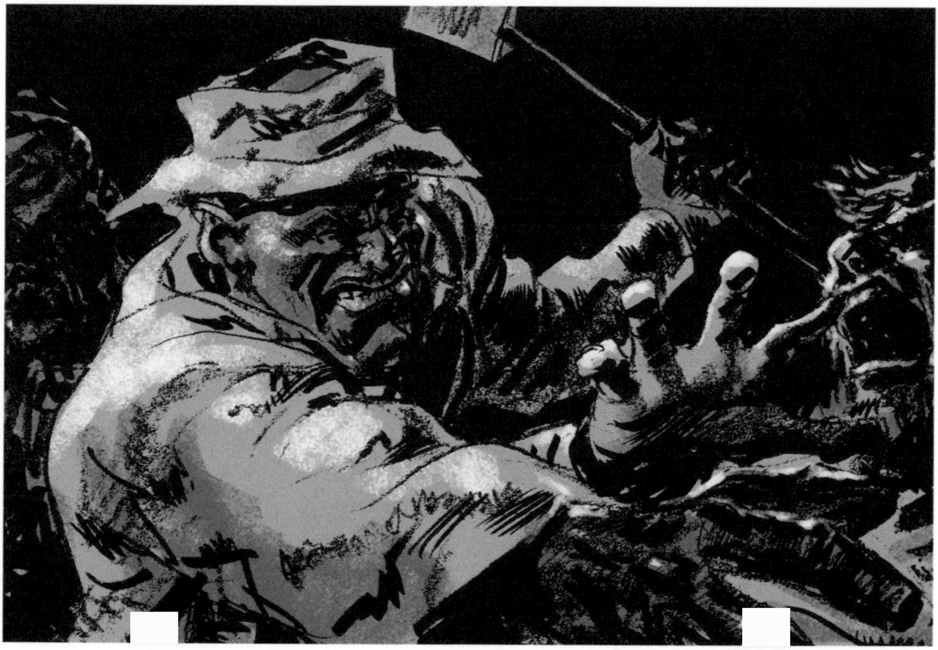

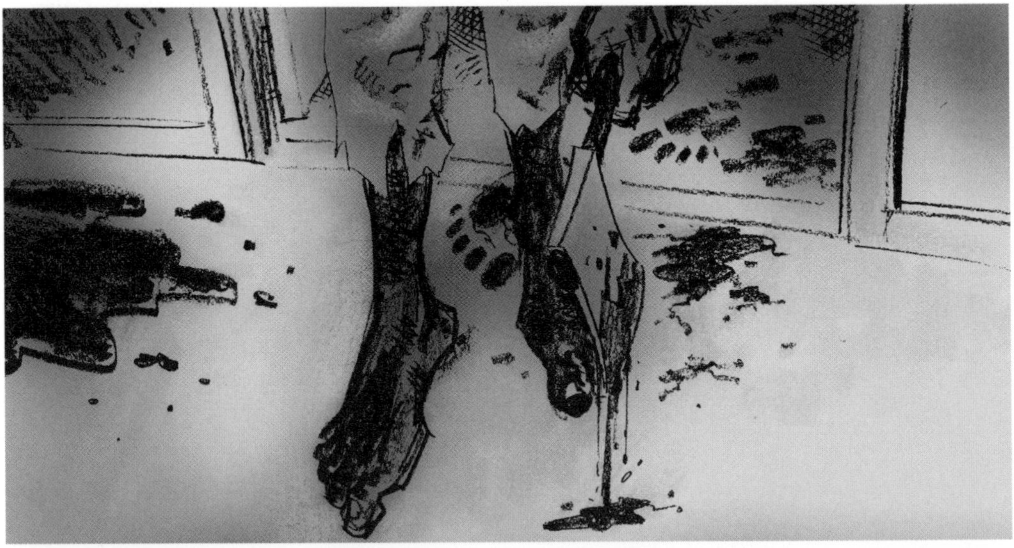

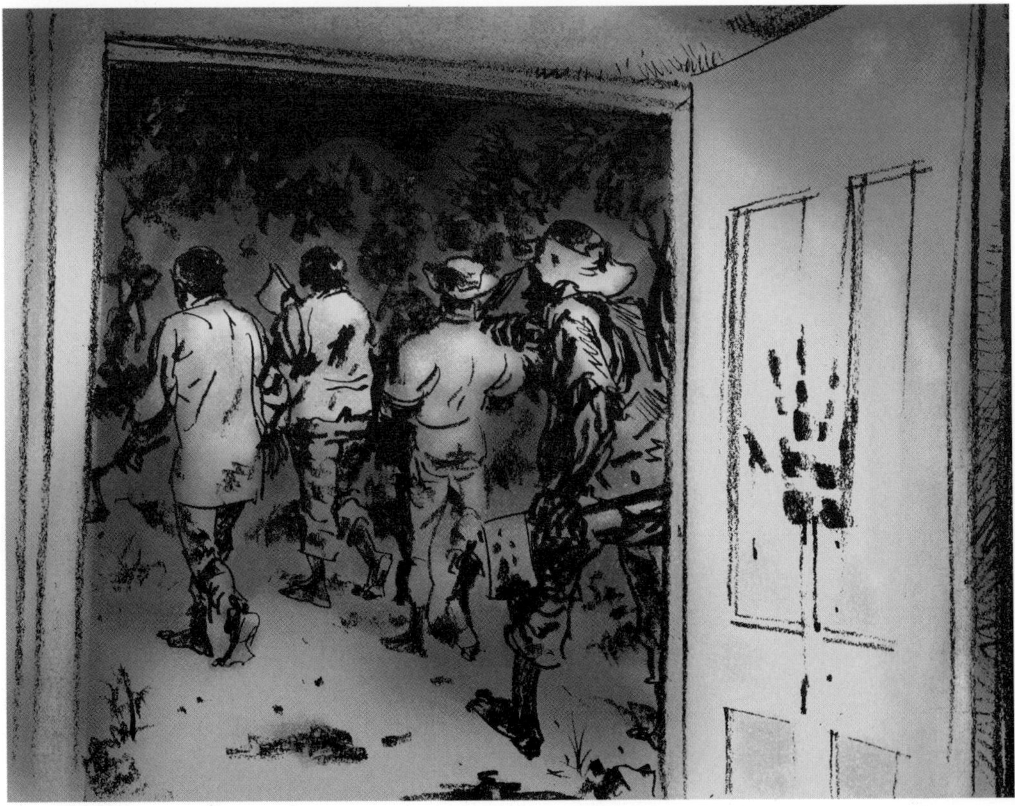

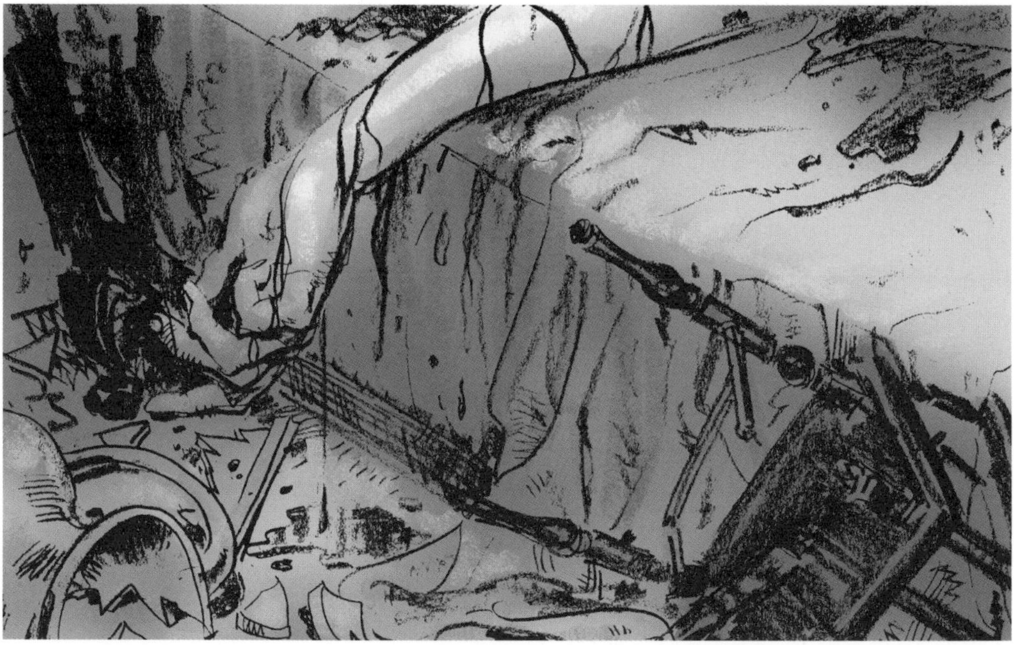

"THE MURDER OF THIS FAMILY, FIVE IN NUMBER, WAS THE WORK OF A MOMENT.

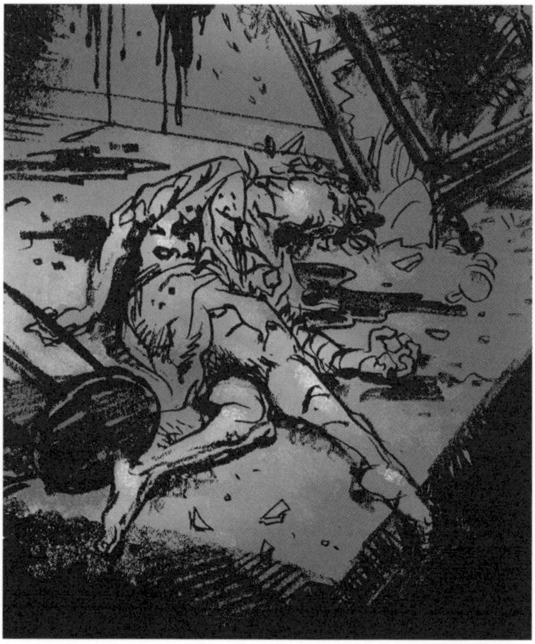

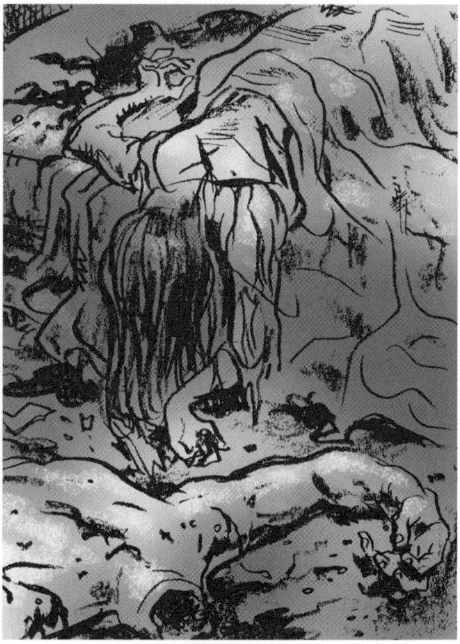

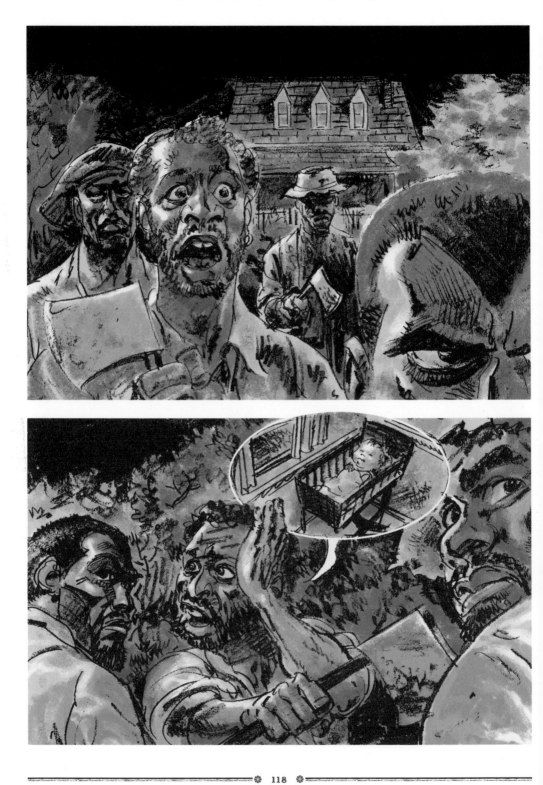

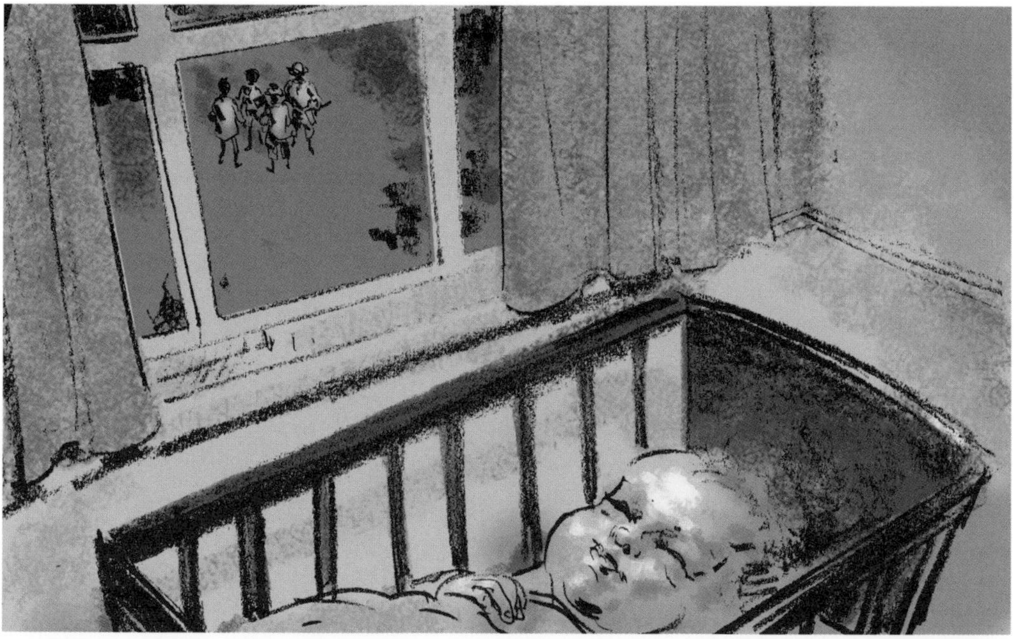

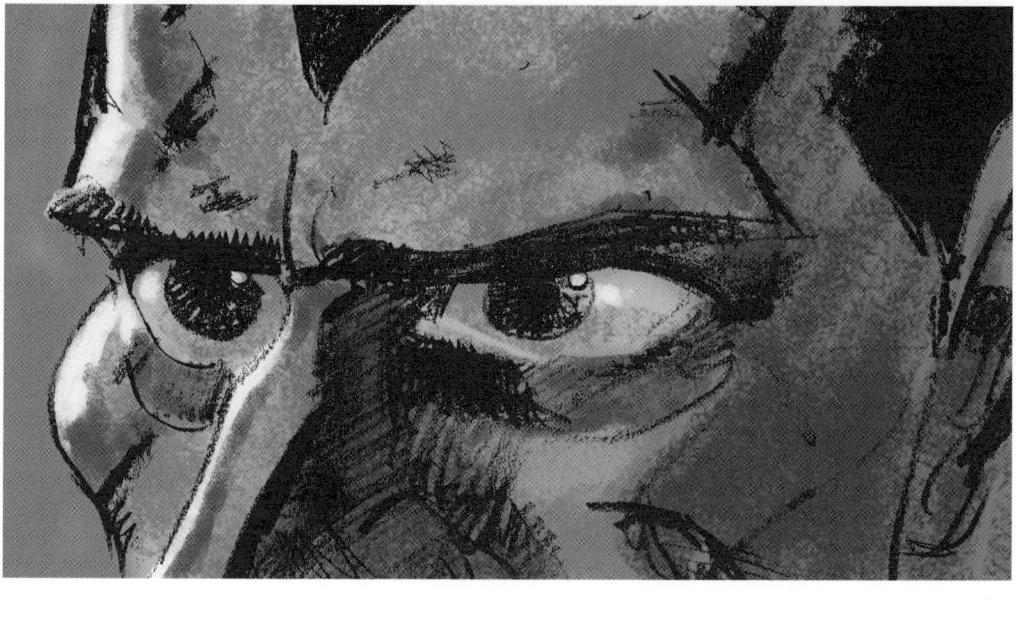

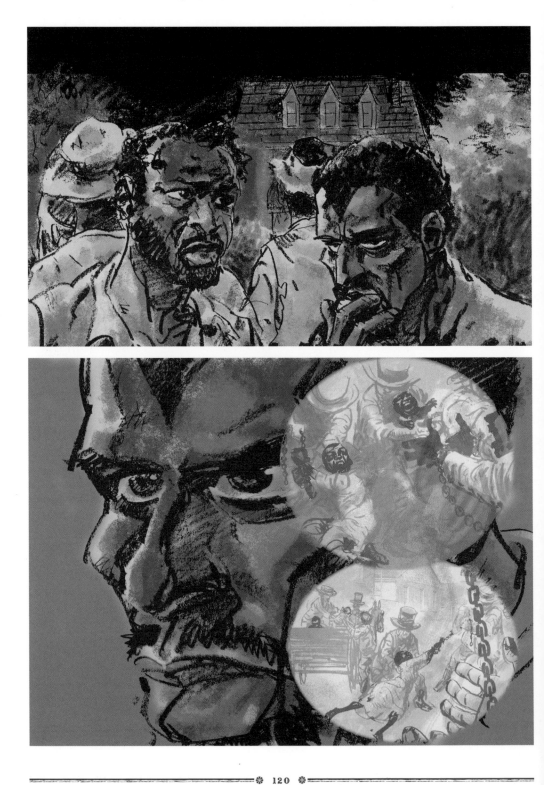

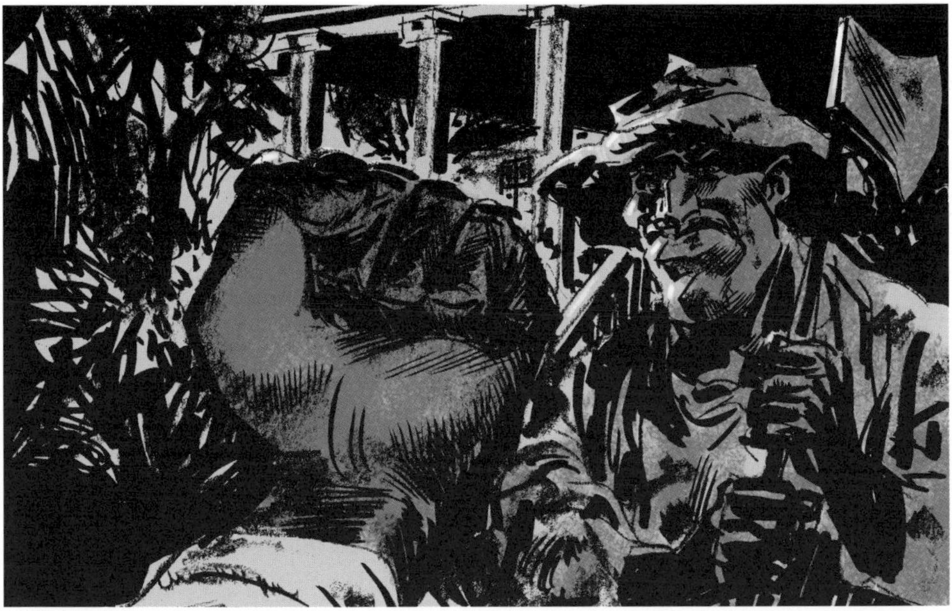

"THERE WAS A LITTLE INFANT SLEEPING IN A CRADLE, THAT WAS FORGOTTEN, UNTIL we had left the house and gone some distance, when Henry and Will returned and killed it.

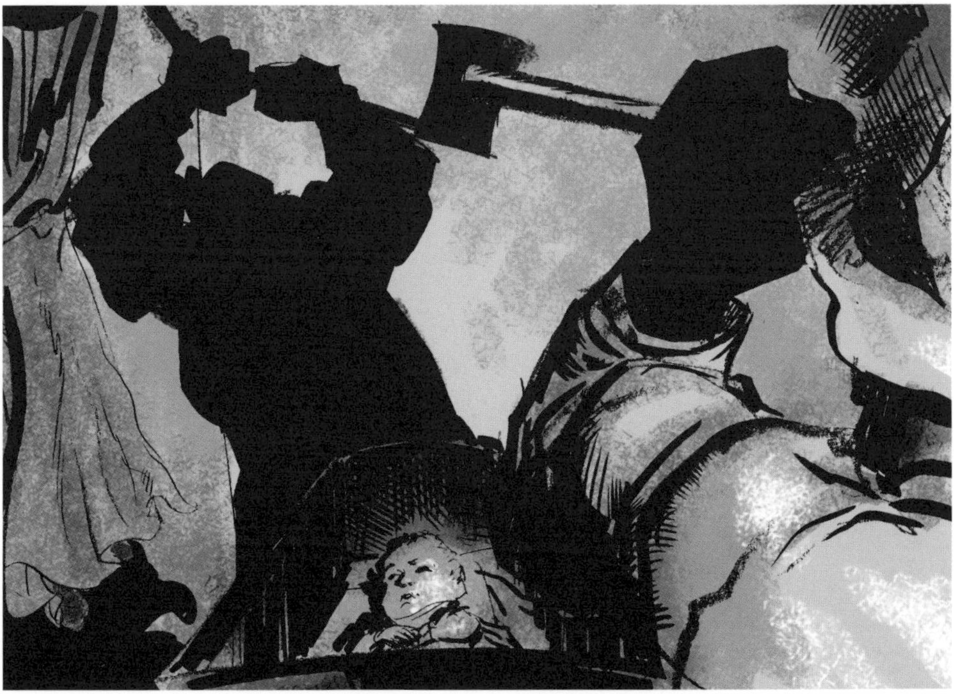

"WE GOT HERE, FOUR GUNS THAT WOULD
shoot, and several old muskets, with a pound
or two of powder.

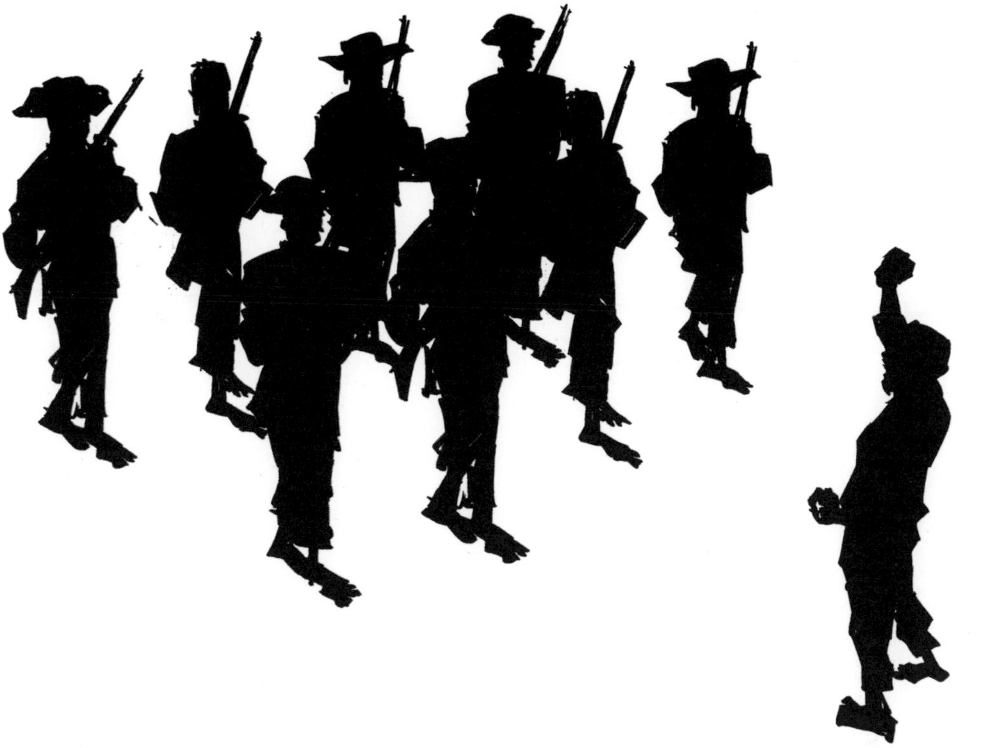

"WE REMAINED SOME TIME AT THE BARN, WHERE WE PARADED; I FORMED THEM IN A LINE as soldiers, and after carrying them through all the maneuvers I was master of, marched them off to Mr. Salathul Francis's, about six hundred yards distant.

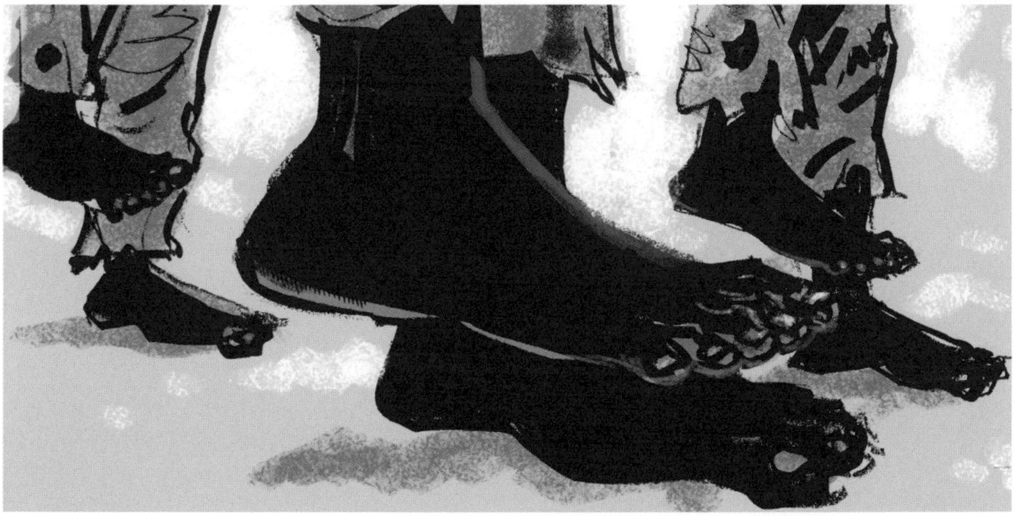

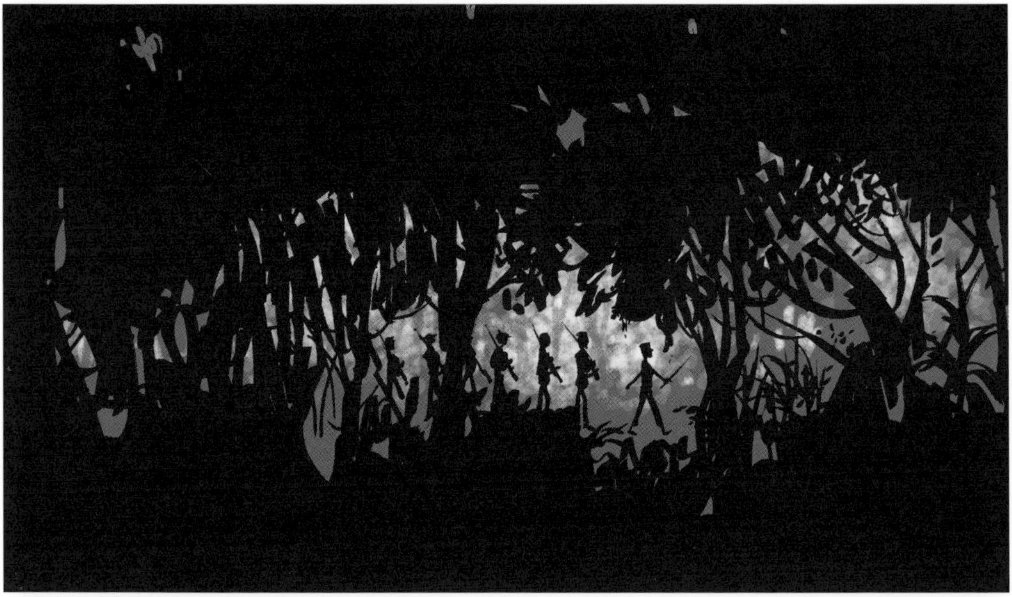

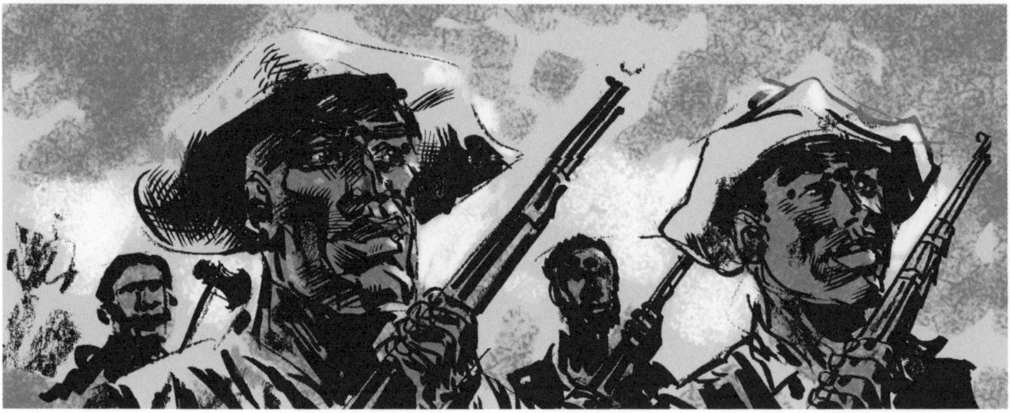

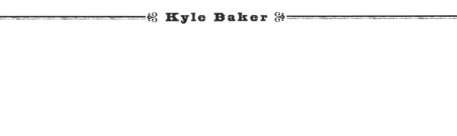

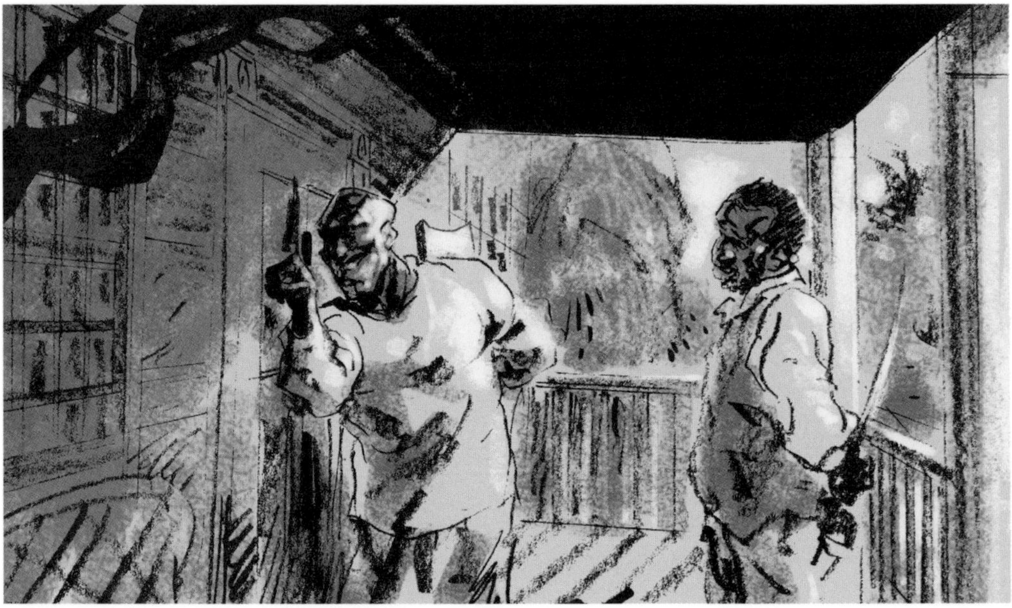

"SAM AND WILL WENT TO THE DOOR AND KNOCKED. MR. FRANCIS ASKED WHO WAS THERE,

Sam replied it was him, and he had a letter for him, on which he got up and came to the door.

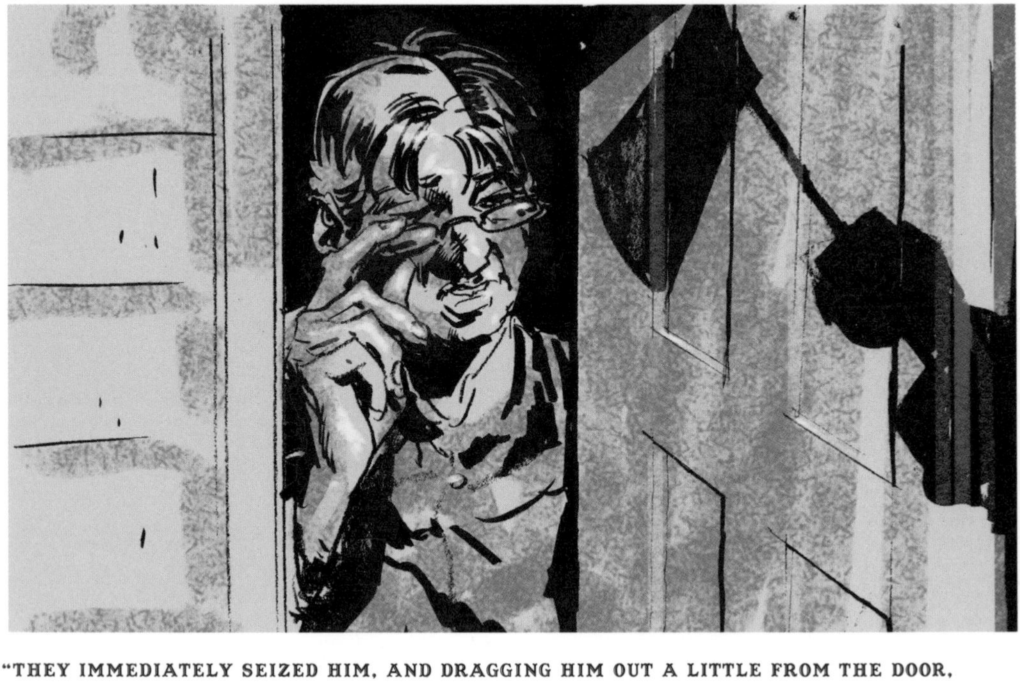

"THEY IMMEDIATELY SEIZED HIM, AND DRAGGING HIM OUT A LITTLE FROM THE DOOR,

he was dispatched by repeated blows on the head; there was no other white person in the family.

"WE STARTED FROM THERE FOR MRS. REESE'S. maintaining the most perfect silence on our march, where finding the door unlocked, we

entered, and murdered Mrs. Reese in her bed, while sleeping. Her son awoke, but it was only to sleep the sleep of death;

he had only time to say 'Who is that', and he was no more. From Mrs. Reese's we went to Mrs. Turner's, a mile distant, which we reached about sunrise, on Monday morning. Henry, Austin, and Sam went to the still, where, finding Mr. Peebles, Austin shot him, and the rest of us went to the house; as we approached, the family discovered us, and shut the door. Vain hope! Will, with one stroke of his

axe, opened it, and we entered and found Mrs. Turner and Mrs. Newsome in the middle of a room, almost frightened to death. Will immediately killed

Mrs. Turner, with one blow of his axe. I took Mrs. Newsome by the hand, and with the sword I had when I was apprehended, I struck her several blows over the head, but not being able to kill her, as the sword was dull. Will turning around and discovering it, dispatched her also.

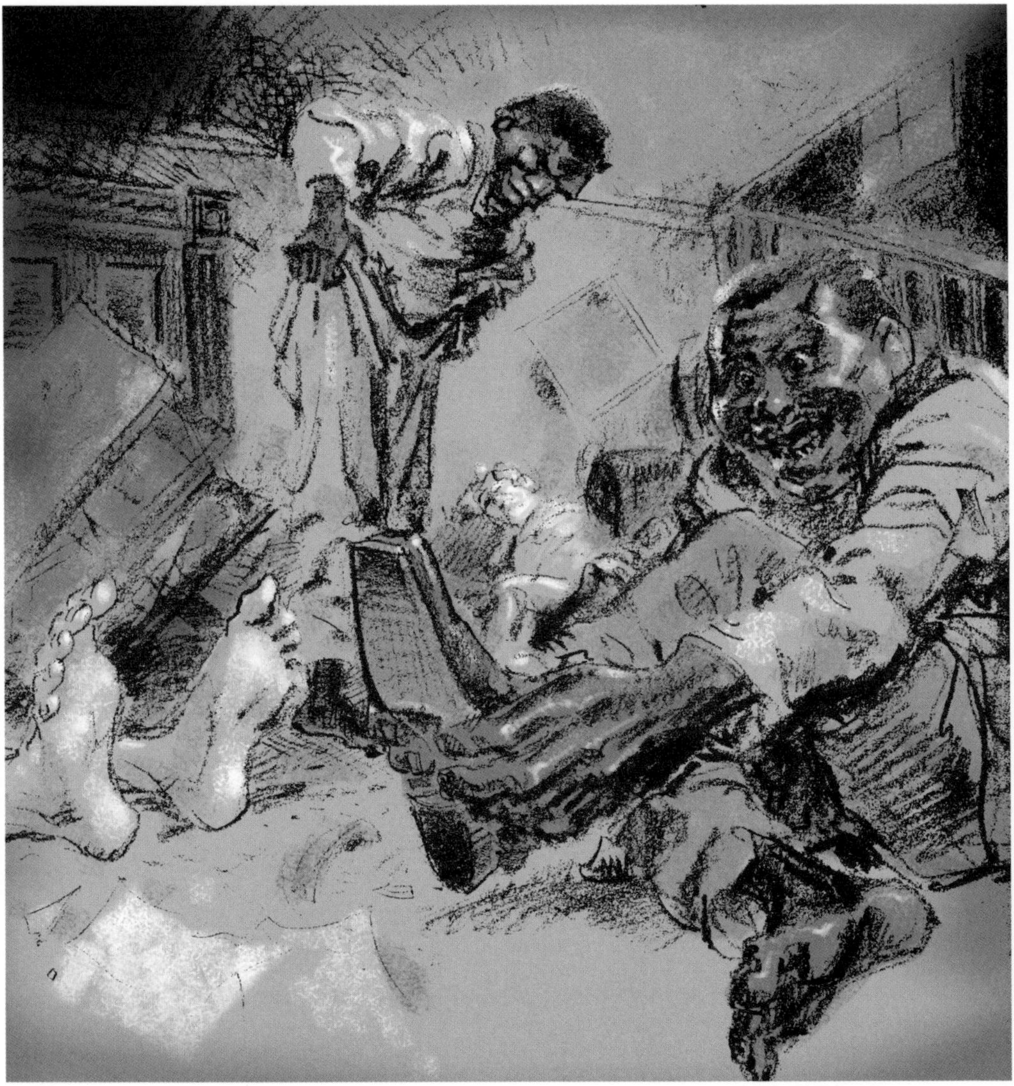

"A GENERAL DESTRUCTION OF PROPERTY AND SEARCH FOR MONEY AND AMMUNITION,

always succeeded the murders.

"BY THIS TIME MY COMPANY AMOUNTED TO fifteen, and nine men mounted, who started for Mrs. Whitehead's, (the other six were to go through a byway to Mr. Bryant's, and rejoin us at Mrs. Whitehead's). As we approached the house we discovered Mr. Richard Whitehead standing in the cotton patch, near the lane fence; we called him over into the lane, and Will, the executioner, was near at hand, with his fatal axe, to send him to an untimely grave. As we pushed on

to the house, I discovered someone run round the garden, and thinking it was some of the white family, I pursued them, but finding it was a servant girl belonging to the house,

I returned to commence the work of death, but they whom I left, had not been idle; all the family were already murdered, but Mrs. Whitehead and her daughter Margaret. As I came round to the door I saw Will pulling Mrs. Whitehead out of the house, and at the step he nearly severed her head from her body with his broad axe. Miss Margaret, when I discovered her, had concealed herself in the corner formed by the projection of the cellar cap from the house; on my approach she fled, but was soon overtaken, and after repeated blows with a sword, I killed her by a blow on the head with a fence rail. By this time, the six who had gone by Mr. Bryant's rejoined us, and informed me they had done the work of death assigned them.

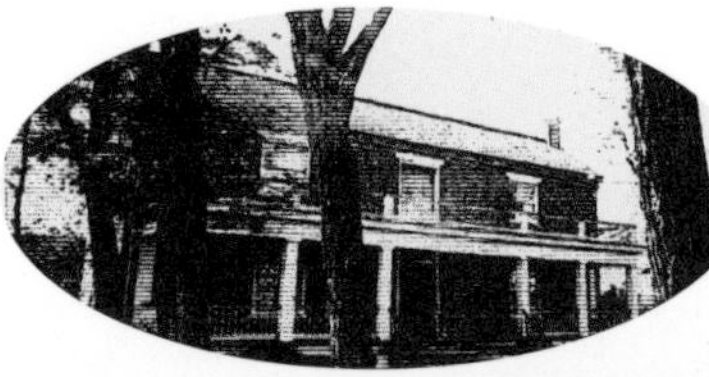

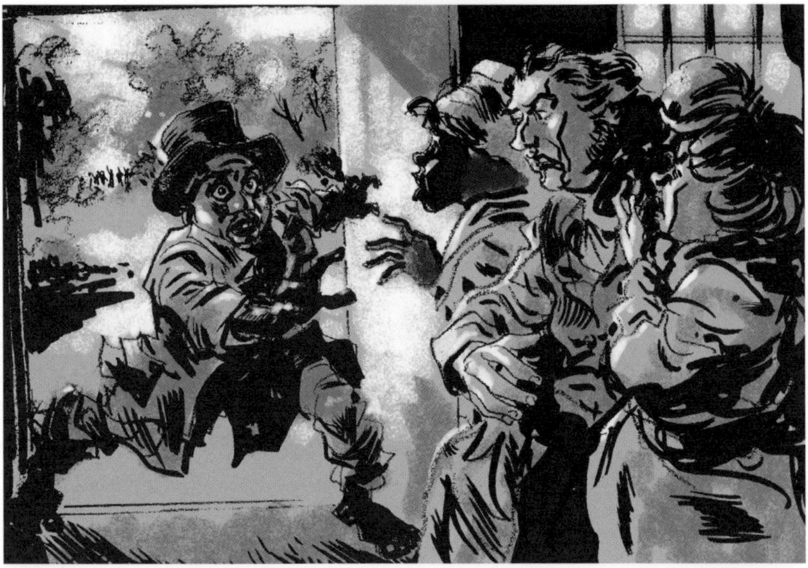

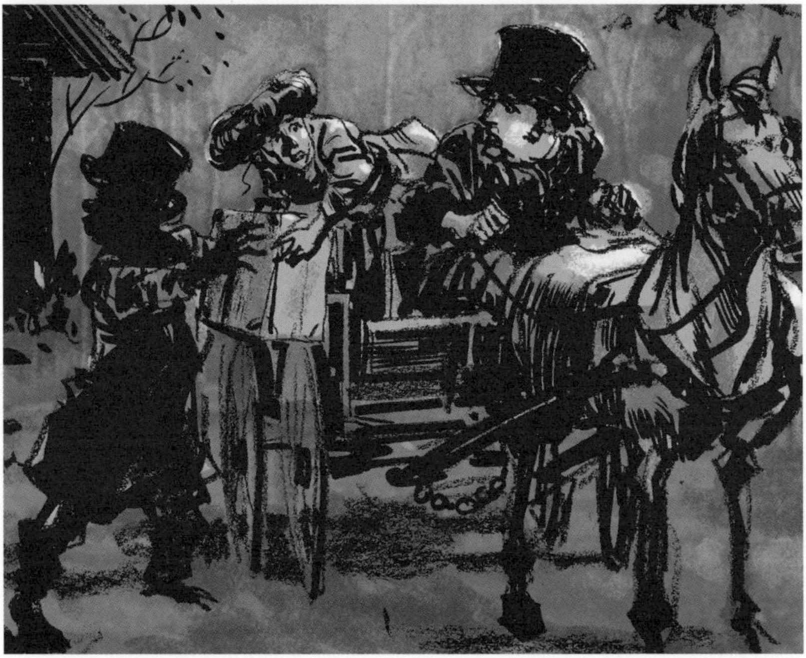

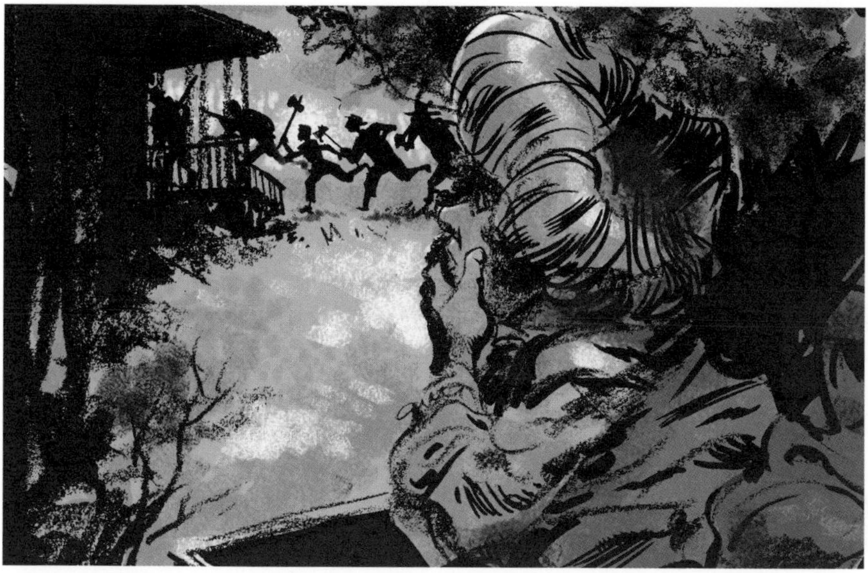

"WE AGAIN DIVIDED, PART GOING TO MR. RICHARD PORTER'S, AND FROM thence to Nathaniel Francis's, the others to Mr. Howell Harris's, and Mr. T. Doyle's. On my reaching Mr. Porter's, he had escaped with his family. I understood there, that the alarm had already spread.

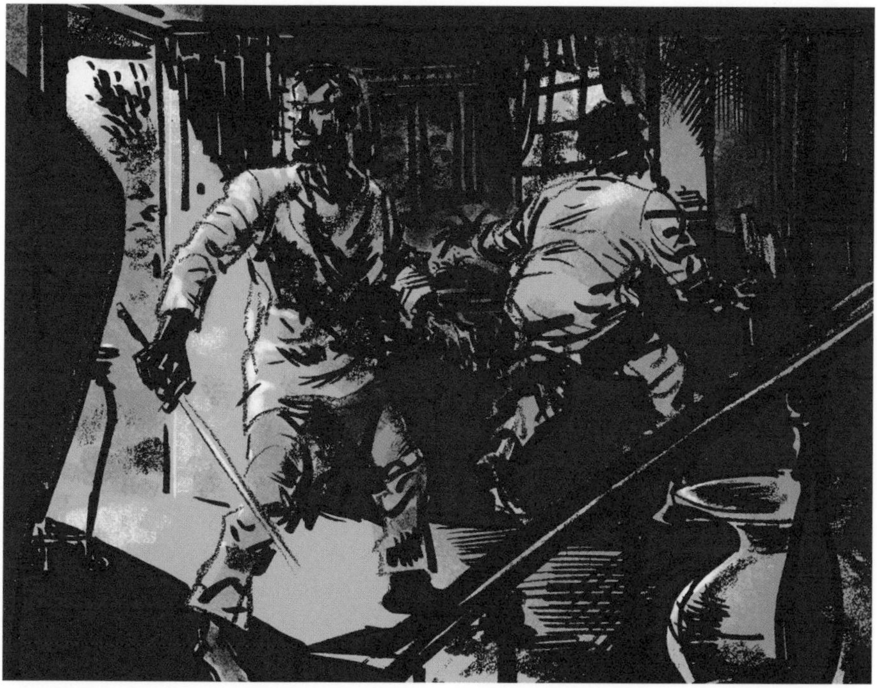

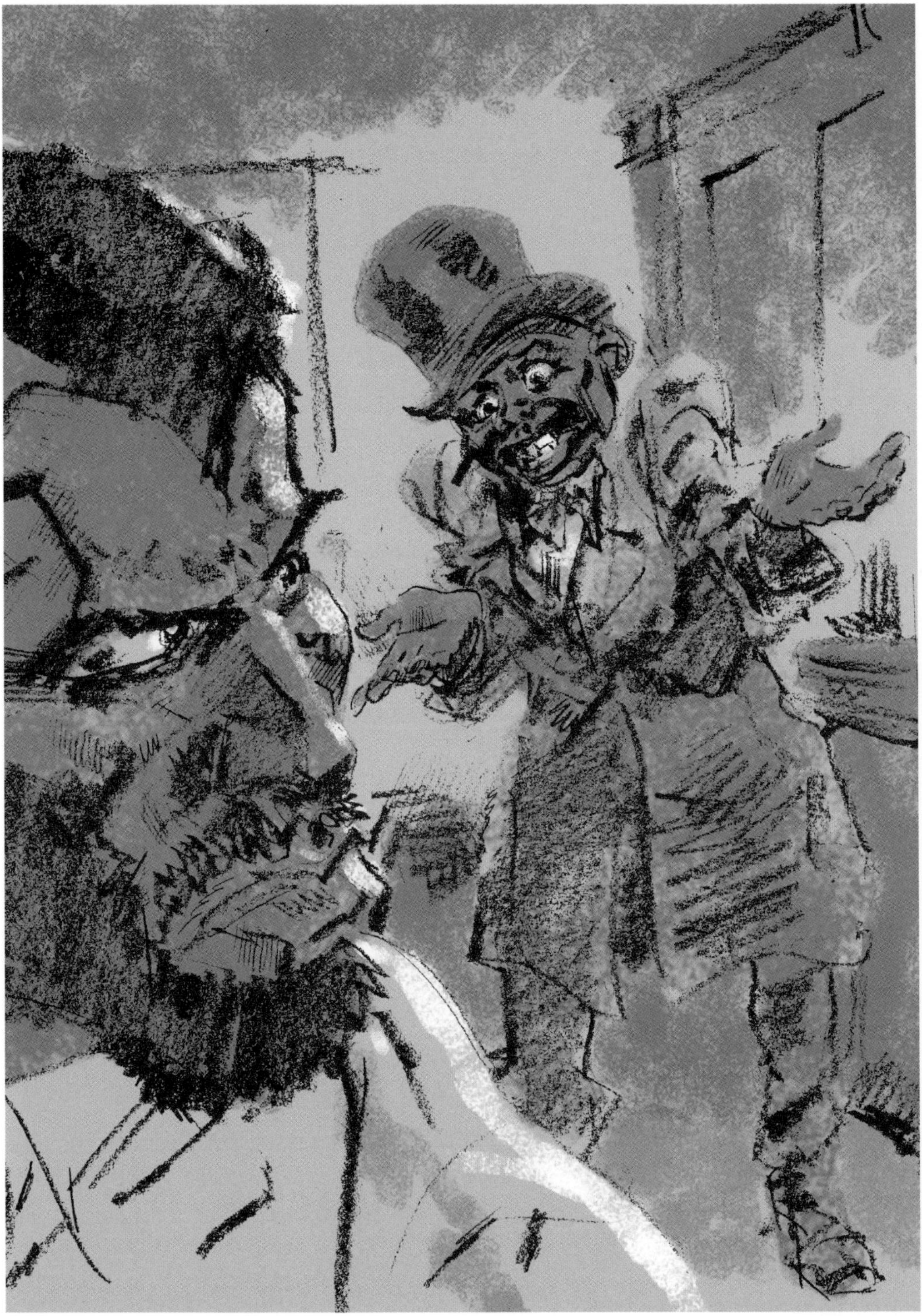

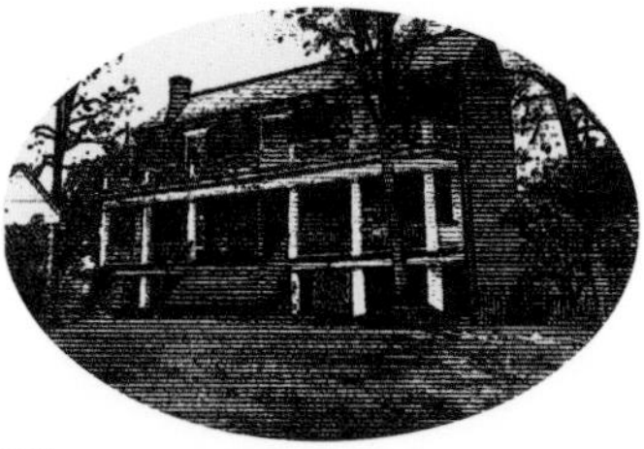

"I IMMEDIATELY RETURNED to bring up those sent to Mr. Doyle's, and Mr. Howell Harris's;

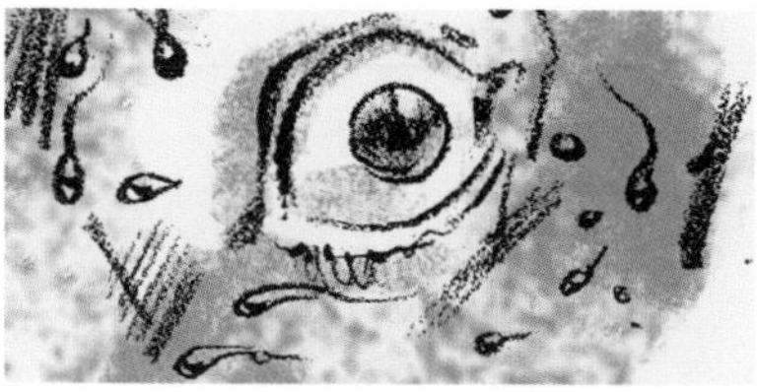

the party I left going on to Mr. Francis's, having told them I would join them in that neighborhood. I met these sent to Mr. Doyle's and Mr. Harris's returning, having met Mr. Doyle on the road and killed him; and learning from some who joined them, that Mr. Harris was

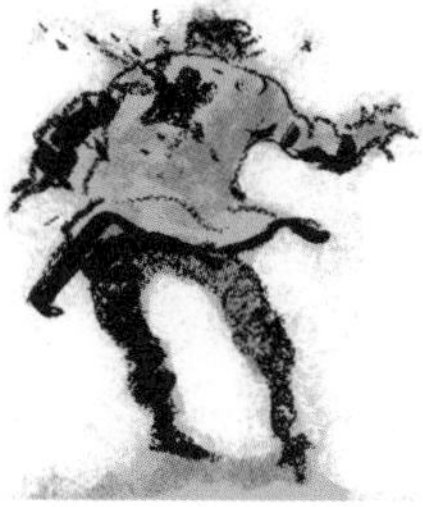

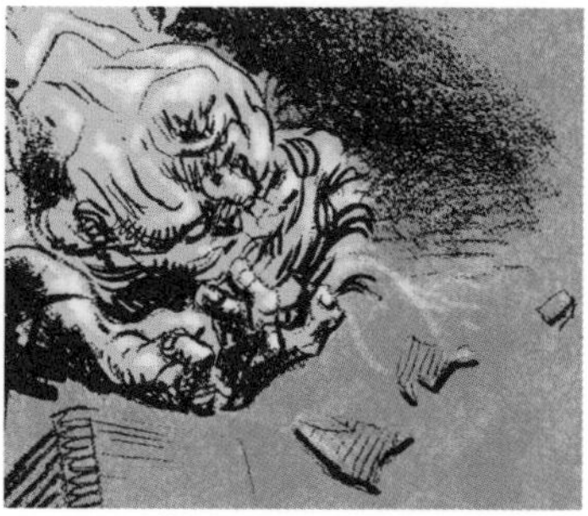

from home, I immediately pursued the course taken by the party gone on before; but knowing they would complete the work of death and pillage at Mr. Francis's before I could get there, I went to Mr. Peter Edwards's, expecting to find them there, but they had been here also. I then went to Mr. John T. Barrow's; they had been here and murdered him.

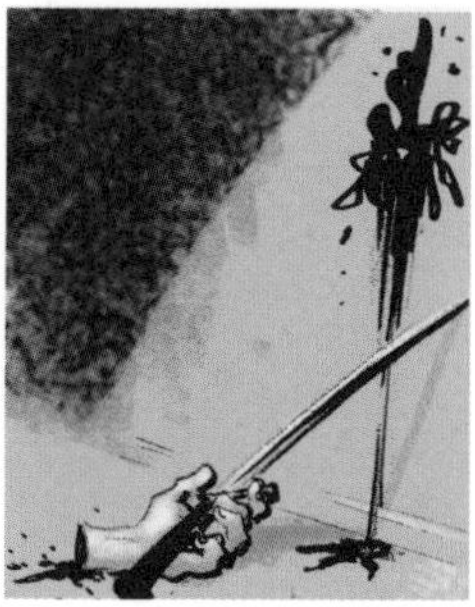

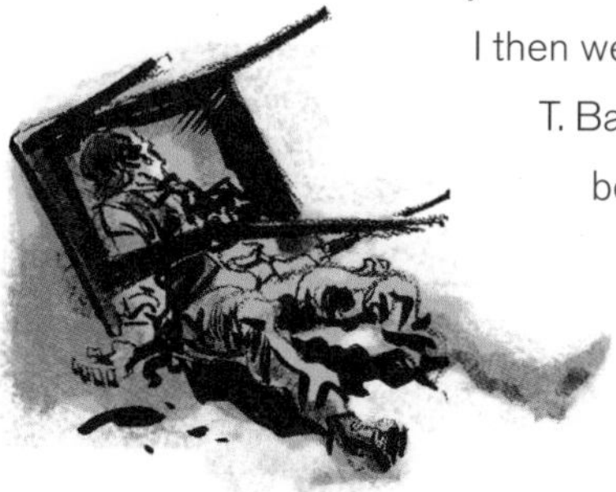

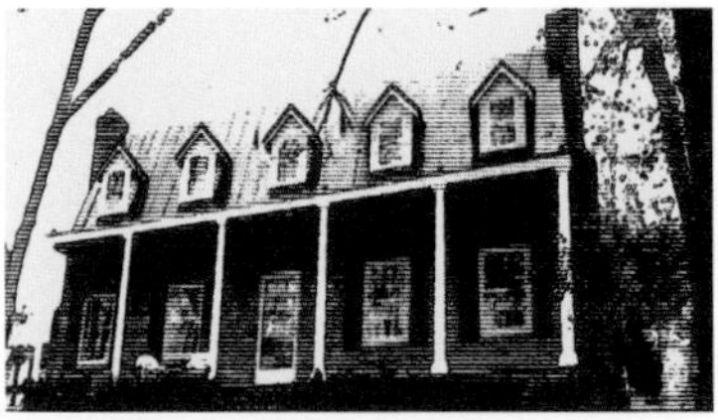

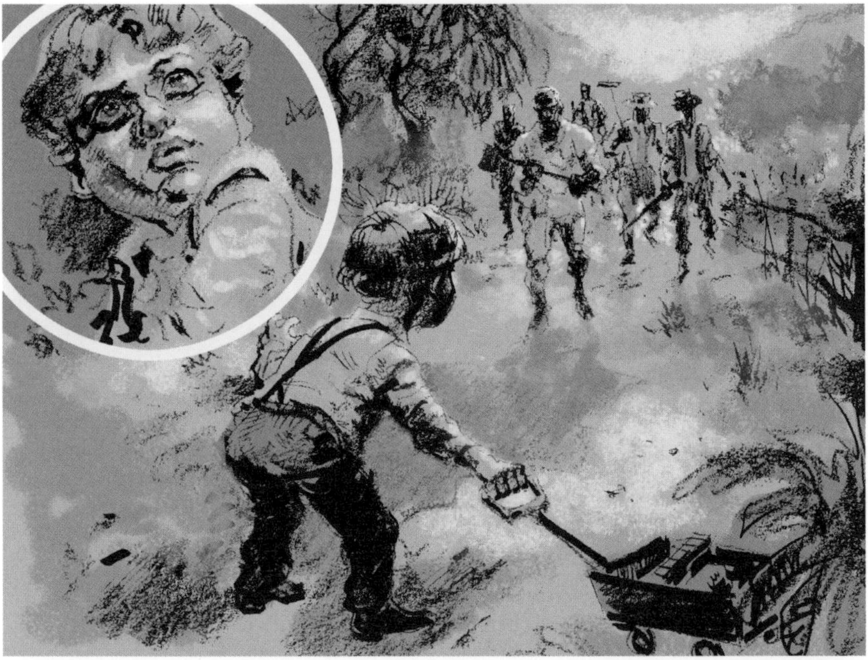

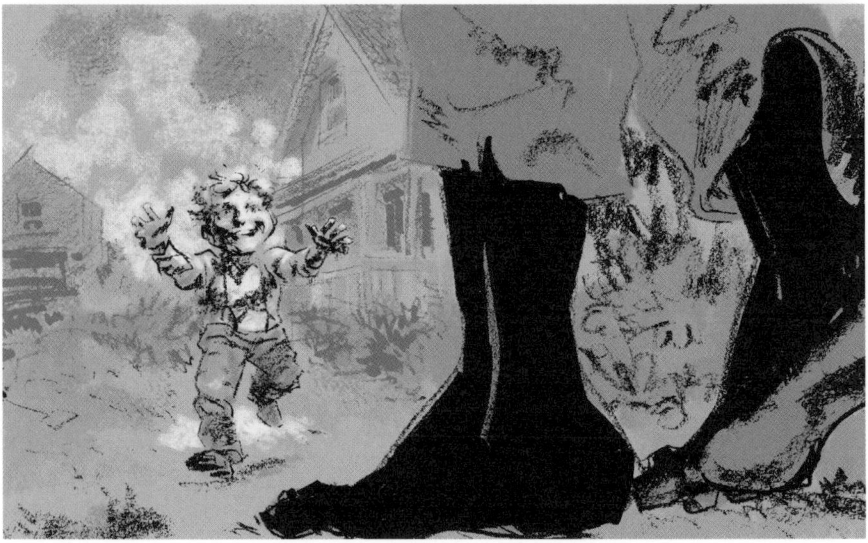

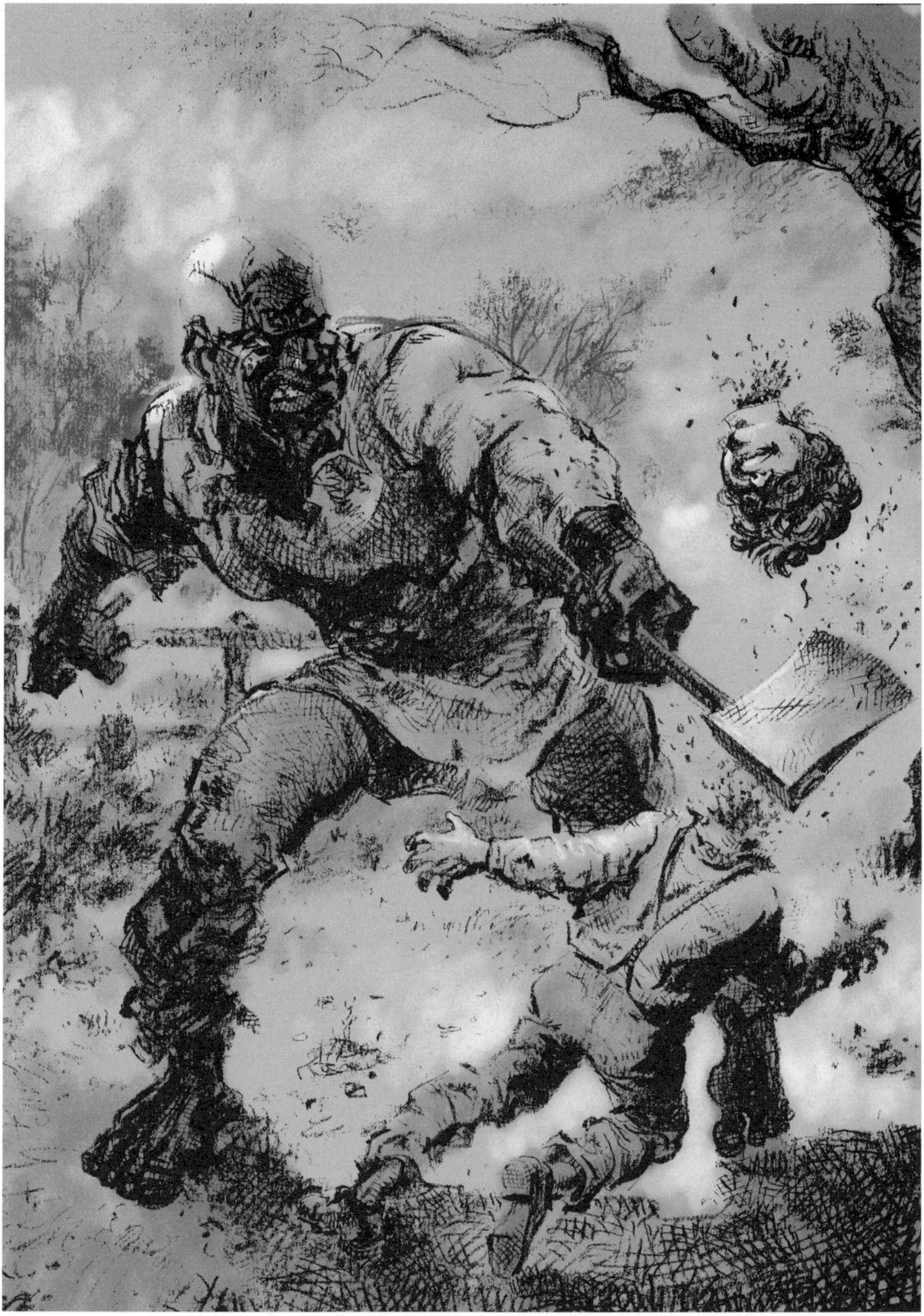

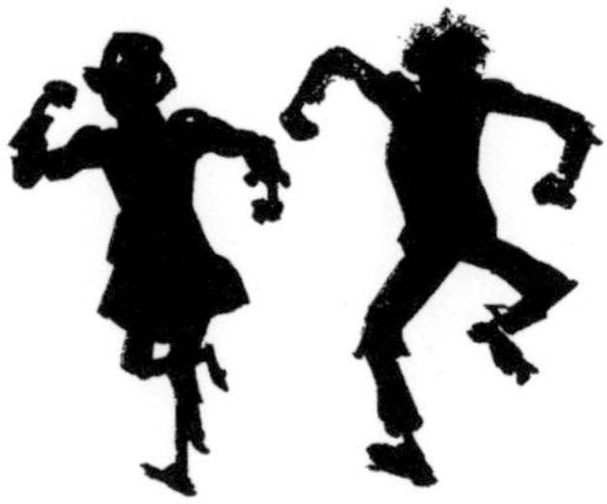

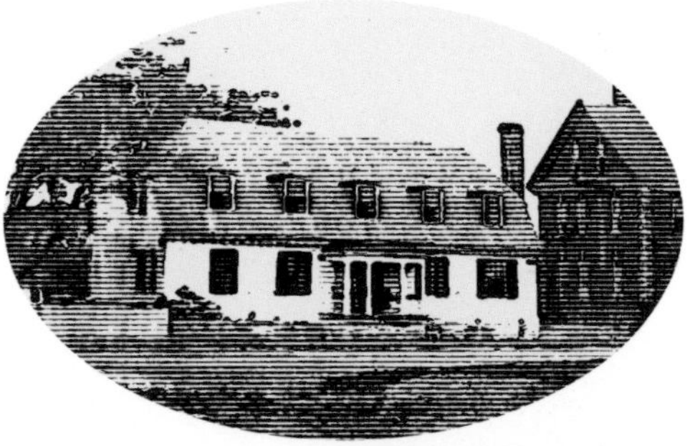

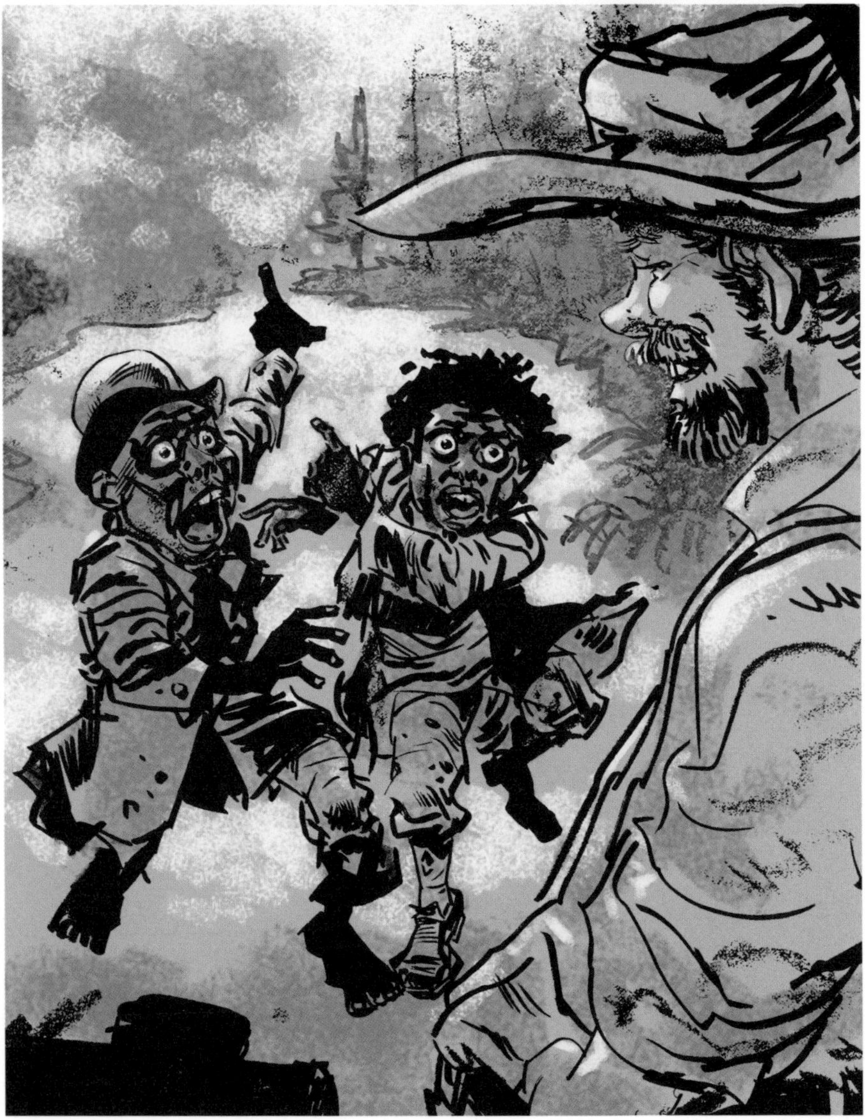

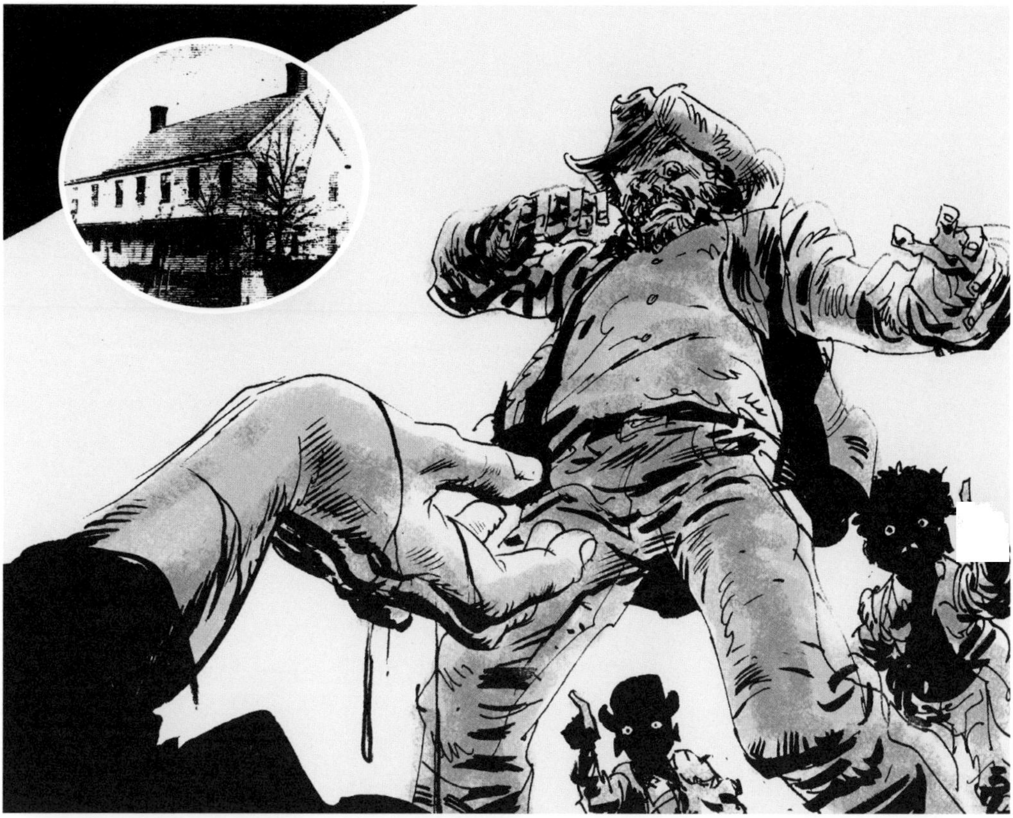

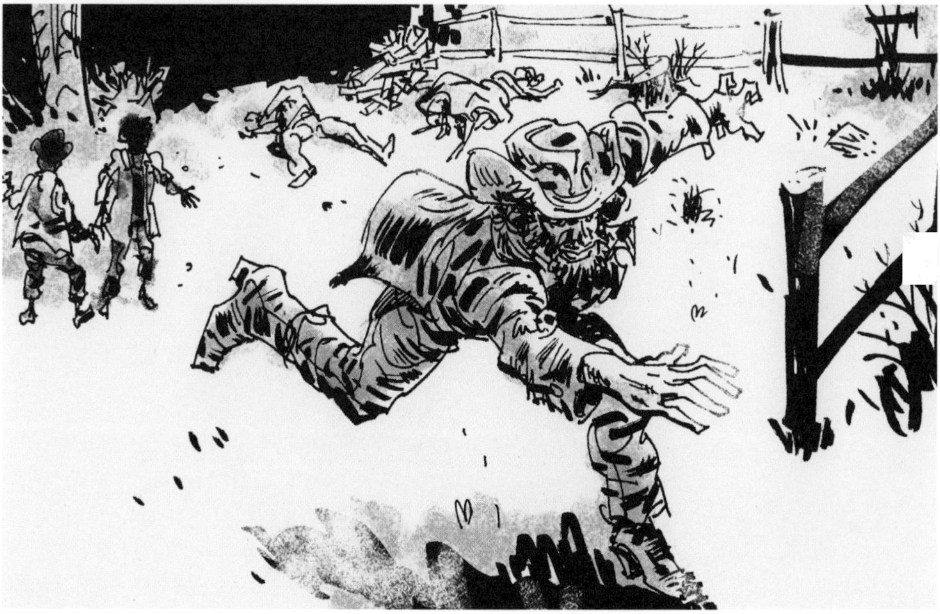

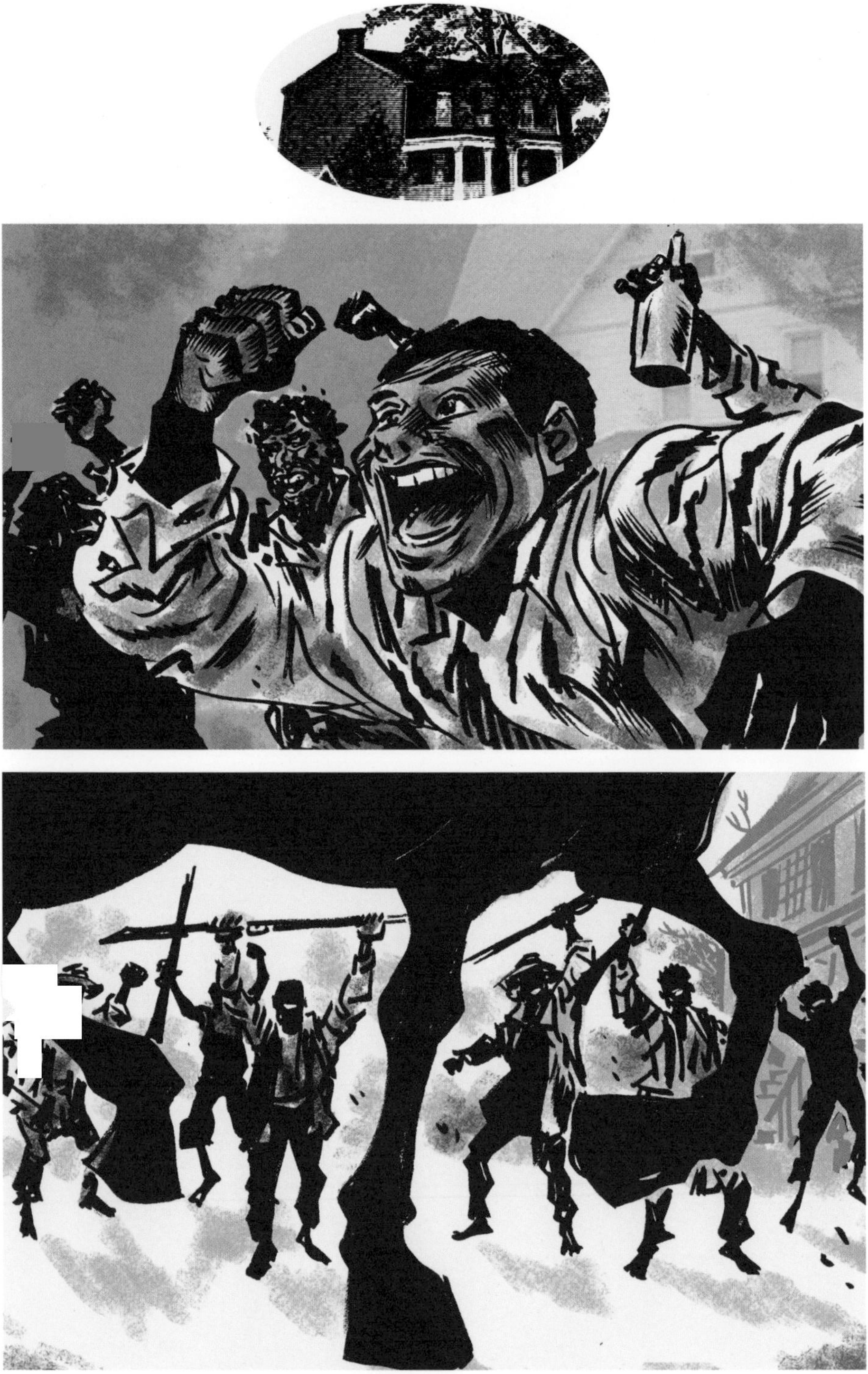

"I PURSUED ON THEIR TRACK TO CAPT. NEWIT HARRIS'S, WHERE I FOUND THE greater part mounted, and ready to start.

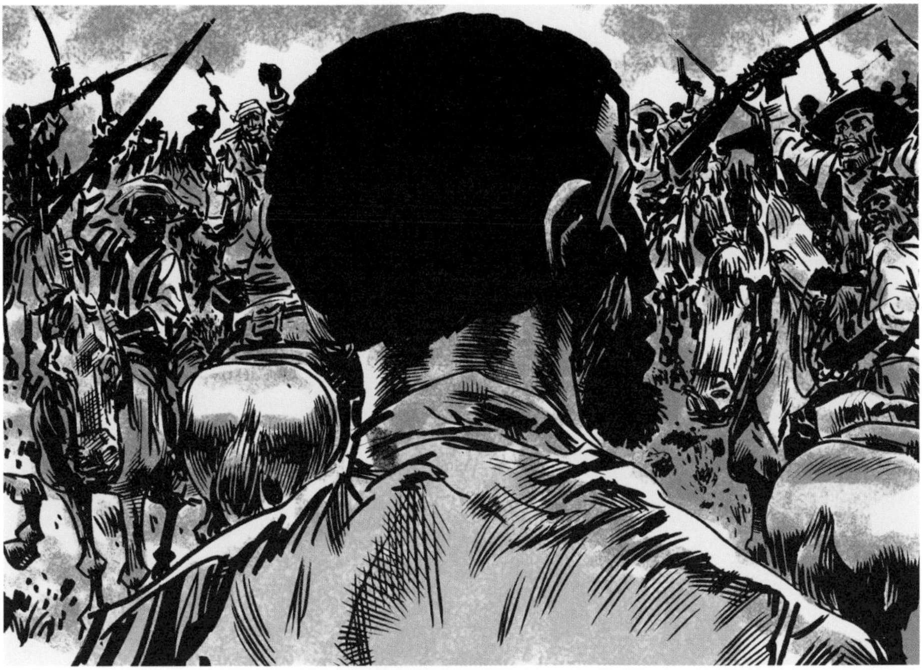

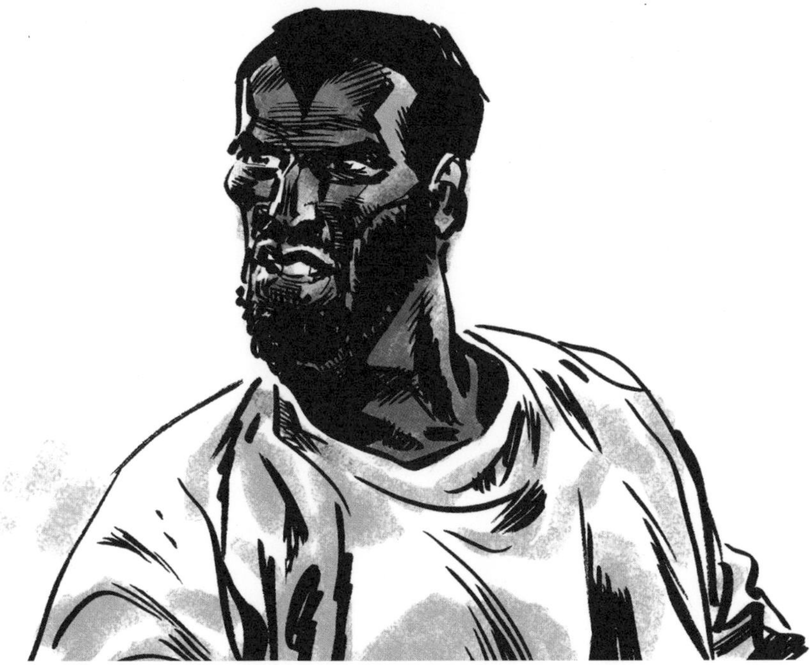

"THE MEN NOW AMOUNTING TO ABOUT FORTY, SHOUTED AND HURRAHED AS I RODE UP.

Some were in the yard, loading their guns, others drinking.

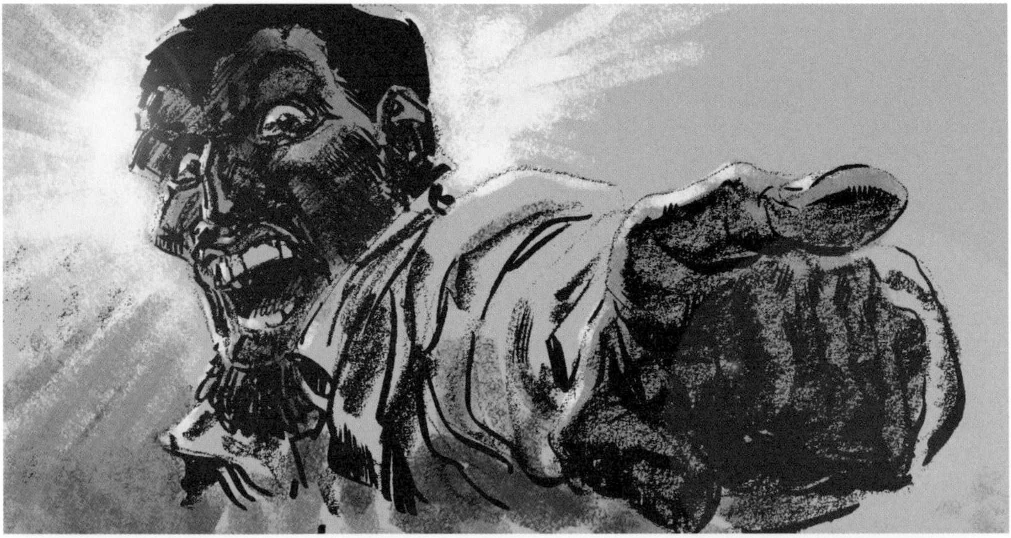

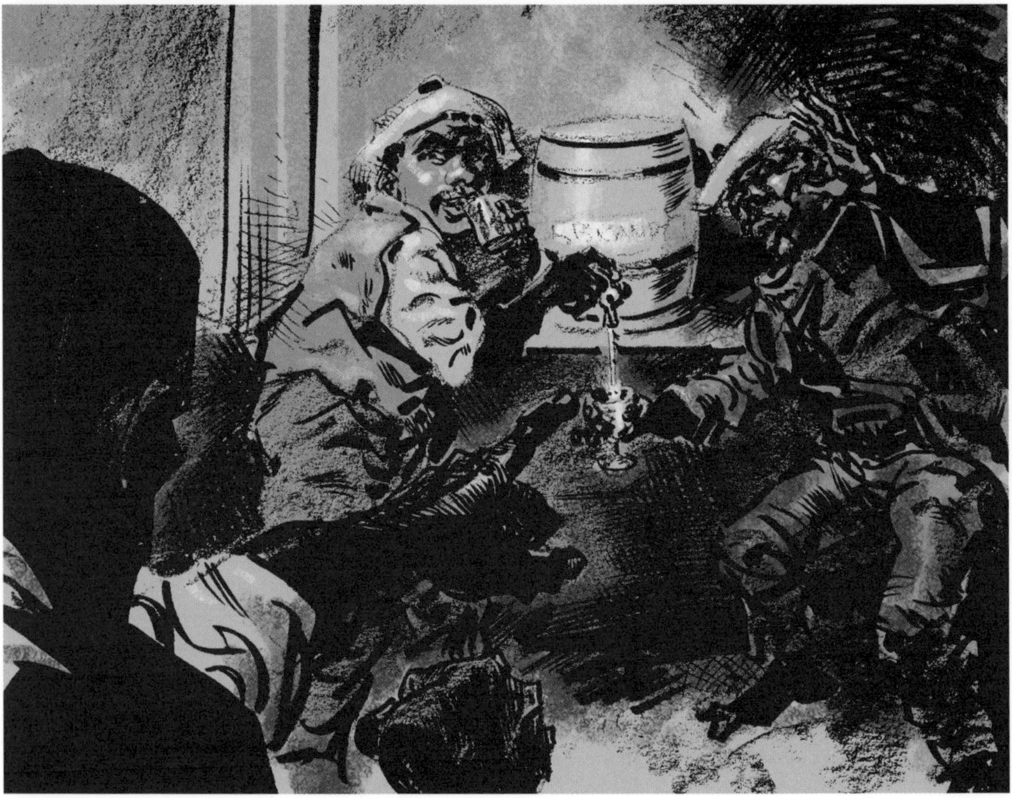

"THEY SAID CAPTAIN HARRIS AND HIS FAMILY HAD ESCAPED, THE PROPERTY in the house they destroyed, robbing him of money and other valuables. I ordered them to mount and march instantly; this was about nine or ten o'clock, Monday morning.

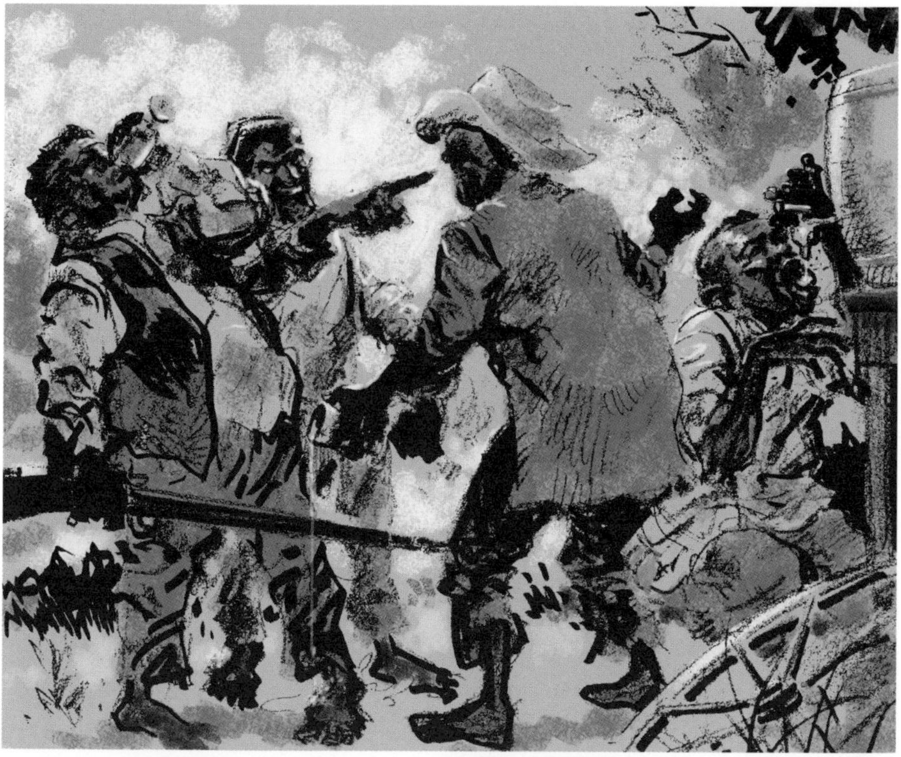

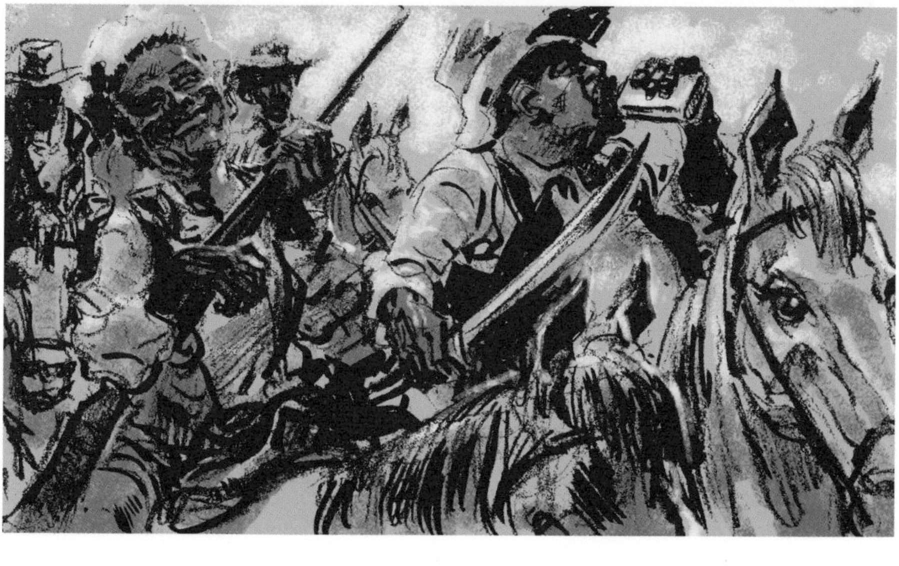

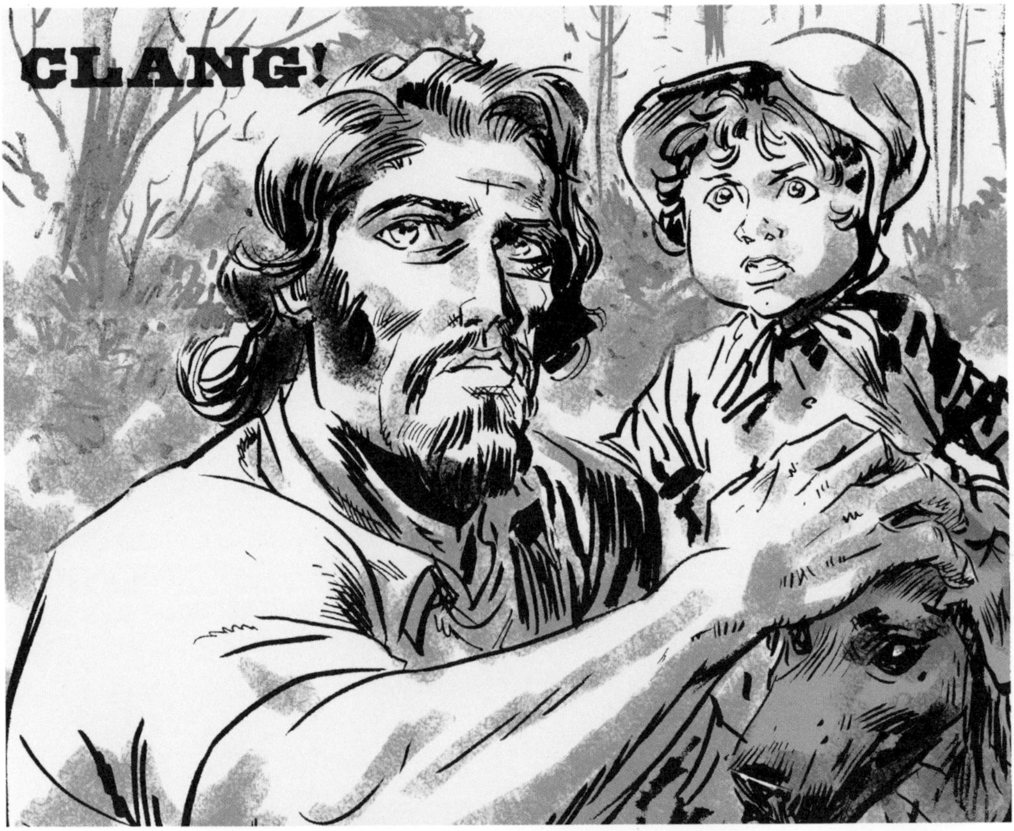
CLANG!

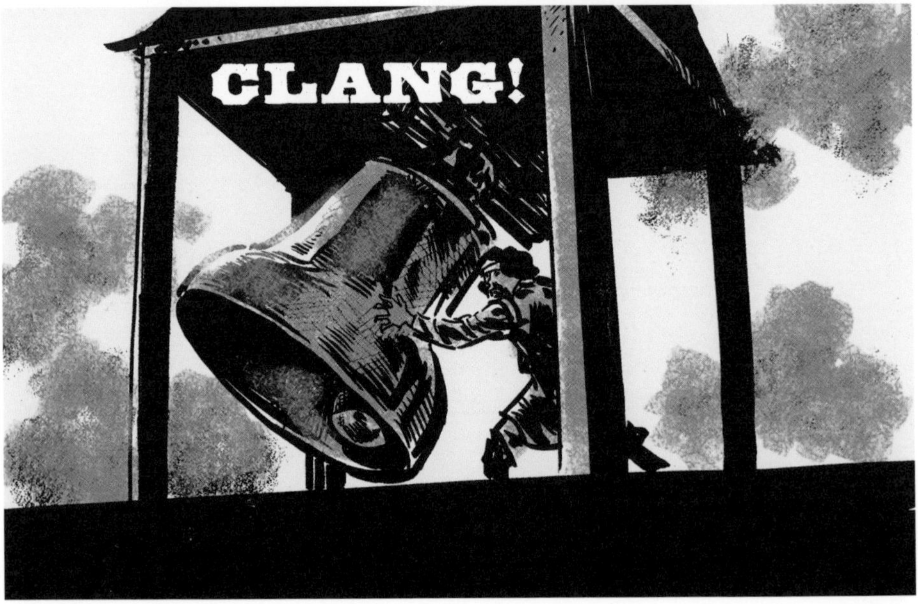
CLANG!

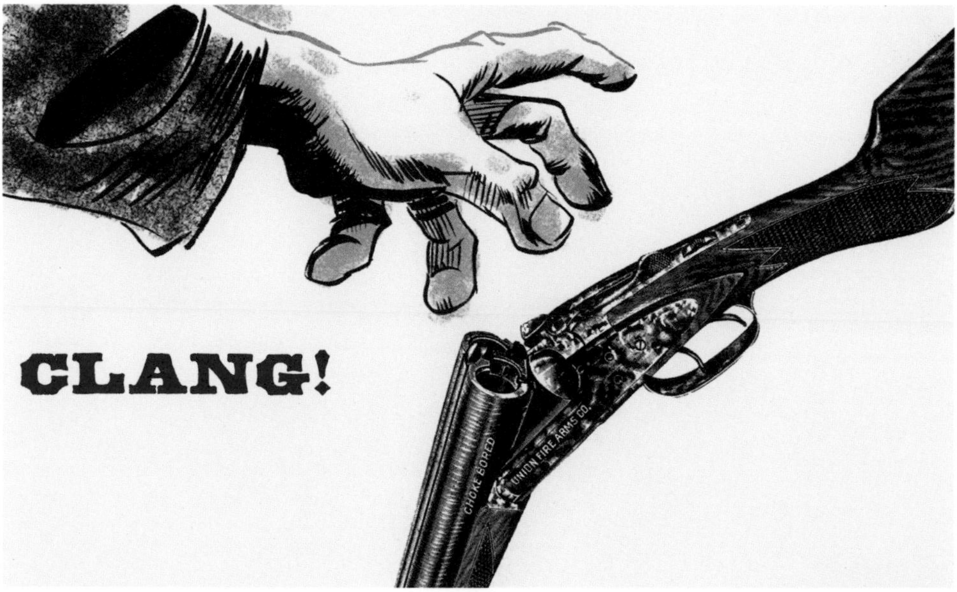
CLANG!
CHOKE BORED
UNION FIRE ARMS CO.

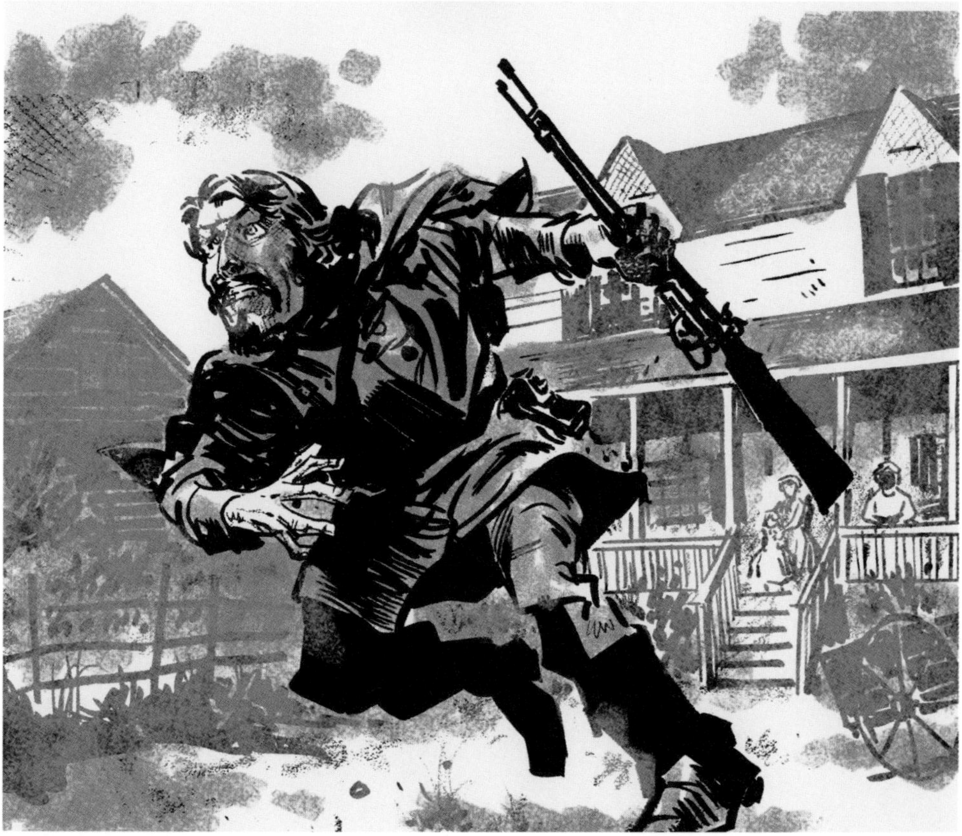

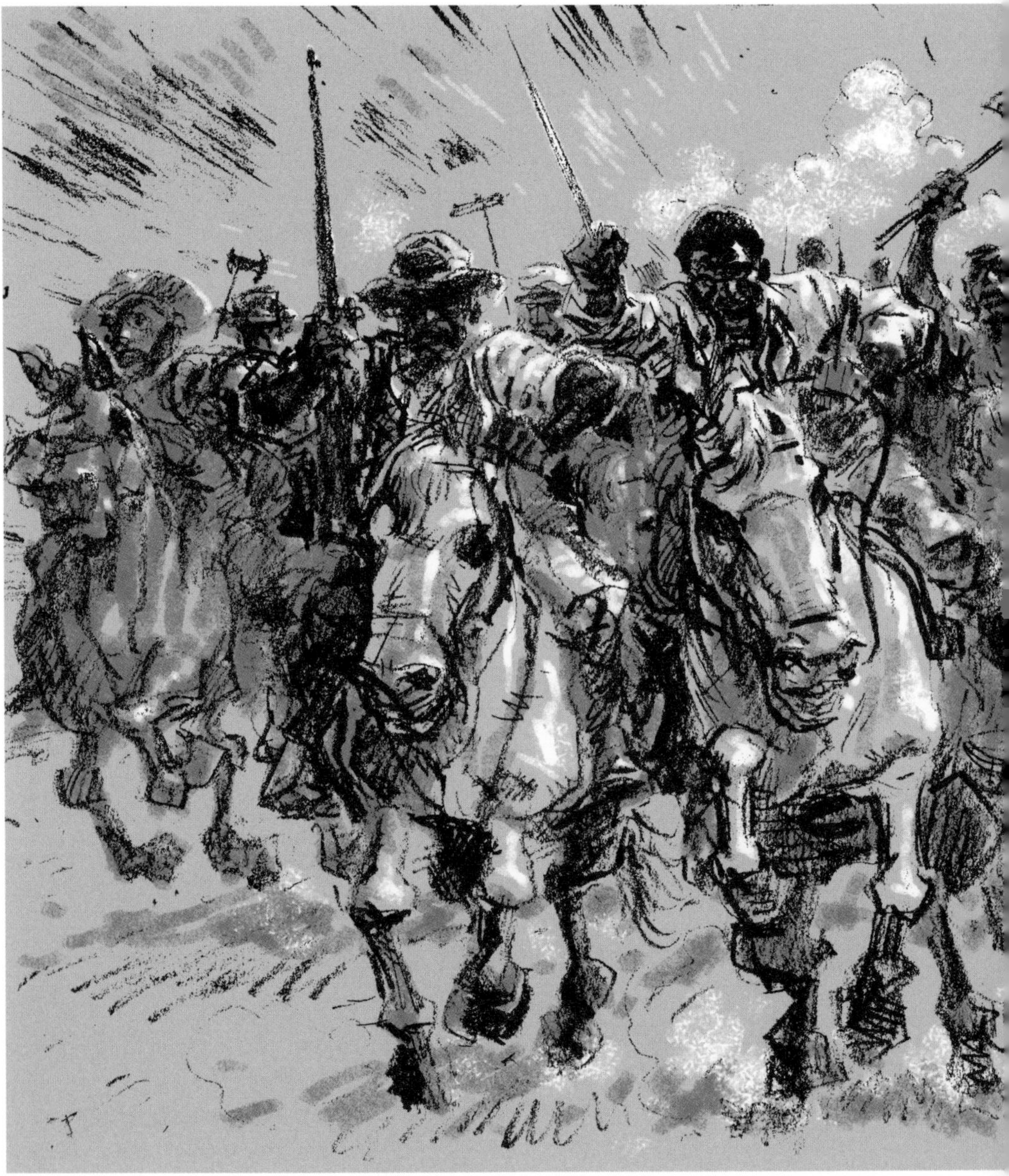

"I PROCEEDED TO MR. LEVI WALLER'S, TWO or three miles distant. As it was my object to carry terror and devastation wherever we went, I placed fifteen or twenty of the best-armed and most to be relied on in front, who generally approached the houses as fast as their horses could run. This was for two purposes: to prevent their escape, and strike terror to the inhabitants.

"HAVING MURDERED MRS. WALLER AND TEN children we started for Mr. William Williams's— killing him and two little boys that were there; while engaged in this, Mrs. Williams fled and got some distance from the

house, but she was pursued, overtaken, and compelled to get up behind one of the company, who brought her back, and after showing her the mangled body of her lifeless husband, she was told to get down and lay by his side, where she was shot dead.

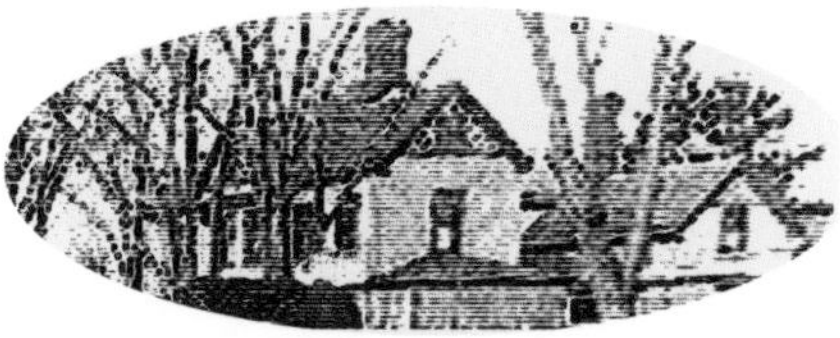

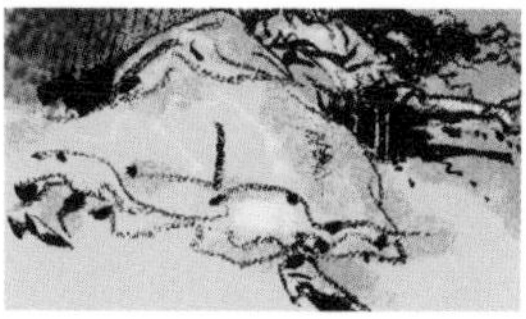

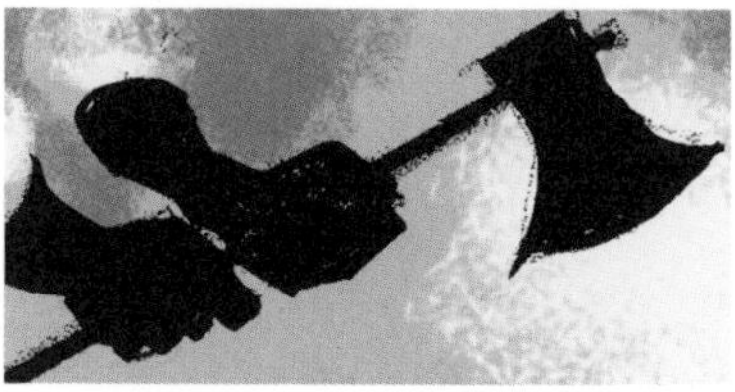

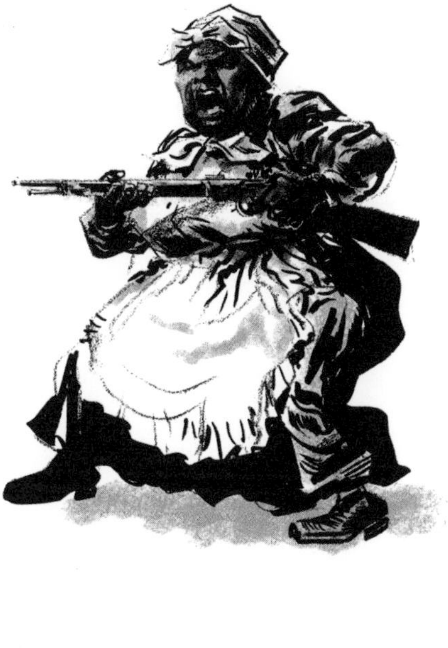

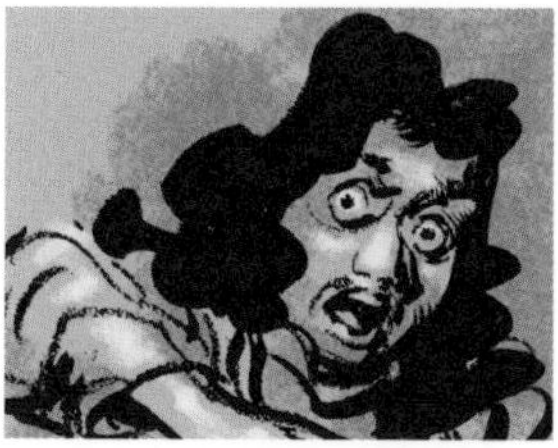

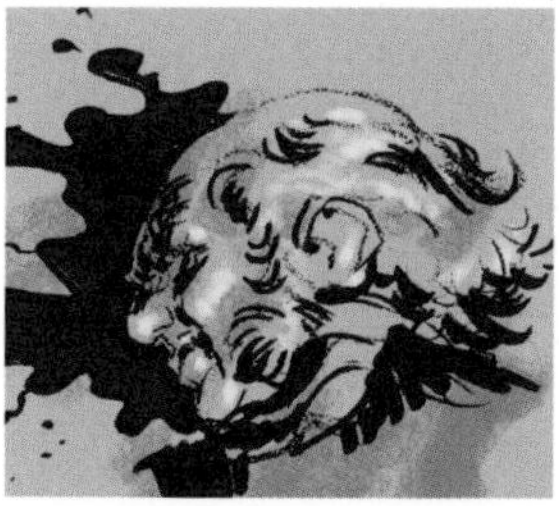

"I THEN STARTED FOR MR. JACOB WILLIAMS'S, where the family were murdered. Here we found

a young man named Drury, who had come on business with Mr. Williams— he was pursued, overtaken, and shot. Mrs. Vaughan's was

the next place we visited—and after murdering the family here, I determined on starting for Jerusalem."

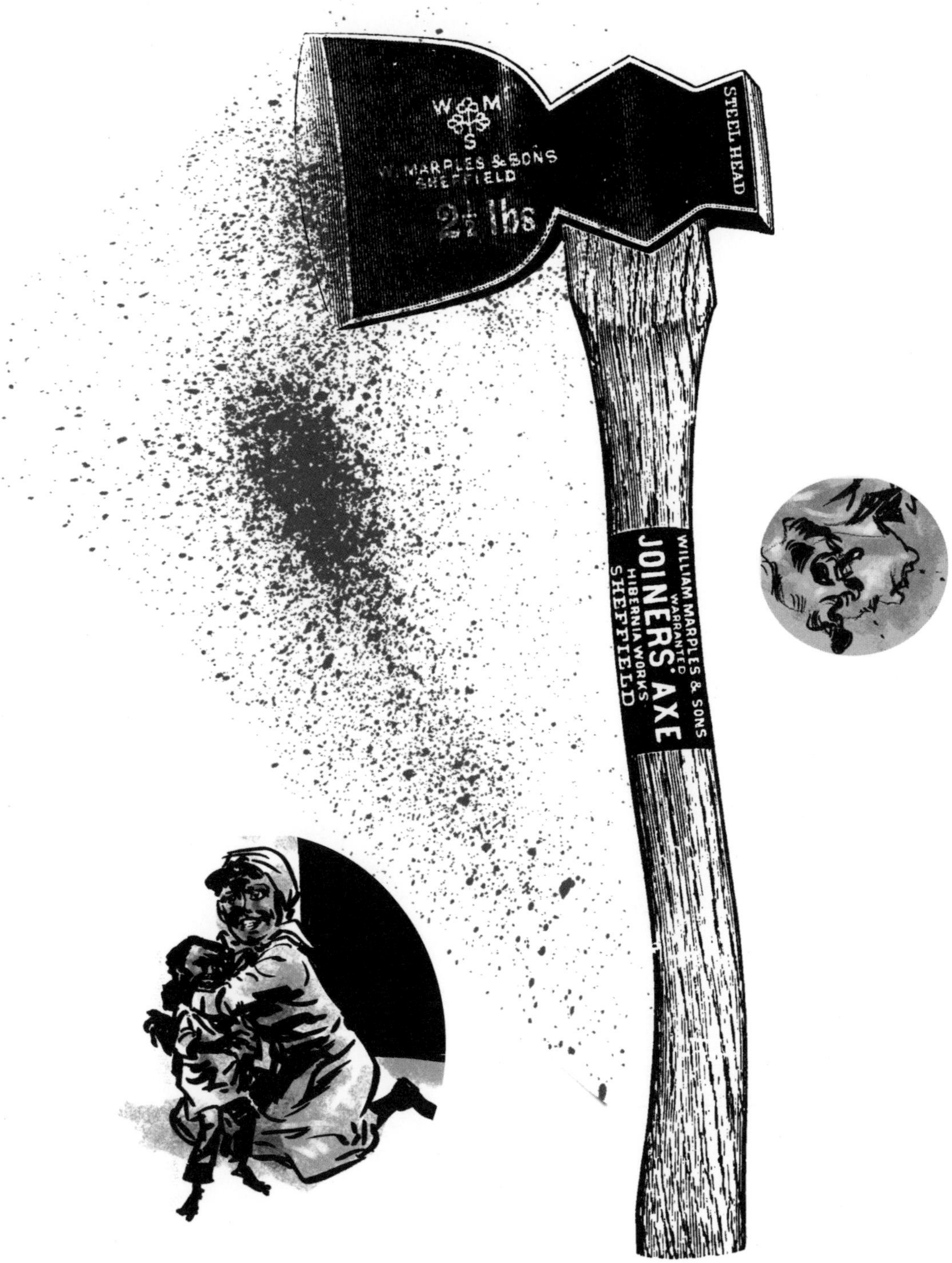
W M
S
W. MARPLES & SONS
SHEFFIELD
2½ lbs
STEEL HEAD
WILLIAM MARPLES & SONS
WARRANTED
JOINERS' AXE
HIBERNIA WORKS
SHEFFIELD

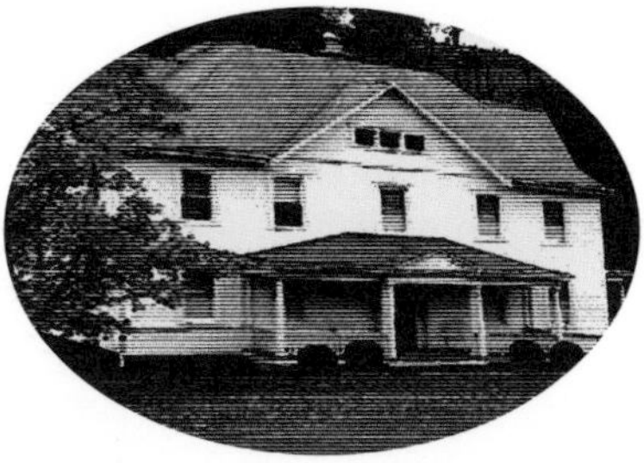

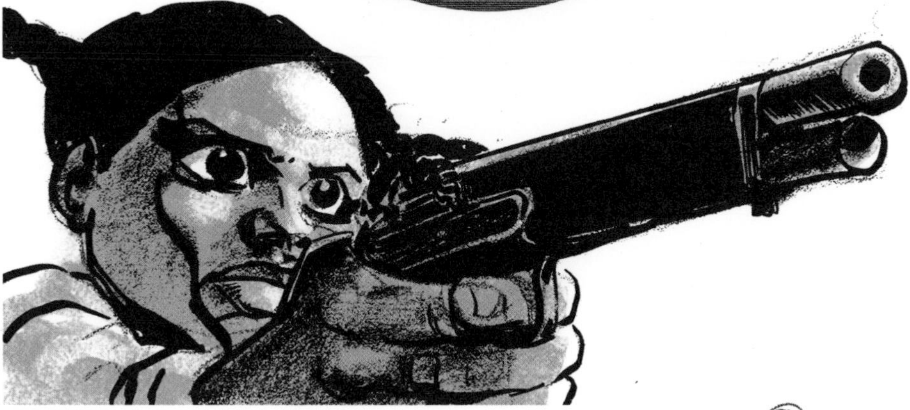

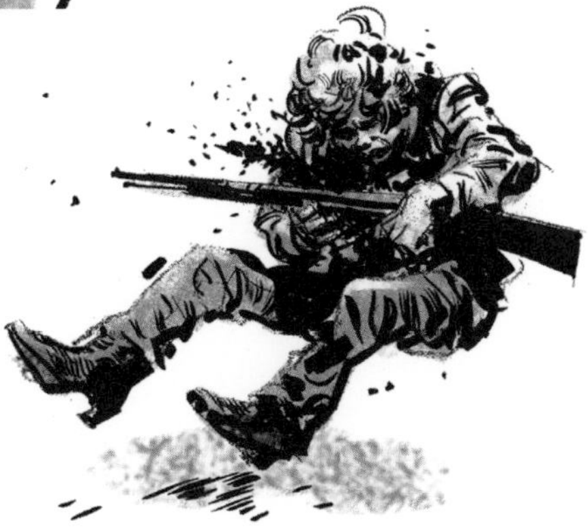

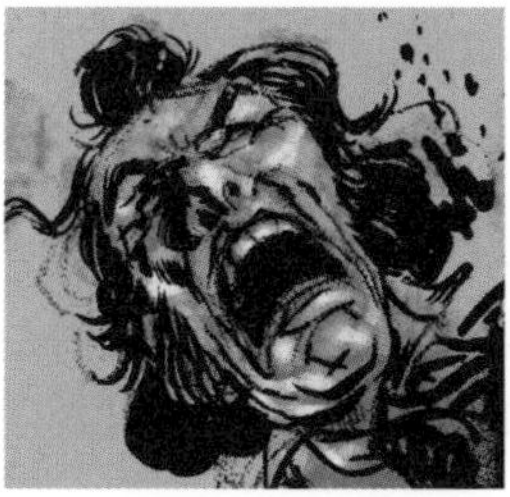

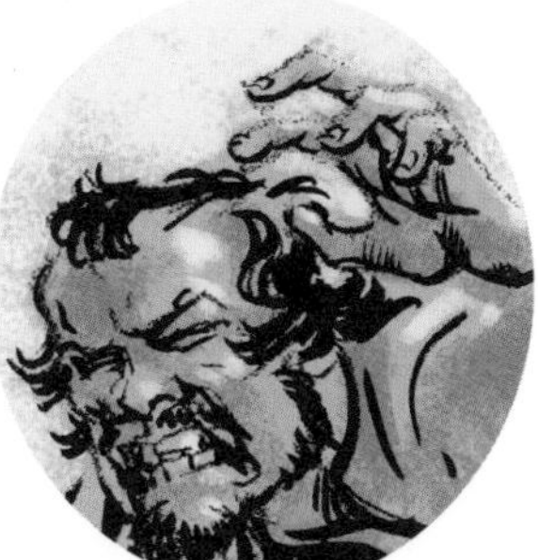

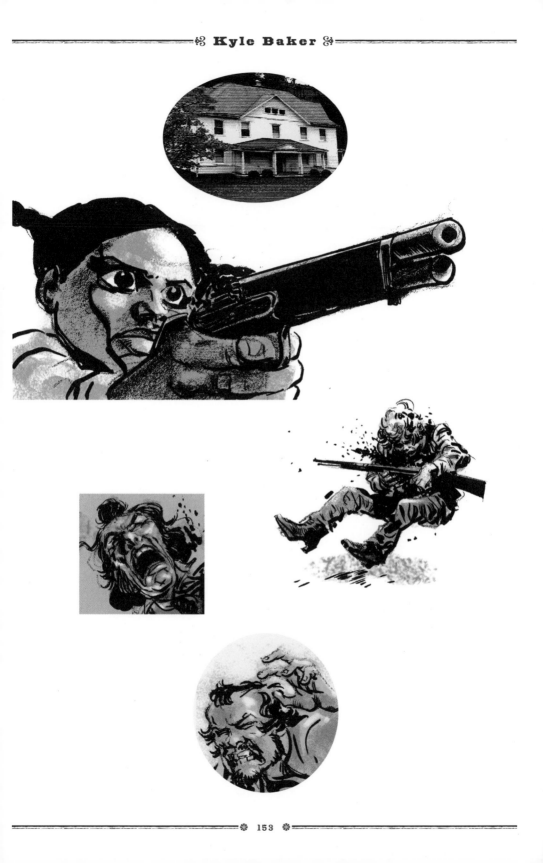

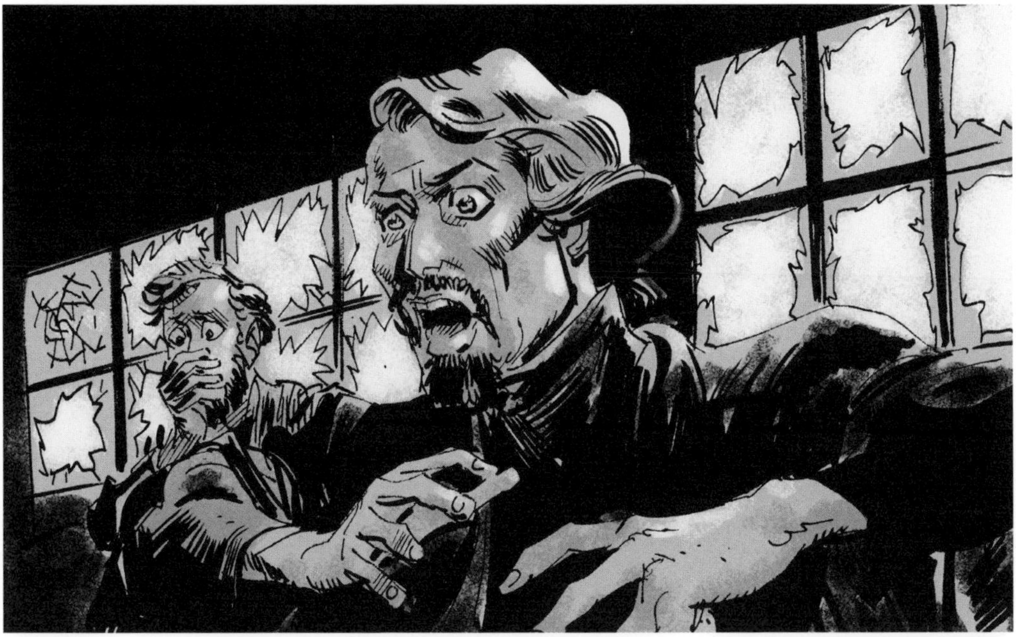

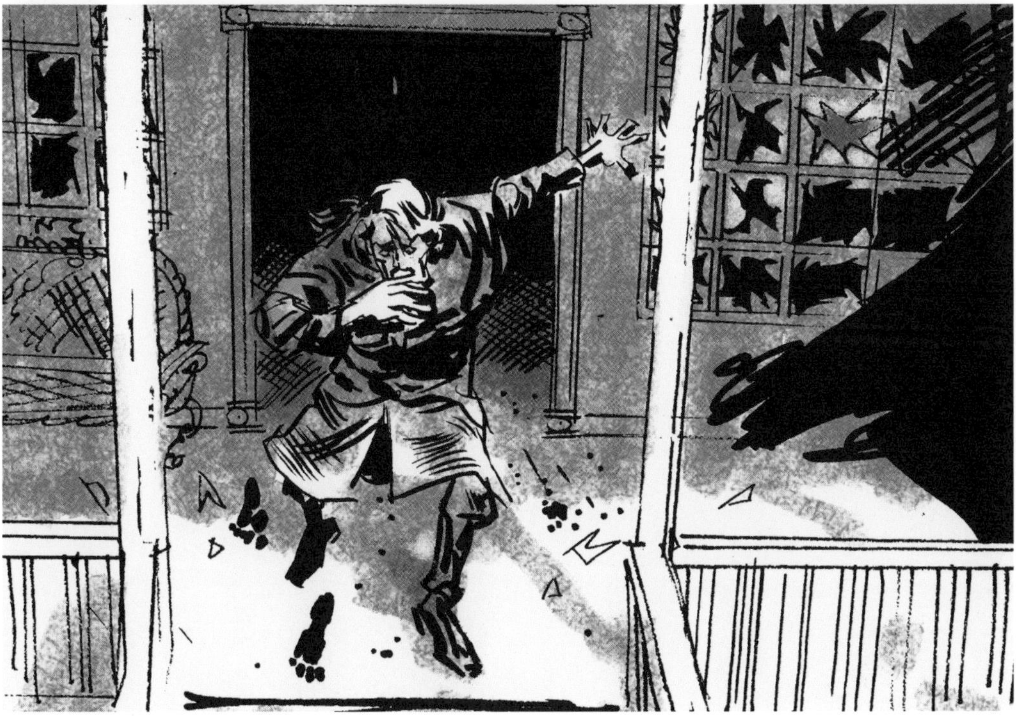

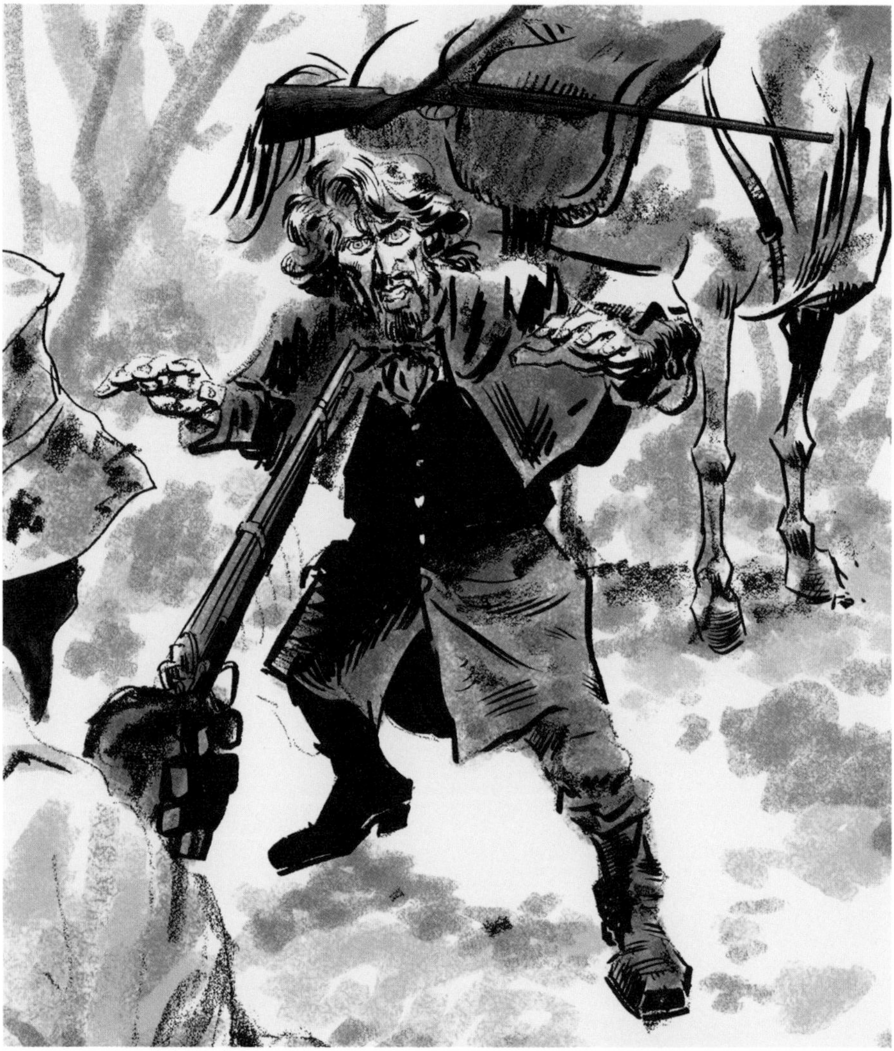

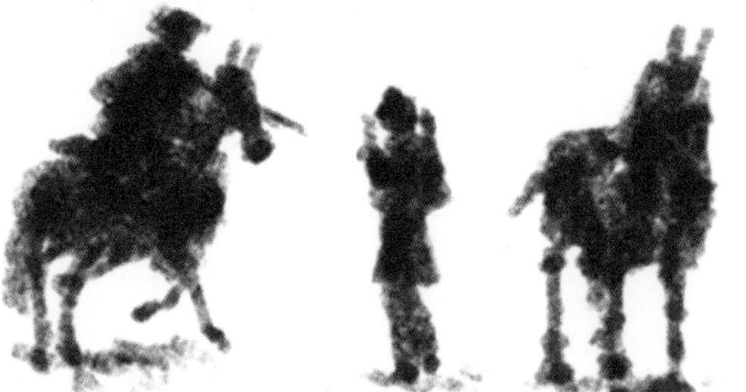

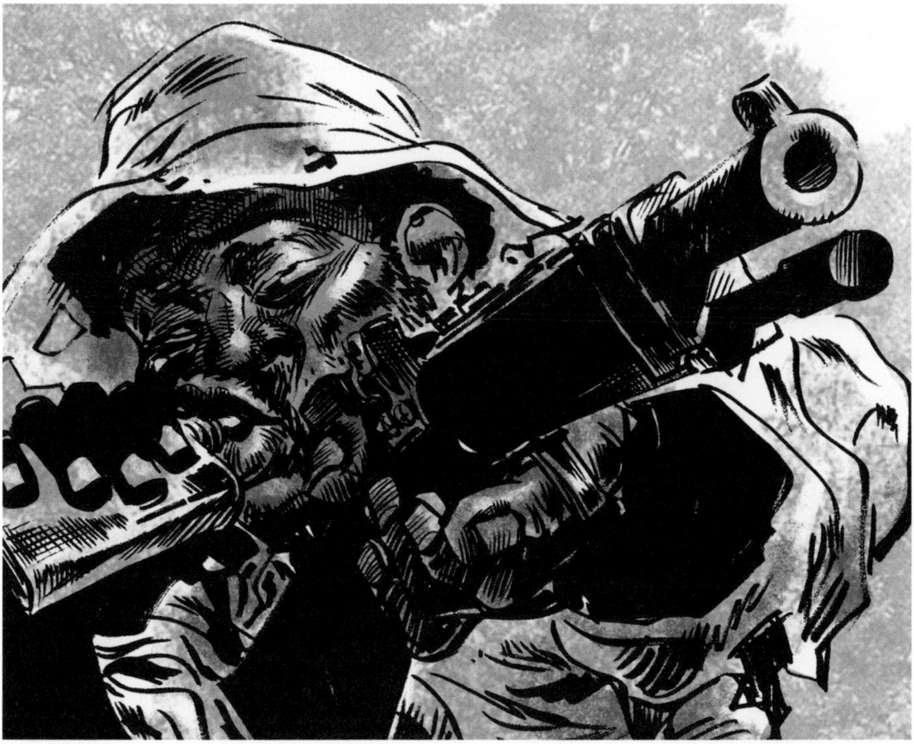

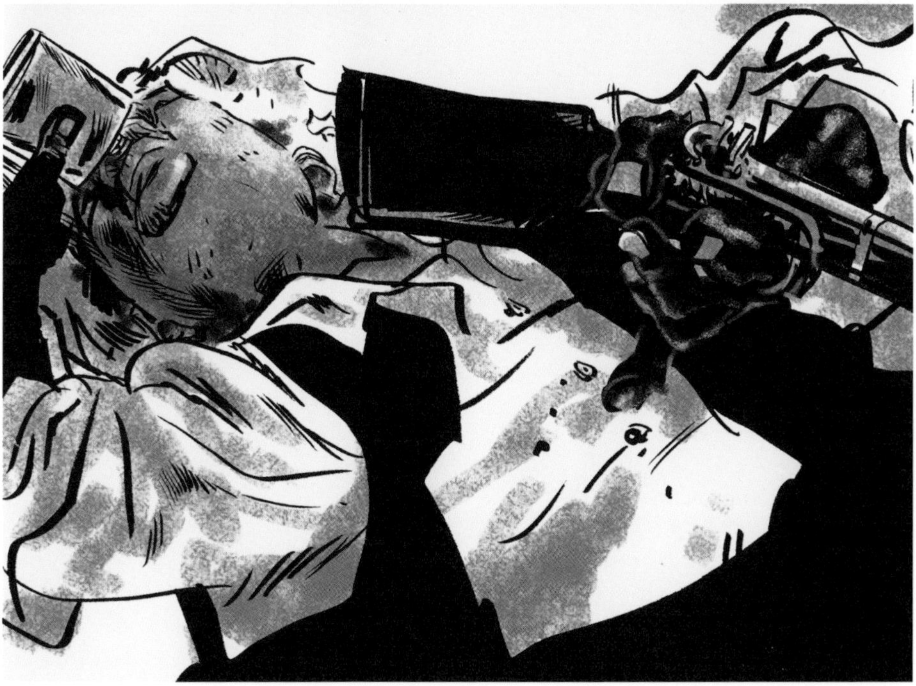

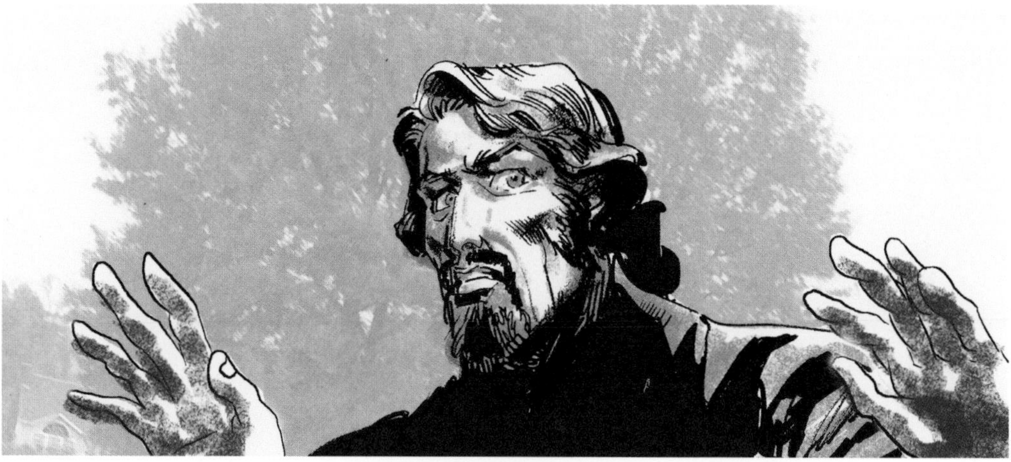

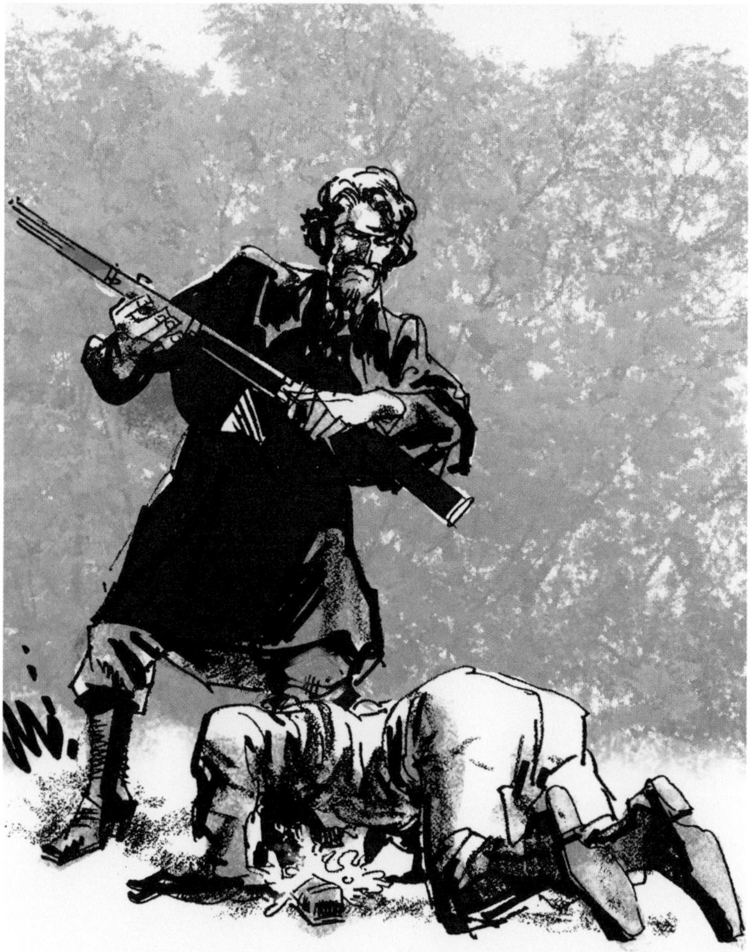

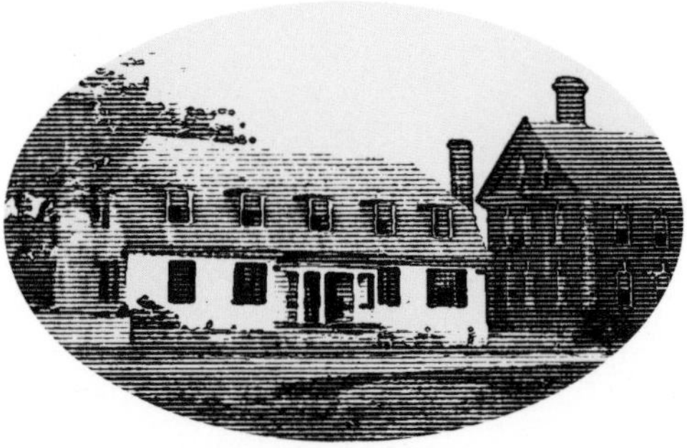

FROM THE CONFESSIONS OF NAT TURNER

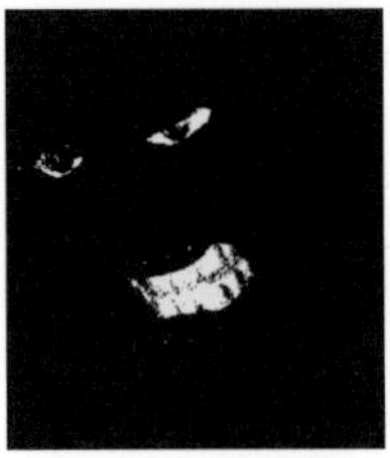

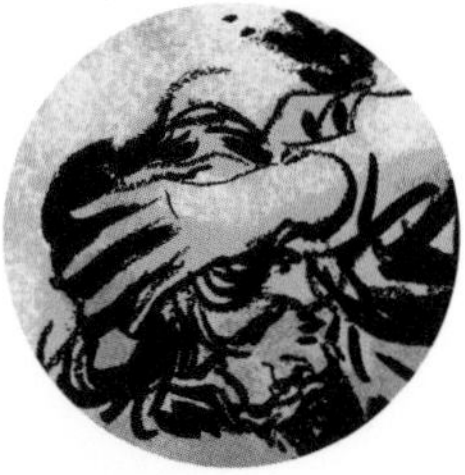

"Our number amounted now to fifty or sixty, all mounted and armed with guns, axes, swords, and clubs. On reaching Mr. James W. Parker's gate, immediately on the road leading to Jerusalem, and about three miles distant, it was proposed to me to call there, but I objected, as I knew he was gone to Jerusalem, and my object was to reach there as soon as possible; but some of the men having relations at Mr. Parker's, it was agreed that they might call and get his people. I remained at the gate on the road, with seven or eight; the others going across the field to the house, about half a mile off.

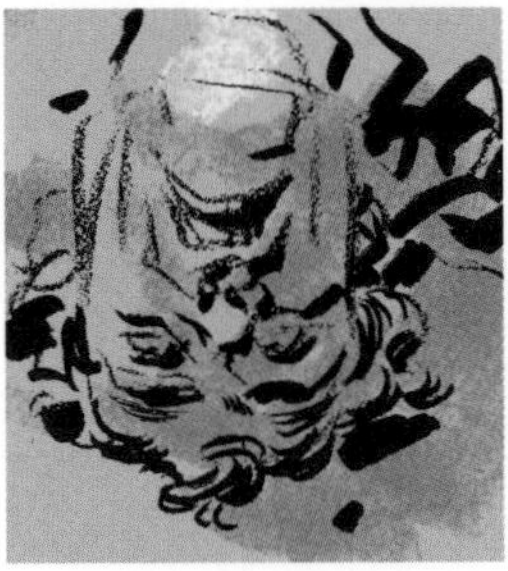

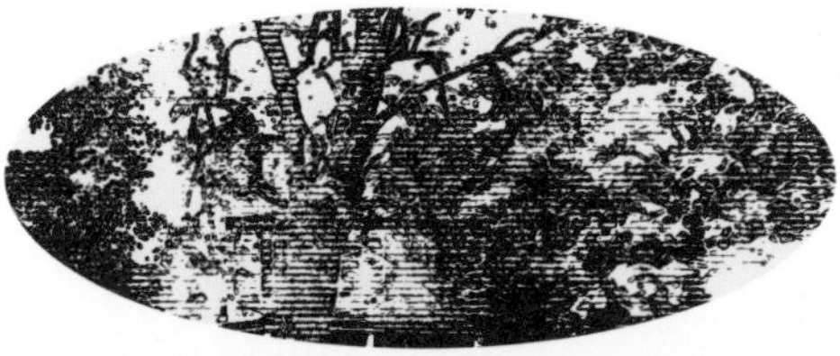

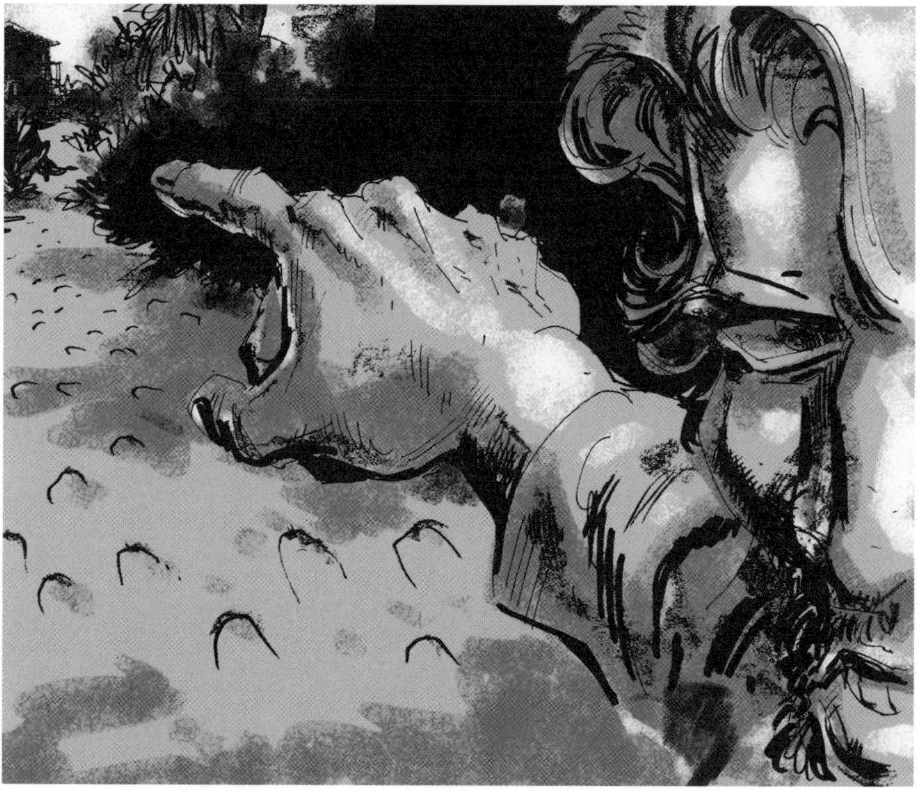

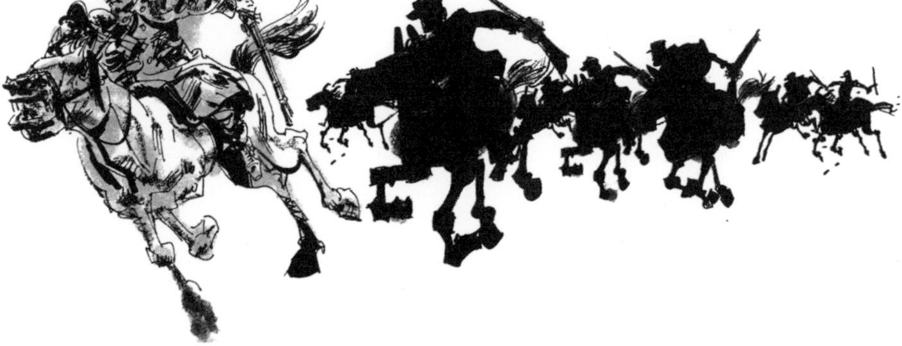

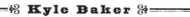

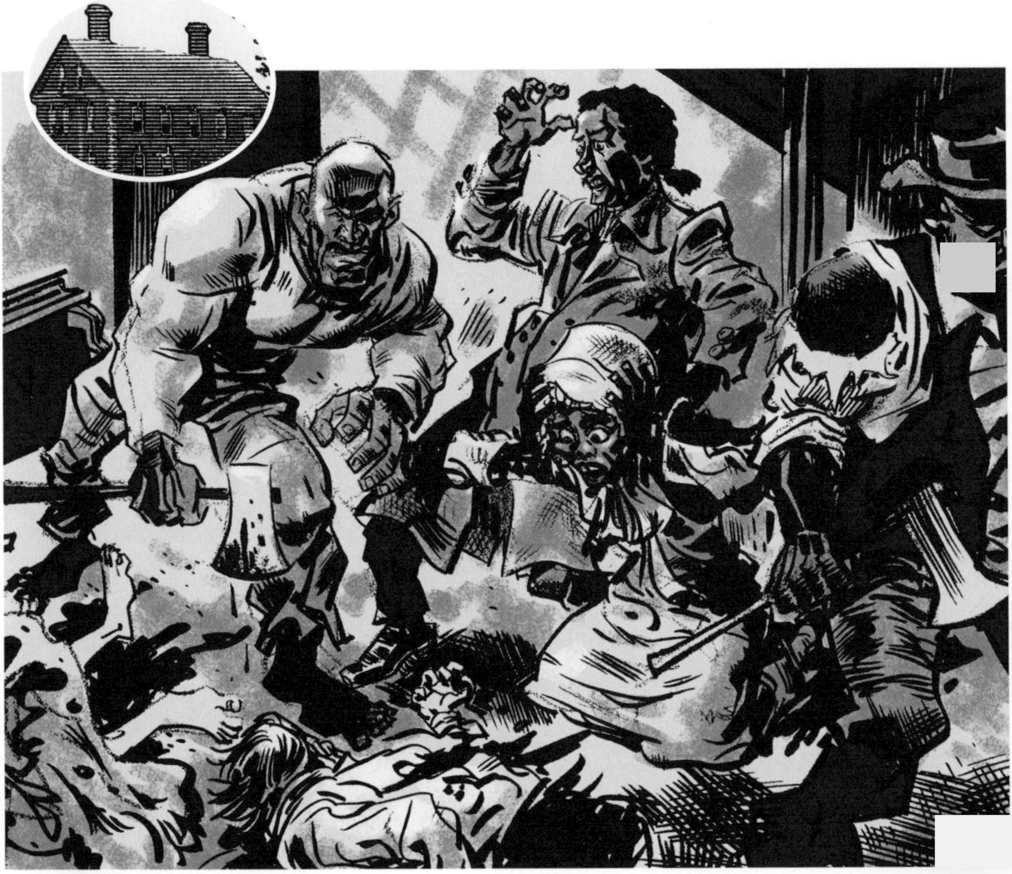

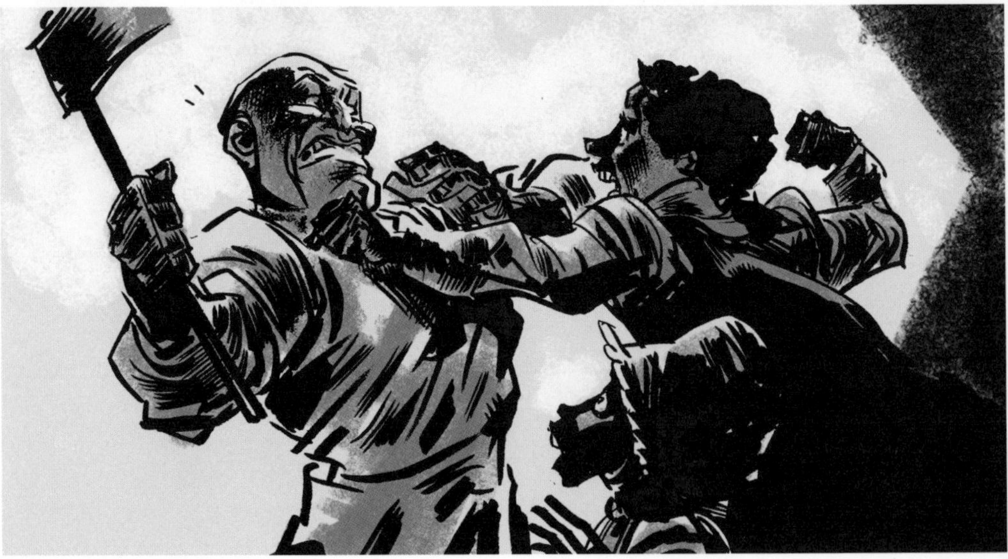

"AFTER WAITING SOME TIME FOR THEM, I BECAME impatient—and started to the house for them...

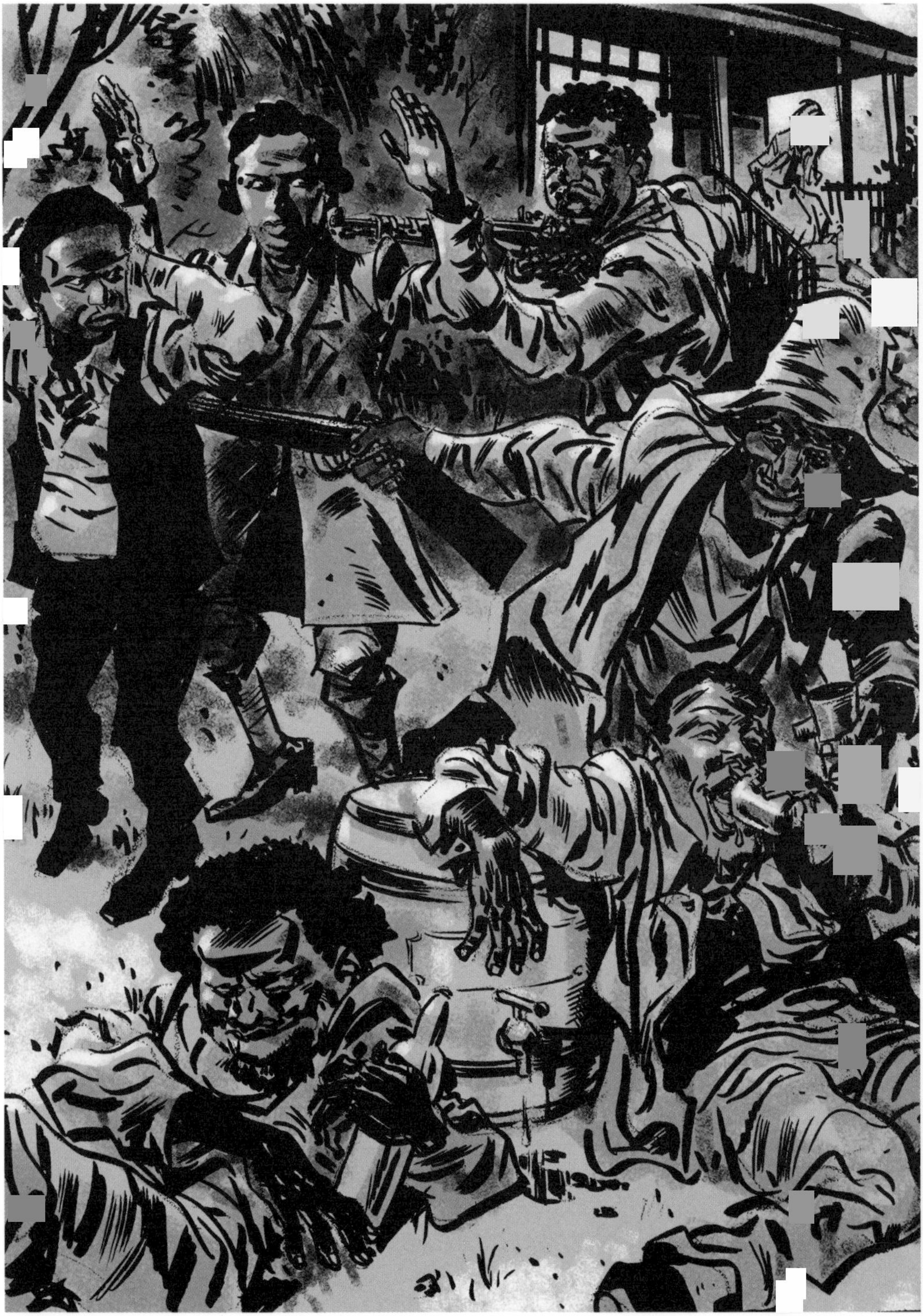

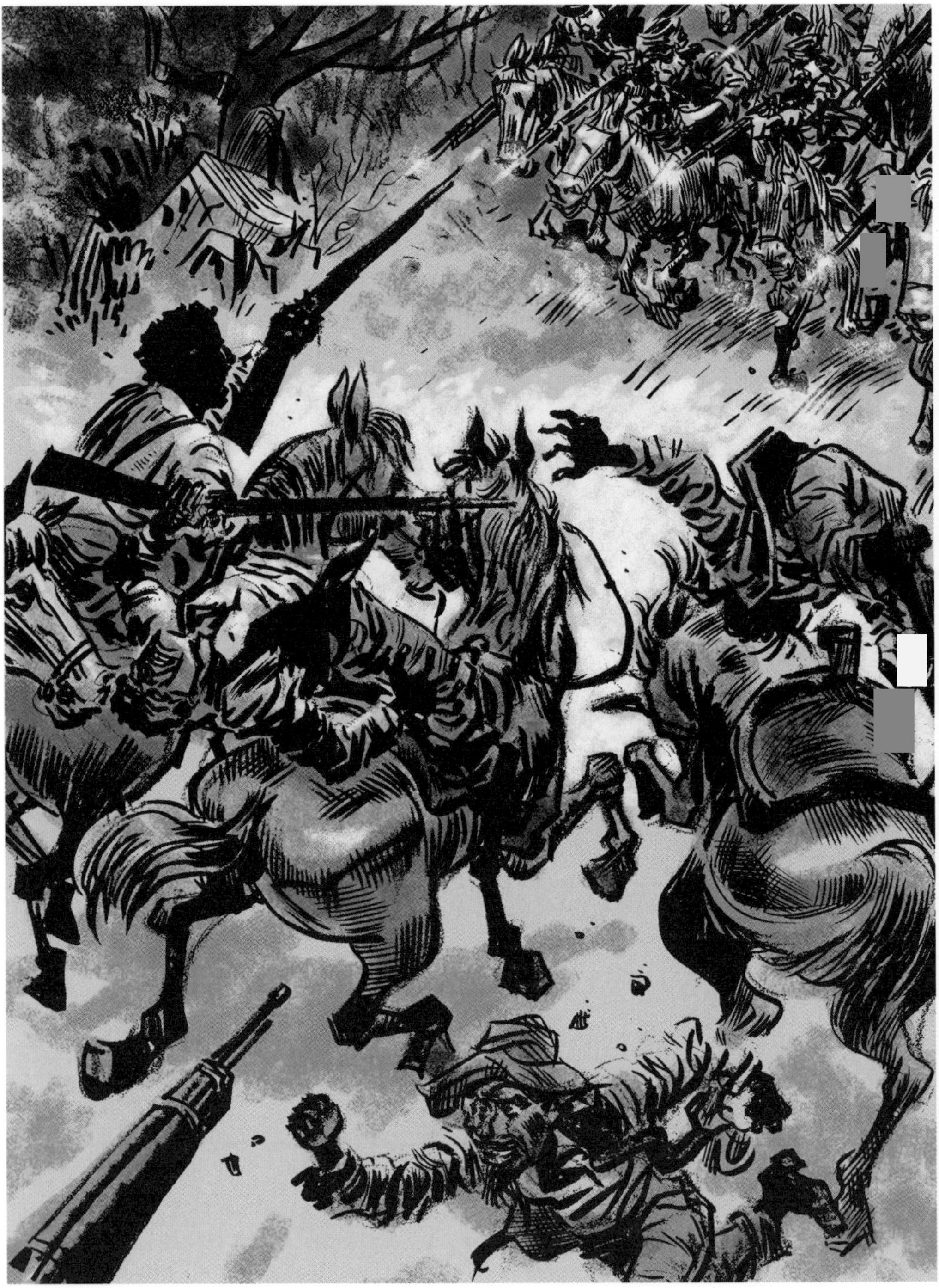

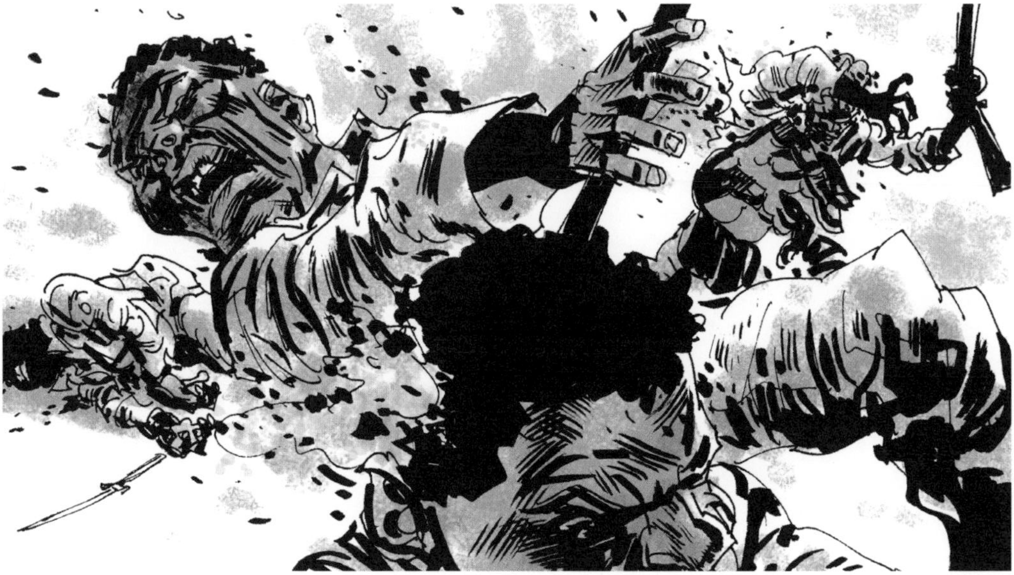

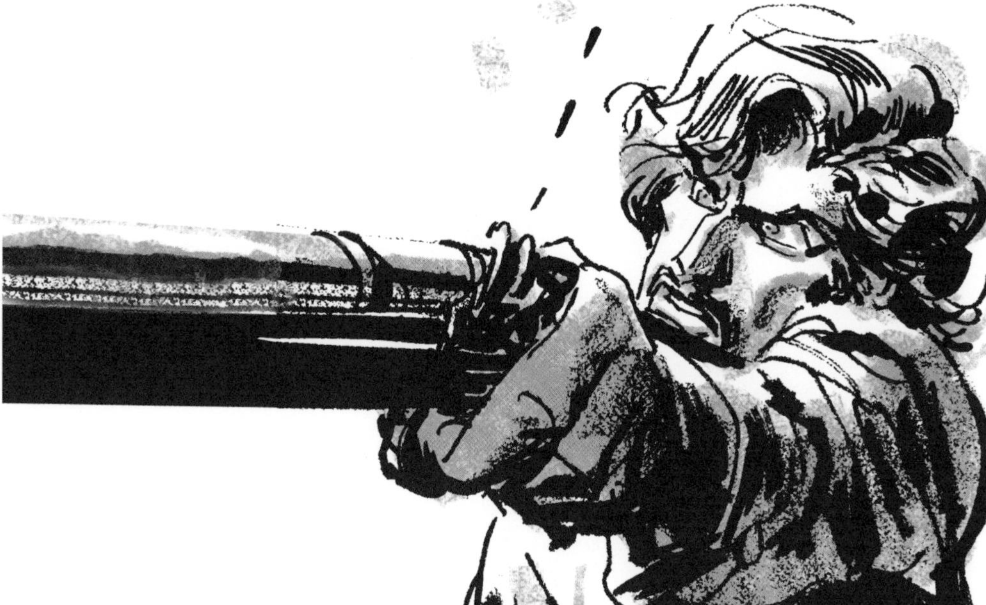

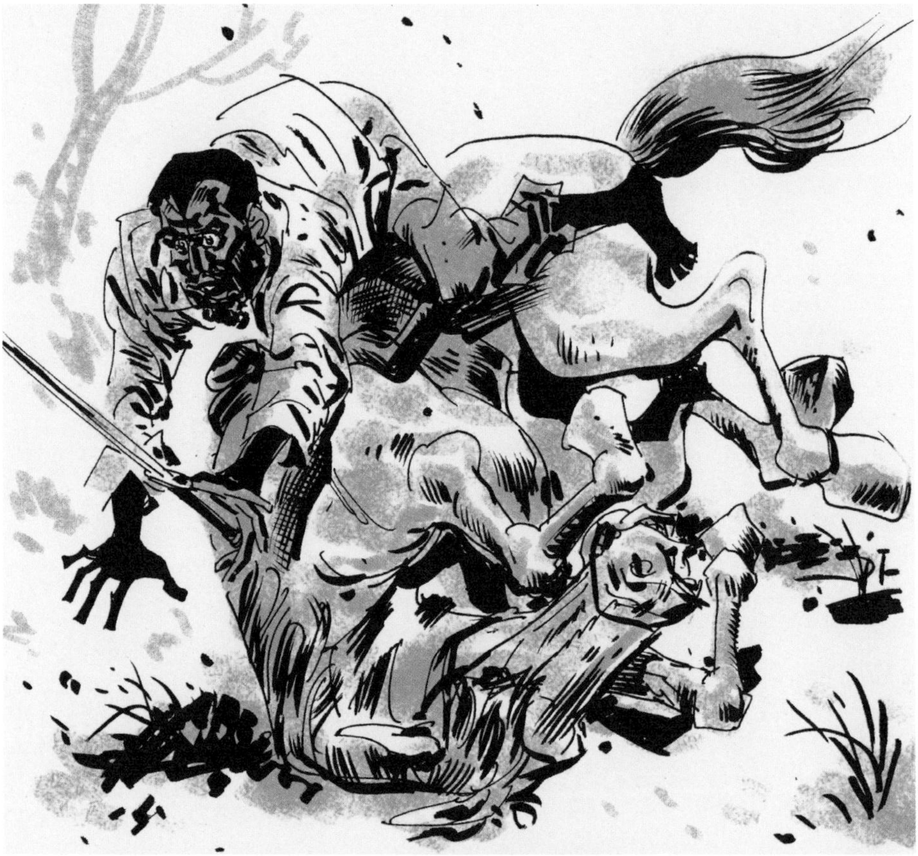

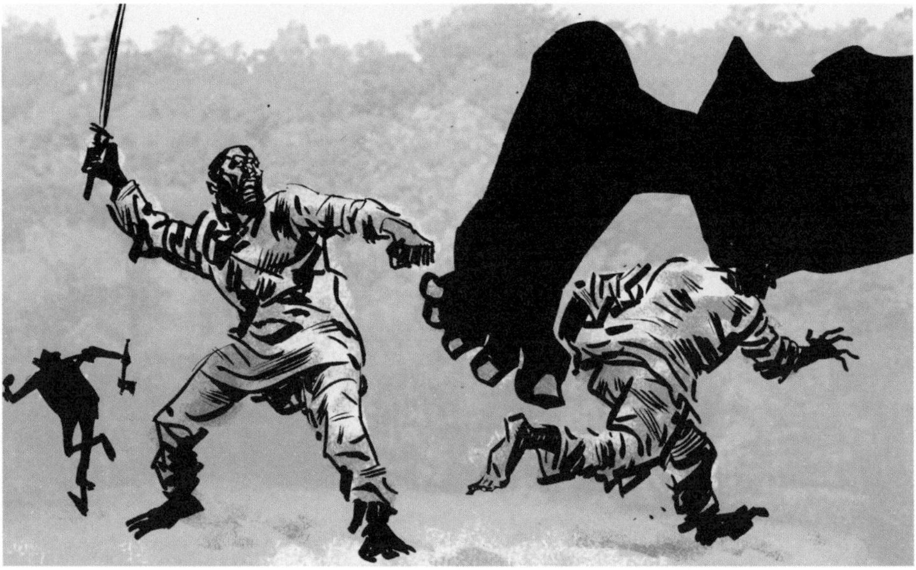

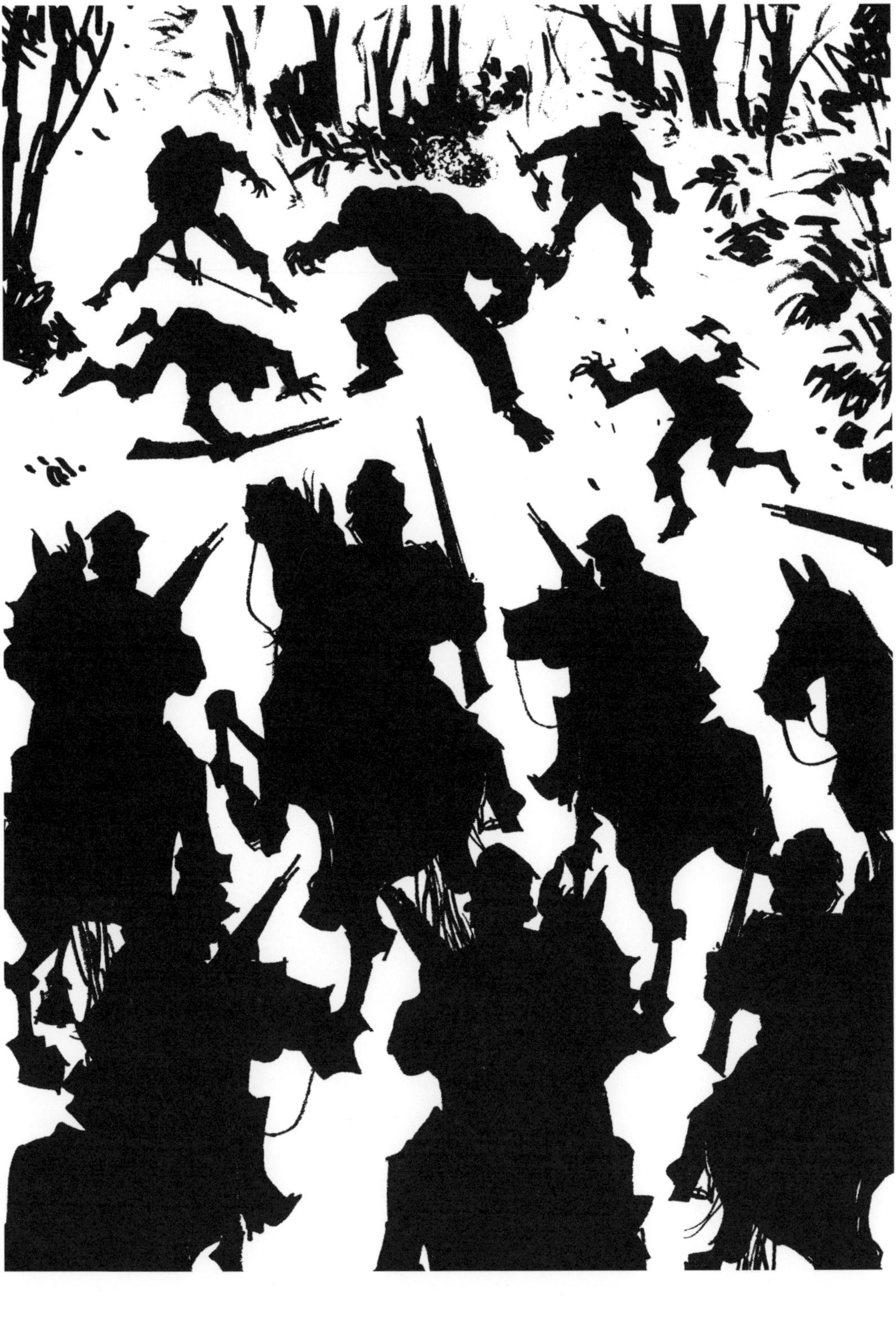

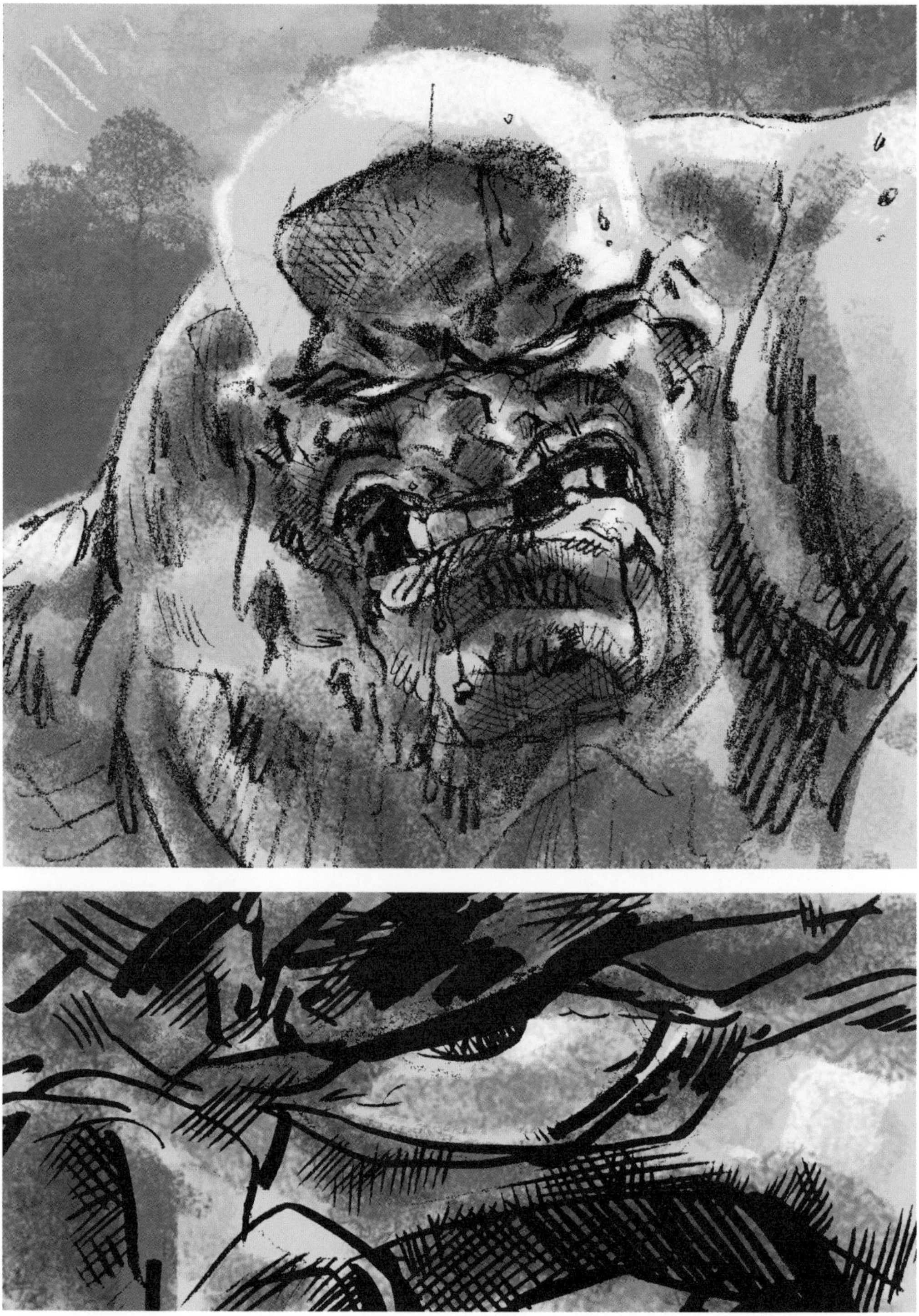

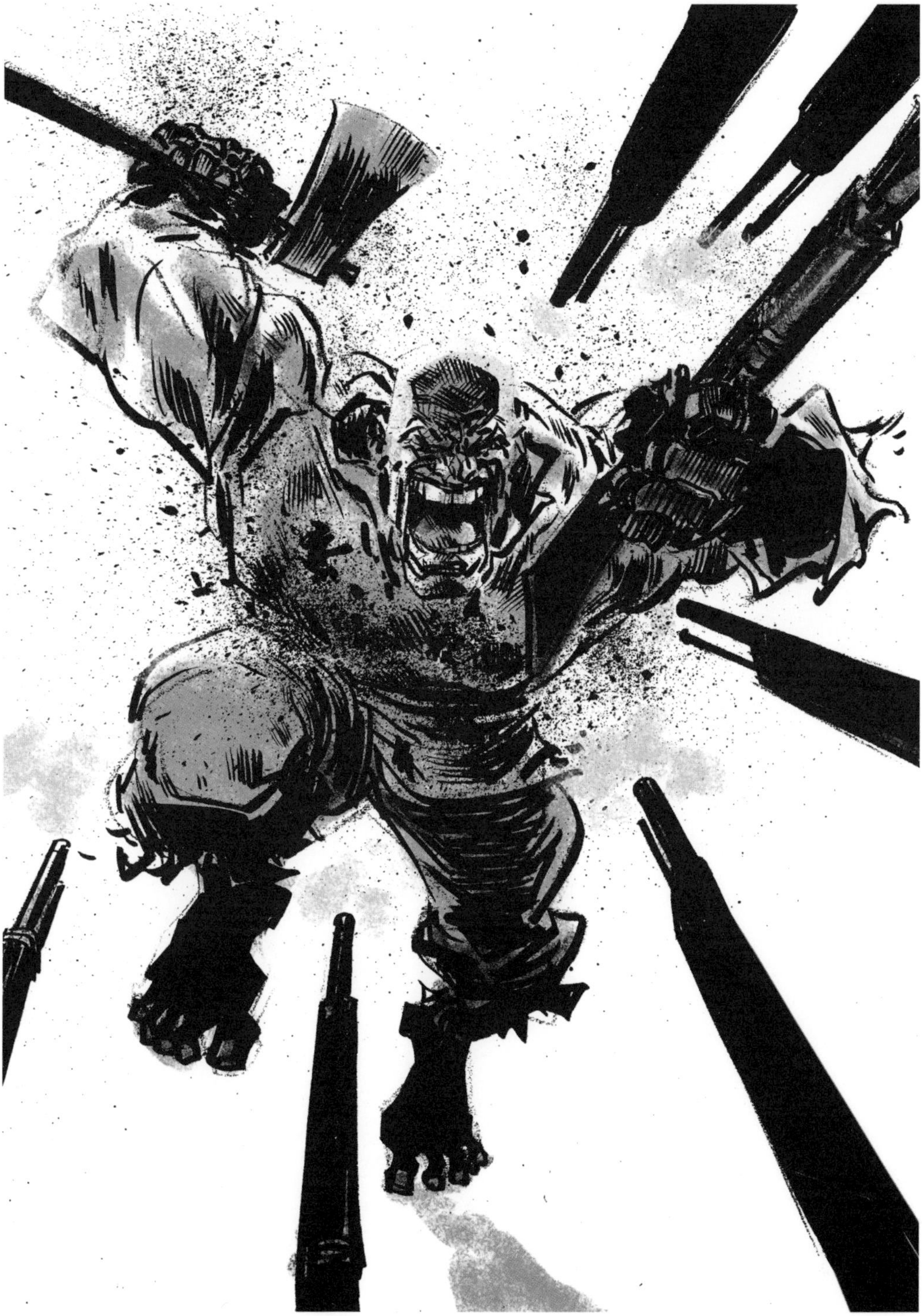

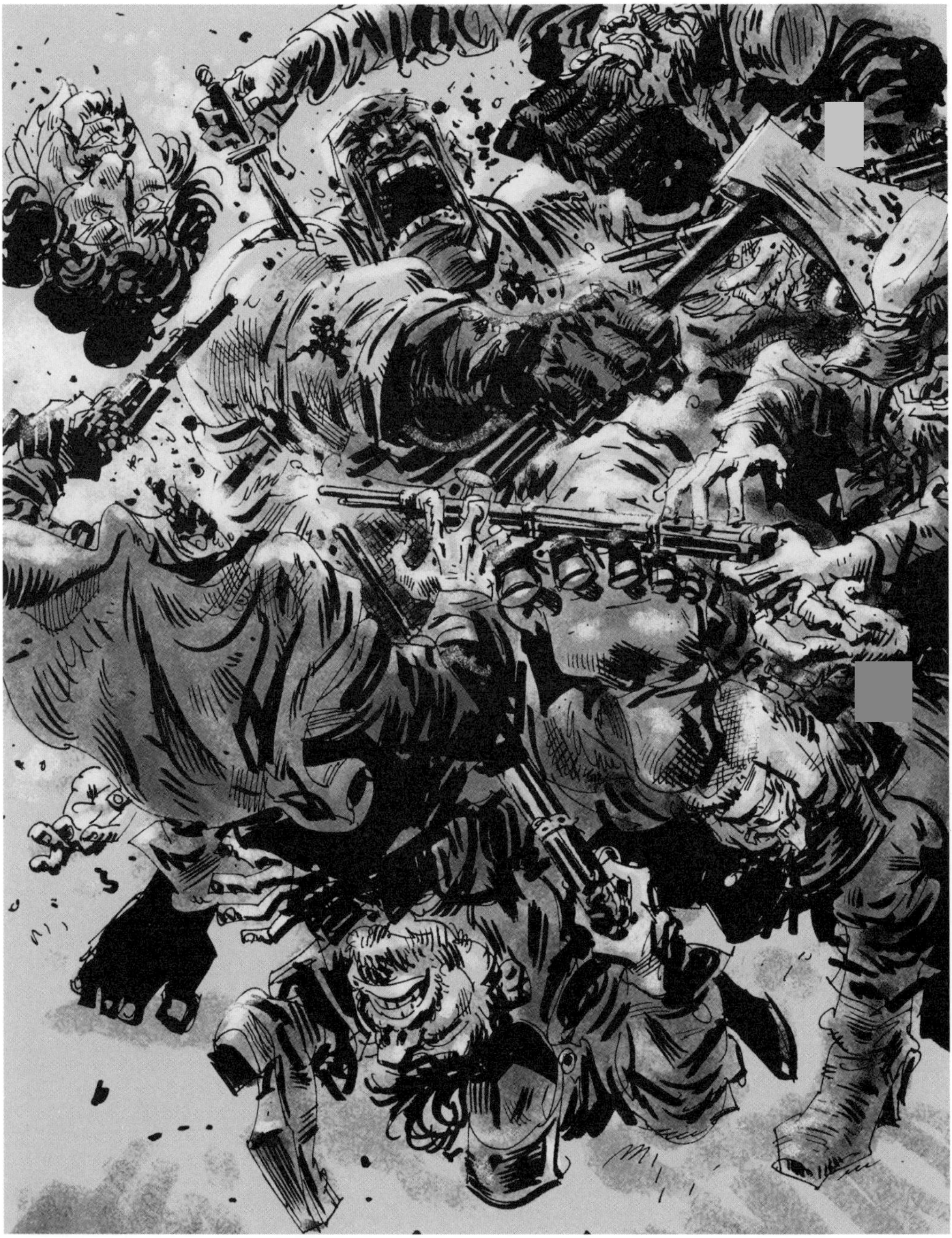

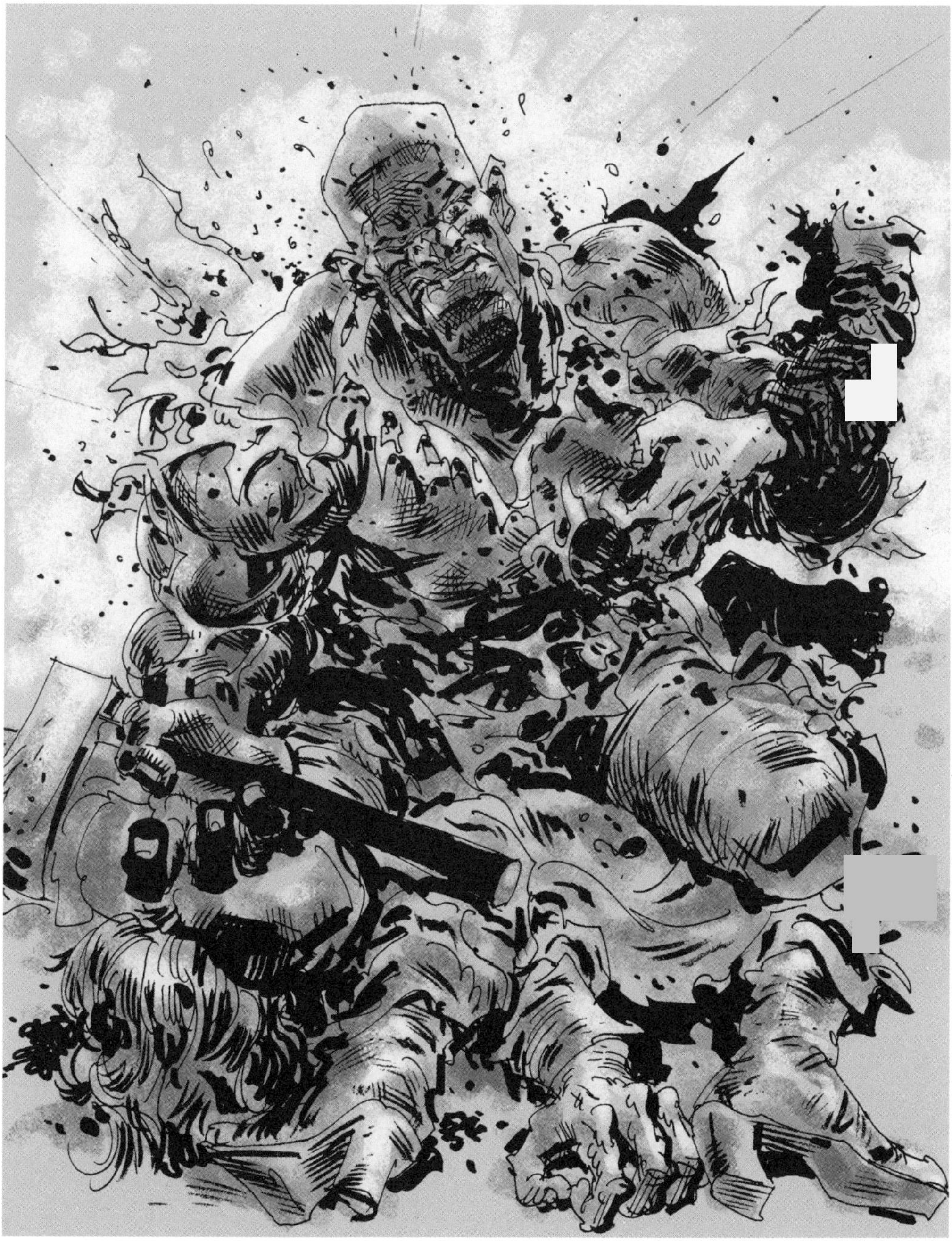

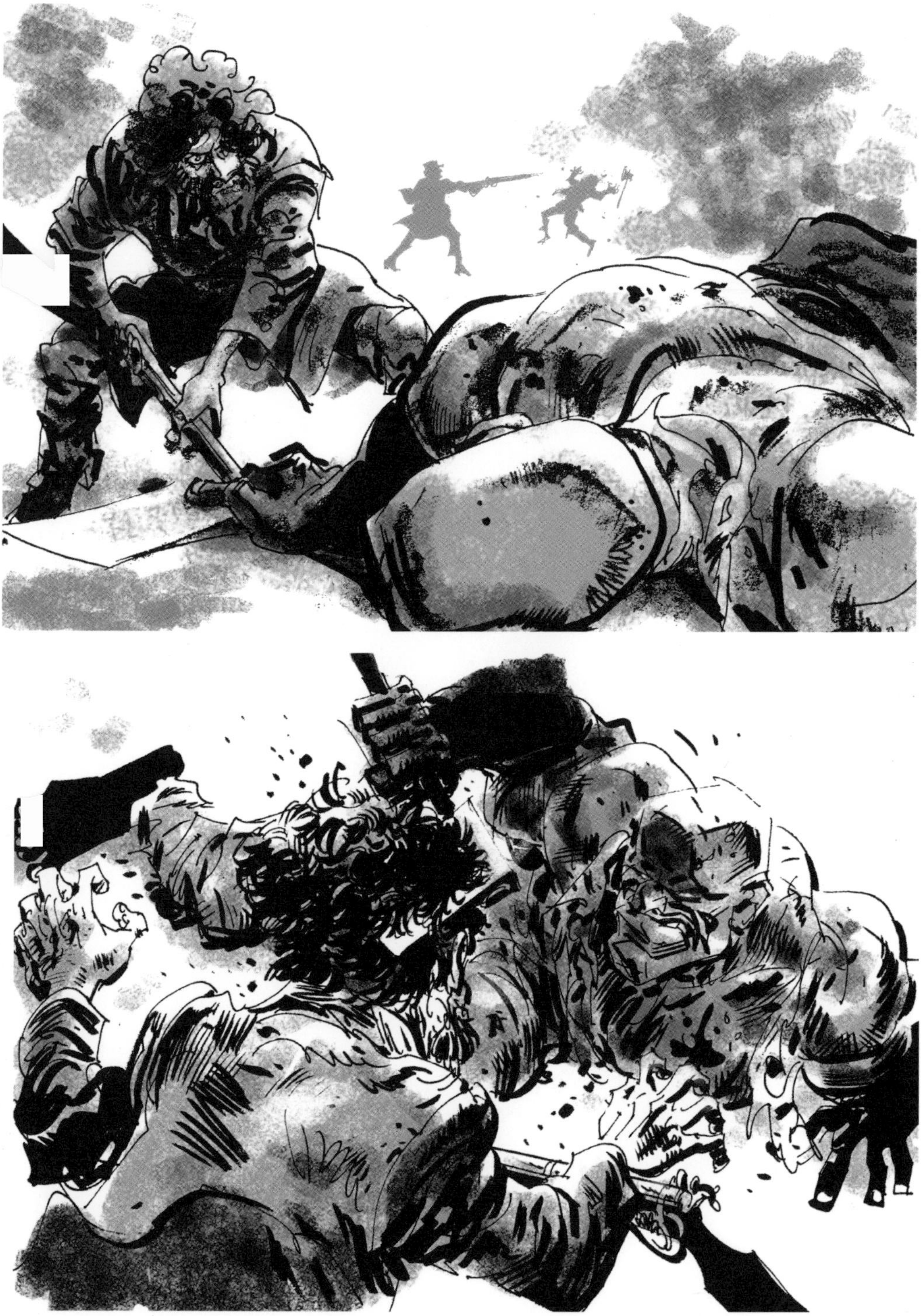

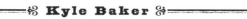

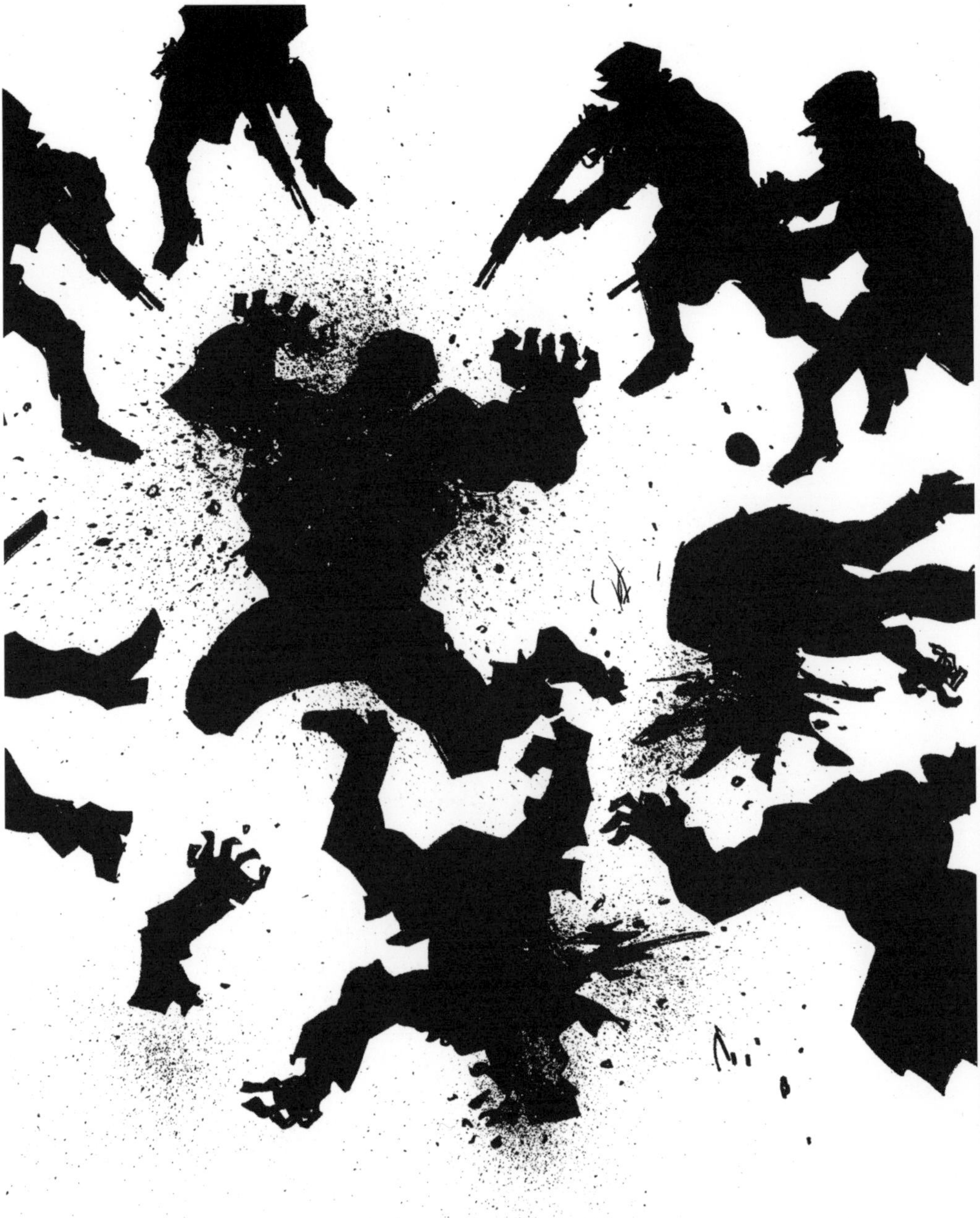

A LIST OF PERSONS MURDERED IN THE INSURRECTION, ON THE 21ST AND 22ND OF AUGUST 1831—

* Joseph Travers and wife and three children,

* Mrs. Elizabeth Turner,

* Hartwell Prebles,

* Sarah Newsome,

* Mrs. P. Reese and son William,

* Trajan Doyle,

* Henry Bryant and wife and child, and wife's mother,

* Mrs. Catherine Whitehead, son Richard, and four daughters and grandchild,

* Salathul Francis,

* Nathaniel Francis's overseer and two children,

* John T. Barrow,

* George Vaughan,

* Mrs. Levi Waller and ten children,

* William Williams, wife and two boys,

* Mrs. Caswell Worrell and child,

* Mrs. Rebecca Vaughan,

* Ann Eliza Vaughan and son Arthur,

* Mrs. John K. Williams and child,

* Mrs. Jacob Williams and three children,

* and Edwin Drury

—AMOUNTING TO FIFTY-FIVE.

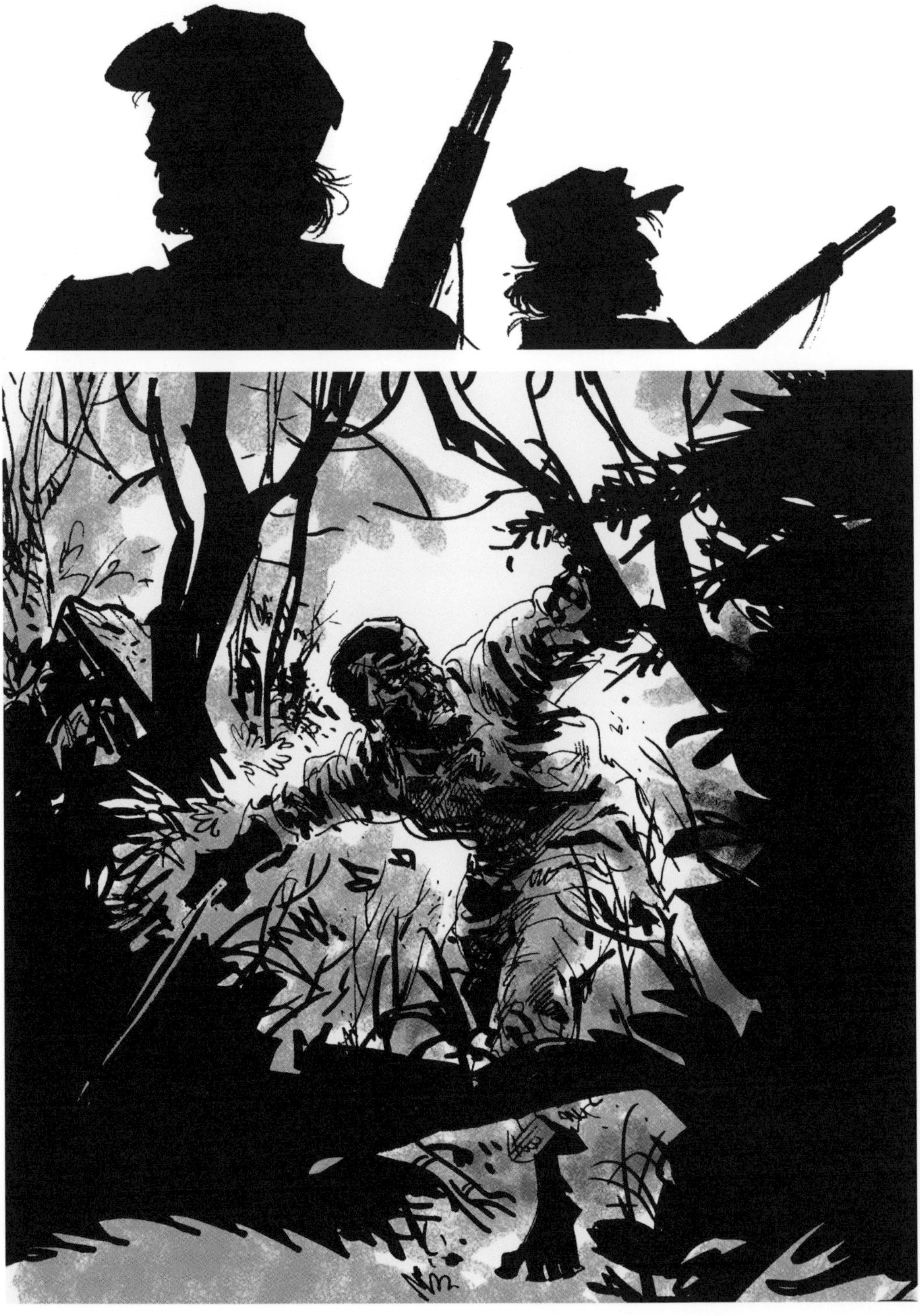

"PURSUING OUR COURSE BACK, AND COMING
in sight of Captain Harris's, where we had been
the day before, we discovered a party of white
men at the house, on which all deserted me but
two (Jacob and Nat). We concealed ourselves
in the woods until near night, when I sent them
in search of Henry, Sam, Nelson, and Hark, and
directed them to rally all they could, at the place
we had had our dinner the Sunday before, where
they would find me, and I accordingly returned
there as soon as it was dark, and remained until
Wednesday evening, when discovering white
men riding around the place as though they
were looking for someone, and none of my men
joining me, I concluded Jacob and Nat had been
taken, and compelled to betray me. On this
I gave up all hope for the present.

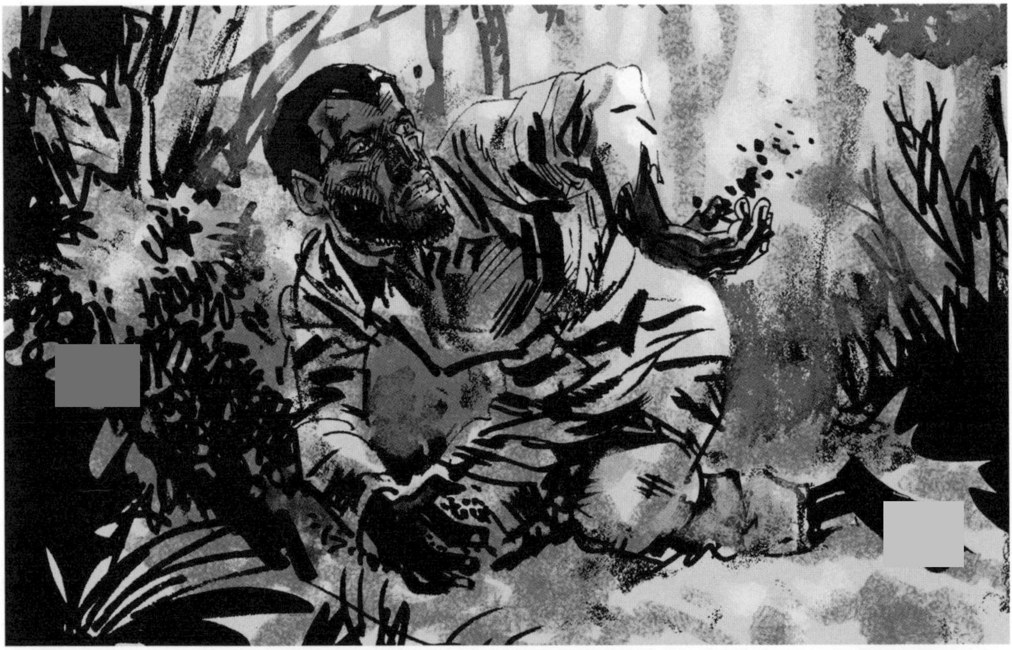

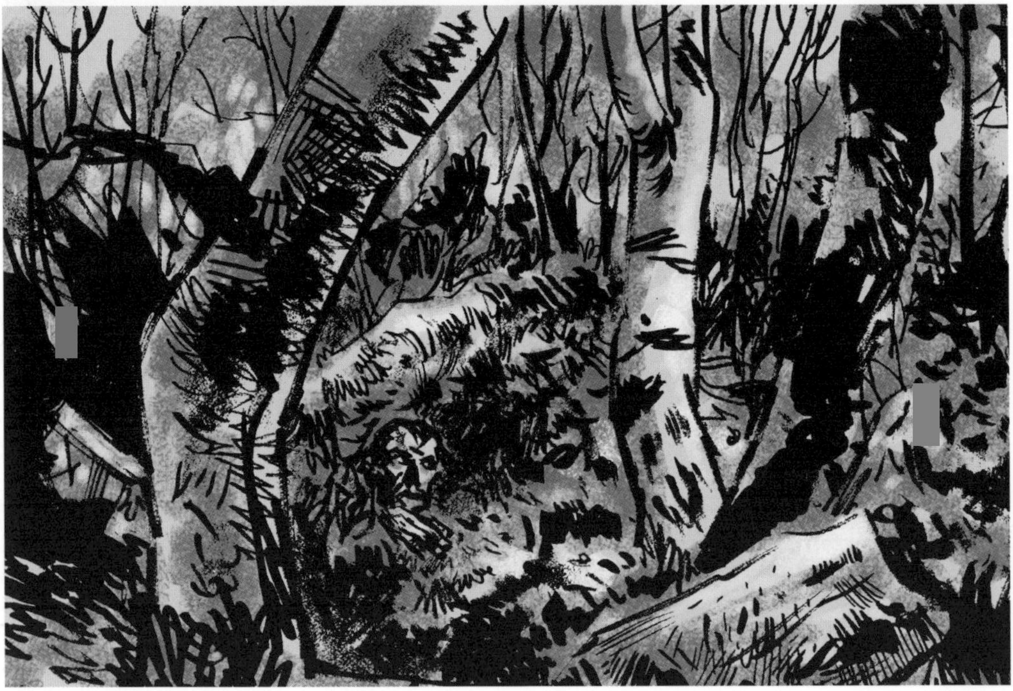

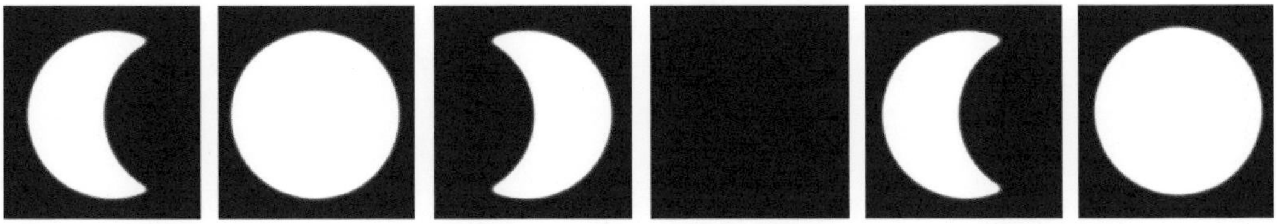

"I CONCEALED MYSELF FOR SIX WEEKS, NEVER LEAVING MY HIDING PLACE BUT FOR A FEW minutes in the dead of night to get water, which was very near; thinking by this time I could venture out, I began to go about in the night and eavesdrop the houses in the neighborhood; pursuing this course for about a fortnight and gathering little or no intelligence, afraid of speaking to any human being, and returning every morning to my cave before the dawn of day.

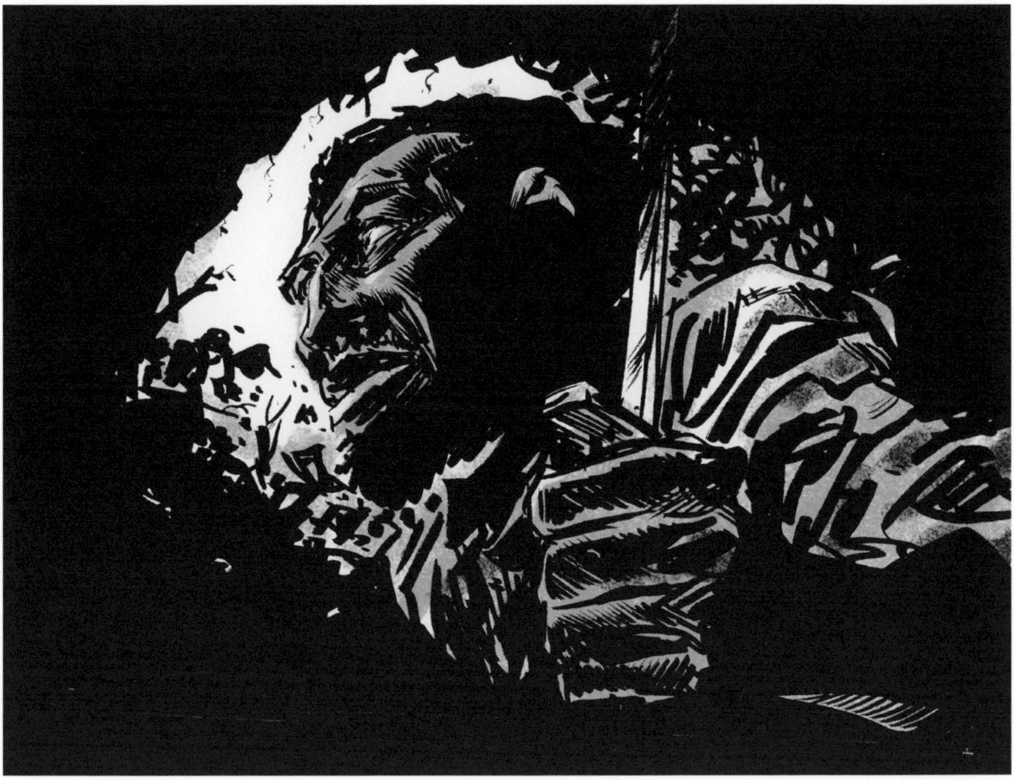

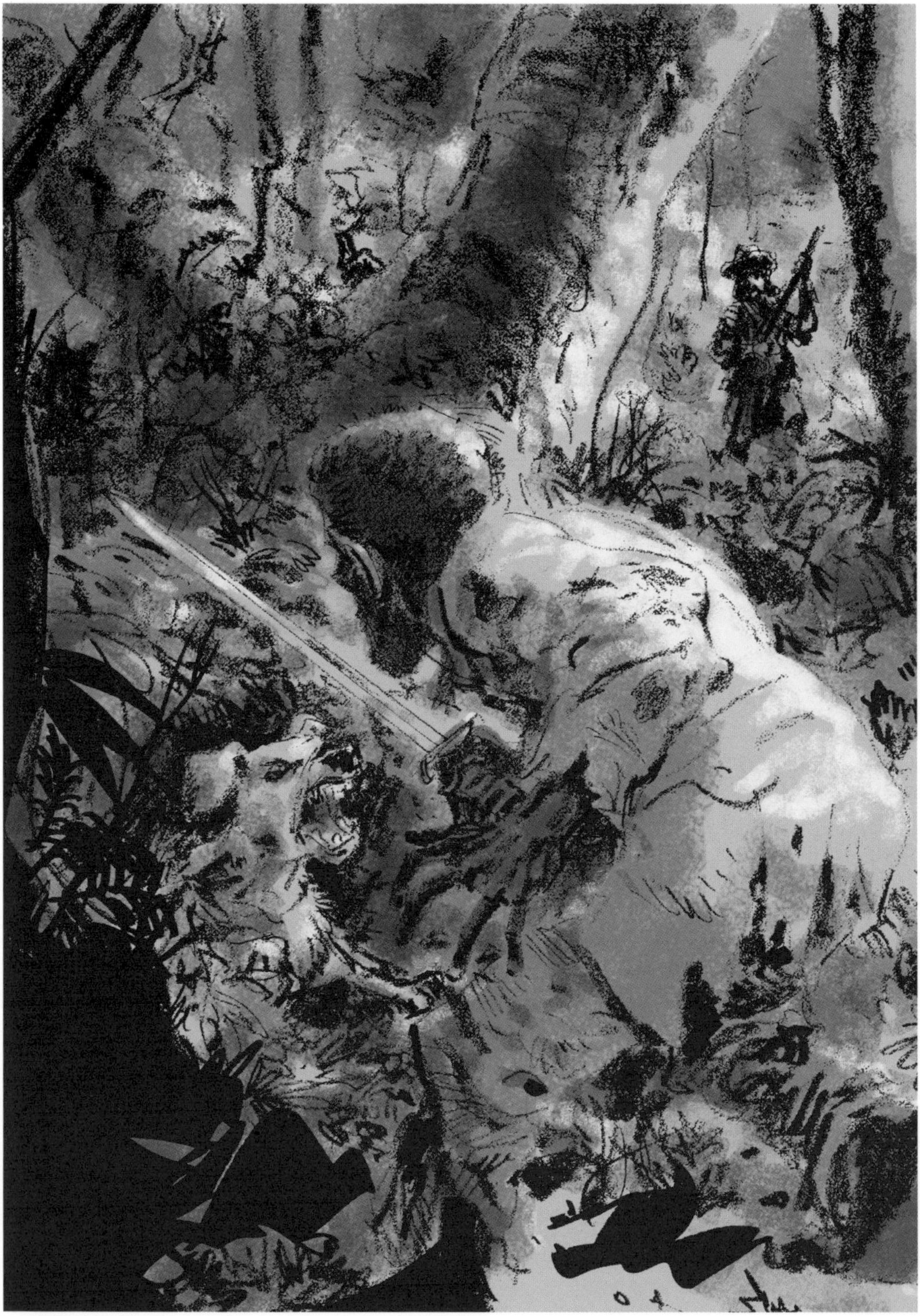

"I KNOW NOT HOW LONG I MIGHT HAVE LED this life, if accident had not betrayed me. A dog in the neighborhood passing by my hiding place one night while I was out, was attracted by some meat I had in my cave, and crawled in and stole it, and was coming out just as I returned...

"ON MR. PHIPPS DISCOVERING THE PLACE OF my concealment, he cocked his gun and aimed at me. I requested him not to shoot, and I would give up, upon which he demanded my sword. I delivered it to him, and he brought me to prison. During the time I was pursued, I had many hair-breadth escapes, which your time will not permit you to relate. I am here loaded with chains, and willing to suffer the fate that awaits me."

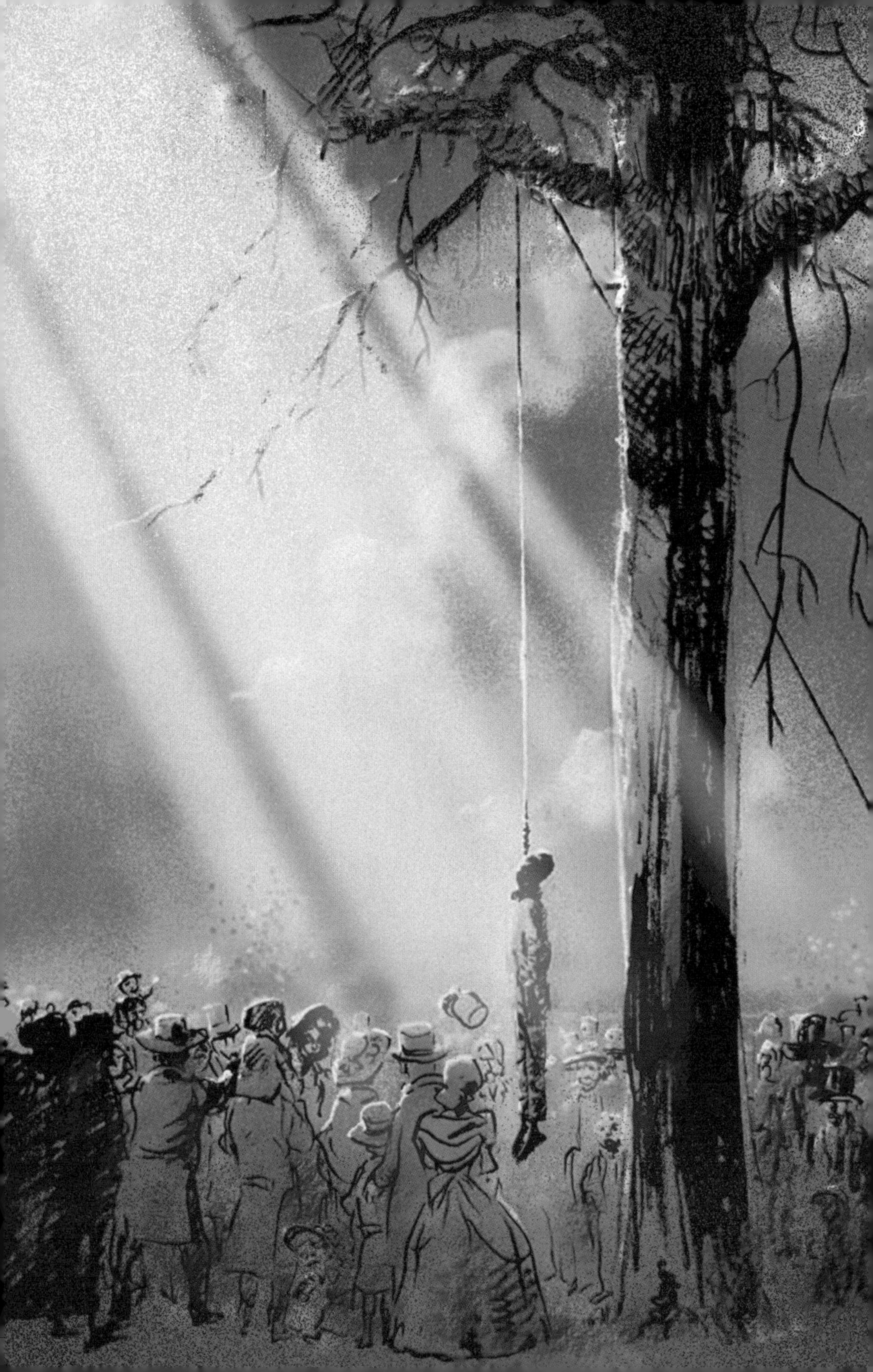

IV

TRIUMPH

FROM THE RECORD OF THOMAS R. GRAY

"I shall not attempt to describe the effect of his narrative, as told and commented on by himself, in the condemned hole of the prison. The calm, deliberate composure with which he spoke of his late deeds and intentions, the expression of his fiend-like face when excited by enthusiasm, still bearing the stains of the blood of helpless innocence about him; clothed with rags and covered with chains; yet daring to raise his manacled hands to heaven, with a spirit soaring above the attributes of man; I looked on him and my blood curdled in my veins.

QUESTION:

"Do you not find yourself mistaken now?"

ANSWER:

"Was not Christ crucified?"

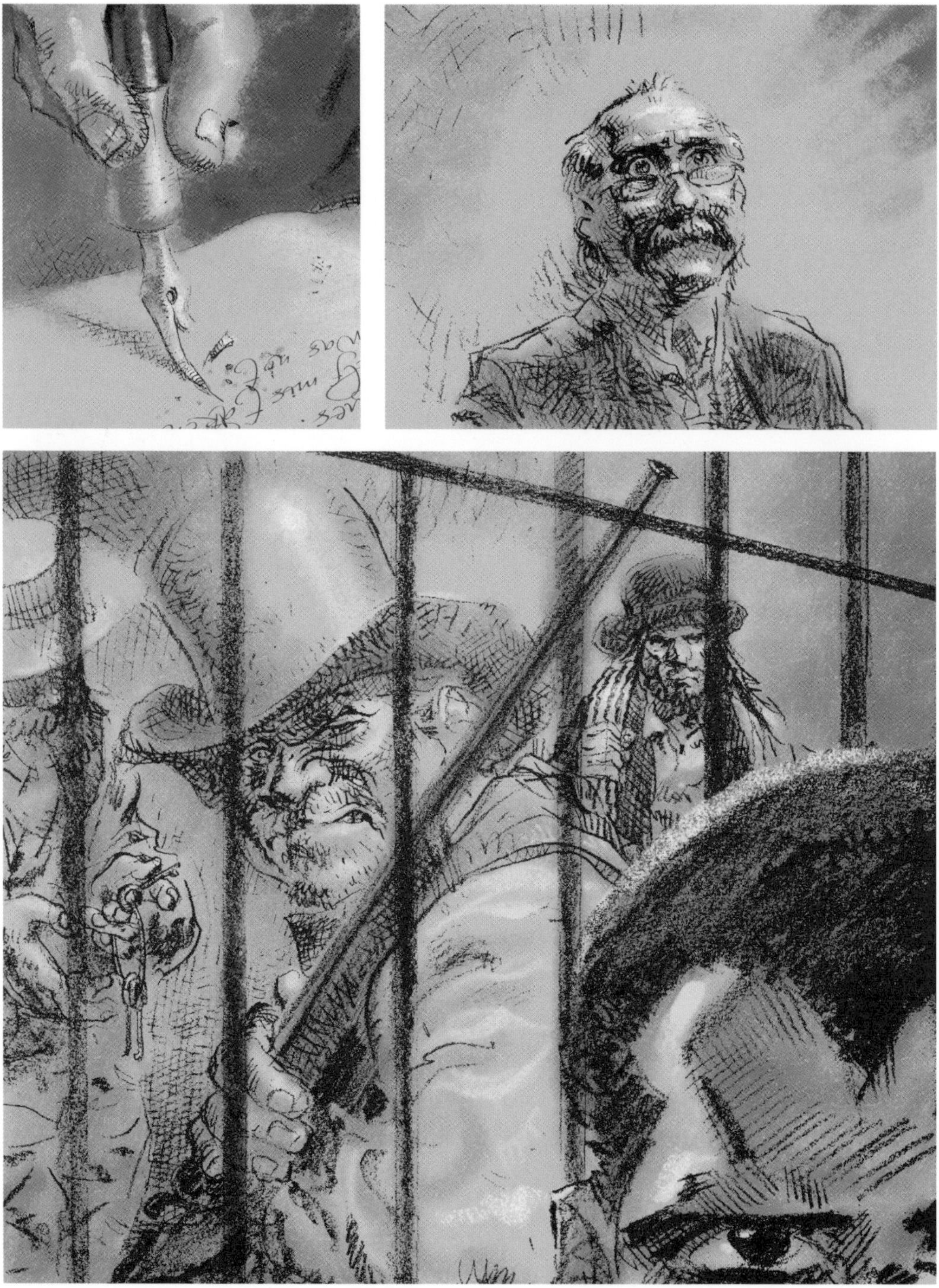

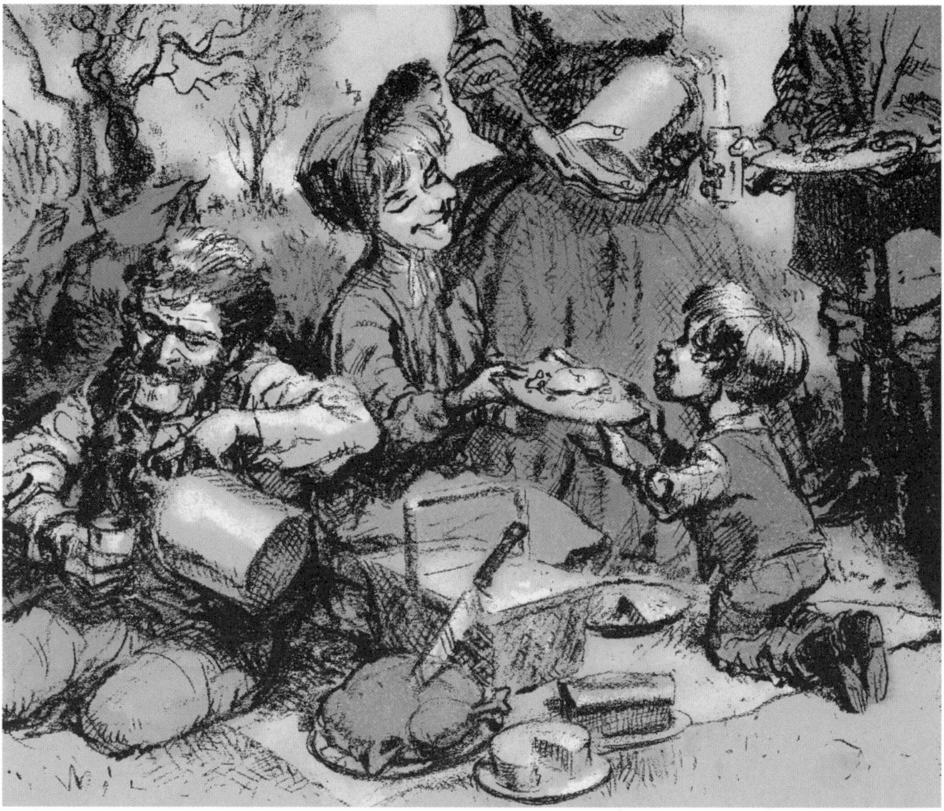

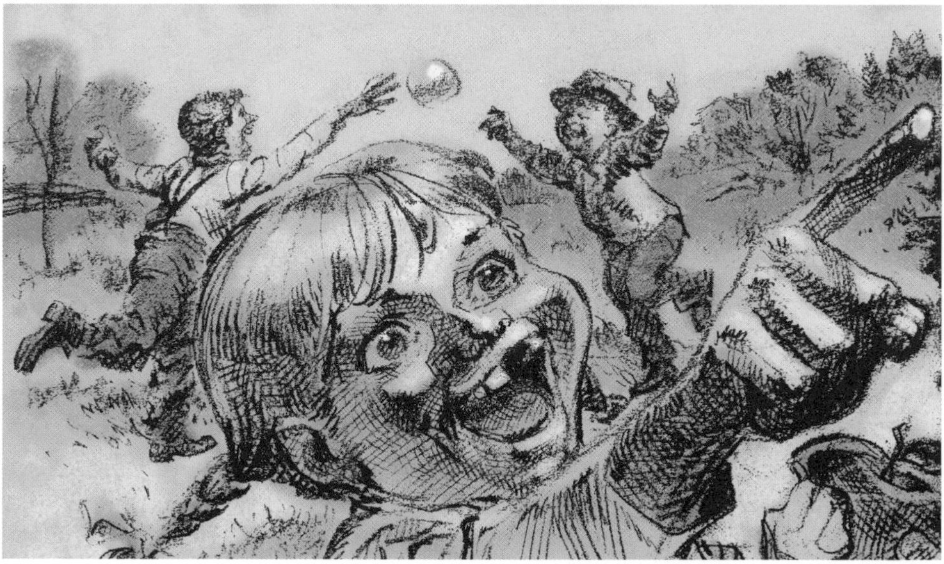

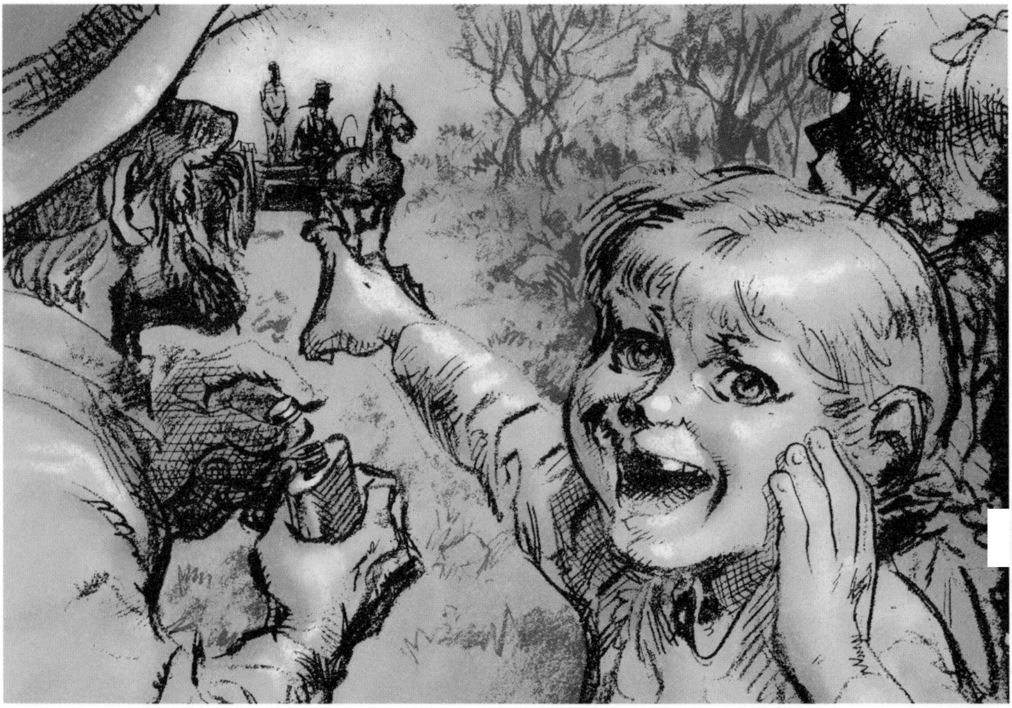

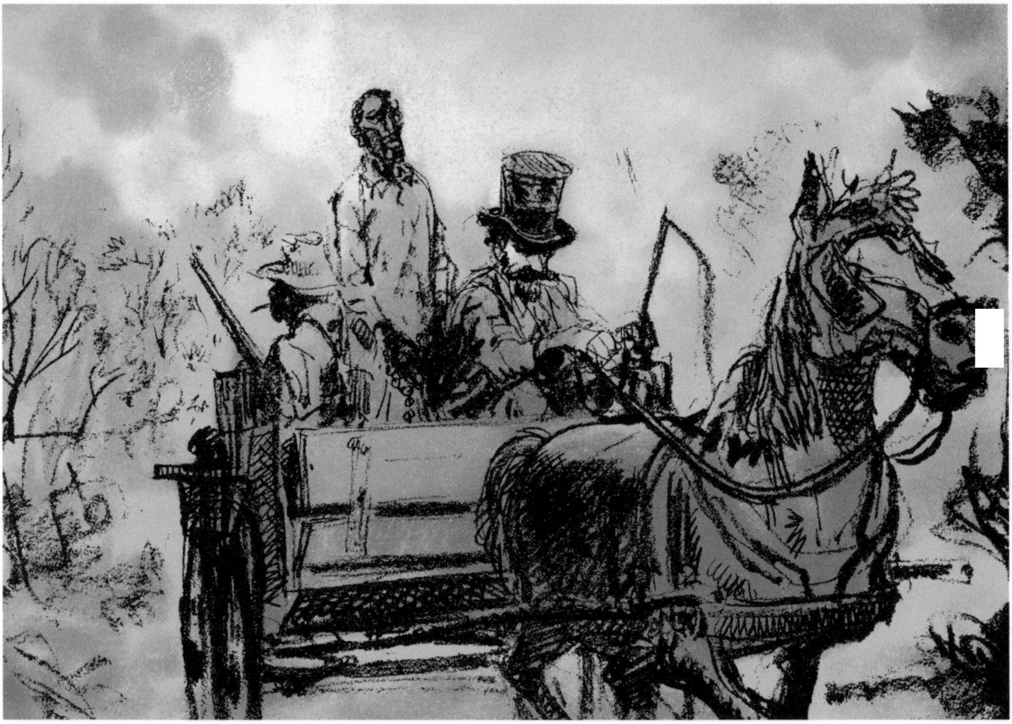

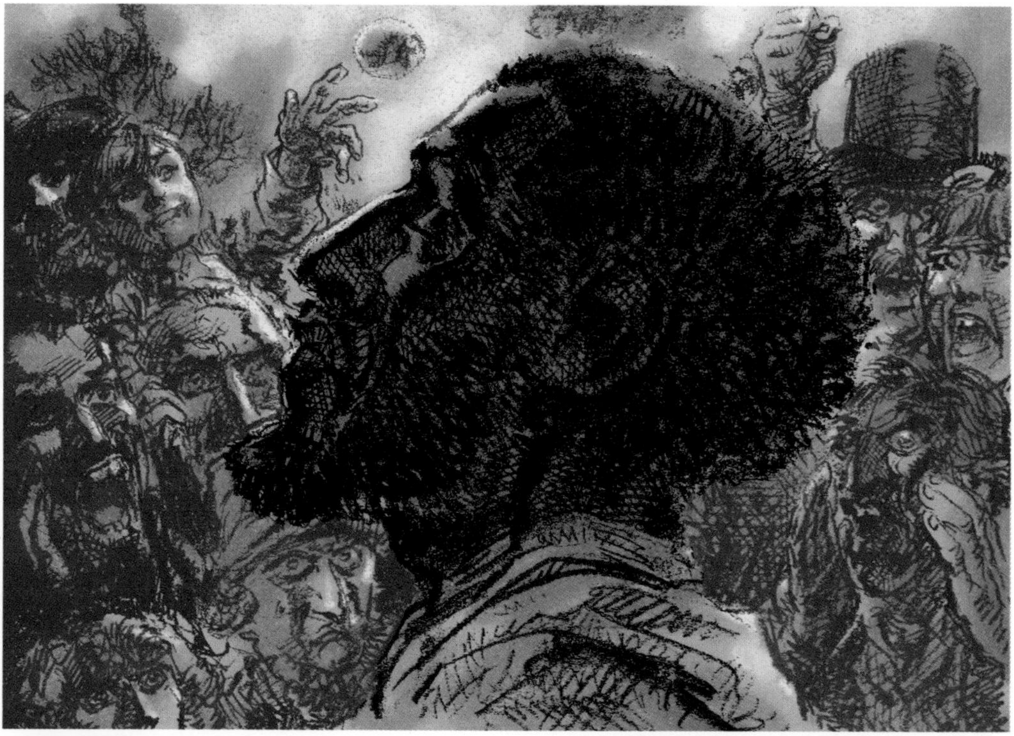

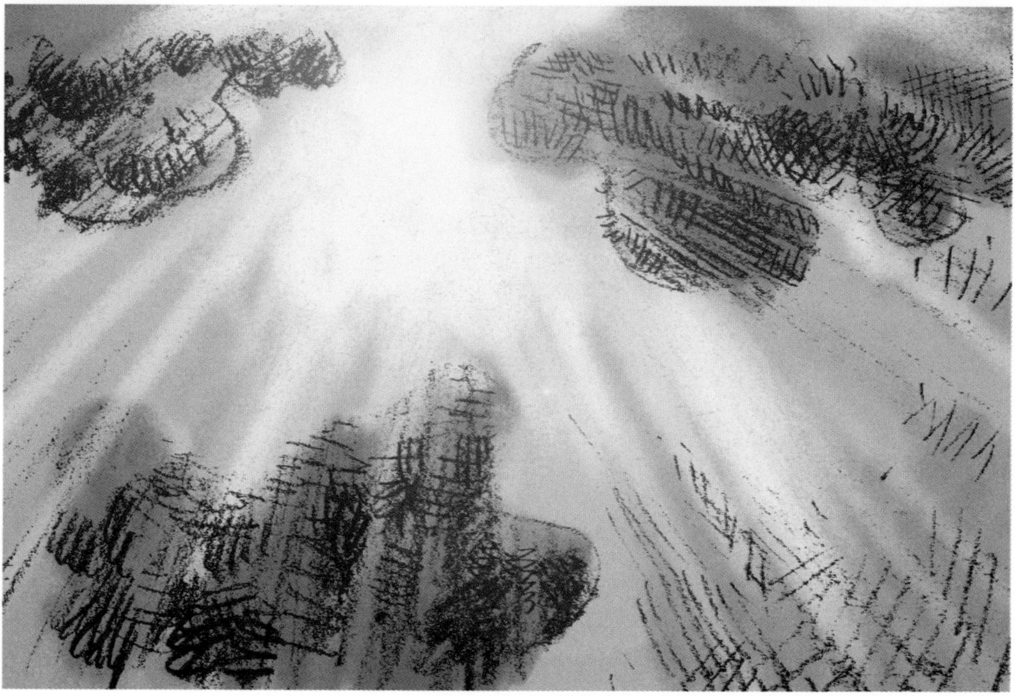

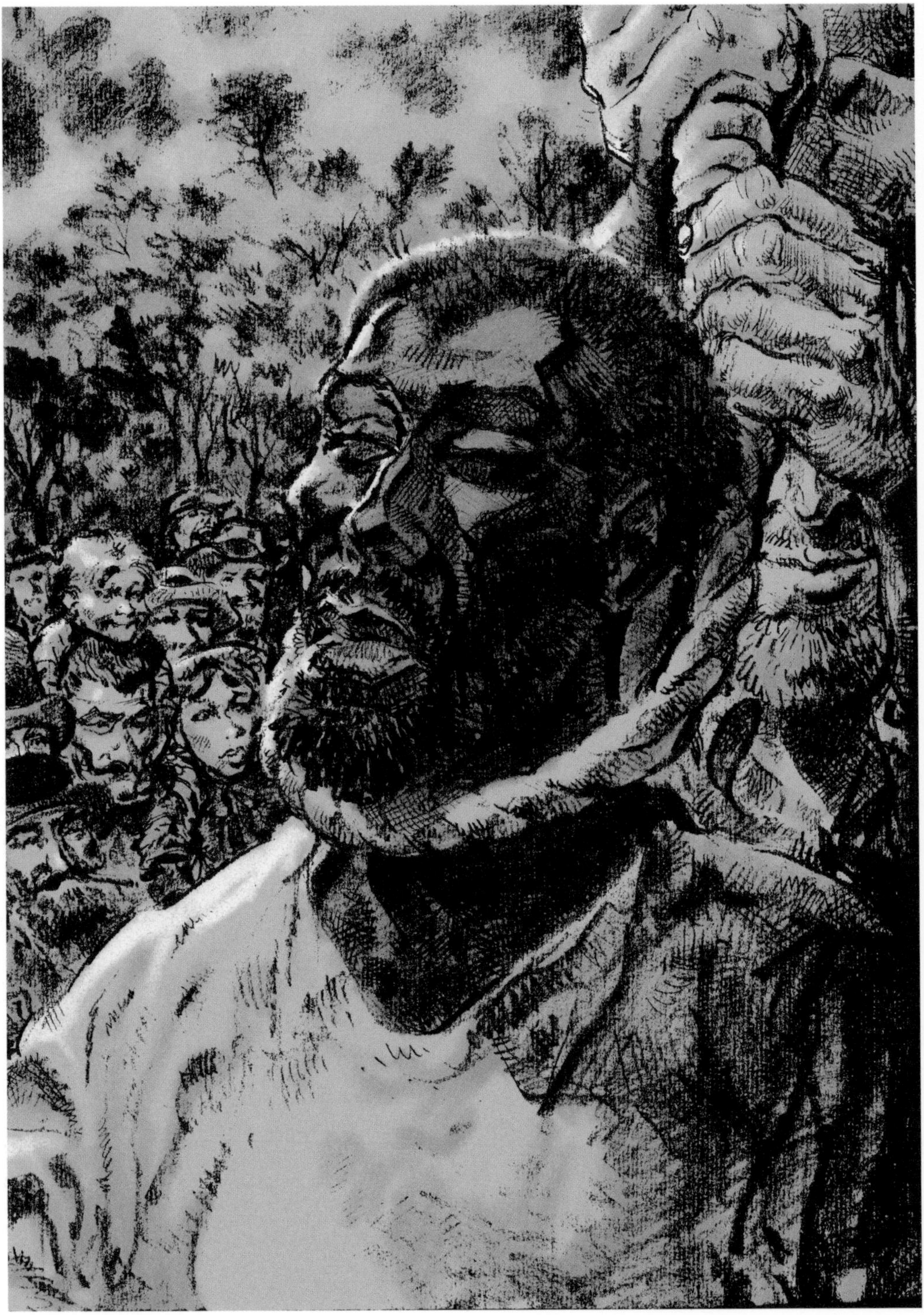

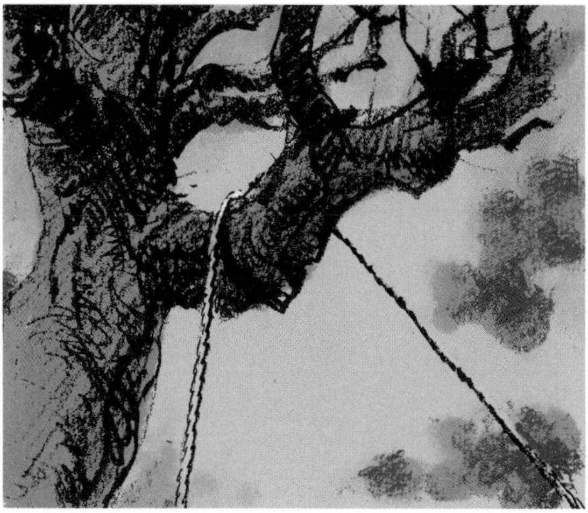

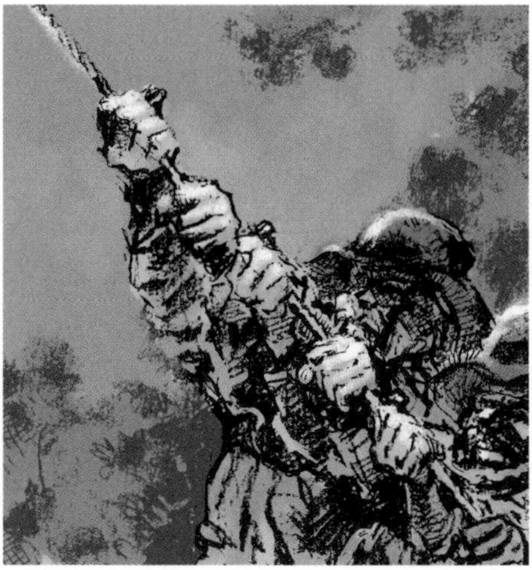

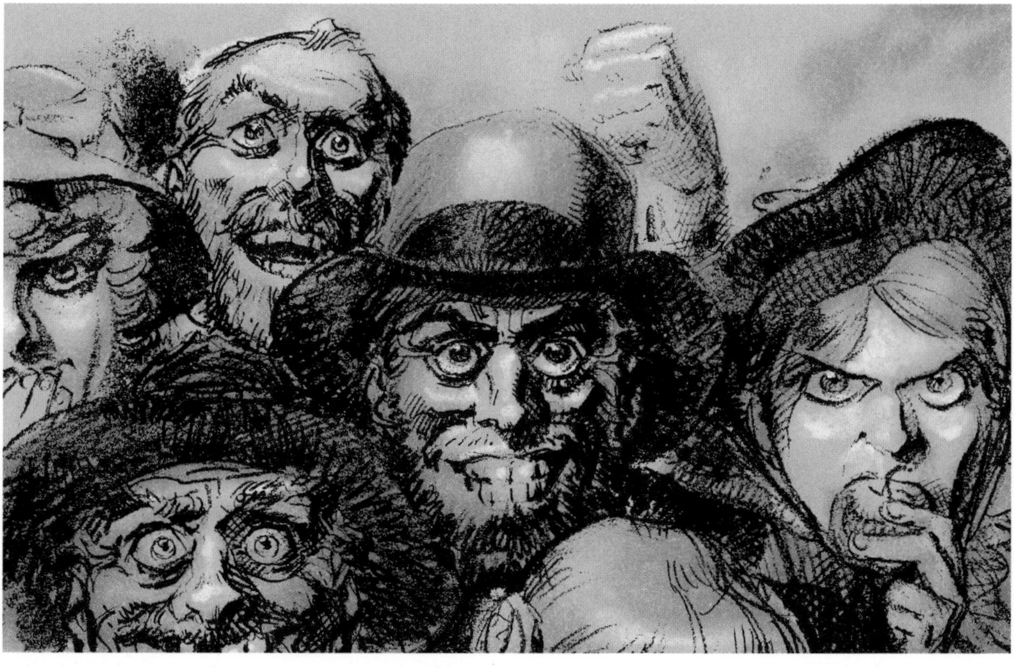

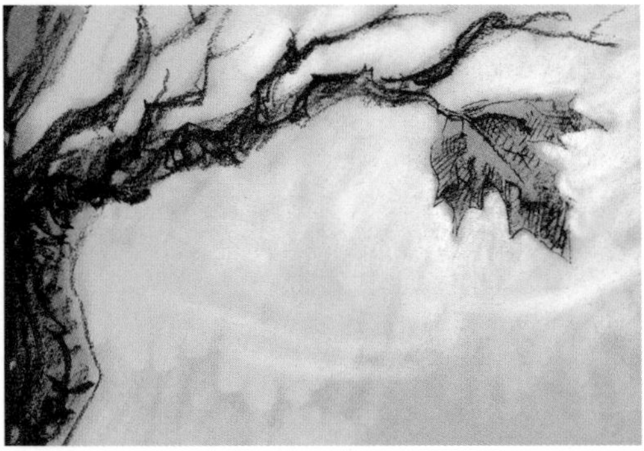

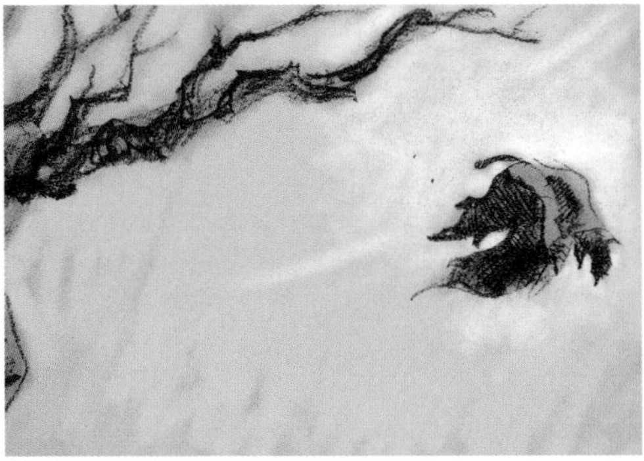

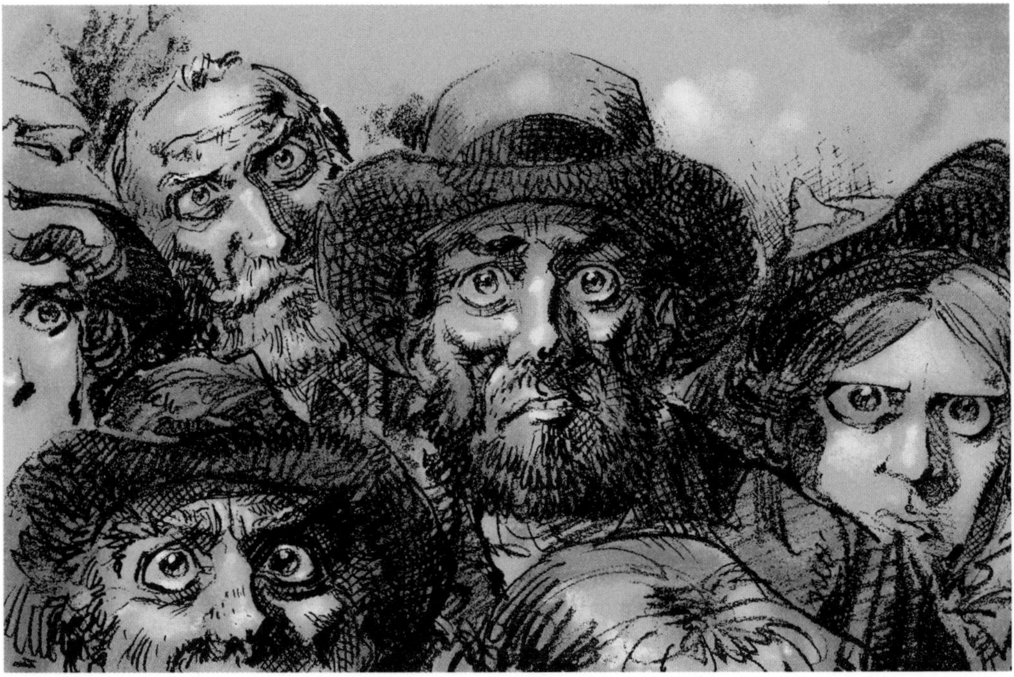

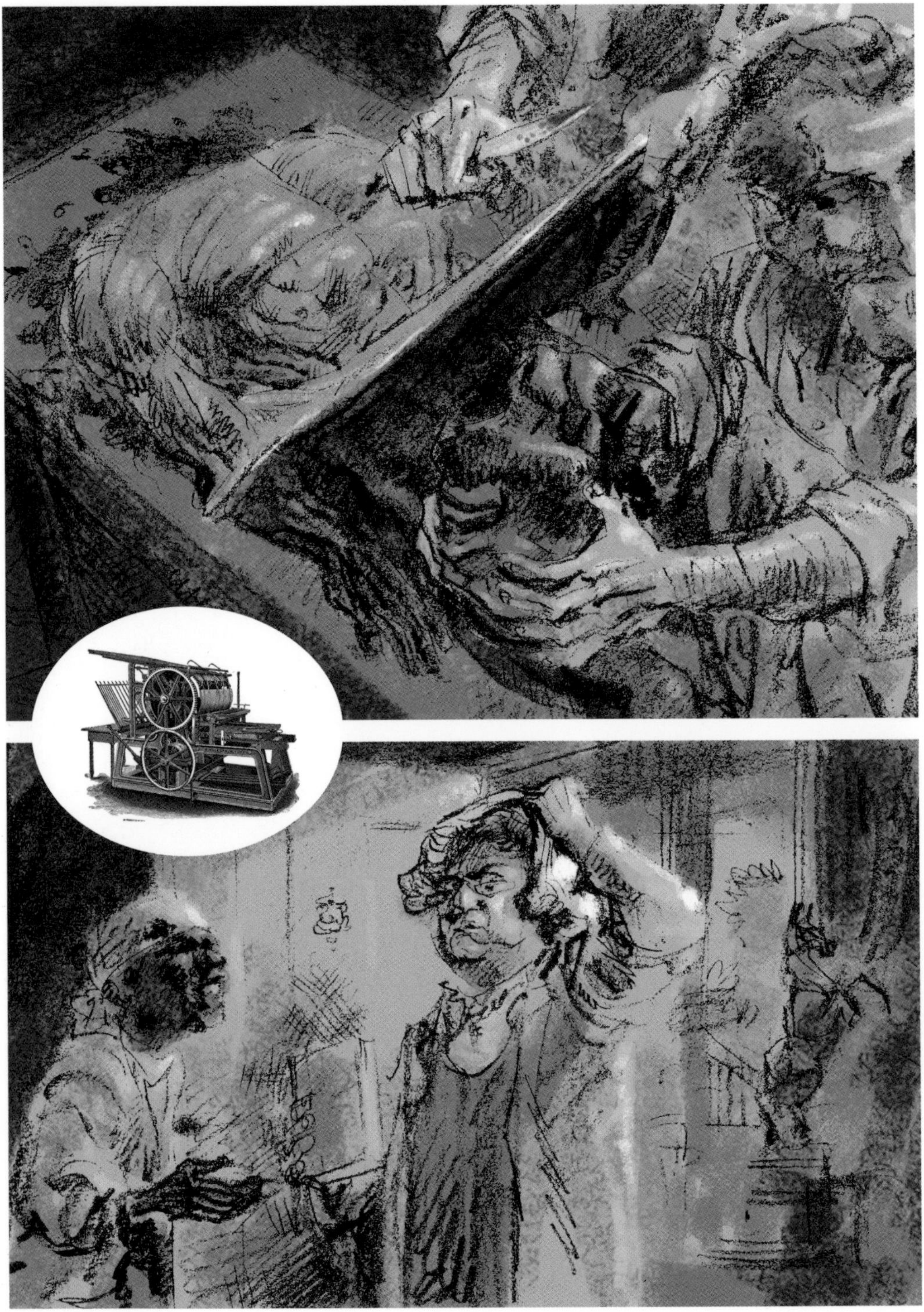

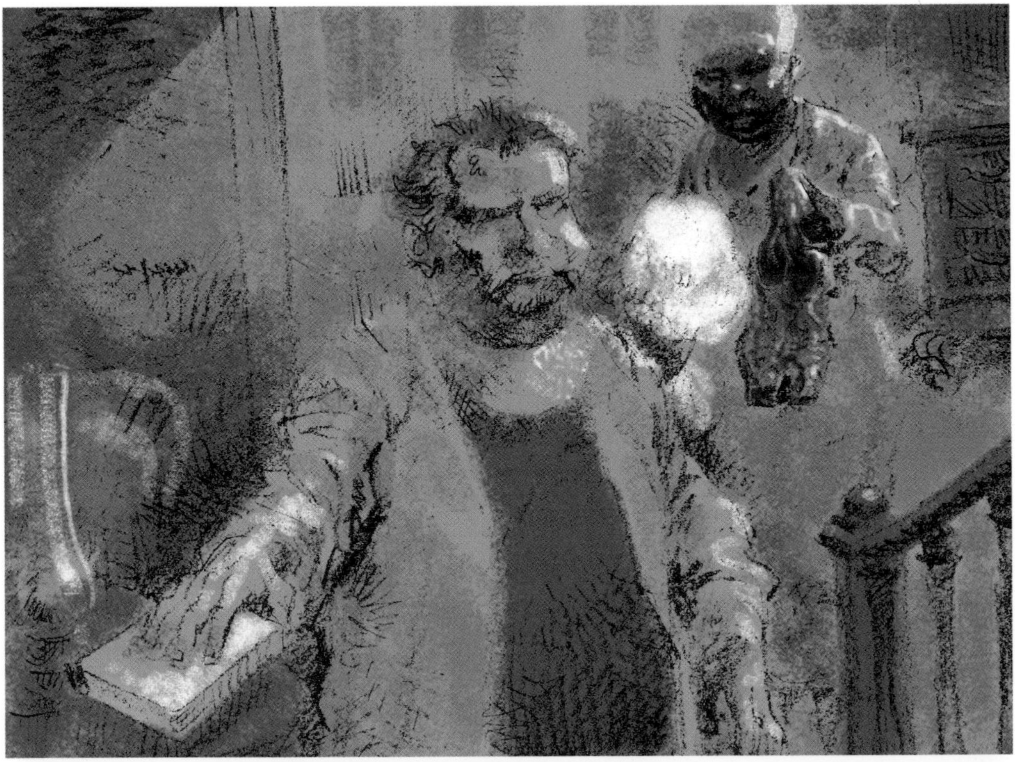

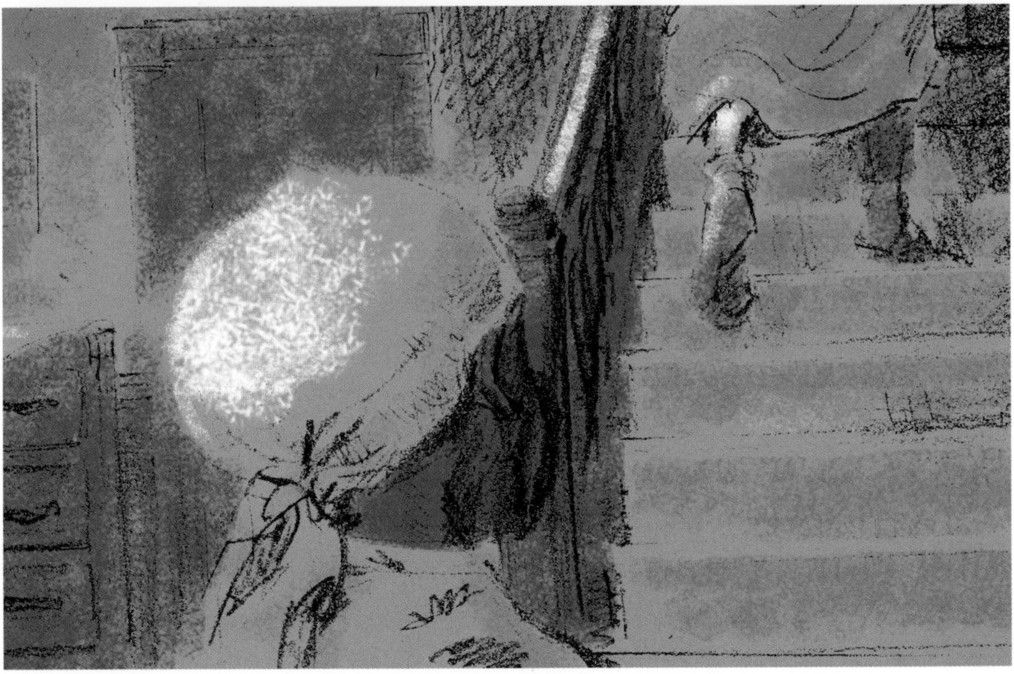

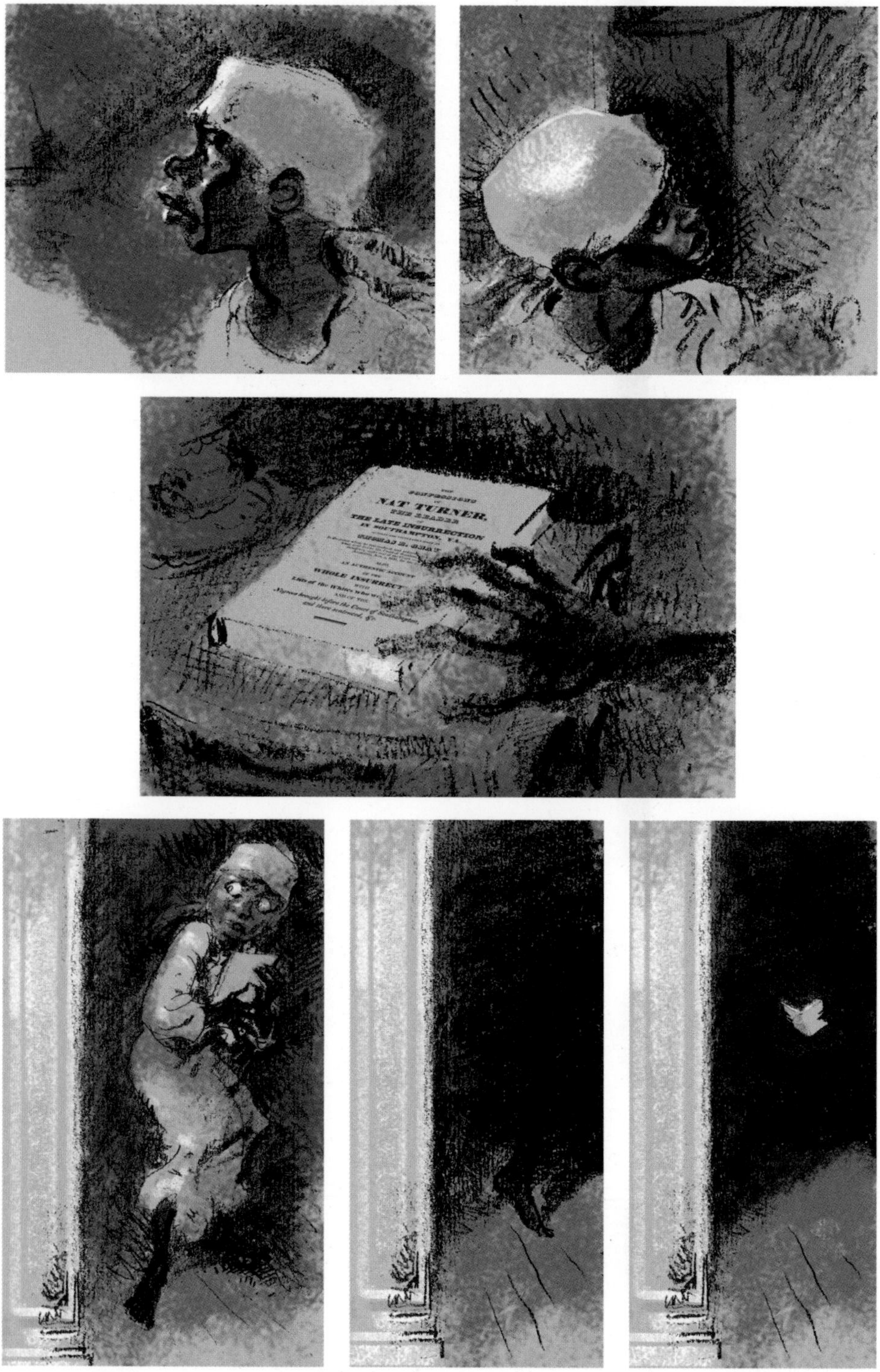
NAT TURNER,
THE LATE INSURRECTION
IN SOUTHAMPTON, VA.
WHOLE INSURRECT

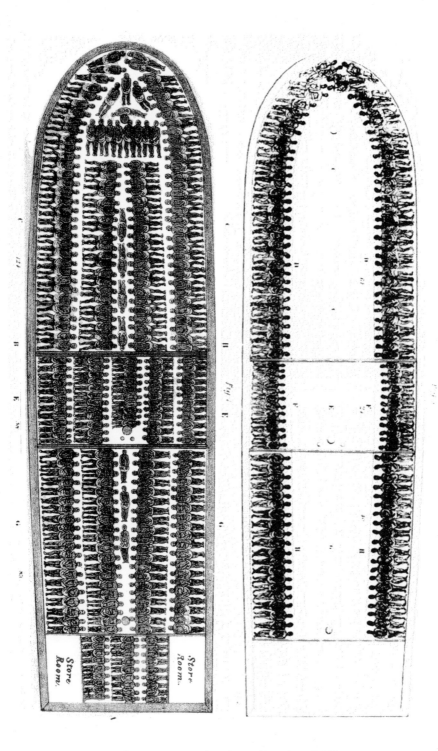

Cross-section of a slave ship, circa 1700s.

BIBLIOGRAPHY

Bisson, Terry. *Nat Turner: Slave Revolt Leader.* Danbury, CT: Grolier, 1988.

Bok, Francis. *Escape from Slavery: The True Story of My Ten Years in Captivity—and My Journey to Freedom in America.* With Edward Tivnan. New York: St. Martin's Press, 2003.

Canot, Theodore, Capt. *Adventures of an African Slaver.* New York: Dover Publications, 2002.

Gray, Thomas R. *The Confessions of Nat Turner: The Leader of the Late Insurrection in Southampton, Virginia.* Baltimore, MD: Lucas & Deaver, 1831.

Library of Congress. *Born in Slavery: Slave Narratives from the Federal Writers' Project, 1936–1938.* Washington, DC: Library of Congress, 2001. http://memory.loc.gov:8081/ammem/snhtml/snhome.html

Oates, Stephen B. *The Fires of Jubilee: Nat Turner's Fierce Rebellion.* New York: Harper & Row, 1975.

Ploski, Harry A., ed. *Reference Library of Black America.* Philadelphia, PA: Afro-American Press, 1990.

Thomas, Velma Maia. *Lest We Forget: The Passage from Africa to Slavery to Emancipation.* New York: Crown Publishing Group, 1997.

NOTES

PAGE 15: African slave catchers were often paid with guns, which gave them an advantage over other tribes armed with only bows and spears.

PAGE 29: Two out of five captives did not survive the forced march to the coast, a journey of up to one thousand miles on foot.

PAGE 39: Packs of hungry sharks routinely followed slave ships, to feast on the hundreds of dead bodies that went overboard.

PAGE 43: It is estimated that about twenty percent of the captives died in the rat-infested ships.

PAGE 68: Many laws such as the Mississippi Black Codes outlawed drums, which Africans used for communication.

PAGE 70: "We were not regularly allowanced. Our food was coarse corn meal boiled. This was called MUSH. It was put into a large wooden tray or trough, and set down upon the ground. The children were then called, like so many pigs, and like so many pigs they would come and devour the mush; some with oyster-shells, others with pieces of shingle, some with naked hands, and none with spoons. He that ate fastest got most; he that was strongest secured the best place; and few left the trough satisfied." —Frederick Douglass, *Narrative of the Life of Frederick Douglass, An American Slave* (1845)

PAGE 71: It was illegal to teach slaves how to read and write.

PAGE 72: With drums banned, slaves passed secret messages from plantation to plantation by song. Slaves brought from the tribal cultures of Africa the custom of creating songs to transmit factual information. In America, slaves turned song into codes that secretly transmitted information they wished to keep from whites. A reference to "River Jordan" in song might secretly be a reference to escape routes up the Mississippi River.

PAGE 196: Onlookers were reportedly unsettled by the fact that Turner did not die kicking and suffering as hanged men usually do. He simply rose into the air, breathing his last, peacefully without twitching a muscle.

PAGE 198: Turner's body was skinned and beheaded.

THE
CONFESSIONS
OF

NAT TURNER

Leader of the late
Insurrection in Southampton, Va.

As fully and voluntarily made to
THOMAS R. GRAY,

In the prison where he was confined,
and acknowledged by him to be such when read before
the Court of Southampton; with the certificate,
under seal of the Court convened at Jerusalem,
November 5, 1831, for his trial.

ᘓ

Also, an authentic
Account of the whole insurrection
With lists of the whites who were murdered,
and of the negroes brought before the court
of Southampton, and there sentenced, &c.

BALTIMORE: PUBLISHED BY THOMAS R. GRAY.
LUCAS & DEAVER, PRINT. 1831.

AGREEABLE TO HIS OWN APPOINTMENT, ON THE EVENING HE WAS COMMITTED
TO PRISON, WITH PERMISSION OF THE JAILER, I VISITED NAT ON TUESDAY
THE 1ST NOVEMBER, WHEN, WITHOUT BEING QUESTIONED AT ALL, HE COMMENCED
HIS NARRATIVE IN THE FOLLOWING WORDS:

SIR,—You have asked me to give a history of the motives which induced me to undertake the late insurrection, as you call it—To do so I must go back to the days of my infancy, and even before I was born.

I was thirty-one years of age the 2nd of October last, and born the property of Benj. Tuner, of this county. In my childhood a circumstance occurred which made an indelible impression on my mind, and laid the ground work of that enthusiasm, which has terminated so fatally to many, both white and black, and for which I am about to atone at the gallows.
It is here necessary to relate this circumstance—trifling as it may seem, it was the commencement of that belief which has grown with time, and even now, sir, in this dungeon, helpless and forsaken as I am, I cannot divest myself of.

Being at play with other children, when three or four years old, I was telling them something, which my mother overhearing, said it had happened before I was born—I stuck to my story, however, and related some thing's which went, in her opinion, to confirm it—others being called on were greatly astonished, knowing that these things had happened, and caused them to say in my hearing, I surely would be a prophet, as the Lord had shewn me things that had happened before my birth. And my father and mother strengthened me in this my first impression, saying in my presence, I was intended for some great purpose, which they had always thought from certain marks on my head and breast—[a parcel of excrescence's which I believe are not at all uncommon, particularly among Negroes, as I have seen several with the same. In this case he has either cut them off or they have nearly disappeared]—

My grandmother, who was very religious, and to whom I was much attached—my master, who belonged to the church, and other religious persons who visited the house, and whom I often saw at prayers, noticing the singularity of my manners, I suppose, and my uncommon intelligence for a child, remarked I had too much sense to be raised, and if I was, I would never be of any service to any one as a slave—To a mind like mine, restless, inquisitive and observant of every thing that was passing, it is easy to suppose that religion was the subject to which it would be directed, and although this subject principally occupied my thoughts—there was nothing that I saw or heard of to which my attention was not directed—

The manner in which I learned to read and write, not only had great influence on my own mind, as I acquired it with the most perfect ease, so much so, that I have no recollection whatever of learning the alphabet—but to the astonishment of the family, one day when a book was shewn to me to keep me from crying , I began spelling the names of different objects—this was a source of wonder to all in the neighborhood, particularly the blacks— and this learning was constantly improved at all opportunities—

When I got large enough to go to work, while employed, I was reflecting on many things that would present themselves to my imagination, and whenever an opportunity occurred of looking at a book, when the school children were getting their lessons, I would find many things that the fertility of my own imagination had depicted to me before; all my time, not devoted to my master's service, was spent either in prayer, or in making experiments in casting different things in molds made of earth, in attempting to make paper, gun-powder and many other experiments, that although I could not perfect, yet convinced me of its practicability if I had the means.

I was not addicted to stealing in my youth, nor have ever been—Yet such was the confidence of the Negroes in the neighborhood, even at this early period of my life, in my superior judgment, that they would often carry me with them when they were going on any roguery, to plan for them. Growing up among them with this confidence in my superior judgment, and when this, in their opinions, was perfected by Divine inspiration, from the circumstances already alluded to in my infancy, and which belief was ever afterwards zealously inculcated by the austerity of my life and manners, which became the subject of remark by white and black.

Having soon discovered to be great, I must appear so, and therefore studiously avoided mixing in society, and wrapped myself in mystery, devoting my time to fasting and prayer—

By this time, having arrived to man's estate, and hearing the scriptures commented on at meetings, I was struck with that particular passage which says: "Seek ye the kingdom of Heaven and all things shall be added unto you." I reflected much on this passage, and prayed daily for light on this subject—As I was praying one day at my plough, the spirit spoke to me, saying "Seed ye the kingdom of Heaven and all things shall be added unto you."

Question—what do you mean by the Spirit. *Ans.* The Spirit that spoke to the prophets in former days—

and I was greatly astonished, and for two years prayed continually, whenever my duty would permit—and then again I had the same revelation, which fully confirmed me in the impression that I was ordained for some great purpose in the hands of the Almighty.

~J

The rest of Nat Turner's actual confession is continued online at:

http://www.wfu.edu/~zulick/340/natturner.html

http://www.melanet.com/nat/nat.html

THIS BOOK IS DEDICATED
TO FREE PEOPLE EVERYWHERE

ACKNOWLEDGMENTS

Thanks to my entire family.

Editor: Charles Kochman
Editorial Assistant: Sofia Gutiérrez
Designer: Sarah Gifford
Production Manager: Jules Thomson

Cataloging-in-Publication Data for the hardcover edition has been applied for and may be obtained from the Library of Congress. Hardcover ISBN: 978-0-8109-9535-2. Paperback ISBN: 978-0-8109-7227-8.

Hardcover and paperback editions published simultaneously in 2008 by Abrams, an imprint of Harry N. Abrams, Inc.

For information about special discounts for bulk purchases, please contact Harry N. Abrams Special Sales at *specialsales@hnabooks.com* or phone 212-229-7109.

Printed and bound in China
10 9 8 7 6 5 4 3 2 1

HNA
harry n. abrams, inc.
a subsidiary of La Martinière Groupe
115 West 18th Street
New York, NY 10011
www.hnabooks.com